To Grace

Merry Christmas 1993

Love Always Mom

Better Homes and Gardens ®

NEW DIETER'S COOK BOOK

WE CARE!

All of us at Better Homes and Gardens® Books are dedicated to providing you with the information and ideas you need to create tasty foods. We welcome your comments or suggestions. Write us at: Better Homes and Gardens® Books, Cook Book Editorial Department, LS-348, 1716 Locust Street, Des Moines, Iowa 50309-3023

If you would like to order any additional copies of our books, call 1-800-678-2803 or check with your local bookstore.

Our seal assures you that every recipe in the **New Dieter's Cook Book** has been tested in the Better Homes and Gardens® Test Kitchen. This means that each recipe is practical and reliable, and meets our high standards of taste appeal. We guarantee your satisfaction with this book for as long as you own it.

NEW DIETER'S COOK BOOK

Editor: Heidi McNutt
Graphic Designer: Mary Schlueter Bendgen
Project Manager: Liz Anderson

Associate Department Editor: Rosemary C. Hutchinson
Associate Art Director: Neoma Thomas
Publishing Systems Text Processor: Paula Forest
Food Stylists: Lynn Blanchard, Janet Herwig
Contributing Photographer: Scott Little

BETTER HOMES AND GARDENS® BOOKS
An Imprint of Meredith® Books

Vice President and Editorial Director: Elizabeth P. Rice
Food and Family Life Editor: Sharyl Heiken
Art Director: Ernest Shelton
Managing Editor: David A. Kirchner
Art Production Director: John Berg
Test Kitchen Director: Sharon Stilwell

President, Book Group: Joseph J. Ward
Vice President, Retail Marketing: Jamie L. Martin
Vice President, Book Clubs: Richard L. Rundall

On cover: Curried Beef and Potatoes (see recipe, page 101)

INTRODUCTION

Whether you've been on and off diets since you were a teenager or have just now decided to trim a few pounds, the *New Dieter's Cook Book* will help you begin a new pattern of nutritious eating.

In these pages, you'll find the delicious low-calorie recipes you need to lose those extra pounds. By preparing the recipes in this book, you'll feel good about yourself and still eat delicious, satisfying meals. What's more, even the nondieting members of your family will enjoy the dishes you prepare.

In the *New Dieter's Cook Book* we've compiled hundreds of low-calorie recipes that we've published over the years. You'll find everything from elegant, sure-to-impress menus to quick-and-easy recipes. Each recipe gives a preparation time to help you fit healthy eating into your family's schedule. Also, look for the special designations of "Low Fat," "Low Sodium," or "Low Cholesterol" that appear at the top of appropriate recipes. At the end of each recipe, you'll find per-serving nutrition information to help you make positive changes in your eating habits.

Turn to the *New Dieter's Cook Book* when you're preparing any meal—whether it's breakfast, a take-along lunch, a family supper, or a holiday dinner. With the help of these low-calorie recipes and information-filled pages, you'll soon be on your way to shedding those extra pounds.

CONTENTS

3 INTRODUCTION

5 GETTING STARTED

19 BEGIN-YOUR-DIET MENUS
Week One 20
Week Two 38

56 CALORIE-TRIMMED CLASSICS

73 MAIN-DISH SALADS

86 BEEF MAIN DISHES

122 PORK AND HAM MAIN DISHES
Pork 123
Ham 142

158 LAMB AND VEAL MAIN DISHES
Lamb 159
Veal 167

173 POULTRY MAIN DISHES

223 FISH AND SHELLFISH MAIN DISHES
Fish 224
Shellfish 237

259 MEATLESS MAIN DISHES

280 MICROWAVE MAIN DISHES

316 SIDE DISHES
Vegetables 317
Rice and Pasta 327
Soups 342
Salads 347

353 MICROWAVE SIDE DISHES

368 BREADS AND DESSERTS
Breads 369
Desserts 382

415 SNACKS AND BEVERAGES
Snacks 416
Beverages 427

436 BREAKFAST AND BRUNCH CHOICES

451 TAKE-ALONG LUNCHES

466 CALORIE TALLY

471 INDEX

480 METRIC CONVERSIONS

GETTING STARTED

CAESAR-STYLE CHICKEN SALAD *(see page 80)*

DO-IT-YOURSELF REDUCING

So you've decided to lose a few unwanted pounds. It may seem easier said than done. But with the help of the 427 delicious, low-calorie recipes and all the information in the *New Dieter's Cook Book*, you'll find that it's easier than ever to trim off those extra pounds. And keep them off.

Of course, the first step before beginning any diet is to check with your doctor and follow his or her medical advice. If you get the go-ahead to diet, don't try to shed pounds too quickly. Instead, take it slow and easy. One or two pounds per week is generally the safest and most effective way to reach your desired-weight goal.

On the following pages, you'll read more about calories and how to estimate desirable weight and calorie needs. You'll also find some suggestions for modifying eating habits plus some pointers on cutting calories when cooking.

VARIETY IN DIET MENUS

Variety, balance, and moderation. Those are the keys to a well-planned weight-loss diet. By selecting a variety of low-calorie, nutrient-dense foods in the appropriate amounts, you can make every calorie worthwhile.

You don't have to give up all of your favorite foods. The items you eat while reducing should be the kinds of foods you will enjoy eating after you've reached your goal. And they should be foods that will fit into your life-style. If a diet doesn't fit your likes and needs, you probably won't stick with it. With the wide variety of recipes in this cookbook, you're sure to find many choices to please your palate.

Another tip: Be sure to include plenty of water and fiber (from foods such as fresh fruits) in your weight-loss plan. Water is necessary for normal body functioning and fiber aids digestion.

ALL ABOUT CALORIES

Calories are what dieting is all about. Simply put, calories measure energy—both the energy the body uses and the energy in food. The body needs calories for bodily processes, such as breathing and heartbeat, for physical activity, and for digestion.

Body weight is maintained when you eat the same number of calories that you burn on a given day. When you take in more calories than the body needs for basic body functions and activity, you gain weight. Conversely, when you eat less than your body needs, you lose weight.

Therefore, to lose weight, there are three choices to consider: 1) Eat less (reduce caloric intake); 2) Increase physical activity (burn up more calories); 3) Combine the two (consume fewer calories and increase physical activity).

One pound of body fat equals about 3,500 calories. So, by cutting 500 calories from your diet each day for a week (500 calories x 7 days = 3,500 calories), you can lose about one pound.

Some people need more calories than others. For example, physically active people need more calories to fuel their exercise. A lean, muscular body requires more calories than a body of the same weight with less muscle and more body fat.

In addition, people with large body frames need more calories to sustain their weight than smaller people do. That's one reason most men need more calories than women. Women who are pregnant or breast-feeding need more calories to sustain the needs of two people.

But, as people get older, metabolic rates slow down. For every decade of life, the metabolic rate drops by about 10 percent. Consequently, as a person grows older, he or she needs fewer calories to keep body processes going.

CALORIE SOURCES

Proteins, carbohydrates, and fats are the nutrient sources of calories. Carbohydrates and proteins yield four calories per gram, and fats yield nine calories per gram. Alcohol also contributes calories—about seven calories per gram—but it has very little nutritional value.

Notice that fats have more than twice the calories per gram of proteins and carbohydrates. Therefore, foods high in fat are usually high in calories.

ESTIMATING YOUR DESIRABLE WEIGHT

You might think there's one ideal weight for you based on your height, but that's not true. Normal weights for healthy people will vary greatly depending on body structure and composition. Ask your doctor for guidance in determining your desirable weight. To determine if you are overweight:

■ Stand in front of a mirror. Do you see telltale bulges, such as "spare tires"?
■ Or, use the "pinch test" to estimate your body fat. Using your thumb and index finger, gently pinch the skin on the back of your arm, on your thigh, or at the waist. Gently pull the skin away from the muscle so you pinch only skin and fat. Do the test in several places, since most people carry weight unevenly.

If you pinch ½ to 1 inch, your body fat level is probably normal. If you pinch less than ½ inch, you may be underweight. More than 1 inch may suggest excess body fat. A doctor or dietitian can measure your body composition more precisely.

■ Or, look at a height-weight table and find your height and body frame. Remember that these tables give only guidelines.

ESTIMATING YOUR CALORIC NEEDS

How many calories you need each day depends on several factors, including your age, body size, and activity level. The chart below gives guidelines for women and men in different age ranges. Because energy needs vary from one person to the next, a range of calorie recommendations is given:

AGE	WOMEN	MEN
19-22	1,700-2,500 cal.	2,500-3,300 cal.
23-50	1,600-2,400 cal.	2,300-3,100 cal.
51-75	1,400-2,200 cal.	2,000-2,800 cal.
76+	1,200-2,000 cal.	1,650-2,450 cal.

To *estimate* the calories needed to maintain your weight:
1. Determine the calories you burn per pound each day based on your average level of activity:

    12 calories/pound for inactivity
    14 calories/pound for light activity (office work plus 20-minute walk)
    20 calories/pound for moderate activity (office work plus ½-hour aerobic exercise)
    25 calories/pound for extensive activity

2. Multiply calories you burn per pound each day by your current weight in pounds to estimate your daily caloric needs.

To lose weight, you need to eat fewer calories than your daily caloric needs or increase your activity level without increasing your caloric intake. *Do not restrict food intake too much.* It's difficult to get all the necessary nutrients in a diet with less than 1,200 calories. *Never* go on a diet below 800 calories unless supervised by a doctor.

The calorie count is given for each recipe in this cookbook so it's easy to keep track of calories as you use these recipes.

DIETING TIPS

EATING HABITS

Here are some suggestions you might consider while dieting:

■ Eat slowly so your brain has time to acknowledge the food you eat and starts sending messages to your body that you're no longer hungry. Cut and chew each bite deliberately. Putting your fork down between bites may help you slow down. And, of course, be sure to leave the table or at least stop eating when you feel full.

■ Smaller plates may help since they limit the amount of food you can put on your plate.

■ Watch portion size. Measure portions of foods until you can accurately estimate the size of a particular portion. Each recipe in this book contains the calorie count for one serving. If you eat a portion larger than the serving size, remember to add extra calories as well.

■ Snack sensibly. Replace cookies and chips with fresh fruits and vegetables. Snacks should make contributions to a healthy diet. Remember that all calories count, so make your snacks sources of good nutrition, not empty calories.

■ Try eating four to six "minimeals" per day instead of three regular-size meals. You might set aside some food from the regular meal for those minimeals. Some dieters find they don't get as hungry between meals if they eat minimeals throughout the day. But, others find it more difficult to keep the calorie counts under control and keep track of the foods consumed when more meals are eaten. Do whatever works best for you, but try to eat at regularly scheduled times.

■ Limit eating to the kitchen and the dining room areas.

■ Avoid doing something else while you eat. You can unconsciously eat too much if you nibble while watching television or while reading. Instead, try working a crossword puzzle or doing needlework in front of the TV.

CHANGE YOUR HABITS

Think of ways to add physical activity to your daily life. For example, park your car farther from your destination and walk, or use the stairs instead of the elevator.

Grocery shop after you've eaten. Shopping when you're hungry may lead to impulse buying, particularly of junk food.

Use a shopping list. A list may help you avoid buying tempting, high-calorie foods.

CALORIE-TRIMMING COOKING METHODS

A variety of cooking methods and techniques help hold down calories. Many of them are also quick-cooking methods so you can get in and out of the kitchen in little time.

Stir-frying allows you to cook small amounts of meat with lots of fresh vegetables. And, very little, if any, fat is used in the cooking process. Use a nonstick spray coating on a cold skillet or wok to get your cooking started.

Broiling and grilling allow fat to drip from meats, poultry, and fish during cooking, thus reducing calories.

Poaching in a low-calorie liquid is another calorie-trimming method. Just quickly simmer fish, poultry, or eggs till done.

Micro-cooking allows you to cook many foods without additional fat. Because micro-cooking dries foods less than conventional cooking, adding fat often is not necessary.

Another calorie-trimming technique is draining the excess fat from browned ground meat. Use either a wire mesh strainer or a metal colander held well above the pool of draining fat.

And, instead of sautéing vegetables in butter, margarine, or cooking oil, precook onions, green peppers, celery, and other vegetables by simmering them in a little water, then drain.

CALORIE-TRIMMED INGREDIENTS

■ Select low-fat and diet salad dressings instead of regular dressings.
■ Buy lean meat, fish, and poultry, and trim off any visible fat. Remove all skin from chicken and turkey pieces before cooking.
■ Switch to low-fat dairy products.
■ Serve naturally sweet desserts, such as fresh fruits.
■ When preparing your own recipes, use slimming ingredients such as these:

Plain low-fat yogurt instead of dairy sour cream (145 versus 495 calories per cup).

Part skim-milk mozzarella cheese instead of cheddar cheese (72 versus 115 calories per ounce).

Unsweetened applesauce instead of sweetened applesauce (53 versus 98 calories per ½ cup).

Reduced-calorie mayonnaise instead of regular mayonnaise (50 versus 100 calories per tablespoon).

WEIGHT MAINTENANCE

Once you've reached your weight goal, continue eating a balanced diet but increase portion sizes so you consume the same number of calories your body burns. But there's no reason to stop following the healthy eating habits you used while reducing. If pounds creep back on, adjust your caloric intake or activity level.

DAILY GUIDELINES

Here are some simple daily nutrient and calorie guidelines for moderately active women 23 to 50 years old (in general, men, teenagers, and pregnant women need more calories):

Calories	2,000
Protein	About 15% of calories
Fat	No more than 30% of calories
Carbohydrate	About 55% of calories
Cholesterol	300 milligrams or less
Sodium	500 to 3,000 milligrams
Potassium	2,000 to 5,600 milligrams

IN THE NEW DIETER'S COOK BOOK

Each recipe in this cookbook lists the calorie count and the amount in grams or milligrams of protein, carbohydrate, fat, cholesterol, sodium, and potassium per serving. Use this information to keep track of what you eat.

SPECIALLY MARKED RECIPES

Recipes marked with the "Low Cholesterol" designation meet the following guidelines for milligrams of cholesterol per serving:
■ Main dish: Less than 100 milligrams
■ Side dish, snack, dessert: Less than 25 milligrams

Recipes marked with the "Low Sodium" designation meet the following guidelines for milligrams of sodium per serving:
■ Main dish: Less than 140 milligrams
■ Bread: Less than 75 milligrams
■ Side dish: Less than 60 milligrams
■ Dessert: Less than 50 milligrams

A recipe marked with "Low Fat" derives no more than 30 percent of its calories from fat.

HOW WE ANALYZED THE NUTRIENTS

At the end of each recipe, you'll find a listing of nutrition information per serving. Remember the following when using this information:
■ When two or more ingredient options appear in a recipe, such as "margarine or butter," the first ingredient choice was used for the analysis.
■ We omitted optional ingredients from the nutrition analysis.
■ We based the nutrition analysis on the first serving size if a recipe gives variable serving sizes (such as "4 to 6 servings").
■ When lean ground beef is an ingredient, we used 85 percent lean beef (15 percent fat) for the recipe analysis.

9

REMEMBER THE DIETARY GUIDELINES

The following information will help you choose what you can eat. Remember that the best diet for you is the one that improves your personal health. A physician or registered dietitian can help you assess your own pluses and minuses. He or she also can help you distinguish fact from fiction in the overwhelming and often confusing collection of nutrition information. And he or she can help you select the best foods for your own health.

DIETARY GUIDELINES

As researchers have learned more about the relationship between food and health, they have identified dietary concerns that affect many individuals. For example, in 1990, the U.S. Surgeon General reemphasized the importance of seven dietary changes originally proposed by researchers with the U.S. Department of Agriculture and the U.S. Department of Health and Human Services. They are:

1. Eat a variety of foods.
2. Maintain a healthy weight.
3. Choose a diet low in fat, saturated fat, and cholesterol.
4. Choose a diet with plenty of vegetables, fruits, and grain products.
5. Use sugars only in moderation.
6. Use salt and sodium only in moderation.
7. If you drink alcoholic beverages, do so in moderation.

The next few pages will examine five concerns related to these guidelines: weight, fat and cholesterol, fiber, sodium, and sugar.

DIETARY CONCERNS: WEIGHT, FAT, CHOLESTEROL

MAINTAIN A HEALTHY WEIGHT

Although weight is only one aspect of our health, it is a primary concern because it affects several other elements of our health. Being either significantly overweight or underweight can be dangerous.

Weight is related to heredity, exercise, and diet. You can't change your genes, but you can control your exercising and eating habits.

The recipes and information in the *New Dieter's Cook Book* provide the tools you need to follow the eat-less approach to weight loss. But remember that total good health involves more than just counting calories. The foods you choose also must provide the necessary variety of nutrients in reasonable amounts. That is why it is so important to eat a variety of foods and why it can be harmful to eat fewer than 1,200 calories per day.

CHOOSE A DIET LOW IN FAT AND SATURATED FAT

Because fats have more than twice as many calories as carbohydrates and proteins (nine calories per gram instead of four), reducing the amount of fat you eat is especially good advice when you are trying to reduce or maintain your weight. But limiting the amount of fat you eat also can improve your chances for long-lasting good health.

How much fat is too much? It is estimated that 36 to 40 percent of total calories in an average American's diet comes from fat. However, health scientists recommend that no more than 30 percent of our calories should come from fat.

To monitor your own diet, look at the nutrition analyses of recipes and at the labels of purchased foods to find the number of grams of fat in the foods you consume. Your total fat grams per day should be no higher than the maximum given in the table on this page.

Some foods, such as main dishes, are naturally higher in fats than other foods, such as fruits. Therefore, your goal should be to balance your use of foods high and low in fat so your daily average over a week matches or stays below the 30 percent suggested maximum.

One of the guidelines in developing all the recipes for the *New Dieter's Cook Book* was that they be low in fat. Thus, the recipes follow low-fat preparation methods, such as broiling instead of frying, and use low-fat ingredients, such as low-fat dairy products.

In some recipes, however, the low-calorie guideline was met by substantially reducing the fat in a traditionally high-fat food. While the resulting recipe is healthier than the original, the amount of fat used may still be higher than allowed in a medically prescribed low-fat diet.

Besides monitoring how much total fat you consume, you should also watch the type of fat you eat. Saturated, monounsaturated, and polyunsaturated fats are equal in calories, but they differ in chemical structure and do not react equally in your body.

Saturated fats are found most often in foods of animal origin as well as in some oils, including coconut and palm. They are almost always solid at room temperature. Monounsaturated and polyunsaturated fats are soft or liquid at room temperature. They usually come from plant foods. Examples are corn, safflower and soybean oils.

The American diet traditionally has been high in saturated fats. Health scientists now recommend cutting the amount of saturated fat from 15 percent of total calories in your diet to not more than 10 percent. The table at the bottom of this page gives specific guidelines for the fat consumption in your diet based on your total calorie intake.

CHOOSE A DIET LOW IN CHOLESTEROL

Much has been written about cholesterol—the so-called villain in our diets. But five facts are most important.

1. **Cholesterol is essential to life.** The human body makes cholesterol because it is a necessary part of cell structure.
2. **Cholesterol is only found in foods of animal origin.** Meat, eggs, fish, poultry, and dairy products all contain cholesterol. Fruits, nuts, seeds, vegetables, grains, and cereals do not.
3. **Cholesterol content in animal foods is similar.** Since cholesterol is an integral part of animal cells, all muscle meats from beef, pork, lamb, fish, and poultry have about 20 milligrams of cholesterol per ounce. Eggs and organ meats have higher concentrations of cholesterol.
4. **Cholesterol is not the same as fat.** The two are often linked, but they are separate food components. For example, removing the skin from chicken removes most of the fat but only some of the cholesterol. The same is true when visible fat is trimmed from pork chops. For dairy foods, the amount of

GRAM EQUIVALENTS FOR LOW-FAT GUIDELINES IN VARIOUS DIET PLANS

Guideline	1,200 calories	1,500 calories	2,000 calories
30% fat	40 grams maximum	50 grams maximum	66 grams maximum
10% saturated fat	13 grams maximum	16 grams maximum	22 grams maximum

cholesterol varies with the amount of fat. And even though plant foods have no cholesterol, two examples—palm and coconut oils—are especially high in saturated fats and should be used with discretion.

5. **Blood cholesterol is different from dietary cholesterol.** The amount of cholesterol you eat can affect the amount of cholesterol in your blood, but it is not the only factor. Heredity, gender, age, total diet, and other health habits also influence your blood cholesterol.

How concerned you should be about dietary cholesterol depends on your blood cholesterol level and family health history. The American Heart Association recommends an average of no more than 300 milligrams of cholesterol per day. However, it is estimated that the average American consumes 400 to 500 milligrams per day.

If a blood test shows that your cholesterol is over 200 milligrams per deciliter (mg/dl), your doctor will probably recommend that you reduce your cholesterol intake. If your cholesterol level and/or family health history puts you in a high-risk category for cardiovascular disease, your doctor probably will suggest diet changes and additional cholesterol testing.

WHEN THE FAT DOESN'T ADD UP

You may notice that some recipes in this book contain 0 grams of fat, but are marked "Low Fat" rather than "No Fat."

This occurs because we've rounded the numbers to the nearest whole gram. For example, a serving of Saucy Rhubarb and Strawberries on page 403 actually contains 0.19 gram total fat. We rounded the total fat down to 0 grams. So although the amount of fat per serving is extremely small, there is a small precentage of calories coming from fat, making it a "Low Fat" recipe.

DIETARY CONCERNS: SODIUM, FIBER, SUGAR

USE SALT AND SODIUM ONLY IN MODERATION

Sodium is an essential nutrient. It helps regulate blood volume and is needed for normal functioning of nerves and muscles. Eating too much sodium has been linked to high blood pressure. It's not the only factor leading to high blood pressure, but it is one individuals can control.

The Food and Drug Administration has defined the following five labeling levels for low-sodium products.

Sodium free: Less than 5 milligrams sodium per serving.

Very low sodium: Less than 35 milligrams sodium per serving.

Low sodium: Less than 140 milligrams sodium per serving.

Reduced sodium: At least 75 percent reduction in the usual level of sodium in that food.

Unsalted: No salt added during processing to a food normally processed with salt.

Even if you don't need to watch your blood pressure, it's a good idea to monitor your sodium intake by checking labels on packaged foods, asking questions at restaurants, and reducing your use of high-sodium condiments. But be aware that some salt-free seasonings substitute potassium, which can sometimes lead to other health problems. Read labels carefully and check with a dietitian or physician before using salt substitutes.

Choose a Diet with Plenty Of Vegetables, Fruits, and Grain Products

Unlike the previously discussed concerns, this one focuses on eating more instead of less. The average American eats an estimated 15 to 20 grams of dietary fiber daily. Many health scientists recommend increasing that amount to 35 grams.

Knowing whether you meet such a specific recommendation is hard, however, because of the difficulty in measuring all the various types of food fibers. Authorized, complete tables of analysis are not as readily available as those for other nutrients. However, some foods that have been analyzed for fiber are listed at *right*.

The easiest way to put fiber in your diet is to include daily servings of complex carbohydrates, such as whole grain breads and cereals, pasta, or rice; starchy vegetables such as potatoes, corn, and peas; dried beans or peas; and whole fruits. All of these foods are easy to fit into your low-calorie meals. Just make sure that you do not season these foods with high-calorie ingredients, such as butter, margarine, or sour cream.

Use Sugars Only in Moderation

Although sugar—as a carbohydrate—has half as many calories as fat, it remains a prime suspect in causing weight problems. At 16 calories per teaspoon, sugar may not seem too harmful. The problem is that sugar provides no vitamins, minerals, or other nutrients. When you're watching your weight, you want as many nutrients as possible from the foods you eat. Check the sugar content of a food by reading the ingredient list on package labels. If sugar, sucrose, glucose, dextrose, maltose, lactose, fructose, or syrup appear at or near the top of the list, you may want to reconsider buying the product.

Food	Dietary Fiber (g)
½ cup whole bran cereal or ½ cup baked beans	8.8
½ cup cooked kidney beans	7.3
½ cup cooked navy beans	6.0
½ cup cooked lima beans	4.5
½ cup cooked lentils	3.7
1 medium apple with skin	3.5
½ large pear with skin, or ¼ cup raisins, or ½ cup raspberries	3.1
3 prunes or 1 cup strawberries	3.0
2 slices whole wheat bread or 1 cup shredded cabbage	2.8
½ cup cooked parsnips	2.7
1 medium orange	2.6
1 medium potato with skin	2.5
1 medium banana	2.4
½ cup cooked brussels sprouts	2.3
½ cup cooked broccoli	2.2
½ cup cooked spinach	2.1
1 medium peach with skin or 3 dates	1.9
3 apricots or 1 cup mushrooms	1.8
¾ cup cooked oatmeal or ½ cup cooked green beans	1.6
1 medium tomato, raw	1.5
1 medium potato without skin or 10 peanuts	1.4
1 cup raw spinach	1.2
½ cup cooked spaghetti	1.1
½ cup cooked brown rice	1.0
5 plums or 1 cup lettuce or ½ cup sliced raw mushrooms	0.9
2 tablespoons peanut butter or 1 cup cucumber or 2 slices white bread	0.8
1 plain bagel	0.6

Source: E. Lanza, R. Butrum: Provisional Dietary Fiber Table, National Institute of Health. Journal of the American Dietetic Association. Vol. 86, No. 6, 1986.

MAKING "DIET" HABITS LIFELONG HABITS

For most people, dieting is a long-term—not a one-shot—commitment. People who are most successful in maintaining their weight have learned to balance their eating and exercising habits. You can do it too by following the tips below.

Recognize your progress: If you've been following the guidelines introduced earlier in this book, you've already started forming habits that will make it possible for you to monitor your weight for the rest of your life. For example, you know that good health requires eating a variety of foods in reasonable amounts—not just counting calories. You know that carbohydrates and protein have half as many calories as fats, so they should dominate your food choices.

You also know that weight loss occurs when you burn more calories than you take in and that regular exercise not only makes you feel better, but also burns up some of those calories. You've examined your attitude about exercise and started thinking positively about *using* energy instead of conserving it.

Most important, you know that no one can force you to eat or to exercise. You control your own actions.

Naturally, it will be easier to continue to make the right choices if you surround yourself with people who offer support, rather than temptation. You may need to actively look for formal support groups or ask family and friends to help you. Remember, also, that you win every time you make a healthy decision, such as snacking on an apple instead of a candy bar or walking two blocks instead of driving.

Review the benefits: Whenever you feel bogged down in your weight program, stop and think about your reasons for monitoring your weight. For example, losing weight makes you feel more attractive and boosts your self-confidence.

More important, your weight is a key factor in determining whether you develop serious health problems. Obesity has been linked with high blood pressure, high levels of blood fats (triglycerides) and cholesterol, heart disease, strokes, the most common types of diabetes, and certain cancers. Many factors affect your overall health, but weight is one you can change.

Regardless of how your weight affects—or seems to affect—your social life, it definitely affects your quality of life. Finding and maintaining your ideal weight is a positive step toward enjoying a healthier life.

DAILY FOOD PATTERN

Your average day's menu should include:

4 servings of breads, cereal, and other whole grain and enriched products (serving: 1 slice; 1 ounce ready-to-eat cereal; ½ to ¾ cup cooked cereal, pasta, or rice).

4 servings of fruits and vegetables (serving: ½ cup or a typical portion such as 1 medium orange, ½ of a medium grapefruit, 1 medium potato, 1 wedge of lettuce).

2 servings of meat, poultry, fish, and beans (serving: 2-3 ounces lean cooked meat, poultry, or fish; 1 to 1½ cups cooked dry beans, peas, or lentils).

2-4 servings of milk, yogurt, cheese (serving: 1 cup milk or yogurt, 2 cups cottage cheese, 1½ ounces cheese).

FOLLOW A SENSIBLE EATING PLAN

Planning is essential in meeting your weight goals. As your planned behaviors become habits, your weight monitoring becomes automatic. Planning involves not only what you eat, but also when you eat, and where you eat. Such planning benefits your whole family—even if other family members aren't concerned about calories. The pattern you develop will likely be followed by your children as well. Setting a good example will help your children learn healthy habits that may help prevent weight problems later in their lives.

Remember, the best eating plan gives you a variety of foods and allows flexibility for changing circumstances.

Planning what to eat: Living with a daily calorie quota is like managing a budget—you'll be most successful when every calorie provides as many nutrients as possible. Like an estimated budget, your eating plan is a guideline. It can be as simple as thinking about what foods you want to eat and purchasing the needed ingredients. Planning lets you consider flavors, textures, colors, and preparation needs to give maximum variety while averaging the total calories over several days. Making a plan forces you to shop for nutritious foods, and may help you leave junk foods and other temptations on store shelves.

Planning is especially important for snacks. Make low-calorie, nutritious choices readily available. Limit your use of ready-to-eat snack foods that are high in fat, sugar, and sodium. If you avoid buying them, it will be easier to avoid eating them.

Planning when to eat: In our society, food often serves a social purpose. We are as likely to eat because of our emotions as we are because we are really hungry. Establishing a structured eating plan that allows for moderate amounts at regular intervals will help you regulate your food intake. The more satisfied you feel, the less likely you'll be to eat inappropriate snacks. Knowing that you will be eating again in a certain number of hours also can help you avoid overeating at any one time.

Exactly how many times you should eat each day depends on your situation. For example, breakfast is an especially important meal, but it comes at a hectic time of the day for many people. If getting up 15 minutes earlier is out of the question, or if you're one of the many individuals who just can't eat first thing in the morning, plan a mid-morning snack so you won't be tempted to overeat at noon. Yogurt or cottage cheese, fruit, and a whole grain muffin will give you similar nutrients to those provided in the traditional cereal, milk, and juice breakfast. The key is to plan ahead so the foods you should eat are available. Likewise, a planned afternoon snack can help you avoid overeating at dinner.

Planning where to eat: Some diet plans set strict rules for eating in only one room of the house. This may be a way to break the snacking-anywhere habit, but strict rules can become so boring that you quit the whole plan. A sensible, lifetime eating plan includes more flexibility. Set rules if they help you break a constant snacking habit. But if eating with the TV news fits your schedule, try it; just remember your planned, portion-controlled menu.

MAKE EXERCISE PART OF YOUR DIET

Trying to lose weight without increasing your physical activity is like taking a vacation without planning it. It's possible to do, but not likely to be as successful. In a yearlong study by Baylor College of Medicine, for example, individuals who followed a reduced-calorie diet lost 14 pounds, those who exercised without dieting lost 7 pounds, and those who did both lost 22 pounds.

EXERCISE MYTHS

Exercise isn't the magic ingredient that will instantly make you slimmer. However, regular exercise will help you reach your weight-loss goal sooner. Many people delay starting an exercise program because they think it's too hard or too time-consuming. Actually these and many other excuses are based on the following myths rather than on fact.

1. **You have to do many exercises to have any effect on your weight.**

   Wrong. Every little bit of exercise helps because doing something is better than doing nothing. Taking a brisk half-hour walk every day can mean a loss of 17 pounds of body fat in one year, assuming your calorie intake doesn't increase. If you also monitor how much you eat, you could lose even more. And those gradually lost pounds are likely to stay off longer than pounds lost quickly through fad dieting.

2. **Exercising increases your appetite.**

   The truth is that the body's appetite mechanism is more likely to function properly with increased activity than when activity levels are low. Filling your leisure time with exercise may also mean you have less time to snack.

3. **Exercise can make you lose weight in specific body areas.**

   Certain exercises do strengthen and firm muscles in specific areas, improving the figure, but fat actually is lost from stored deposits throughout the body.

4. **Exercise is risky for older adults.**

   More influential than age is an individual's overall health status. Medical problems, such as high blood pressure or a heart murmur, may dictate some modifications. Checking with your doctor is always a good idea before starting an exercise program.

5. **Exercise is too tiring.**

   Pushing yourself to exhaustion is seldom a good idea, especially when you're just beginning an exercise program. Setting a reasonable pace will allow you to build up your endurance without becoming discouraged and quitting. As you stick with your program, you probably also will discover that you feel less tired than you did previously. As you become more fit, you'll also notice your self-confidence building while anxieties and depression decrease.

6. **Exercise is boring.**

   So is sleeping, but that doesn't make it any less necessary. The best way to make exercise fun is to choose an activity you can share with a friend. Better yet, join two or three friends for two or three different activities during the week. If that's not possible, investigate group exercise sessions offered by your community recreation center, health club, or fitness center.

7. **Exercising takes too much time.**

   The real question here is not time, but commitment. Whether you are committed to losing weight, maintaining a desired weight, or just improving your overall health, you owe it to yourself to devote some free time to exercising. Look for opportunities to walk instead of ride, to stand instead of sit, and to be active with family and friends.

8. Exercise produces large muscles.

While it's true that weight lifting and some other forms of exercise practiced in excess can produce an overly muscular physique, moderate overall exercise tends to firm up the body and give you a trimmer look.

FITTING EXERCISE INTO YOUR LIFE

Knowing the importance of exercise doesn't automatically make exercise part of your life. Like any habit, it takes time to develop. Oftentimes the first step involves a change in attitude—thinking positively about using energy rather than saving energy.

The ideal exercise program includes 20 to 30 minutes of aerobic activity at your target heart rate (see tip box at right) combined with both a warm-up and a cooldown composed of flexibility and stretching exercises for your joints and muscles.

The best program for you depends on your general health, including how active you've been recently. If you've been more inactive than active, you'll want to start slowly with daily goals to help reinforce your commitment.

The best exercise activities for individuals who are out of shape or who are easily injured are low-impact or low-stress aerobics, such as walking, biking, or swimming.

Brisk walking. This is one of the most highly recommended exercises for all age groups. The only equipment needed is a good pair of shoes, thick socks, and comfortable, loose-fitting clothes.

Before you begin your walk, do warm-up exercises to stretch your muscles. This will prevent possible injury during exercise and minimize soreness following exercise.

Aim for a smooth stride when you walk. As you feel more comfortable, increase your pace to reach your target heart rate; continue for 15 to 20 minutes then slow down to a comfortable pace; continue a slow walk until your heart rate approaches resting level. Repeat some of the stretches for a cooldown.

Bicycling. Riding a bike to work, for errands, or with family and friends is an excellent way to put variety into your exercise program. Select a bike that fits your body size and life-style, whether it's a 10-speed touring bike or an indoor exercise bike.

Before starting out, be sure to stretch. Start riding slowly, then increase your speed. After maintaining your target heart rate for at least 20 minutes, remember to cool down by pedaling at a slower speed to let your heart reach resting level before dismounting. Then repeat some stretching exercises.

Swimming. This is an excellent exercise choice if you have weak leg muscles or painful joints because the water helps support your weight.

Your long-term goal is to swim continuously for 20 minutes. Before starting to swim, spend about 10 minutes in warm-up exercises. And before getting out of the pool, swim slowly to allow your heart to return to its normal resting rate. Cool down by repeating some of the stretching exercises.

TARGET HEART RATE

The average adult has a resting heart rate of about 70 beats per minute. To find your target heart rate, subtract your age from 220. Multiply this number by 0.7. Using this calculation, a 40-year-old person would have a target rate of 126 beats per minute.

Monitor your heart rate during exercise so that it gradually increases during the warm-up, is maintained at the target rate for 20 to 30 minutes, then is gradually decreased to normal during the cooldown. (To check your heart rate, place the tips of your second and third fingers on one side of your Adam's apple; count the beats for 10 seconds and multiply by 6.)

SET UP A CRISIS-MANAGEMENT STRATEGY

Away-from-home meals and holiday celebrations are unavoidable hazards for the dieter. They often include traditional foods to satisfy emotional and social—rather than nutritional—needs. Such occasions become excuses for overeating foods we might consider off-limits the rest of the year.

How you deal with these temptations is your choice. Some people try to remain aloof and maintain their strict diet plan, while secretly feeling cheated. Others abandon their eating plans and give in totally to the celebrations, later regretting the consequences. Still others manage to maintain a moderate approach, balancing denial and impulse.

An event is less likely to be your downfall, however, if you plan a strategy. Here are some ideas that might help.

1. Be realistic.
The eating plan you develop is a road map. Some detours will be beyond your control, while others will be your own doing; accept this fact. Who's to blame is less important than how fast you get back on track.

2. Identify the situations that are most tempting and look for alternatives.
Food is often used as a catalyst to draw people together. When you give yourself permission to create new reasons for gathering, you remove some temptation. Ask a friend to join you in a craft class or to view a museum exhibit instead of meeting for lunch. Suggest going to a movie, play, or concert instead of a restaurant when you want to celebrate. When eating lunch together is the only practical choice, suggest a restaurant where you know you can eat sensibly. Or, propose a picnic where you can bring your own food and perhaps even get some exercise.

Before holiday celebrations arrive, think about the traditions you most enjoy. How many are related to food? Are some foods prepared because they are expected rather than enjoyed? What's the worst that could happen if some traditional foods were omitted or made in smaller amounts?

3. If you cannot control the situation, remember that you still control what you eat.
Serve yourself small helpings and eat slowly. In a restaurant, ask about portion size before ordering; if appropriate, offer to split an order with your companion. If attending a buffet or party, eat a nutritious snack before you go to take the edge off your hunger. Remind yourself why it's important to reach your weight goal.

Learn to savor the first bite. Take a small helping and remind yourself that additional helpings never taste as good as the first.

HOW TO AVOID HOLIDAY HOLDUPS IN YOUR DIET

1. Review past experiences.
Identify specific instances you will face again. What were the consequences of your past actions?

2. Brainstorm alternatives.
Write down actions you can take to avoid or resist tempting situations.

3. Practice the desired behavior.
Follow your plan in your imagination and in your daily activities.

4. Get enough rest.
Nothing will sabotage your plans faster than being too tired.

BEGIN-YOUR-DIET MENUS

SPINACH SALAD *(see page 55)*

BEGIN-YOUR-DIET MENUS

Here it is! An easy way to start your diet out right. Just by following the daily meal and snack plans in this chapter, you'll limit yourself to around 1,200 calories per day. Use all 14 days of meals or select individual daily menus that fit your tastes and needs. The page references in the menus tell you where the recipes appear.

Besides the foods listed, remember to drink six to eight glasses of water each day. Also, it's difficult to consume an adequate amount of iron when you are dieting. So check with your doctor to see if he or she recommends a multivitamin and/or a mineral supplement.

Good luck!

DAY	BREAKFAST	LUNCH	DINNER	SNACK
One (1,243 total calories)	½ cup blueberries 1 ounce bran flakes ½ cup skim milk	1 serving Salmon- and Pasta-Stuffed Tomatoes **(see page 22)** Whole grain crackers (equaling 75 calories) 1 fresh pear	1 serving Burritos with 1 serving Quick-to-Fix Spanish Rice **(see page 23)** 1 serving tossed salad with dressing* ½ cup skim milk	¼ small cantaloupe (1 cup) *or* other fruit ½ cup skim milk
Two (1,221 total calories)	1 cup sliced fresh strawberries ½ whole wheat and raisin bagel with 1 tablespoon reduced-calorie soft-style cream cheese 1 cup skim milk	1 serving Marinated Vegetable and Turkey Sandwiches **(see page 24)** Carbonated water 1 banana 1 cup skim milk	4 ounces broiled beef tenderloin 1 serving Herbed Vegetable Toss **(see page 25)** 1 serving tossed salad with dressing* 1 fresh plum *or* other fruit	1 fresh peach *or* other fruit
Three (1,194 total calories)	1 serving Pancakes with Orange Sauce **(see page 26)** 1 cup skim milk	1 serving salad with roast beef (3 ounces lean cooked roast beef, 2 cups torn lettuce, 1½ cups torn fresh spinach, and ½ cup broccoli flowerets tossed with 2 tablespoons reduced-calorie salad dressing with less than 15 calories per tablespoon) Whole grain crackers (equaling 75 calories) ¾ cup skim milk	1 serving Chicken and Sweet Pepper Stir-Fry **(see page 27)** ½ cup steamed brown rice 3 small fresh pineapple wedges (½ cup) 1 fortune cookie	2 fresh apricots *or* 1 fresh peach 3 cups popped popcorn (no fat**)

DAY	BREAKFAST	LUNCH	DINNER	SNACK
Four (1,211 total calories)	1 serving Cheese- and Fruit-Topped English Muffins (**see page 28**) ¾ cup skim milk	1 serving Chinese Burritos (**see page 29**) ¾ cup steamed sliced carrots 1 cup fresh red *and/or* green grapes	¾ cup cooked whole wheat spaghetti ½ cup spaghetti sauce with mushrooms and 2 ounces cooked lean ground beef 1 breadstick 1 serving Tossed Italian Salad (**see page 30**)	1 fresh peach *or* other fruit ½ cup skim milk
Five (1,226 total calories)	1 cup mixed fruit topped with ¼ cup lemon low-fat yogurt*** 2 slices whole wheat bread, toasted, with 1 teaspoon reduced-calorie margarine	1 serving Greek-Style Pita Sandwiches (**see page 31**) 1 cup steamed broccoli cuts 1 wedge cantaloupe (1 cup) *or* other fruit ½ cup skim milk	4 ounces broiled skinned chicken breast half 1 serving Lemony-Herbed Asparagus (**see page 32**) 1 serving Fruit Slaw (**see page 33**) 1 whole wheat roll 1 cup skim milk	1 fresh pear *or* other fruit
Six (1,219 total calories)	½ cup low-calorie cranberry juice cocktail *or* ½ cup fresh fruit 1 ounce shredded wheat biscuits 1 cup skim milk	1 serving Ham and Vegetable Soup (**see page 34**) ½ whole wheat English muffin, toasted, with 1 teaspoon reduced-calorie margarine 1 cup watermelon cubes *or* other fruit 1 cup skim milk	3 ounces cooked lean roast pork 1 serving Stuffed Winter Squash (**see page 35**) ½ cup stewed *or* sliced tomatoes 1 whole wheat roll with 1 teaspoon reduced-calorie margarine	1 fresh orange 3 cups popped popcorn (no fat**)

DAY	BRUNCH		DINNER	SNACK
Seven (1,211 total calories)	1 cup assorted fresh fruits 1 serving Puffy Omelet Squares (**see page 36**) ½ whole wheat English muffin, toasted, with 1 teaspoon reduced-calorie margarine 1 cup skim milk		4 ounces grilled salmon steak 1½ cups steamed pea pods 3 boiled new potatoes 1 serving tossed salad with dressing* 1 serving Poached Pears with Raspberry Sauce (**see page 37**)	1 cup cantaloupe *or* other fruit 1 cup skim milk

MENU HINTS

When no beverage is listed with a meal, drink water, tea, or coffee.

* For 1 serving tossed salad, use 2 cups torn spinach and lettuce and ¼ cup each sliced carrot and broccoli tossed with 2 tablespoons reduced-calorie salad dressing with less than 15 calories per tablespoon.

** Pop popcorn without any oil. Do not add any margarine or butter to popped popcorn.

*** Yogurt with less than 150 calories per 8 ounces.

21

SALMON-AND-PASTA-STUFFED TOMATOES   186 calories

Preparation Time: 25 min. ▪ Chilling Time: 4 hrs. ▪ Low Fat ▪ Low Cholesterol

Choose bright red, medium tomatoes. Insert the point of a sharp knife into each tomato near the core and cut out one-half inch of the core. Invert the tomatoes. Then, cut from the top to, but not quite through, the stem end. Repeat to cut each tomato into 6 wedges.

1	cup four-color corkscrew macaroni
1	7½-ounce can salmon, drained, flaked, and skin and bones removed
½	cup plain low-fat yogurt
½	cup shredded cucumber
¼	cup shredded carrot
2	tablespoons reduced-calorie mayonnaise *or* salad dressing
¼	teaspoon dried dillweed
4	medium tomatoes

▪ Cook macaroni according to package directions. Drain; set aside. Combine salmon, yogurt, cucumber, carrot, mayonnaise or salad dressing, dillweed, ¼ teaspoon *salt,* and ⅛ teaspoon *pepper.* Toss with pasta. Cover; chill 4 to 24 hours.

▪ Meanwhile, for tomato cups, cut out ½ *inch* of the core from *each* tomato. Invert tomatoes. For each, cut from top to, *but not quite through,* the stem end, making 6 wedges.

▪ To serve, place tomatoes on plates. Spread wedges slightly apart; fill with salmon-pasta mixture. Makes 4 servings.

Nutrition information per serving: 186 calories, 15 g protein, 19 g carbohydrate, 6 g fat, 3 mg cholesterol, 452 mg sodium, 570 mg potassium.

BURRITOS

Preparation Time: 15 min. ▪ Cooking Time: 10 min. ▪ Low Fat ▪ Low Cholesterol

Spoon the meat filling onto each tortilla just below the center. Fold the bottom edge of each tortilla up and over the filling just till the mixture is covered. Fold opposite sides of each tortilla in, just till they meet. Roll up tortillas.

4	10-inch flour tortillas
½	pound lean ground beef
1	cup chopped onion
1	15-ounce can black beans, drained
1	10-ounce can tomatoes with green chili peppers
2	teaspoons chili powder
	Chopped green onion

▪ Wrap tortillas in foil. Heat in a 350° oven for 10 minutes to soften. Meanwhile, for filling, cook ground beef and onion till meat is brown and onion is tender. Drain. Stir in black beans, *undrained* tomatoes with chili peppers, and chili powder. Simmer, uncovered, 5 minutes or to desired consistency.

▪ Reserve ¼ cup filling; set aside. Spoon *one-fourth* of the remaining filling onto *each* tortilla just below center. Fold bottom edge of tortilla up and over filling. Fold opposite sides of tortilla in, just till they meet. Roll up from the bottom. Top with some of the reserved filling. Sprinkle with green onion. Makes 4 servings.

Note: Serve these meaty burritos with Quick-to-Fix Spanish Rice: Heat together 2 cups cooked rice, 1 cup chopped tomato, and one 4-ounce can diced green chili peppers.

Nutrition information per serving: 386 calories, 23 g protein, 49 g carbohydrate, 12 g fat, 37 mg cholesterol, 324 mg sodium, 635 mg potassium.

VEGETABLE AND TURKEY SANDWICHES   *257 calories*

Preparation Time: 25 min. ▪ Chilling Time: 4 hrs. ▪ Low Fat ▪ Low Cholesterol

½	cup sliced green pepper
½	cup small cauliflower flowerets
1	medium carrot, cut into thin strips (½ cup)
1	medium tomato, chopped
6	pitted ripe olives, sliced
4	green onions, cut into strips
½	cup reduced-calorie Italian salad dressing
½	teaspoon dried basil, crushed
4	club rolls, split
4	slices fully cooked turkey breast (4 ounces total)

▪ Combine green pepper slices, cauliflower, carrot strips, chopped tomato, olive slices, and onion strips. Stir in Italian salad dressing and basil. Cover and refrigerate vegetable mixture for 4 to 24 hours.

▪ To assemble sandwiches, toast rolls, if desired. Top *each* roll half with *half* a turkey slice. Stir vegetable mixture. Using a slotted spoon, spoon vegetable mixture over turkey slices. Makes 4 servings.

Nutrition information per serving: 257 calories, 14 g protein, 36 g carbohydrate, 7 g fat, 22 mg cholesterol, 604 mg sodium, 329 mg potassium.

HERBED VEGETABLE TOSS

170 calories

Preparation Time: 15 min. ▪ Cooking Time: 20 min. ▪ Low Fat ▪ Low Sodium ▪ No Cholesterol

Pair these steamed veggies with a broiled steak for a filling dinner.

12	**whole tiny new potatoes**
4	**medium carrots, bias-sliced into 1-inch pieces (2 cups)**
2	**teaspoons olive oil *or* margarine, melted**
¼	**teaspoon dried rosemary *or* thyme, crushed**

▪ Place a steamer basket in a large saucepan. Add water to just below basket. Bring water to boiling.

▪ Meanwhile, peel a strip around the center of each new potato. Add potatoes and carrots to steamer basket. Cover and steam for 20 to 25 minutes or till vegetables are tender.

▪ Remove vegetables from steamer basket and place in a serving bowl. Sprinkle with oil or melted margarine and rosemary or thyme. Toss lightly to coat. Makes 4 servings.

Nutrition information per serving: 170 calories, 3 g protein, 35 g carbohydrate, 3 g fat, 0 mg cholesterol, 31 mg sodium, 749 mg potassium.

PANCAKES WITH ORANGE SAUCE

233 calories

Preparation Time: 25 min. ▪ Low Fat ▪ Low Cholesterol

Spray a cold griddle or heavy skillet with nonstick spray coating; heat over medium heat till drops of water dance across the surface of the griddle or skillet. Cook pancakes till golden brown, turning to cook second sides when pancakes have bubbly surfaces and slightly dry edges.

¾	**cup whole wheat flour**
¼	**cup all-purpose flour**
1½	**teaspoons baking powder**
¾	**cup skim milk**
1	**tablespoon honey**
1	**teaspoon cooking oil**
2	**stiffly beaten egg whites**
	Nonstick spray coating
	Orange Sauce

▪ Combine flours, baking powder, and ⅛ teaspoon *salt*. Combine milk, honey, and oil; add to dry ingredients. Stir just till moistened. Fold in egg whites.

▪ Spray a *cold* griddle with nonstick spray coating. For *each* pancake, pour about ¼ *cup* batter onto *hot* griddle. Cook till brown, turning when pancakes have bubbly surfaces. Serve with Orange Sauce. Serves 4.

▪ **Orange Sauce:** Combine 2 tablespoons *sugar* and 1 tablespoon *cornstarch*. Stir in ¾ cup *water* and 2 tablespoons frozen *orange juice concentrate*. Cook and stir till thickened and bubbly. Cook and stir 2 minutes more. Stir in one 11-ounce can *mandarin orange sections,* drained, and 1 tablespoon finely chopped *walnuts*. Keep warm.

Nutrition information per serving: 233 calories, 8 g protein, 47 g carbohydrate, 2 g fat, 1 mg cholesterol, 244 mg sodium, 352 mg potassium.

CHICKEN AND SWEET PEPPER STIR-FRY   204 calories

Preparation Time: 10 min. ▪ Marinating Time: 30 min. ▪ Cooking Time: 15 min. ▪ Low Fat ▪ Low Cholesterol

18	**ounces boned skinless chicken breast halves**
3	**tablespoons soy sauce**
1	**tablespoon dry sherry**
	Nonstick spray coating
1	**medium onion, cut into wedges**
2	**medium green *or* sweet red peppers, thinly sliced**
1½	**cups sliced fresh mushrooms**
1	**tablespoon cooking oil**
1	**teaspoon grated gingerroot**
1	**8-ounce can bamboo shoots, drained**
¼	**cup chicken broth**
1	**teaspoon cornstarch**

▪ Cut chicken into ½-inch pieces. Place in a bowl; stir in soy sauce and sherry. Let stand for 30 minutes. Spray a *cold* wok or large skillet with nonstick spray coating; preheat over medium-high heat. Add onion; stir-fry 2 minutes. Add peppers; stir-fry 1 minute. Add mushrooms; stir-fry about 1 minute more or till vegetables are crisp-tender. Remove vegetables from wok or skillet; set aside.

▪ Drain chicken, reserving the marinade. Add oil to wok. Add gingerroot; stir-fry 15 seconds. Add *half* the chicken; stir-fry 3 to 4 minutes or till no longer pink. Remove. Stir-fry remaining chicken for 3 to 4 minutes or till no longer pink. Return all chicken, vegetables, and bamboo shoots to wok; push from center of wok.

▪ Stir broth, cornstarch, and ¼ teaspoon *pepper* into reserved marinade; add to wok. Cook and stir till slightly thickened; toss gently to coat chicken mixture. Measure and refrigerate *2 cups* mixture for Chinese Burritos (see page 29). Serve remaining mixture while hot. Serves 4.

Nutrition information per serving: 204 calories, 30 g protein, 8 g carbohydrate, 6 g fat, 73 mg cholesterol, 613 mg sodium, 621 mg potassium.

CHEESE-TOPPED ENGLISH MUFFINS

236 calories

Preparation Time: 15 min. ▪ Low Fat ▪ Low Cholesterol

Avoid a breakfast scramble by stirring together the cheese mixture the night before.

¾	**cup low-fat ricotta cheese**
¼	**teaspoon finely shredded lime peel**
2	**teaspoons lime juice**
1	**tablespoon sugar**
⅛	**teaspoon ground nutmeg**
4	**whole wheat English muffins, split and toasted**
2	**whole kiwi fruit, sliced, *or* 1 cup sliced strawberries *or* peaches**

▪ In a small bowl combine ricotta cheese, lime peel, lime juice, sugar, and nutmeg. Spread cheese mixture evenly over toasted muffin halves.

▪ Top each muffin half with kiwi fruit slices, strawberry slices, or peach slices. Makes 4 servings.

Nutrition information per serving: 236 calories, 11 g protein, 37 g carbohydrate, 6 g fat, 14 mg cholesterol, 416 mg sodium, 285 mg potassium.

CHINESE BURRITOS

257 calories

Preparation Time: 20 min. ▪ Cooking Time: 5 min. ▪ Low Fat ▪ Low Cholesterol

This south-of-the-border specialty is filled with the Oriental stir-fry reserved from Day Three's dinner menu.

4	**8-inch flour tortillas**
2	**cups Chicken and Sweet Pepper Stir-Fry (see page 27)**
1	**4-ounce can sliced mushrooms, drained**
¼	**cup plum preserves**

▪ Wrap tortillas in foil. Heat in a 350° oven for 10 minutes to soften.

▪ Meanwhile, in a medium saucepan stir together the reserved Chicken and Sweet Pepper Stir-Fry, mushrooms, and plum preserves. Cook and stir over medium heat about 5 minutes or till heated through.

▪ To assemble, spoon *one-fourth* of the chicken mixture down the center of *each* tortilla. Fold in the opposite sides of the tortilla so they overlap. Makes 4 servings.

Nutrition information per serving: 257 calories, 18 g protein, 36 g carbohydrate, 5 g fat, 36 mg cholesterol, 433 mg sodium, 328 mg potassium.

TOSSED ITALIAN SALAD

83 calories

Preparation Time: 25 min. ▪ Low Cholesterol

4	**cups torn fresh spinach**
2	**cups torn red leaf lettuce**
1	**medium green *or* sweet yellow pepper, cut into strips (1 cup)**
⅔	**cup thinly sliced radishes**
1	**small red onion, sliced and separated into rings**
2	**tablespoons red wine vinegar**
4	**teaspoons olive oil *or* salad oil**
½	**teaspoon garlic salt**
½	**teaspoon dried oregano, crushed**
2	**tablespoons grated Parmesan cheese**

▪ For salad, in a large salad bowl place spinach, lettuce, pepper strips, radish slices, and onion rings. Toss lightly.

▪ For dressing, in a screw-top jar combine vinegar, olive oil, garlic salt, oregano, and 1 tablespoon *water.* Cover and shake well to mix.

▪ Pour dressing over salad. Toss lightly to coat. Sprinkle Parmesan cheese over salad. Toss lightly. Sprinkle with coarsely ground pepper, if desired. Serve immediately. Makes 4 servings.

Nutrition information per serving: 83 calories, 4 g protein, 6 g carbohydrate, 6 g fat, 2 mg cholesterol, 364 mg sodium, 466 mg potassium.

GREEK-STYLE PITA SANDWICHES

209 calories

Preparation Time: 25 min. ▪ Cooking Time: 3 min. ▪ Low Cholesterol

½	**pound lean boneless lamb** *or* **pork**
2	**pita bread rounds, halved crosswise**
¼	**cup plain low-fat yogurt**
2	**tablespoons reduced-calorie mayonnaise** *or* **salad dressing**
1	**teaspoon dried dillweed**
	Nonstick spray coating
1	**clove garlic, minced**
¼	**teaspoon onion powder**
1	**small cucumber, thinly sliced (⅔ cup)**
1	**small tomato, thinly sliced**

▪ Partially freeze lamb or pork. Thinly slice across the grain into bite-size strips. Set aside.

▪ Wrap pita halves in foil. Heat in a 350° oven for 10 minutes. In a small bowl combine yogurt, mayonnaise or salad dressing, and dillweed. Set aside.

▪ Meanwhile, spray a *cold* wok or skillet with nonstick spray coating; preheat over medium-high heat. Add lamb or pork, garlic, and onion powder; stir-fry about 3 minutes or till meat is tender. Remove wok or skillet from heat. Stir in ⅛ teaspoon *salt* and ⅛ teaspoon *pepper*.

▪ Spread some of the yogurt mixture inside each warm pita half. Fill pita halves with meat mixture, cucumber slices, and tomato slices. Makes 4 servings.

Nutrition information per serving: 209 calories, 18 g protein, 14 g carbohydrate, 8 g fat, 63 mg cholesterol, 221 mg sodium, 336 mg potassium.

LEMONY HERBED ASPARAGUS

58 calories

Preparation Time: 10 min. ▪ Cooking Time: 5 min. ▪ No Cholesterol ▪ Low Sodium

When fresh asparagus isn't available, use a 10-ounce package of frozen spears and cook it according to the package directions.

1	**pound asparagus spears**
1	**tablespoon olive oil** *or* **margarine**
⅛	**teaspoon dried basil, crushed**
⅛	**teaspoon dried oregano, crushed**
1	**teaspoon lemon juice**

▪ To prepare fresh asparagus, wash and scrape off scales. Snap off and discard the woody bases.

▪ Meanwhile, place a steamer basket in a medium saucepan. Add water to just below basket. Bring water to boiling. Add asparagus to steamer basket. Cover and steam for 5 to 8 minutes or till tender.

▪ Meanwhile, in another saucepan combine olive oil or margarine, basil, oregano, and dash *pepper.* Cook and stir over medium heat till heated through or till margarine melts. Remove from heat. Stir in lemon juice.

▪ Transfer asparagus to a serving platter. Drizzle with lemon mixture. Makes 4 servings.

Nutrition information per serving: 58 calories, 3 g protein, 5 g carbohydrate, 4 g fat, 0 mg cholesterol, 5 mg sodium, 358 mg potassium.

FRUIT SLAW

Preparation Time: 15 min. ▪ Chilling Time: 4 hrs. ▪ No Cholesterol ▪ Low Sodium

Cut the preparation time by starting with a bag of shredded cabbage with carrot.

1	8-ounce can pineapple chunks (juice pack)
2	cups shredded cabbage
⅔	cup chopped apple
½	cup shredded carrot
¼	cup chopped green pepper
1	tablespoon cooking oil
1	tablespoon honey
1	tablespoon lemon juice
⅛	teaspoon ground ginger *or* ¼ teaspoon grated gingerroot

▪ Drain pineapple chunks, reserving 2 tablespoons juice. Set juice aside. For salad, in a large salad bowl combine pineapple, cabbage, apple, carrot, and green pepper.

▪ For dressing, in a screw-top jar combine reserved pineapple juice, oil, honey, lemon juice, ginger or gingerroot, and ⅛ teaspoon *salt.* Cover and shake well to mix. Pour dressing over salad. Toss lightly to coat. Chill 4 to 24 hours. Toss before serving. Serve with a slotted spoon. Makes 4 servings.

Nutrition information per serving: 104 calories, 1 g protein, 19 g carbohydrate, 4 g fat, 0 mg cholesterol, 15 mg sodium, 283 mg potassium.

HAM AND VEGETABLE SOUP

172 calories

Preparation Time: 15 min. ▪ Cooking Time: 17 min. ▪ Low Fat ▪ Low Cholesterol

4½	cups chicken broth
2	medium potatoes, cubed (2 cups)
½	cup chopped onion
1½	cups broccoli flowerets
1	cup cauliflower flowerets
¼	teaspoon ground nutmeg
½	cup chopped, fully cooked ham (about 3 ounces)

■ In a large saucepan combine chicken broth, potatoes, and onion. Bring to boiling; reduce heat. Cover and simmer for 10 minutes.

■ Stir in broccoli, cauliflower, and nutmeg. Simmer about 5 minutes more or till vegetables are crisp-tender. Stir in ham and heat through. Makes 4 servings.

Nutrition information per serving: 172 calories, 14 g protein, 22 g carbohydrate, 3 g fat, 13 mg cholesterol, 1,175 mg sodium, 836 mg potassium.

STUFFED WINTER SQUASH

125 calories

Preparation Time: 13 min. ▪ Cooking Time: 65 min. ▪ Low Fat ▪ No Cholesterol ▪ Low Sodium

From the first forkful to the last bite, this apple-stuffed acorn squash is a real crowd-pleaser.

2	small acorn squash (14 to 16 ounces each)
1½	cups chopped cooking apple
¼	cup chopped celery
2	tablespoons chopped walnuts
1	tablespoon sugar
½	teaspoon ground cinnamon
	Salt

▪ Cut squash in half lengthwise; remove seeds. Place squash halves, cut side down, in a shallow baking dish. Bake in a 350° oven for 40 to 45 minutes or till almost tender.

▪ Meanwhile, stir together apple, celery, walnuts, sugar, and cinnamon. Turn squash halves cut side up. Sprinkle lightly with salt. Spoon apple mixture into squash halves. Return to oven and bake, covered, about 25 minutes more or till apple is tender. Makes 4 servings.

▪ **Microwave directions:** Prepare as above *except* place squash halves, cut side down, in a microwave-safe 12x7½x2-inch baking dish. Micro-cook, uncovered, on 100% power (high) for 8 to 12 minutes or till tender. Turn squash over; sprinkle with salt and fill with apple mixture. Cover with vented plastic wrap and cook on high for 4 to 5 minutes or till apple is tender.

Nutrition information per serving: 125 calories, 2 g protein, 27 g carbohydrate, 3 g fat, 0 mg cholesterol, 12 mg sodium, 551 mg potassium.

PUFFY OMELET SQUARES

144 calories

Preparation Time: 13 min. ▪ Cooking Time: 22 min.

	Nonstick spray coating
6	**egg yolks**
½	**teaspoon onion powder**
¼	**teaspoon salt**
⅛	**teaspoon pepper**
6	**egg whites**
1	**14½-ounce can stewed tomatoes, cut up**
½	**of a medium zucchini, quartered lengthwise and sliced (½ cup)**
⅛	**teaspoon pepper**

■ Spray an 8x8x2-inch baking dish with nonstick spray coating; set aside. For omelet, beat egg yolks, onion powder, salt, and ⅛ teaspoon pepper about 4 minutes or till thick and lemon colored; set aside. Beat egg whites till soft peaks form (tips fold over); fold into egg yolks.

■ Spread egg mixture evenly into prepared dish. Bake in a 350° oven for 22 to 25 minutes or till a knife inserted near the center comes out clean.

■ Meanwhile, for sauce combine *undrained* tomatoes, zucchini, and ⅛ teaspoon pepper. Bring to boiling; reduce heat. Cover and simmer about 5 minutes or till zucchini is tender. Simmer, uncovered, for 10 to 12 minutes more or to desired consistency. To serve, cut omelet into quarters; top with sauce. Makes 4 servings.

Nutrition information per serving: 144 calories, 10 g protein, 7 g carbohydrate, 9 g fat, 411 mg cholesterol, 395 mg sodium, 392 mg potassium.

POACHED PEARS WITH RASPBERRY SAUCE   167 calories

Preparation Time: 43 min. ▪ Chilling Time: 2 hrs. ▪ Low Fat ▪ No Cholesterol ▪ Low Sodium

Wash pears; pat dry. Using an apple corer, core the pears from the bottom, leaving the stems attached; peel. Cut a thin slice off the bottom of the pears so they'll stand upright. Then rub the pears with lemon juice to prevent them from turning brown.

4	**medium pears, cored and peeled**
	Lemon juice
2	**cups water**
2	**cups frozen, lightly sweetened red raspberries, thawed**
⅓	**cup white wine**
4	**teaspoons sugar**

■ Cut a thin slice off the bottom of each pear so it stands; rub pears with lemon juice. In large saucepan, bring water to boiling. Place pears upright in pan. (Add additional water to cover pears, if necessary, to prevent pears from turning brown.) Return to boiling; reduce heat. Cover and simmer for 8 to 10 minutes or till tender. Chill pears in cooking liquid.

■ For sauce, place berries in a blender container or food processor bowl. Cover and blend or process till puréed; press berries through a sieve to remove seeds.

■ Place berries in a small saucepan; stir in wine and sugar. Bring to boiling; reduce heat. Simmer, uncovered, for 15 to 20 minutes or till reduced to about ¾ cup, stirring occasionally. Chill.

■ To serve, spoon most of the raspberry sauce onto 4 serving plates. Remove pears from poaching liquid; place upright in sauce. Spoon remaining sauce over pears. Serves 4.

Nutrition information per serving: 167 calories, 2 g protein, 43 g carbohydrate, 1 g fat, 0 mg cholesterol, 5 mg sodium, 332 mg potassium.

BEGIN-YOUR-DIET MENUS—WEEK TWO

DAY	BREAKFAST	LUNCH	DINNER	SNACK
Eight (1,217 total calories)	1 small wedge honeydew melon garnished with a strawberry 1 serving Apple and Oat Bran Muffins (**see page 40**) 1 cup skim milk	1 cup canned Manhattan-style clam chowder prepared with water Whole grain crackers (equaling 75 calories) 1 fresh pear 1 cup skim milk	1 serving Turkey Paprikash (**see page 41**) 1½ cups steamed broccoli 1 apple *or* other fruit	½ whole wheat bagel with 1 tablespoon reduced-calorie soft-style cream cheese 1 cup carrot and celery sticks
Nine (1,244 total calories)	1 fresh orange 1 ounce oatmeal, cooked 1 cup skim milk	1 serving Vegetarian Chili with Rice (**see page 42**) 1 serving tossed salad with dressing* ½ cup pineapple chunks (fresh or water pack, drained) 1 cup skim milk	4 ounces baked fish steak *or* fillet 1 serving Wild Rice and Bulgur Pilaf (**see page 43**) 1 serving Stuffed Tomatoes (**see page 44**) Carbonated water	1 cup watermelon chunks *or* other fruit
Ten (1,207 total calories)	3 fresh apricots *or* juice-pack canned apricots 1 ounce oat bran cereal, cooked, with 1 teaspoon sugar ½ cup skim milk	1 serving Cheesy Tater Topper (**see page 45**) 1 medium apple	1 serving Ham and Vegetables with Mostaccioli (**see page 46**) ½ cup cooked spinach ¼ small cantaloupe (1 cup) *or* other fruit 1 cup skim milk	2 6-inch breadsticks
Eleven (1,190 total calories)	2 fresh kiwi fruit, sliced and topped with ¼ cup vanilla low-fat yogurt*** ½ whole wheat English muffin *or* bagel with 1 teaspoon reduced-calorie margarine	1 serving Mushroom and Barley Soup (**see page 47**) ½ whole wheat bagel *or* English muffin, toasted, with 1 teaspoon reduced-calorie margarine 1 fresh peach *or* other fruit 1 cup skim milk	4 ounces baked chicken breast 1 serving Mexican-Style Creamed Corn (**see page 48**) 1 serving tossed salad with dressing* ¼ small cantaloupe (1 cup) *or* other fruit 1 cup skim milk	1 fresh pear

DAY	BREAKFAST	LUNCH	DINNER	SNACK
Twelve (1,180 total calories)	½ cup fresh blueberries 1 ounce bran flakes ½ cup skim milk	Pita sandwich (½ whole wheat pita bread round, 3 ounces cooked lean roast beef, ½ cup thin cucumber slices, ½ cup alfalfa sprouts, 2 teaspoons reduced-calorie mayonnaise) 1 cup steamed sliced carrots with 1 teaspoon reduced-calorie margarine	1 serving Oriental Openers (**see page 49**) 1 serving Linguine with Scallops (**see page 50**) 2 or 3 tomato slices 1 serving Fruit Tart (**see page 51**)	1 cup skim milk
Thirteen (1,193 total calories)	1 whole wheat waffle topped with ½ cup raspberries 1 cup skim milk	2 ounces baked turkey breast slices 1 serving Brown Rice Pilaf (**see page 52**) 2 small tomato wedges ¼ small cantaloupe (1 cup) *or* other fruit 1 cup skim milk	4 ounces cooked lean roast beef 1 small baked potato with 1 tablespoon reduced-calorie margarine 1 cup steamed peas and pearl onions 1 serving Peach Daiquiri Ice (**see page 53**)	2 cups popped popcorn (no fat**)
Fourteen (1,212 total calories)	1 fresh orange 1 serving Oatmeal with Fruit and Nuts (**see page 54**) ½ cup skim milk	1 roast beef sandwich (2 slices whole wheat bread, 2 ounces cooked lean roast beef, 3 slices tomato, ½ cup alfalfa sprouts, 2 teaspoons reduced-calorie mayonnaise) 1 cup steamed summer squash	1 serving Spinach Salad (**see page 55**) Grilled shrimp kabob (3 ounces shrimp, ½ cup green pepper squares) 1 whole wheat roll 1 cup fresh strawberries *or* other fruit 1 cup skim milk	1 small banana

MENU HINTS

When no beverage is listed with a meal, drink water, tea, or coffee.

* For 1 serving tossed salad, use 2 cups torn spinach and lettuce and ¼ cup *each* sliced carrot and broccoli tossed with 2 tablespoons reduced-calorie salad dressing with less than 15 calories per tablespoon.

** Pop popcorn without any oil. Do not add any margarine or butter to popped popcorn.

*** Yogurt with less than 150 calories per 8 ounces.

APPLE AND OAT BRAN MUFFINS

124 calories

Preparation Time: 12 min. ▪ Cooking Time: 18 min. ▪ Low Fat ▪ Low Cholesterol

1¼	cups whole wheat flour
1	cup oat bran
⅓	cup packed brown sugar
2½	teaspoons baking powder
¼	teaspoon baking soda
¼	teaspoon salt
¼	teaspoon ground nutmeg
¼	teaspoon ground cinnamon
1	cup buttermilk
2	egg whites
2	tablespoons cooking oil
¾	cup shredded, peeled apple
	Nonstick spray coating

▪ In a medium bowl stir together flour, oat bran, brown sugar, baking powder, baking soda, salt, nutmeg, and cinnamon. Set aside.

▪ In a small bowl combine buttermilk, egg whites, and oil. Add to dry ingredients; stir just till moistened. Stir in shredded apple. Store batter, tightly covered, in the refrigerator for up to 5 days.

▪ To bake, spray muffin cups with nonstick spray coating. Spoon about ¼ *cup* batter into *each* muffin cup. Bake in a 375° oven for 18 to 20 minutes or till a toothpick inserted near the center comes out clean. Makes 12 muffins (12 servings).

Nutrition information per serving: 124 calories, 4 g protein, 22 g carbohydrate, 3 g fat, 1 mg cholesterol, 162 mg sodium, 162 mg potassium.

TURKEY PAPRIKASH

Preparation Time: 30 min. ▪ Low Fat ▪ Low Cholesterol

	Nonstick spray coating
12	**ounces fully cooked turkey breast portion, sliced ¼ inch thick**
1	**medium onion, sliced and separated into rings**
2	**teaspoons paprika**
1	**teaspoon instant chicken bouillon granules**
⅔	**cup plain low-fat yogurt**
2	**tablespoons all-purpose flour**
1	**tablespoon tomato paste**
2	**tablespoons snipped fresh parsley**
3	**cups hot cooked noodles**

▪ Spray a *cold* large skillet with nonstick spray coating. Heat over medium heat for 1 minute. Add turkey slices to skillet. Cover and cook about 3 minutes or till heated through. Remove turkey slices from skillet and keep warm.

▪ For sauce, add onion rings to skillet. Cook and stir till rings are tender but not brown. Carefully stir in paprika, bouillon granules, ¾ cup *water,* and ⅛ teaspoon *pepper.* Combine yogurt, flour, and tomato paste; stir into skillet. Cook and stir till thickened and bubbly. Cook and stir 1 minute more.

▪ Toss parsley with hot cooked noodles. Arrange noodles on a large serving platter. Top with turkey slices. Spoon some sauce over turkey; pass remaining sauce. Makes 4 servings.

Nutrition information per serving: 312 calories, 35 g protein, 38 g carbohydrate, 2 g fat, 72 mg cholesterol, 207 mg sodium, 558 mg potassium.

VEGETARIAN CHILI WITH RICE

316 calories

Preparation Time: 10 min. ▪ Cooking Time: 15 min. ▪ Low Fat ▪ No Cholesterol

1	15½-ounce can red kidney beans, drained
1	15-ounce can great northern beans, drained
1	14½-ounce can tomatoes, cut up
1	8-ounce can tomato sauce
¾	cup chopped green pepper
½	cup chopped onion
1	tablespoon chili powder
1	teaspoon sugar
½	teaspoon dried basil, crushed
2	cloves garlic, minced
2	cups hot cooked rice

▪ In a large saucepan combine kidney beans, great northern beans, *un-drained* tomatoes, tomato sauce, green pepper, onion, chili powder, sugar, basil, garlic, and 1 cup *water*. Bring to boiling; reduce heat. Simmer, covered, for 15 minutes, stirring occasionally.

▪ Top *each* serving of chili with ½ *cup* hot cooked rice. Makes 4 servings.

Nutrition information per serving: 316 calories, 15 g protein, 67 g carbohydrate, 2 g fat, 0 mg cholesterol, 881 mg sodium, 939 mg potassium.

WILD RICE AND BULGUR PILAF

161 calories

Preparation Time: 10 min. ▪ Cooking Time: 50 min. ▪ Low Fat ▪ Low Cholesterol

This easy side dish makes a great accompaniment to fish, game, or poultry dishes.

½	**cup wild rice**
2	**cups chicken broth**
¾	**cup chopped onion**
¼	**teaspoon dried tarragon, crushed**
	Dash pepper
½	**cup bulgur**
¼	**cup snipped fresh parsley**
	Sweet yellow pepper strips (optional)
	Fresh parsley sprigs (optional)

▪ Place *uncooked* wild rice in a strainer. Run cold water over rice for 1 minute, lifting rice to rinse well.

▪ In a medium saucepan combine chicken broth, onion, tarragon, pepper, and rinsed rice. Bring to boiling; reduce heat. Cover and simmer about 45 minutes or till rice is done. Stir in bulgur and parsley. Cover and let stand for 5 minutes. Fluff with a fork. Garnish with yellow pepper strips and parsley sprigs, if desired. Makes 4 servings.

Nutrition information per serving: 161 calories, 7 g protein, 31 g carbohydrate, 1 g fat, 1 mg cholesterol, 395 mg sodium, 288 mg potassium.

43

STUFFED TOMATOES

53 calories

Preparation Time: 15 min. ▪ Cooking Time: 15 min. ▪ Low Fat ▪ Low Cholesterol

This bright and colorful vegetable-stuffed side dish will liven up any dinner plate.

4	**medium tomatoes**
2	**cups loose-pack frozen zucchini, carrots, cauliflower, lima beans, and Italian beans**
2	**tablespoons grated Romano cheese**
⅛	**teaspoon pepper**

▪ Cut tomatoes in half. Spoon out pulp, leaving a ¼-inch-thick shell. Reserve tomato pulp; discard seeds. Chop tomato pulp. Set shells and pulp aside.

▪ In a small saucepan cook frozen vegetables according to package directions. Drain. Stir in chopped tomato pulp. Spoon *one-eighth* of the vegetable mixture into *each* tomato shell. Place tomatoes in a 10x6x2-inch baking dish. Sprinkle with grated cheese and pepper.

▪ Bake in a 350° oven for 15 to 20 minutes or till heated through. Makes 4 servings.

Nutrition information per serving: 53 calories, 3 g protein, 9 g carbohydrate, 1 g fat, 4 mg cholesterol, 63 mg sodium, 255 mg potassium.

CHEESY TATER TOPPER

255 calories

Preparation Time: 14 min.* ▪ Low Fat ▪ Low Cholesterol

Diet food just keeps getting better—now it includes a baked potato smothered with cheese sauce!

1	cup skim milk
1	tablespoon cornstarch
½	teaspoon dry mustard
⅛	teaspoon pepper
¾	cup shredded American cheese
1	10-ounce package frozen mixed vegetables, cooked and drained
4	medium baking potatoes (6 to 8 ounces each), baked*

■ In a small saucepan stir together milk, cornstarch, mustard, and pepper. Cook and stir till thickened and bubbly. Add cheese, stirring till melted. Stir in mixed vegetables and heat through. Serve warm over baked potatoes. Serves 4.

*Note: To bake potatoes, scrub thoroughly and prick with a fork. Bake in a 425° oven for 40 to 60 minutes or till done. Or, prick skin of potatoes; place potatoes in microwave oven. Cook on 100% power (high) for 14 to 17 minutes or till done, rearranging once. Let stand for 5 minutes to finish cooking.

Nutrition information per serving: 255 calories, 10 g protein, 39 g carbohydrate, 7 g fat, 22 mg cholesterol, 352 mg sodium, 748 mg potassium.

HAM AND VEGETABLES WITH MOSTACCIOLI 291 calories

Preparation Time: 38 min. ▪ Low Fat ▪ Low Cholesterol

Here's a saucy one-dish meal—meat, vegetables, and pasta all in one.

4	**ounces mostaccioli (1½ cups)**
2	**cups sliced zucchini**
½	**cup sliced green onion**
4	**teaspoons cornstarch**
¼	**teaspoon dried basil, crushed**
¼	**teaspoon dried marjoram, crushed**
1	**13-ounce can (1⅔ cups) evaporated skim milk**
5	**ounces fully cooked ham, cut into strips (1 cup)**

▪ Cook pasta according to package directions; drain well. Set aside.

▪ In a medium saucepan combine zucchini, onion, and ¼ cup *water*. Bring to boiling; reduce heat. Simmer, covered, for 4 to 5 minutes or till vegetables are crisp-tender; drain well. Return to saucepan.

▪ Meanwhile, for sauce, in a small saucepan combine cornstarch, basil, marjoram, a little of the evaporated milk, and ⅛ teaspoon *pepper*. Stir in remaining milk all at once. Cook and stir till thickened and bubbly. Stir sauce, ham, and pasta into vegetables. Heat through. Makes 4 servings.

Nutrition information per serving: 291 calories, 21 g protein, 46 g carbohydrate, 3 g fat, 23 mg cholesterol, 540 mg sodium, 696 mg potassium.

MUSHROOM AND BARLEY SOUP

179 calories

Preparation Time: 12 min. ▪ Cooking Time: 18 min. ▪ Low Fat ▪ Low Cholesterol

5½	cups beef broth
⅔	cup quick-cooking barley
½	cup chopped onion
2	cloves garlic, minced
1	teaspoon dried basil, crushed
½	teaspoon Worcestershire sauce
⅛	teaspoon pepper
2	cups sliced fresh mushrooms
½	cup shredded carrot
2	tablespoons cornstarch
2	tablespoons water
1	tablespoon snipped fresh parsley

▪ In a large saucepan bring beef broth to boiling. Stir in barley, onion, garlic, basil, Worcestershire sauce, and pepper. Cover and simmer about 10 minutes or till barley is nearly tender. Stir in mushrooms and carrot. Simmer, covered, for 5 minutes more.

▪ Meanwhile, in a small bowl combine cornstarch and water; stir into saucepan. Cook and stir till slightly thickened and bubbly. Cook and stir 2 minutes more. Sprinkle with parsley. Makes 4 servings.

Nutrition information per serving: 179 calories, 8 g protein, 36 g carbohydrate, 1 g fat, 1 mg cholesterol, 1,090 mg sodium, 467 mg potassium.

MEXICAN-STYLE CREAMED CORN

94 calories

Preparation Time: 5 min. ▪ Cooking Time: 8 min. ▪ Low Fat ▪ No Cholesterol

Diced green chili peppers give this quick-to-fix side dish a hint of Mexican flavor.

1	**10-ounce package frozen whole kernel corn**
¼	**cup chopped green pepper**
¼	**cup chopped sweet red pepper**
¼	**cup chopped celery**
¼	**cup reduced-calorie soft-style cream cheese**
½	**of a 4-ounce can (¼ cup) diced green chili peppers**
1	**tablespoon skim milk**

▪ In a medium saucepan combine corn, green pepper, red pepper, celery, and ½ cup *water*. Cook about 5 minutes or till corn is tender. Drain.

▪ Stir in cream cheese, chili peppers, milk, ¼ teaspoon *salt*, and dash *pepper*. Heat through. Makes 4 servings.

Nutrition information per serving: 94 calories, 4 g protein, 17 g carbohydrate, 3 g fat, 0 mg cholesterol, 215 mg sodium, 144 mg potassium.

ORIENTAL OPENERS

Preparation Time: 30 min. ▪ Low Cholesterol

50 calories

Use a sharp knife to split the pea pods open lengthwise. Then, put the filling in a clear plastic bag. Snip off one corner of the bag and squeeze the filling into each pea pod. Or, put the filling in a decorating bag with a round tip; pipe the filling into the pea pods.

⅓	**cup low-fat ricotta cheese**
2	**tablespoons reduced-calorie soft-style cream cheese**
2	**tablespoons finely shredded radish**
1	**tablespoon snipped fresh chives**
	Dash onion salt
24	**fresh pea pods**

▪ For filling, stir together ricotta cheese, cream cheese, shredded radish, chives, and onion salt. Mix well. Set aside.

▪ With a sharp knife, split pea pods open lengthwise. Stuff each pea pod with filling. Chill till serving time. Serves 6 (4 pea pods each).

Nutrition information per serving: 50 calories, 3 g protein, 3 g carbohydrate, 3 g fat, 4 mg cholesterol, 73 mg sodium, 79 mg potassium.

LINGUINE WITH SCALLOPS

362 calories

Preparation Time: 25 min. ▪ Low Fat ▪ Low Cholesterol

1	**pound fresh *or* frozen scallops**
12	**ounces linguine**
1	**teaspoon margarine**
1	**teaspoon olive oil *or* cooking oil**
1½	**cups chicken broth**
¾	**cup dry vermouth *or* dry white wine**
3	**tablespoons lemon juice**
¾	**cup sliced green onion**
¾	**cup snipped fresh parsley**
2	**tablespoons capers, drained**
1	**teaspoon dried dillweed**
¼	**teaspoon pepper**

▪ Thaw scallops, if frozen. Halve any large scallops; set aside. Cook linguine according to package directions.

▪ Meanwhile, in a large skillet heat margarine and oil over medium-high heat. Add scallops; cook and stir about 2 minutes or till opaque. Remove scallops with a slotted spoon, leaving juices in skillet.

▪ Stir broth, vermouth or white wine, and lemon juice into skillet. Bring to boiling. Boil for 10 to 12 minutes or till liquid is reduced to about 1 cup. Stir in onion, parsley, capers, dillweed, and pepper. Reduce heat and simmer, uncovered, for 1 minute. Add scallops, stirring just till heated through. Pour over linguine; toss gently. Makes 6 servings.

Nutrition information per serving: 362 calories, 28 g protein, 54 g carbohydrate, 4 g fat, 40 mg cholesterol, 407 mg sodium, 619 mg potassium.

FRUIT TART

Preparation Time: 45 min. ▪ No Cholesterol

153 calories

⅓	**cup whole wheat flour**
⅓	**cup all-purpose flour**
1	**tablespoon sugar**
3	**tablespoons margarine**
2	**tablespoons ice water**
2	**teaspoons sugar**
1	**teaspoon cornstarch**
½	**cup orange juice**
1	**kiwi fruit, peeled and sliced**
¾	**cup thinly sliced banana**
1	**cup thinly sliced strawberries**

▪ For crust, combine flours and the 1 tablespoon sugar. Cut in margarine till mixture resembles coarse crumbs. Sprinkle with ice water; toss till crumbly. Form dough into a ball. Press dough into a circle on waxed paper; cover with another sheet of waxed paper. Roll into a 10-inch circle. Remove top sheet of waxed paper; invert onto an ungreased baking sheet. Remove remaining waxed paper. Crimp pastry edge. Prick with a fork.

▪ Bake crust in a 400° oven for 12 to 15 minutes or till lightly browned. Cool. Meanwhile, for glaze, combine the 2 teaspoons sugar and cornstarch. Stir in orange juice. Cook and stir till thickened and bubbly. Remove from heat; cool.

▪ Place crust on a serving plate. Arrange kiwi fruit in the center. Arrange bananas around kiwi and berries around bananas. Spoon glaze over fruit. Serve immediately or chill for 1 hour. Makes 6 servings.

Nutrition information per serving: 153 calories, 2 g protein, 24 g carbohydrate, 6 g fat, 0 mg cholesterol, 68 mg sodium, 232 mg potassium.

BROWN RICE PILAF

104 calories

Preparation Time: 5 min. ▪ Cooking Time: 17 min. ▪ Low Fat ▪ No Cholesterol

Specks of carrot and green onion make this a colorful side dish.

½	teaspoon instant chicken bouillon granules
1	cup sliced fresh mushrooms
¾	cup quick-cooking brown rice
½	cup shredded carrot
¼	teaspoon dried marjoram, crushed
¼	cup thinly sliced green onion
2	tablespoons snipped fresh parsley

▪ In a medium saucepan stir together bouillon granules and 1 cup *water*. Bring to boiling. Stir in mushrooms, brown rice, carrot, marjoram, and dash *pepper*. Reduce heat and simmer, covered, for 12 minutes.

▪ Remove from heat; let stand for 5 minutes. Add green onion and parsley; toss lightly with a fork. Serve immediately. Makes 4 servings.

Nutrition information per serving: 104 calories, 3 g protein, 21 g carbohydrate, 1 g fat, 0 mg cholesterol, 105 mg sodium, 205 mg potassium.

PEACH DAIQUIRI ICE

108 calories

Preparation Time: 8 min. ▪ Freezing Time: 4 hrs. ▪ Low Fat ▪ No Cholesterol ▪ Low Sodium

Oh, so easy and, oh, so good!

1	16-ounce can peach slices (juice pack)
¼	cup sugar
2	tablespoons rum
¼	teaspoon finely shredded lime peel
2	tablespoons lime juice

■ Drain peaches, reserving 2 tablespoons juice. In a blender container or food processor bowl combine peach slices, sugar, rum, lime peel, lime juice, and reserved peach juice. Cover and blend or process till smooth. Pour peach mixture into an 8x4x2-inch loaf pan.

■ Cover and freeze at least 4 hours or till firm. Let stand at room temperature about 5 minutes before serving. Serves 4.

Nutrition information per serving: 108 calories, 0 g protein, 25 g carbohydrate, 0 g fat, 0 mg cholesterol, 1 mg sodium, 6 mg potassium.

OATMEAL WITH FRUIT AND NUTS

204 calories

Preparation Time: 5 min. ▪ Cooking Time: 8 min. ▪ Low Fat ▪ Low Cholesterol

Warms you on a subzero winter morning.

3	cups water
½	teaspoon ground cinnamon
¼	teaspoon salt
1⅓	cups regular rolled oats
1	small apple, chopped
¼	cup pitted whole dates, snipped
2	tablespoons sliced almonds
1	tablespoon brown sugar
2⅔	cups skim milk

■ In a medium saucepan combine water, cinnamon, and salt. Bring to boiling; stir in oats. Cook for 5 minutes, stirring occasionally. Let stand, covered, till of desired consistency.

■ Divide oatmeal mixture among four serving bowls. Top each bowl of oatmeal with some chopped apple, snipped dates, sliced almonds, and brown sugar. Divide milk among serving bowls. Makes 4 servings.

Nutrition information per serving: 204 calories, 7 g protein, 38 g carbohydrate, 4 g fat, 1 mg cholesterol, 146 mg sodium, 315 mg potassium.

SPINACH SALAD

141 calories

Preparation Time: 30 min. ▪ Low Fat ▪ No Cholesterol

Grilled or broiled shrimp, a roll, and fresh fruit complete this tasty meal.

6	**cups torn fresh spinach**
2	**medium oranges, peeled and sectioned**
1	**small red onion, sliced and separated into rings**
½	**of an 8-ounce can (½ cup) sliced water chestnuts, drained**
2	**tablespoons orange juice**
1	**tablespoon olive oil *or* cooking oil**
1	**tablespoon honey**
1	**teaspoon toasted sesame seed**
1	**teaspoon prepared mustard**

▪ For salad, in a large salad bowl place spinach, orange sections, onion rings, and water chestnuts. Sprinkle with ¼ teaspoon *pepper*.

▪ For dressing, in a screw-top jar combine orange juice, oil, honey, sesame seed, and mustard. Cover and shake well. Pour dressing over salad. Toss lightly to coat. Serve immediately. Makes 4 servings.

Nutrition information per serving: 141 calories, 4 g protein, 24 g carbohydrate, 4 g fat, 0 mg cholesterol, 87 mg sodium, 807 mg potassium.

CALORIE-TRIMMED CLASSICS

DEEP-DISH APPLE PIE *(see page 68)*

STROGANOFF-STYLE BEEF

349 calories

Preparation Time: 30 min. ▪ Cooking Time: 10 min. ▪ Low Cholesterol

¾	pound boneless beef round steak
1	8-ounce carton plain low-fat yogurt
2	tablespoons all-purpose flour
1	tablespoon tomato paste
1	teaspoon instant beef bouillon granules
2	teaspoons Worcestershire sauce
½	teaspoon dried thyme, crushed
¼	teaspoon dry mustard
2	cups sliced fresh mushrooms
½	cup chopped onion
1	tablespoon margarine
2	tablespoons dry white wine
2	cups hot cooked noodles

▪ Partially freeze meat. Trim separable fat from meat and thinly slice meat across the grain into bite-size strips.

▪ In a small bowl stir together yogurt and flour. Stir in tomato paste, bouillon granules, Worcestershire sauce, thyme, mustard, and ⅛ teaspoon *pepper*. Set aside.

▪ In a large skillet cook mushrooms and onion in margarine till tender; remove from skillet.

▪ Add beef to skillet. Cook 2 to 4 minutes or till no longer pink. Remove from skillet.

▪ Add wine and ⅓ cup *water* to skillet. Bring to boiling. Stir yogurt mixture into skillet. Return meat, mushrooms, and onion to skillet. Cook and stir till thickened and bubbly. Cook 1 minute more. Serve over noodles. Makes 4 servings.

Nutrition information per serving: 349 calories, 28 g protein, 30 g carbohydrate, 12 g fat, 89 mg cholesterol, 254 mg sodium, 582 mg potassium.

PORK CHOPS WITH BARBECUE SAUCE

146 calories

Preparation Time: 10 min. ▪ Cooking Time: 28 min. ▪ Low Cholesterol

Serve refreshing coleslaw on the side.

1	8-ounce can tomato sauce
½	cup finely chopped onion
½	cup finely chopped green pepper
2	cloves garlic, minced
2	tablespoons vinegar
2	tablespoons molasses
1	tablespoon Worcestershire sauce
¼	teaspoon pepper
	Few dashes bottled hot pepper sauce
6	pork loin chops, cut ½ inch thick (2 pounds total)

▪ For sauce, in a small saucepan combine tomato sauce, onion, green pepper, garlic, vinegar, molasses, Worcestershire sauce, pepper, and hot pepper sauce. Bring to boiling; reduce heat. Cover and simmer for 15 minutes. Uncover and simmer about 10 minutes more or till of desired consistency.

▪ Reserve *½ cup* of the sauce for pork chops. Cover and refrigerate remaining sauce for another use.

▪ Meanwhile, trim separable fat from pork chops. Place meat on the unheated rack of a broiler pan. Broil 3 to 4 inches from the heat for 5 minutes. Turn and broil 5 minutes more or till nearly done. Turn chops and spoon reserved sauce over chops. Broil 3 to 5 minutes more or till pork chops are no longer pink. Makes 6 servings.

Nutrition information per serving: 146 calories, 18 g protein, 4 g carbohydrate, 6 g fat, 55 mg cholesterol, 148 mg sodium, 345 mg potassium.

FRIED CHICKEN WITH CREAM GRAVY

219 calories

Preparation Time: 30 min. ▪ Cooking Time: 40 min. ▪ Low Cholesterol

Choose mashed potatoes or rice pilaf, and steamed carrots to complete your hearty meal.

6	**medium chicken breast halves, skinned (2¼ pounds total)**
¼	**cup all-purpose flour**
½	**teaspoon salt**
½	**teaspoon paprika**
⅛	**to ¼ teaspoon pepper**
2	**tablespoons cooking oil**
½	**cup evaporated skim milk**
½	**cup chicken broth**

▪ Rinse chicken pieces; pat dry with paper towels.

▪ In a plastic bag combine flour, salt, paprika, and pepper. Add a few chicken breasts at a time to the bag; shake to coat. Remove chicken from bag, shaking off any excess coating in the bag. Reserve remaining flour mixture.

▪ In a 12-inch skillet heat cooking oil. Add chicken and cook, uncovered, over medium heat for 10 to 15 minutes, turning to brown evenly.

▪ Reduce heat; cover tightly. Cook 30 minutes. Uncover and cook 10 to 15 minutes more or till chicken is tender and no longer pink. Drain chicken on paper towels. Keep warm.

▪ Pour fat from skillet and discard.

▪ For gravy, in a small bowl slowly stir milk into reserved flour mixture. Stir in chicken broth. Add mixture to skillet. Cook and stir till thickened and bubbly. Cook and stir 1 to 2 minutes more. Serve gravy over chicken. Makes 6 servings.

Nutrition information per serving: 219 calories, 29 g protein, 6 g carbohydrate, 8 g fat, 73 mg cholesterol, 332 mg sodium, 313 mg potassium.

LOBSTER NEWBURG

225 calories

Preparation Time: 10 min. ▪ Cooking Time: 10 min. ▪ Low Fat

Impress dinner guests with this easy-to-fix classic. Everyone will love the flavor that goes along with the reduced calories and fat.

2	teaspoons margarine
1	tablespoon all-purpose flour
¼	teaspoon salt
1½	cups milk
1	beaten egg
8	ounces cubed fresh *or* frozen cooked lobster *or* frozen lobster-flavored, tail-shape fish pieces, thawed and chopped
1	tablespoon dry sherry
	Dash ground red pepper
	Dash white *or* black pepper
2	English muffins, split and toasted

▪ In a medium saucepan melt margarine. Stir in flour and salt. Add milk all at once. Cook and stir till thickened and bubbly. Cook and stir 1 minute more.

▪ Stir about *half* of the hot mixture into the beaten egg. Return all to saucepan. Cook and stir mixture till thickened, but *do not boil.*

▪ Stir in lobster, dry sherry, ground red pepper, and white or black pepper. Heat through. Serve over English muffin halves. Makes 4 servings.

Nutrition information per serving: 225 calories, 20 g protein, 23 g carbohydrate, 5 g fat, 116 mg cholesterol, 435 mg sodium, 364 mg potassium.

EGGS BENEDICT

Preparation Time: 12 min. ▪ Cooking Time: 6 min.

To poach eggs, break them, one at a time, into a small dish or measuring cup. Hold the dish close to the simmering water and slip the egg into the pan.

¼	**cup plain low-fat yogurt**
¼	**cup reduced-calorie mayonnaise**
2	**teaspoons skim milk**
¼	**teaspoon dry mustard**
	Dash ground red pepper
	Nonstick spray coating
4	**eggs**
4	**ounces Canadian-style bacon (4 slices)**
2	**English muffins, split and toasted**

▪ For sauce, in a small saucepan combine yogurt, mayonnaise, milk, dry mustard, and ground red pepper; set aside.

▪ Spray an 8-inch skillet with nonstick spray coating. Fill the skillet halfway with water. Bring to boiling; reduce heat so water is simmering. To poach eggs, break 1 egg into a small dish and slide egg into water. Repeat with remaining eggs. Simmer, uncovered, for 3 to 5 minutes or till eggs are just soft-cooked.

▪ Meanwhile, in a large skillet lightly brown bacon over medium heat for 3 minutes on each side. Cover; keep warm.

▪ Cook and stir sauce over low heat just till heated through, but *do not boil.*

▪ To serve, top each muffin half with 1 slice bacon, 1 egg, and *one-fourth* of the sauce. Makes 4 servings.

Nutrition information per serving: 254 calories, 16 g protein, 18 g carbohydrate, 12 g fat, 296 mg cholesterol, 563 mg sodium, 205 mg potassium.

CHEESY SCALLOPED POTATOES

118 calories

Preparation Time: 25 min. ▪ Cooking Time: 65 min. ▪ Low Fat ▪ Low Cholesterol

Boost the cheese flavor by using sharp cheddar.

1½	cups skim milk
2	tablespoons all-purpose flour
½	teaspoon salt *or* seasoned salt
⅛	teaspoon pepper
⅛	teaspoon garlic powder (optional)
½	cup chopped onion
	Nonstick spray coating
4	medium potatoes, peeled and thinly sliced
½	cup shredded cheddar cheese (2 ounces)
	Snipped fresh parsley (optional)

▪ For sauce, in a small saucepan, stir together milk, flour, salt, pepper, and garlic powder, if desired. Cook and stir over medium heat till thickened and bubbly. Stir in onion.

▪ Spray a 1½-quart casserole with nonstick spray coating. Place *half* of the potatoes in the casserole. Top with *half* of the sauce. Repeat layers with remaining potatoes and sauce.

▪ Bake, covered, in a 350° oven about 65 minutes or till potatoes are tender, stirring once. Remove from oven and sprinkle with cheese. Cover and let stand 1 to 2 minutes or till cheese is melted. If desired, garnish with parsley. Serves 8.

Nutrition information per serving: 118 calories, 5 g protein, 19 g carbohydrate, 3 g fat, 8 mg cholesterol, 208 mg sodium, 339 mg potassium.

SKILLET SWEET POTATOES

134 calories

Preparation Time: 10 min. ▪ Cooking Time: 25 min. ▪ Low Fat ▪ No Cholesterol

1	**pound sweet potatoes, peeled and sliced***
½	**teaspoon finely shredded orange peel**
½	**cup orange juice**
1	**tablespoon molasses *or* brown sugar**
¼	**teaspoon salt**
¼	**teaspoon ground cinnamon**
⅛	**teaspoon ground allspice**

■ In a large skillet bring 1 inch of water to boiling. Add sweet potatoes; reduce heat. Cover and simmer for 20 minutes or till tender. Drain well.

■ Meanwhile, for sauce, in a small bowl combine orange peel, orange juice, molasses or brown sugar, salt, cinnamon, and allspice. Pour over potatoes in skillet.

■ Cook and stir gently till bubbly. Simmer, uncovered, for 5 minutes or till potatoes are glazed, spooning sauce over potatoes occasionally. Makes 4 servings.

***Note:** If desired, substitute *one 18-ounce can sweet potatoes* for fresh sweet potatoes. Cut potatoes into 2-inch pieces. Place in a 1-quart casserole. Pour sauce over sweet potatoes. Bake, uncovered, in a 350° oven about 30 minutes or till heated through and sauce is bubbly.

Nutrition information per serving: 134 calories, 2 g protein, 31 g carbohydrate, 0 g fat, 0 mg cholesterol, 149 mg sodium, 323 mg potassium.

BOSTON BAKED BEANS

133 calories

Preparation Time: 1¼ hrs. ▪ Cooking Time: 4½ hrs. ▪ Low Fat ▪ No Cholesterol

1¼	**cups dry navy beans *or* dry great northern beans (½ pound total)**
1	**cup chopped onion**
½	**cup chopped celery**
½	**cup chopped carrots**
¼	**cup molasses**
½	**teaspoon salt**
½	**teaspoon dry mustard**
⅛	**teaspoon pepper**

▪ Rinse beans. In a medium saucepan combine beans and 3 cups *water.* Cover and let stand overnight. (Or, bring to boiling; reduce heat. Simmer for 2 minutes. Remove from heat. Cover and soak for 1 hour.) Rinse and drain beans.

▪ In a 1½-quart casserole or bean pot combine soaked beans, onion, celery, and carrots. Stir in molasses, salt, mustard, pepper, and 2 cups *water.*

▪ Bake, covered, in a 325° oven for 4½ to 5 hours or till beans are tender and most of the liquid is absorbed, stirring occasionally and adding more water as needed (up to 1 cup). Makes 8 servings.

Nutrition information per serving: 133 calories, 7 g protein, 26 g carbohydrate, 1 g fat, 0 mg cholesterol, 155 mg sodium, 529 mg potassium.

CREAMY POTATO SALAD

130 calories

Preparation Time: 20 min. ▪ Cooking Time: 25 min. ▪ Chilling Time: 4 hrs.

Tote a tasty potato salad with you to your next picnic. It's so flavorful, no one will guess it's a lower-calorie recipe.

4	medium potatoes (1¼ pounds total)
1	cup sliced celery
¼	cup finely chopped onion
2	tablespoons dill *or* sweet pickle relish
½	cup reduced-calorie mayonnaise
½	cup plain low-fat yogurt
2	tablespoons skim milk
2	teaspoons prepared mustard
½	teaspoon salt
¼	to ½ teaspoon celery seed
1	hard-cooked egg, chopped

▪ Scrub potatoes. Cook potatoes, covered, in boiling water for 25 to 30 minutes or till tender. Drain and cool.

▪ Peel and cube potatoes. Transfer to a large bowl. Stir in celery, onion, and pickle relish.

▪ In a small mixing bowl combine mayonnaise, yogurt, milk, mustard, salt, and celery seed. Pour over potatoes. Toss lightly to coat potatoes. Carefully fold in chopped egg.

▪ Cover and chill for 4 to 24 hours. Serve in a lettuce-lined bowl, if desired. Makes 8 servings.

▪ **Microwave directions:** Pierce the skin of each potato in several places. Micro-cook on 100% power (high) for 14 to 17 minutes or till tender, rearranging once. Cool.

Nutrition information per serving: 130 calories, 3 g protein, 17 g carbohydrate, 6 g fat, 41 mg cholesterol, 300 mg sodium, 322 mg potassium.

CARROT SNACK CAKE

156 calories

Preparation Time: 20 min. ▪ Cooking Time: 20 min.

Now and then you deserve a special dessert, so dive into this reduced-calorie carrot cake. It has less than half the calories of the traditional version.

¼	cup margarine, softened
½	cup sugar
1	egg
¼	cup skim milk
½	teaspoon vanilla
½	cup finely shredded carrot
1	cup all-purpose flour
1¼	teaspoons baking powder
¼	teaspoon ground cinnamon
⅛	teaspoon salt
	Dash ground nutmeg
	Nonstick spray coating
2	teaspoons sifted powdered sugar

▪ In a small mixer bowl beat margarine and sugar till blended. Beat in egg, milk, and vanilla. Stir in carrot.

▪ In another bowl combine flour, baking powder, cinnamon, salt, and nutmeg. Add to carrot mixture and stir till blended.

▪ Spray an 8x8x2-inch baking pan with nonstick spray coating. Pour batter evenly into pan.

▪ Bake in a 350° oven for 20 to 25 minutes or till a toothpick inserted near the center of the cake comes out clean. Cool on wire rack. (If desired, remove from pan after cooling 10 minutes. Then, cool completely.)

▪ Place a paper doily on top of the cake. Lightly sift the powdered sugar evenly over the doily. Then, carefully remove the doily. Makes 9 servings.

Nutrition information per serving: 156 calories, 2 g protein, 23 g carbohydrate, 6 g fat, 31 mg cholesterol, 145 mg sodium, 55 mg potassium.

Strawberry-Topped Cheesecake

206 calories

Preparation Time: 20 min. ▪ Cooking Time: 40 min. ▪ Chilling Time: several hrs.

½	**cup graham cracker crumbs**
4	**teaspoons margarine, melted**
1	**cup low-fat cottage cheese**
2	**8-ounce containers reduced-calorie soft-style cream cheese**
¾	**cup sugar**
2	**tablespoons all-purpose flour**
1¼	**teaspoons vanilla**
3	**eggs**
¼	**cup skim milk**
¼	**cup plain low-fat yogurt**
2	**teaspoons skim milk**
1	**cup fresh strawberries, sliced**

■ In a small bowl stir together graham cracker crumbs and melted margarine. Press onto the bottom only of an 8-inch springform pan. Set aside.

■ With an electric mixer beat *undrained* cottage cheese till smooth. Add cream cheese, sugar, flour, and *1 teaspoon* of the vanilla; beat till smooth. Add eggs and beat just till combined. *Do not overbeat.* Stir in the ¼ cup milk. Pour mixture into pan. Place on a baking sheet or in a shallow baking pan.

■ Bake in a 375° oven for 40 to 45 minutes or till set.* Cool 10 minutes. Using a metal spatula, loosen the sides of the cheesecake from pan. (This helps keep the cheesecake edges from cracking.) Cool 35 minutes more, then remove the sides of pan. Cover and chill thoroughly.

■ In a small bowl combine yogurt, remaining milk, and remaining vanilla. To serve, arrange sliced strawberries on top of cheesecake and drizzle with yogurt mixture. Serves 12.

*****Note:** To test your cheesecake for doneness, gently shake the sides of the pan. The center should appear *nearly* set.

Nutrition information per serving: 206 calories, 9 g protein, 21 g carbohydrate, 10 g fat, 93 mg cholesterol, 353 mg sodium, 161 mg potassium.

DEEP-DISH APPLE PIE

157 calories

Preparation Time: 30 min. ▪ Cooking Time: 40 min. ▪ Low Fat ▪ No Cholesterol

6	cups thinly sliced peeled apples (2 pounds total)
¼	cup sugar
1	teaspoon ground cinnamon
1	tablespoon cornstarch
⅛	teaspoon salt
¾	cup all-purpose flour *or* ½ cup all-purpose flour plus ¼ cup whole wheat flour
	Dash ground nutmeg
3	tablespoons margarine
2 to 3	tablespoons cold water
	Skim milk

▪ Place apples in a 10x6x2-inch baking dish.

▪ In a small mixing bowl combine sugar and cinnamon; set aside *1 teaspoon* of the mixture. Stir cornstarch and salt into remaining sugar mixture and mix well. Sprinkle evenly over apples in dish.

▪ In a medium mixing bowl stir together flour and nutmeg. Cut in margarine till mixture resembles coarse crumbs. Sprinkle *1 tablespoon* of the water over part of the mixture; gently toss with a fork. Push to side of bowl. Repeat till all is moistened. Form into a ball.

▪ On a floured surface roll dough into a 12x8-inch rectangle. Cut decorative vents in pastry. Carefully place pastry atop apples; flute edges to sides of dish, but not over the edge. Brush pastry with milk and sprinkle with the reserved sugar mixture.

▪ Bake in a 375° oven about 40 minutes or till apples are tender and crust is golden brown. Serve warm. Serves 8.

Nutrition information per serving: 157 calories, 1 g protein, 29 g carbohydrate, 5 g fat, 0 mg cholesterol, 84 mg sodium, 109 mg potassium.

CREAM PUFFS

160 calories

Preparation Time: 25 min. ▪ Cooking Time: 30 min.

	Nonstick spray coating
1	cup water
¼	cup margarine
¼	teaspoon salt
1	cup all-purpose flour
4	eggs
⅓	cup sugar
3	tablespoons cornstarch
⅛	teaspoon salt
3	cups skim milk
1	slightly beaten egg
2	teaspoons vanilla
1	drop yellow food coloring (optional)
12	large strawberries, sliced

▪ Spray a baking sheet with nonstick spray coating. Bring water, margarine, and the ¼ teaspoon salt to boiling. Add flour all at once, stirring vigorously. Cook and stir till mixture forms a ball that doesn't separate. Cool 10 minutes.

▪ Add the 4 eggs, one at a time, beating till smooth after each addition. Drop batter by heaping tablespoons, 3 inches apart onto baking sheet, making 12 mounds. Bake in a 400° oven for 30 minutes or till golden brown and puffy. Cool. Split cream puffs and remove any soft dough from inside.

▪ Meanwhile, for pudding, in a saucepan combine sugar, cornstarch, and ⅛ teaspoon salt. Stir in milk. Cook and stir till bubbly. Cook and stir 2 minutes more. Remove from heat.

▪ Gradually stir 1 cup of the hot mixture into the beaten egg. Return all to saucepan; cook and stir 2 minutes more. Remove from heat. Stir in vanilla and food coloring, if desired. Pour into a bowl; cover surface with clear plastic wrap. Chill.

▪ To serve, fill cream puffs with pudding and strawberries. Serves 12.

Nutrition information per serving: 160 calories, 6 g protein, 20 g carbohydrate, 6 g fat, 116 mg cholesterol, 172 mg sodium, 170 mg potassium.

BROWNIE BITES

104 calories

Preparation Time: 8 min. ▪ Cooking Time: 20 min. ▪ No Cholesterol

Satisfy that urge for chocolate with this lower-calorie favorite. It makes a small batch so there won't be a lot of leftovers to tempt you later.

2	tablespoons margarine
⅓	cup sugar
¼	cup cold water
½	teaspoon vanilla
½	cup all-purpose flour
2	tablespoons unsweetened cocoa powder
½	teaspoon baking powder
2	tablespoons finely chopped walnuts *or* pecans
	Nonstick spray coating
1	teaspoon powdered sugar

■ In a small saucepan melt margarine; remove from heat. Stir in sugar, water, and vanilla. Stir in flour, cocoa powder, and baking powder till well mixed. Stir in chopped nuts.

■ Spray the bottom only of an 8x4x2-inch loaf pan with nonstick spray coating. Pour batter into pan.

■ Bake in a 350° oven about 20 minutes or till a toothpick inserted near the center comes out clean. Cool thoroughly. Remove from pan. Cut into 8 bars. Sprinkle with the powdered sugar. Makes 8 servings.

Nutrition information per serving: 104 calories, 1 g protein, 16 g carbohydrate, 4 g fat, 0 mg cholesterol, 68 mg sodium, 28 mg potassium.

CINNAMON ROLLS WITH ORANGE GLAZE 131 calories

Preparation Time: 45 min. ▪ Cooking Time: 20 min. ▪ Low Fat ▪ Low Cholesterol

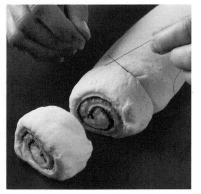

To slice the dough into 12 pieces, put a piece of heavy-duty thread under the dough. Criss-cross the thread over the dough and pull quickly.

1	1-pound loaf frozen bread dough, thawed
1	tablespoon margarine, melted
1	tablespoon sugar
1	teaspoon ground cinnamon
	Nonstick spray coating
½	cup powdered sugar
¼	teaspoon finely shredded orange peel
2	to 3 teaspoons orange juice

■ On a floured surface, roll dough into a 12x8-inch rectangle. (If the dough is difficult to roll out, let it rest for a short time and roll again. Repeat as necessary.)

■ Brush dough with melted margarine; sprinkle evenly with the 1 tablespoon sugar and the cinnamon.

■ Roll up dough, beginning from one of the long sides. Seal seam. Slice into twelve 1-inch pieces.

■ Spray a 9x1½-inch round baking pan with nonstick spray coating. Place rolls in pan with one cut side down. Cover and let rise in a warm place till nearly double, about 30 minutes.

■ Bake in a 375° oven for 20 to 25 minutes or till lightly browned. Cool slightly; remove from pan.

■ For glaze, in a small bowl stir together powdered sugar, orange peel, and enough orange juice to make of desired consistency. Drizzle over warm rolls. Serve warm. Serves 12.

Nutrition information per serving: 131 calories, 3 g protein, 23 g carbohydrate, 3 g fat, 2 mg cholesterol, 194 mg sodium, 34 mg potassium.

STRAWBERRY SHORTCAKE

231 calories

Preparation Time: 1 hr. 10 min. ▪ Cooking Time: 10 min.

We've cut more than half the calories and fat from the traditional fruity favorite.

3	cups sliced fresh strawberries
2	tablespoons sugar
1⅔	cups all-purpose flour
1	tablespoon sugar
2	teaspoons baking powder
¼	teaspoon baking soda
3	tablespoons margarine
1	beaten egg
½	cup buttermilk *or* skim milk
	Nonstick spray coating
1	1.4-ounce envelope whipped dessert topping mix
½	cup skim milk

▪ Combine strawberries and the 2 tablespoons sugar. Cover and let stand in the refrigerator at least 1 hour.

▪ In a mixing bowl stir together flour, the 1 tablespoon sugar, baking powder, and baking soda. Cut in margarine till mixture resembles coarse crumbs. Combine egg and buttermilk. Add to flour mixture all at once, stirring till combined.

▪ Spray an 8-inch round baking pan with nonstick spray coating. With lightly floured hands, pat dough into pan. Bake in a 450° oven about 10 minutes or till golden. Cool in pan 10 minutes. Remove from pan and cool completely, or serve shortcake warm.

▪ Meanwhile, prepare whipped dessert topping mix according to package directions using the skim milk.

▪ Split shortcake into 2 layers. Place the bottom layer on a serving plate. Top with some of the berries, then add the second layer of shortcake. Spoon dessert topping and the remaining strawberries on top of cake. Makes 8 servings.

Nutrition information per serving: 231 calories, 5 g protein, 35 g carbohydrate, 8 g fat, 47 mg cholesterol, 193 mg sodium, 251 mg potassium.

Main-Dish Salads

ANTIPASTO SALAD *(see page 85)*

BEEF SALAD WITH FRESH BASIL DRESSING   212 calories

Preparation Time: 30 min. ▪ Low Cholesterol

Chill the dressing in the freezer to cool it fast!

½	cup buttermilk
3	tablespoons reduced-calorie mayonnaise *or* salad dressing
1	tablespoon snipped fresh basil *or* 1 teaspoon dried basil, crushed
1	tablespoon lemon juice
1	teaspoon sugar
	Dash pepper
6	cups torn mixed greens
8	ounces lean cooked beef, cut into thin strips
1	small parsnip, thinly sliced
1	medium carrot, thinly sliced
½	of a small zucchini, sliced
½	cup broccoli flowerets
½	of a 16-ounce can julienne beets, well drained

▪ For the dressing, in a small mixing bowl stir together buttermilk, mayonnaise or salad dressing, basil, lemon juice, sugar, and pepper. Cover and chill in the refrigerator.

▪ For salad, toss together the mixed greens, beef, parsnip, carrot, zucchini, and broccoli. Add the chilled dressing and toss to coat. Spoon onto 4 individual serving plates. Garnish with drained beets. Makes 4 servings.

Nutrition information per serving: 212 calories, 20 g protein, 13 g carbohydrate, 9 g fat, 53 mg cholesterol, 254 mg sodium, 684 mg potassium.

TACO SALAD

Preparation Time: 35 min. ▪ Cooking Time: 10 min. ▪ Low Cholesterol

For the tortilla bowls, carefully press a warm corn tortilla into a 10-ounce custard cup. (Using a warm tortilla makes it easier to press it into the cup without tearing it.) Adjust the tortilla to fit by fluting the edges as necessary.

4	6- or 8-inch corn tortillas
	Nonstick spray coating
¾	pound lean ground beef *or* turkey
1	medium onion, chopped
1	clove garlic, minced
1	8-ounce can tomato sauce
1	tablespoon vinegar
½	teaspoon ground cumin
¼	teaspoon crushed red pepper
4	cups shredded lettuce
½	cup chopped green *or* sweet red pepper
¼	cup finely shredded cheddar cheese (1 ounce)
12	cherry tomatoes, halved

▪ Wrap tortillas in foil. Warm in a 350° oven for 10 minutes.

▪ Spray four 10-ounce custard cups with nonstick spray coating. Carefully press 1 tortilla into each cup. Bake in a 350° oven for 15 minutes or till crisp. Cool; remove from custard cups.

▪ Meanwhile, in a large skillet cook meat, onion, and garlic till meat is no longer pink and onion is tender. Drain fat.

▪ Stir in tomato sauce, vinegar, cumin, and red pepper. Bring to boiling; reduce heat. Simmer, uncovered, for 10 minutes.

▪ Divide lettuce among 4 serving plates. Place a tortilla on each plate. Spoon beef mixture into tortillas. Sprinkle with green or sweet red pepper and cheese. Serve with cherry tomato halves. Makes 4 servings.

Nutrition information per serving: 278 calories, 23 g protein, 24 g carbohydrate, 11 g fat, 67 mg cholesterol, 440 mg sodium, 661 mg potassium.

PORK AND NOODLE SALAD

350 calories

Preparation Time: 20 min. ▪ Chilling Time: 2 hrs. ▪ Low Cholesterol

4	**ounces Chinese egg noodles *or* fine noodles, broken in half**
¼	**cup soy sauce**
2	**tablespoons rice vinegar *or* vinegar**
1	**tablespoon salad oil**
1	**tablespoon honey**
1	**teaspoon sesame oil (optional)**
1	**10-ounce package frozen cut asparagus**
1	**large carrot, cut into thin strips**
1	**cup bean sprouts**
8	**ounces cooked lean pork, cut into thin strips**
¼	**cup thinly sliced green onion**

▪ Cook the noodles according to package directions; drain. Cover the noodles with ice water and let stand till thoroughly chilled. Drain well.

▪ Meanwhile, for dressing, in a screw-top jar combine soy sauce, rice vinegar or vinegar, oil, honey, and sesame oil, if desired. Cover and shake to mix well. Chill.

▪ Cook asparagus according to package directions; drain.

▪ Arrange noodles on a large serving platter. Arrange asparagus and carrot in a circle atop noodles. Place bean sprouts and pork in center of carrot and asparagus ring. Sprinkle with green onion. Cover and chill 2 to 24 hours.

▪ To serve, pour dressing over salad; toss lightly. Serves 4.

Nutrition information per serving: 350 calories, 27 g protein, 35 g carbohydrate, 12 g fat, 82 mg cholesterol, 1,099 mg sodium, 668 mg potassium.

HOT HAM AND APPLE SLAW

188 calories

Preparation Time: 20 min. ▪ Cooking Time: 10 min. ▪ Low Fat ▪ Low Cholesterol

Team a serving of this sweet-sour main dish with a tasty corn bread muffin.

⅓	**cup apple juice**
1	**tablespoon vinegar**
2	**teaspoons cornstarch**
½	**teaspoon celery seed**
⅛	**teaspoon pepper**
	Nonstick spray coating
½	**cup chopped onion**
2	**cups coarsely shredded cabbage**
1	**cup shredded carrots**
1	**teaspoon cooking oil (optional)**
12	**ounces fully cooked ham, cubed**
1	**medium apple, coarsely chopped**

▪ For sauce, stir together apple juice, vinegar, cornstarch, celery seed, and pepper. Set aside.

▪ Spray a wok or large skillet with nonstick spray coating. Preheat over medium-high heat. Add onion and stir-fry for 2 minutes. Add cabbage and carrots; stir-fry about 2 minutes or till vegetables are crisp-tender. Remove from wok.

▪ Add oil to hot wok, if necessary. Add ham and stir-fry 2 to 3 minutes or till heated through. Push ham from center of wok.

▪ Stir sauce; add to center of wok. Cook and stir till thickened and bubbly. Cook and stir for 1 minute more. Return vegetables to wok. Add apple. Stir all ingredients together to coat with sauce. Cook and stir for 1 minute. Garnish with additional apple slices, if desired. Makes 4 servings.

Nutrition information per serving: 188 calories, 19 g protein, 17 g carbohydrate, 5 g fat, 45 mg cholesterol, 1,040 mg sodium, 523 mg potassium.

HAM AND PASTA SALAD

175 calories

Advance Preparation Time: 25 min. ▪ Chilling Time: 4 hrs. ▪ Final Preparation Time: 15 min. ▪ Low Cholesterol

½	cup orzo, tripolini, tiny tube macaroni, *or* tiny star macaroni
1	cup frozen mixed peas and carrots
8	ounces fully cooked boneless ham, cut into ½-inch cubes
4	green onions, sliced
½	cup plain low-fat yogurt
2	tablespoons reduced-calorie creamy cucumber dressing
¼	teaspoon dried dillweed
2	medium tomatoes, sliced
1	green pepper, cut into half rings
	Lettuce leaves

■ In a medium saucepan bring a large amount of water to boiling. Add pasta and frozen mixed peas and carrots. Return to boiling, then reduce heat slightly. Boil, uncovered, for 5 to 8 minutes or till pasta and carrots are tender. Immediately drain mixture in a colander, then rinse with *cold* water and drain again.

■ In a medium mixing bowl stir together pasta, peas and carrots, ham, and green onions. In a small mixing bowl stir together yogurt, cucumber dressing, and dillweed. Pour yogurt mixture over pasta and vegetable mixture. Toss till well coated. Cover and chill for at least 4 hours.

■ To serve, arrange the tomato slices and green pepper on 4 lettuce-lined salad plates. Stir the pasta mixture and divide mixture among plates. Makes 4 servings.

Nutrition information per serving: 175 calories, 17 g protein, 16 g carbohydrate, 6 g fat, 38 mg cholesterol, 800 mg sodium, 531 mg potassium.

STIR-FRIED CHICKEN SALAD

179 calories

Preparation Time: 15 min. ▪ Marinating Time: 2 hrs. ▪ Cooking Time: 4 min. ▪ Low Fat ▪ Low Cholesterol

9	**ounces boned skinless chicken breast halves, cut into thin strips**
3	**tablespoons white wine vinegar**
1	**tablespoon olive _or_ cooking oil**
2	**teaspoons Dijon-style mustard**
½	**teaspoon sugar**
¼	**teaspoon salt**
⅛	**teaspoon paprika**
⅛	**teaspoon pepper**
4	**cups torn fresh spinach**
10	**cherry tomatoes, halved**
½	**cup shredded carrot**
½	**cup jicama peeled and cut into thin bite-size strips***
¼	**cup sliced radishes**
	Nonstick spray coating

▪ Place chicken in a plastic bag set in a deep bowl.

▪ In a small bowl stir together vinegar, oil, mustard, sugar, salt, paprika, and pepper. Pour over chicken; close bag. Marinate chicken in the refrigerator for 2 to 5 hours, turning bag frequently.

▪ Meanwhile, in a large bowl combine spinach, tomatoes, carrot, jicama, and radishes. Cover and chill till serving time.

▪ Spray a cold wok or large skillet with nonstick spray coating. Preheat over medium-high heat. Drain chicken, reserving marinade. Stir-fry chicken for 2 to 3 minutes or till no longer pink. Add marinade and heat till boiling.

▪ Pour hot chicken mixture over salad mixture. Toss to combine. Serve immediately. Makes 4 servings.

*Note: If desired, substitute ½ cup sliced _water chestnuts_ for the jicama.

Nutrition information per serving: 179 calories, 22 g protein, 9 g carbohydrate, 6 g fat, 54 mg cholesterol, 308 mg sodium, 626 mg potassium.

CAESAR-STYLE CHICKEN SALAD　　　207 calories

Advance Preparation Time: 30 min. ▪ Chilling Time: 4 hrs. ▪ Final Preparation Time: 5 min. ▪ Low Cholesterol

Next time you're cooking chicken, cook a few extra pieces to use later in this main-dish salad.

⅔ cup reduced-calorie mayonnaise *or* salad dressing
¼ cup grated Parmesan cheese
¼ cup lemon juice
2 cloves garlic, minced
1 tablespoon anchovy paste (optional)
6 cups torn romaine
2 cups cooked chicken *or* turkey cut into thin bite-size strips
2 cups sliced fresh mushrooms
1 cup small cherry tomatoes, halved

▪ In a small mixing bowl stir together mayonnaise or salad dressing, Parmesan cheese, lemon juice, garlic, and, if desired, anchovy paste. Set mayonnaise mixture aside.

▪ In a deep 3- or 3½-quart bowl toss together romaine, chicken or turkey, mushrooms, and cherry tomatoes. Carefully spread mayonnaise mixture evenly over top of romaine mixture, sealing to edge of bowl. Cover tightly with plastic wrap. Refrigerate for 4 to 24 hours.

▪ To serve, lightly toss salad mixture till well coated. Spoon mixture onto salad plates. Makes 6 servings.

Nutrition information per serving: 207 calories, 17 g protein, 6 g carbohydrate, 13 g fat, 55 mg cholesterol, 273 mg sodium, 424 mg potassium.

ORANGE CHICKEN TABBOULEH

273 calories

Preparation Time: 40 min. ▪ Chilling Time: 4 hrs. ▪ Low Fat ▪ Low Cholesterol

1½	cups boiling water
¾	cup bulgur
2	oranges
1½	cups cubed cooked chicken *or* turkey
2	cups chopped seeded cucumber
2	tablespoons snipped fresh parsley
2	tablespoons chopped green onion
1	tablespoon snipped fresh mint *or* 1 teaspoon dried mint, crushed
1	tablespoon olive oil *or* salad oil
½	teaspoon salt
	Romaine lettuce leaves

▪ In a medium mixing bowl pour boiling water over bulgur. Let stand 30 minutes. Drain off excess liquid.

▪ Meanwhile, finely shred enough peel from oranges to make *2 teaspoons* peel. Section oranges over a bowl to catch juice. Cover and chill orange sections till serving time. Measure and reserve *¼ cup* orange juice.

▪ In a large mixing bowl stir together drained bulgur, orange peel, orange juice, chicken, cucumber, parsley, green onion, mint, oil, and salt.

▪ Cover and chill 4 to 24 hours, stirring occasionally.

▪ Just before serving, fold in orange sections. Serve on lettuce-lined plates. Makes 4 servings.

Nutrition information per serving: 273 calories, 19 g protein, 32 g carbohydrate, 8 g fat, 47 mg cholesterol, 320 mg sodium, 436 mg potassium.

CURRIED CHICKEN AND RICE SALAD

261 calories

Preparation Time: 30 min. ▪ Chilling Time: 30 min. ▪ Low Cholesterol

For pineapple boats, use a sharp knife to cut the pineapple, crown and all, into quarters. Cut the fruit away from the rind, leaving about a ½-inch-thick shell.

1	small fresh pineapple*
1½	cups *cold* cooked rice *or* brown rice
1½	cups cubed cooked chicken *or* turkey (8 ounces)
1	cup sliced celery
¼	cup raisins
½	cup plain low-fat yogurt
¼	cup reduced-calorie mayonnaise
2	tablespoons skim milk
1	to 1½ teaspoons curry powder
½	teaspoon instant chicken bouillon granules

▪ For pineapple boats, cut 1 small pineapple, crown and all, into quarters. Cut fruit from rind, leaving a ½-inch-thick shell. Remove core from loosened fruit and discard. Chop enough fruit to equal ½ cup. Cover and chill the remaining fruit for another use. Cover and chill pineapple boats till serving time.

▪ In a medium mixing bowl stir together the ½ cup pineapple, cold rice, chicken or turkey, celery, and raisins.

▪ For dressing, in a small bowl stir together yogurt, mayonnaise, milk, curry powder, and bouillon granules. Pour over chicken mixture and toss to coat. Cover and chill for ½ hour to 24 hours.

▪ To serve, stir an additional 1 to 2 tablespoons skim milk into salad to moisten, if necessary. Divide the salad among pineapple boats. Makes 4 servings.

*Note: If desired, substitute ½ cup drained canned crushed pineapple for the fresh pineapple. Serve salad on lettuce-lined plates.

Nutrition information per serving: 261 calories, 19 g protein, 25 g carbohydrate, 9 g fat, 57 mg cholesterol, 222 mg sodium, 390 mg potassium.

CHILLED CHICKEN AND VEGETABLE SALAD   181 calories

Preparation Time: 20 min. ▪ Chilling Time: 4 hrs.

Toast English muffins or bagels to serve on the side.

½	**cup low-fat cottage cheese**
1	**tablespoon catsup**
1	**hard-cooked egg, chopped**
1	**tablespoon thinly sliced green onion**
1	**tablespoon pickle relish**
⅛	**teaspoon salt**
1½	**cups chopped cooked chicken**
½	**cup chopped celery**
½	**cup chopped green *or* sweet red pepper**
	Lettuce leaves
2	**tablespoons toasted sliced almonds**

▪ For dressing, in a blender container combine cottage cheese and catsup. Cover and blend till smooth.

▪ In a small mixing bowl stir together cottage cheese mixture, egg, onion, pickle relish, and salt. Set dressing aside.

▪ In a medium mixing bowl combine chicken, celery, and green or red pepper. Add dressing and toss gently to mix. Cover and chill for 4 to 24 hours.

▪ To serve, divide salad among 4 lettuce-lined salad plates. Garnish with almonds. Makes 4 servings.

Nutrition information per serving: 181 calories, 22 g protein, 6 g carbohydrate, 7 g fat, 117 mg cholesterol, 330 mg sodium, 315 mg potassium.

SALADE NIÇOISE

308 calories

Preparation Time: 40 min. ▪ Chilling Time: 2 hrs.

1	**pound small potatoes, sliced ¼ inch thick**
½	**pound whole green beans***
⅓	**cup lemon juice**
2	**tablespoons cooking oil**
1½	**teaspoons sugar**
4	**teaspoons brown mustard _or_ Dijon-style mustard**
¾	**teaspoon dried dillweed**
	Lettuce leaves
1	**6½-ounce can tuna (water pack), drained and broken into chunks**
2	**medium tomatoes, seeded and cut into chunks**
½	**small red onion, thinly sliced and separated into rings**
2	**hard-cooked eggs, cut into wedges**

■ In a large saucepan bring 2 inches of water to boiling. Add potatoes and green beans. Cover and simmer 10 minutes or just till tender. Remove beans with a slotted spoon; drain potatoes. Cover and chill for 2 to 24 hours.

■ Meanwhile, for dressing, in a screw-top jar combine lemon juice, oil, sugar, mustard, dillweed, 2 tablespoons _water,_ ¼ teaspoon _salt,_ and ⅛ teaspoon _pepper._ Cover and shake well to blend. Chill for 2 to 24 hours.

■ To serve, place lettuce leaves on a platter. Arrange potatoes, beans, tuna, tomatoes, onion, and eggs atop lettuce. Shake dressing and drizzle over salad. Serves 4.

*Note: If desired, substitute one 9-ounce package frozen cut _green beans,_ thawed, for the fresh beans. Add to the potatoes the last 5 minutes of cooking.

Nutrition information per serving: 308 calories, 21 g protein, 34 g carbohydrate, 11 g fat, 166 mg cholesterol, 269 mg sodium, 966 mg potassium.

ANTIPASTO SALAD

Preparation Time: 20 min. ▪ Low Cholesterol

1	9-ounce package frozen artichoke hearts
¼	cup red wine vinegar
2	tablespoons olive oil *or* salad oil
1	tablespoon snipped fresh basil *or* 1 teaspoon dried basil, crushed
1	tablespoon snipped fresh parsley
	Lettuce leaves
2	medium tomatoes, cut into wedges
1	6½-ounce can tuna (water pack), drained and broken into chunks
2	cups small fresh mushrooms
4	ounces part-skim mozzarella cheese, cut into strips

▪ Cook artichoke hearts according to package directions; drain well.

▪ Meanwhile, for salad dressing, combine vinegar, olive oil, basil, parsley, a dash *salt,* and a dash *pepper.* Set aside.

▪ Arrange lettuce leaves on 4 individual serving plates. Arrange artichoke hearts, tomatoes, tuna, mushrooms, and cheese atop lettuce. Drizzle with salad dressing. Serves 4.

Nutrition information per serving: 244 calories, 24 g protein, 11 g carbohydrate, 13 g fat, 44 mg cholesterol, 237 mg sodium, 585 mg potassium.

BEEF
MAIN DISHES

BEEF DIJON *(see page 91)*

MUSHROOM-STUFFED BEEF ROAST

175 calories

Preparation Time: 30 min. ▪ Marinating Time: 6 hrs. ▪ Cooking Time: 1¼ hrs. ▪ Low Cholesterol

1	**2-pound beef eye of round roast**
¼	**cup dry white wine**
8	**ounces fresh mushrooms, finely chopped (3 cups)**
¼	**cup water**
¼	**teaspoon dried dillweed *or* fennel seed, crushed**
⅛	**teaspoon salt**
⅓	**cup thinly sliced green onion**
1	**tablespoon reduced-calorie mayonnaise *or* salad dressing**
½	**cup plain low-fat yogurt**
1	**tablespoon all-purpose flour**
⅛	**teaspoon pepper**
½	**cup beef broth**

▪ Trim excess fat from roast. Then, cut 8 evenly spaced crosswise slits or pockets in roast, making each 3 inches deep. Place roast in a plastic bag set in a deep bowl. Pour wine over roast. Seal bag. Marinate roast in the refrigerator for 6 to 24 hours, turning bag occasionally.

▪ For filling, in medium saucepan combine mushrooms, water, dillweed or fennel seed, and salt. Cook, uncovered, over medium heat for 15 minutes or till liquid is evaporated. Cool. Stir in onion and mayonnaise or salad dressing.

▪ Remove roast from bag, discarding marinade. Spoon filling into pockets in roast. Place roast in a shallow roasting pan. Bake in a 325° oven for 1¼ to 1½ hours or till meat thermometer registers 140°. Remove from oven. Keep warm.

▪ For sauce, in a small saucepan stir together yogurt, flour, and pepper. Stir in beef broth. Cook and stir over medium heat till thickened and bubbly. Then, cook and stir for 1 minute more. To serve, slice meat between filled pockets. Serve with sauce. Makes 8 servings.

Nutrition information per serving: 175 calories, 25 g protein, 4 g carbohydrate, 6 g fat, 56 mg cholesterol, 153 mg sodium, 475 mg potassium.

GARLIC-WINE POT ROAST

290 calories

Preparation Time: 12 min. ▪ Cooking Time: 2 hrs. ▪ Low Cholesterol ▪ Low Sodium

	Nonstick spray coating
1	**3-pound boneless beef round rump roast, trimmed of separable fat**
¾	**cup water**
½	**cup dry red wine**
1	**large onion, sliced**
4	**cloves garlic, minced**
2	**teaspoons instant beef bouillon granules**
¼	**teaspoon dried thyme, crushed**
¼	**teaspoon pepper**
1	**pound carrots, cut into 2-inch-long pieces**
1	**16-ounce package frozen cut green beans**
2	**tablespoons cornstarch**
2	**tablespoons water**

▪ Spray a *cold* Dutch oven with nonstick spray coating, then preheat over medium heat. Brown roast on both sides in the Dutch oven. Drain any fat. Add the ¾ cup water, wine, onion, garlic, bouillon granules, thyme, and pepper. Cover and simmer for 1 hour.

▪ Add carrots to Dutch oven and simmer for 40 minutes. Then, add beans and simmer for 10 minutes more or till beans and meat are tender. Transfer roast and vegetables to a serving platter. Keep warm while making gravy.

▪ For gravy, skim fat from pan juices. Stir together cornstarch and 2 tablespoons water. Stir mixture into pan juices. Cook and stir till thickened and bubbly. Then, cook and stir for 2 minutes more. To serve, spoon gravy over meat and vegetables. Makes 10 servings.

Nutrition information per serving: 290 calories, 34 g protein, 12 g carbohydrate, 11 g fat, 98 mg cholesterol, 138 mg sodium, 590 mg potassium.

GRILLED FLANK STEAK

240 calories

Preparation Time: 15 min. ▪ Grilling Time: 12 min. ▪ Low Cholesterol

Score the flank steak on both sides by making shallow diagonal cuts about 1 inch apart in a diamond pattern.

¼	**cup chopped onion**
1	**clove garlic, minced**
½	**teaspoon chili powder**
1	**tablespoon margarine**
½	**cup tomato sauce**
2	**tablespoons vinegar**
1	**tablespoon honey**
¼	**teaspoon salt**
¼	**teaspoon pepper**
1½	**pounds beef flank steak, cut ¾ inch thick**

■ For sauce, in a small saucepan cook onion, garlic, and chili powder in margarine till tender. Stir in tomato sauce, vinegar, honey, salt, and pepper. Bring to boiling, stirring constantly. Boil 5 minutes or till sauce is slightly thickened.

■ Meanwhile, trim fat from flank steak. Score steak diagonally into diamonds on both sides. (See photo above.) Brush with sauce. Grill steak on an uncovered grill directly over *medium* coals for 7 minutes. Turn and grill to desired doneness, allowing 5 to 7 minutes more for medium. Brush occasionally with the remaining sauce.

■ To serve, thinly slice the flank steak across the grain. Makes 6 servings.

■ **Broiling directions:** Place meat on the unheated rack of a broiler pan. Broil 3 inches from the heat for 6 minutes. Turn and broil to desired doneness, allowing 6 to 8 minutes more for medium. Brush occasionally with sauce.

Nutrition information per serving: 240 calories, 21 g protein, 5 g carbohydrate, 14 g fat, 58 mg cholesterol, 304 mg sodium, 436 mg potassium.

MUSHROOM-STUFFED FLANK STEAK ROLL   313 calories

Preparation Time: 15 min. ▪ Cooking Time: 55 min. ▪ Low Cholesterol

¾	**pound beef flank steak**
1	**cup sliced fresh mushrooms**
	Nonstick spray coating
1	**cup vegetable juice cocktail**
1	**tablespoon Worcestershire sauce**
1½	**cups water**
½	**cup chopped onion**
1	**teaspoon instant beef bouillon granules**
1	**cup quick-cooking barley**
3	**tablespoons snipped fresh parsley**
2	**tablespoons cornstarch**
2	**tablespoons water**

▪ Score steak on both sides by making shallow cuts at 1-inch intervals diagonally across steak in a diamond pattern. Using a meat mallet, pound steak into a 10x8-inch rectangle.

▪ Spread mushrooms on top of steak. Roll up meat, starting from one short side. Secure with wooden skewers.

▪ Spray a *cold* large skillet with nonstick spray coating. In the skillet brown steak roll on all sides. Add vegetable juice cocktail and Worcestershire sauce. Cover and simmer 55 to 60 minutes or till meat is tender, turning steak roll occasionally.

▪ Meanwhile, in a medium saucepan heat the 1½ cups water, onion, and bouillon granules to boiling. Add barley. Cover and simmer for 10 to 12 minutes or till water is absorbed. Remove from heat and stir in parsley.

▪ Transfer roll to a cutting board. Stir together cornstarch and 2 tablespoons water. Stir into liquid in skillet. Cook and stir till thickened and bubbly. Cook and stir 2 minutes more. To serve, remove skewers from meat and slice. Arrange slices on barley mixture. Spoon gravy on top. Serves 4.

Nutrition information per serving: 313 calories, 21 g protein, 33 g carbohydrate, 11 g fat, 45 mg cholesterol, 416 mg sodium, 613 mg potassium.

BEEF DIJON

256 calories

Preparation Time: 13 min. ▪ Cooking Time: 12 min. ▪ Low Cholesterol

Elegant, simple, delicious, and low in calories—what more can you ask for?

2	teaspoons whole black peppers
1	pound beef flank steak
1	cup sliced fresh mushrooms
½	cup thinly sliced green onion
¼	cup water
½	teaspoon instant beef bouillon granules
⅓	cup plain low-fat yogurt
1	tablespoon all-purpose flour
2	teaspoons Dijon-style mustard
1	10-ounce package frozen asparagus spears *or* 1 pound fresh asparagus spears, cooked and drained

▪ Coarsely crack the black peppers. Rub *half* of the peppers into *each* side of the steak. Place steak on the unheated rack of a broiler pan. Broil 3 inches from heat for 6 minutes. Turn steak over and broil for 6 to 8 minutes more or till steak is to desired doneness.

▪ Meanwhile, for sauce, in a saucepan combine mushrooms, green onion, water, and bouillon granules. Cover and cook over medium heat about 5 minutes or till mushrooms are tender. Stir together yogurt, flour, and mustard. Stir yogurt mixture into mushroom mixture. Cook and stir till thickened and bubbly. Then, cook and stir for 1 minute more.

▪ To serve, thinly slice steak diagonally across the grain. Arrange steak slices and asparagus on dinner plates. Serve with sauce. Makes 4 servings.

Nutrition information per serving: 256 calories, 26 g protein, 8 g carbohydrate, 14 g fat, 61 mg cholesterol, 208 mg sodium, 680 mg potassium.

DEVILED STEAK

195 calories

Preparation Time: 5 min. ▪ Grilling Time: 12 min. ▪ Low Cholesterol

1	**tablespoon catsup**
1	**tablespoon water**
1	**tablespoon Worcestershire sauce**
1	**teaspoon dry mustard**
¼	**teaspoon salt**
	Dash pepper
1	**pound boneless beef tenderloin** *or* **sirloin steak, cut 1 inch thick**

▪ For sauce, combine catsup, water, Worcestershire sauce, dry mustard, salt, and pepper.

▪ Trim fat from meat. Grill meat on an uncovered grill directly over *medium-hot* coals for 6 minutes. Brush with sauce. Turn and grill to desired doneness, allowing 6 to 9 minutes more for medium, brushing frequently with sauce. Brush any remaining sauce over meat before serving. Makes 4 servings.

▪ **Broiling directions:** Place meat on the unheated rack of a broiler pan. Broil 3 inches from the heat for 6 minutes. Turn and broil to desired doneness, allowing 7 to 11 minutes more for medium. Brush frequently with sauce.

Nutrition information per serving: 195 calories, 24 g protein, 2 g carbohydrate, 10 g fat, 73 mg cholesterol, 269 mg sodium, 352 mg potassium.

SHERRIED FILLET STEAKS

210 calories

Preparation Time: 2 min. ▪ Cooking Time: 4 min. ▪ Low Cholesterol

Serve with either pasta or Cauliflower Amandine (see page 361) and a tossed salad, and you have a complete meal in minutes.

	Nonstick spray coating
2	**4-ounce beef tenderloin steaks, cut ½ inch thick and trimmed of separable fat**
2	**tablespoons dry sherry**
⅛	**teaspoon salt**
⅛	**teaspoon cracked pepper**
	Dash dried tarragon, crushed
1	**tablespoon snipped fresh chives *or* parsley**

▪ Spray a *cold* 8-inch skillet with nonstick spray coating. Heat skillet over medium-high heat. Add steaks and cook for 2 to 3 minutes on each side or till steaks are to desired doneness. Transfer steaks to a serving platter.

▪ For sauce, carefully add sherry to the skillet. Then add salt, pepper, and tarragon. Cook and stir for 1 minute. To serve, pour sauce over steaks and sprinkle with snipped chives or parsley. Makes 2 servings.

Nutrition information per serving: 210 calories, 23 g protein, 1 g carbohydrate, 10 g fat, 73 mg cholesterol, 185 mg sodium, 351 mg potassium.

PEANUT SATÉ

222 calories

Preparation Time: 15 min. ▪ Marinating Time: 4 hrs. ▪ Cooking Time: 7 min. ▪ Low Cholesterol

1	pound lean boneless beef sirloin
1	small onion, cut up
2	tablespoons soy sauce
2	tablespoons lime juice
1	teaspoon sugar
1	teaspoon ground cumin
1	clove garlic, minced
⅓	cup chicken broth
2	tablespoons peanut butter
1	tablespoon molasses
1	teaspoon soy sauce
¼	teaspoon crushed red pepper
1	clove garlic, minced

■ Cut beef into 1½-inch pieces. Place in a plastic bag set in a deep bowl.

■ For marinade, in a blender container or food processor bowl place onion, the 2 tablespoons soy sauce, lime juice, sugar, cumin, and garlic. Cover and blend or process till smooth. Pour over meat in bag; close bag.

■ Marinate meat in the refrigerator for 4 hours, turning bag occasionally. Drain meat, reserving marinade.

■ For sauce, in a saucepan stir broth into peanut butter. Stir in molasses, the 1 teaspoon soy sauce, crushed red pepper, and garlic. Cook and stir till heated through. Keep warm.

■ Thread meat onto four 8-inch skewers. Arrange on the unheated rack of a broiler pan. Broil 3 to 4 inches from the heat for 7 to 9 minutes or to desired doneness, turning occasionally and brushing with marinade. Serve sauce with meat for dipping. Makes 4 servings.

Nutrition information per serving: 222 calories, 25 g protein, 6 g carbohydrate, 11 g fat, 66 mg cholesterol, 368 mg sodium, 448 mg potassium.

BEEF ROULADES

247 calories

Preparation Time: 25 min. ▪ Cooking Time: 1 hr. 10 min. ▪ Low Cholesterol

Try a combination of red, yellow, orange, and green sweet peppers for a colorful stuffing.

1	pound boneless beef round steak, cut ½ inch thick and trimmed of separable fat
1	tablespoon Dijon-style mustard
8	4-inch green pepper strips *or* 8 green onions, cut into 4-inch lengths
	Nonstick spray coating
1	medium onion, chopped (½ cup)
1½	cups beef broth
1	tablespoon all-purpose flour
2	cups chopped carrots

▪Cut steak into 4 serving-size pieces. Using a meat mallet, pound each piece to ⅛-inch thickness.

▪Spread one side of *each* beef piece with *one-fourth* of the mustard. Place *2* green pepper strips or *2* green onions at a short end of *each* beef piece and roll up. Secure with wooden toothpicks.

▪Spray a *cold* large skillet with nonstick spray coating. Heat skillet over medium heat. Add beef rolls; brown on all sides. Remove rolls from skillet. Add chopped onion to skillet and cook for 3 minutes or till onion is nearly tender.

▪In a small mixing bowl stir together beef broth and flour. Pour mixture into the skillet. Cook and stir till thickened and bubbly. Then, add chopped carrots and beef rolls. Cover and simmer about 1 hour or till beef is tender. Makes 4 servings.

Nutrition information per serving: 247 calories, 29 g protein, 10 g carbohydrate, 9 g fat, 82 mg cholesterol, 465 mg sodium, 565 mg potassium.

ITALIAN BEEF SKILLET

213 calories

Preparation Time: 20 min. ▪ Cooking Time: 1 hr. 20 min. ▪ Low Cholesterol

Serve Cheesy Polenta Squares (see page 334) as an Italian side-dish alternative to pasta.

1	pound beef round steak
	Nonstick spray coating
2	cups sliced fresh mushrooms
1	cup chopped onion
1	cup chopped green pepper
½	cup chopped celery
2	cloves garlic, minced
1	14½-ounce can tomatoes, cut up
½	teaspoon dried basil, crushed
¼	teaspoon dried oregano, crushed
⅛	teaspoon crushed red pepper
2	tablespoons grated Parmesan cheese

▪ Trim separable fat from round steak, then cut meat into 5 serving-size pieces. Spray a *cold* large skillet with nonstick spray coating. Add meat pieces to skillet; brown both sides of each piece. Remove meat from skillet.

▪ Add mushrooms, onion, green pepper, celery, and garlic to the skillet. Cook till vegetables are nearly tender. Then, stir in *undrained* tomatoes, basil, oregano, and red pepper. Add meat to skillet, spooning vegetable mixture over the meat. Cover and simmer about 1¼ hours or till meat is tender, stirring occasionally.

▪ Transfer meat to a serving platter. Spoon vegetable mixture over meat and sprinkle with Parmesan cheese. Makes 5 servings.

Nutrition information per serving: 213 calories, 25 g protein, 10 g carbohydrate, 8 g fat, 67 mg cholesterol, 227 mg sodium, 654 mg potassium.

HERBED STEAK AND ONIONS

237 calories

Preparation Time: 15 min. ▪ Marinating Time: overnight ▪ Grilling Time: 18 min. ▪ Low Cholesterol

To marinate your steak, place a plastic bag in a deep bowl. Pour the marinade into the bag and add the steak. Seal the bag, then turn it to coat the steak with marinade. Marinating this way keeps the meat covered with the marinade and makes cleanup a cinch. Just throw out the bag.

1	cup tomato juice
1	tablespoon olive oil *or* cooking oil
½	teaspoon dried basil, crushed
½	teaspoon dried oregano, crushed
¼	teaspoon pepper
1	clove garlic, minced
1	pound beef top round steak, cut 1 inch thick
2	large onions, thinly sliced and separated into rings

▪ For marinade, combine tomato juice, oil, basil, oregano, pepper, and garlic. Set aside.

▪ Trim fat from steak and cut steak into four equal portions. Place meat in a plastic bag set in a deep bowl. Pour marinade over steak. Seal bag; turn to coat steak well. Marinate overnight in the refrigerator. Then, drain steak, reserving marinade.

▪ Place onions on an 18-inch square of heavy foil. Turn edges of foil up slightly. Drizzle *½ cup* of the reserved marinade over onions. Fold foil tightly to seal. Grill onion packet and steak on an uncovered grill directly over *medium* coals for 10 minutes. Turn onion packet and steak; brush steak with marinade. Grill steak to desired doneness, allowing 8 to 10 minutes more for medium. Grill onions 8 minutes more or till tender.

▪ Unwrap onions and place on a serving plate. Arrange meat atop onion. Spoon any remaining sauce from onions over the meat. Makes 4 servings.

Nutrition information per serving: 237 calories, 28 g protein, 9 g carbohydrate, 9 g fat, 71 mg cholesterol, 273 mg sodium, 655 mg potassium.

SUKIYAKI

245 calories

Preparation Time: 35 min. ▪ Cooking Time: 8 min. ▪ Low Fat ▪ Low Cholesterol

½	pound beef top round steak
2	ounces cellophane noodles
⅓	cup beef broth
2	tablespoons sake *or* dry sherry
2	tablespoons soy sauce
	Nonstick spray coating
2	cups sliced bok choy
1	cup green onions bias sliced into ½-inch pieces
1	cup fresh bean sprouts
1	8-ounce can bamboo shoots *or* sliced water chestnuts, drained
1	cup sliced fresh mushrooms
1	tablespoon cooking oil
8	ounces tofu, cubed

▪ Partially freeze beef; trim separable fat. Thinly slice across the grain into bite-size strips. Set aside.

▪ In a bowl pour boiling water over cellophane noodles to cover; let stand 10 minutes. Drain. With kitchen shears, cut noodles into 2-inch lengths.

▪ In a mixing bowl stir together beef broth, sake or dry sherry, soy sauce, and ¼ teaspoon *pepper;* set aside.

▪ Spray a large skillet or wok with nonstick spray coating. Preheat over medium heat. Add bok choy and green onions; stir-fry 2 to 3 minutes or till vegetables are crisp-tender. Remove from skillet. Add bean sprouts, bamboo shoots, and mushrooms; stir-fry 1 to 2 minutes or till mushrooms are tender. Remove vegetable mixture from skillet.

▪ Add oil to hot skillet; swirl to coat. Add beef; stir-fry 2 to 3 minutes or till beef is no longer pink.

▪ Add tofu and broth mixture to skillet. Cook and stir till bubbly. Return all vegetables to skillet. Add noodles. Cover and cook 2 to 3 minutes or till heated through. Serves 4.

Nutrition information per serving: 245 calories, 20 g protein, 20 g carbohydrate, 9 g fat, 33 mg cholesterol, 629 mg sodium, 530 mg potassium.

PINEAPPLE BEEF

337 calories

Preparation Time: 15 min. ▪ Marinating Time: 15 min. ▪ Cooking Time: 7 min. ▪ Low Fat ▪ Low Cholesterol

¾	**pound beef top round steak, cut ½ inch thick**
1	**8-ounce can pineapple slices (juice pack)**
2	**tablespoons dry sherry *or* water**
1	**tablespoon soy sauce**
1	**tablespoon molasses *or* brown sugar**
⅛	**to ¼ teaspoon crushed red pepper**
	Nonstick spray coating
4	**green onions, cut into ½-inch pieces**
1	**tablespoon cornstarch**
1	**medium tomato, cut into wedges**
1	**6-ounce package frozen pea pods, thawed**
2	**cups hot cooked rice**

▪ Trim separable fat from round steak. Partially freeze meat; then, cut on bias into thin bite-size strips. Drain pineapple, reserving juice. Cut pineapple slices into quarters; set aside.

▪ In a bowl stir together reserved pineapple juice, dry sherry or water, soy sauce, molasses or brown sugar, and red pepper. Add meat; stir till coated. Cover and marinate meat at room temperature for 15 minutes. Drain, reserving marinade.

▪ Spray a *cold* large skillet or wok with nonstick spray coating. Add *half* of meat to skillet or wok. Stir-fry for 2 to 3 minutes or till browned. Remove meat. Stir-fry remaining meat and onions for 2 to 3 minutes or till meat is browned. Return all meat to skillet. Push meat from center of skillet.

▪ For sauce, stir cornstarch into reserved marinade. Add sauce to center of skillet. Cook and stir till thickened and bubbly. Add tomato, pea pods, and pineapple. Stir ingredients together until coated with sauce. Cook and stir about 2 minutes more or till heated through. Serve over hot cooked rice. Makes 4 servings.

Nutrition information per serving: 337 calories, 23 g protein, 47 g carbohydrate, 6 g fat, 57 mg cholesterol, 296 mg sodium, 497 mg potassium.

BEEF STIR-FRY WITH ORANGE SAUCE

294 calories

Preparation Time: 30 min. ▪ Cooking Time: 6 min. ▪ Low Fat ▪ Low Cholesterol

Partially freeze the meat till it's firm but not hard (about 30 to 45 minutes). Hold a sharp knife at a 45-degree angle to the cutting board while you thinly slice the meat. Cutting at this angle creates the most tender slice of meat.

¾	**pound beef top round steak**
	Orange Sauce
	Nonstick spray coating*
4	**green onions, bias-sliced into 1-inch pieces**
1	**clove garlic, minced**
1	**tablespoon cooking oil (optional)**
6	**cups torn fresh spinach**
½	**of an 8-ounce can (⅓ cup) sliced water chestnuts, drained**
2	**cups hot cooked rice**

▪ Partially freeze meat. Then, thinly slice meat across the grain into bite-size strips.

▪ Prepare Orange Sauce; set aside.

▪ Spray a wok or 12-inch skillet with nonstick spray coating. Heat over medium-high heat. Stir-fry onions and garlic for 1 minute; remove from wok. If necessary, add 1 tablespoon oil. Stir-fry meat for 2 to 3 minutes or till done. Push meat away from center of wok.

▪ Stir Orange Sauce and pour into the center of wok. Cook and stir till thickened and bubbly. Stir in spinach, water chestnuts, and onion mixture. Cover and cook for 1 minute. Serve over rice. Makes 4 servings.

▪ **Orange Sauce:** In a small bowl stir together 1 tablespoon *cornstarch,* 1 teaspoon *sugar,* and 1 teaspoon *instant beef bouillon granules.* Stir in 1 teaspoon finely shredded *orange peel,* ½ cup *orange juice,* and 1 tablespoon *soy sauce.*

*Note: You may need to cook the beef in the oil to keep it from sticking to the wok. If you do, add 25 calories to the calorie count of each serving.

Nutrition information per serving: 294 calories, 20 g protein, 37 g carbohydrate, 7 g fat, 46 mg cholesterol, 428 mg sodium, 648 mg potassium.

CURRIED BEEF AND POTATOES

251 calories

Preparation Time: 30 min. ▪ Cooking Time: 12 min. ▪ Low Fat ▪ Low Cholesterol

Save a step and use your leftover baked or boiled potatoes.

¾	**pound beef top round steak**
2	**small potatoes, halved and thinly sliced (½ pound total)**
½	**cup beef broth**
2	**teaspoons cornstarch**
¼	**teaspoon salt**
	Nonstick spray coating
¾	**cup chopped onion**
¾	**cup chopped green *or* sweet red pepper**
1	**tablespoon cooking oil**
1	**teaspoon curry powder**
1	**medium tomato, coarsely chopped**

▪ Partially freeze meat. Thinly slice across the grain into bite-size strips. Set aside.

▪ Cook sliced potatoes in boiling water about 5 minutes or till tender. Drain and set aside.

▪ Meanwhile, for sauce, stir together beef broth, cornstarch, and salt.

▪ Spray a wok or large skillet with nonstick spray coating. Heat over medium-high heat. Add onion and stir-fry 2 minutes. Add green pepper and stir-fry about 2 minutes more or till vegetables are crisp-tender. Remove from wok.

▪ Add oil to hot wok. Add beef and curry powder. Stir-fry 2 to 3 minutes or till beef is done. Push beef from center of wok.

▪ Stir sauce and add to center of wok. Cook and stir till thickened and bubbly. Stir in onion mixture, potatoes, and tomato. Cook and stir all ingredients for 1 minute or till heated through. Makes 4 servings.

Nutrition information per serving: 251 calories, 23 g protein, 21 g carbohydrate, 8 g fat, 53 mg cholesterol, 414 mg sodium, 714 mg potassium.

BEEF AND BREW

348 calories

Preparation Time: 10 min. ▪ Cooking Time: 1 hr. 20 min. ▪ Low Fat

¾	cup light beer
¾	cup water
1	bay leaf
½	teaspoon dried thyme, crushed
⅛	teaspoon ground pepper
1	pound beef round steak, trimmed of separable fat and cut into 1-inch pieces
2	medium onions, cut into wedges
2	medium green *or* sweet red peppers, cut into thin strips
¼	cup water
2	tablespoons all-purpose flour
2	cups hot, cooked egg noodles

▪ In large saucepan stir together beer, the ¾ cup water, bay leaf, ½ teaspoon *salt,* thyme, and ground pepper. Stir in meat. Bring to boiling. Reduce heat. Cover and simmer for 55 minutes. Add onions and green or red peppers and simmer about 20 minutes or till beef is tender. Remove bay leaf.

▪ Stir together the ¼ cup water and flour. Stir flour mixture into meat mixture. Cook and stir till thickened and bubbly. Cook and stir for 2 minutes more. Serve over hot egg noodles. Makes 4 servings.

Nutrition information per serving: 348 calories, 32 g protein, 29 g carbohydrate, 10 g fat, 106 mg cholesterol, 316 mg sodium, 493 mg potassium.

BARBECUE BEEF SANDWICHES

278 calories

Advance Preparation Time: 2¼ hrs. ▪ Final Preparation Time: 8 min. ▪ Low Fat ▪ Low Cholesterol

To shred the meat, be sure to cook the meat till it is very tender. *Then, transfer the meat to a cutting board. Using the tines of two forks, pull the meat across the grain to form shreds.*

1	**2-pound beef round steak, cut ¾ inch thick**
	Nonstick spray coating
1	**14½-ounce can tomatoes, cut up**
1	**large onion, chopped**
1	**large carrot, chopped**
2	**tablespoons Worcestershire sauce**
2	**tablespoons vinegar**
1	**tablespoon brown sugar**
2	**teaspoons chili powder**
1	**teaspoon dried oregano, crushed**
1	**clove garlic, minced**
1	**bay leaf**
8	**hamburger buns**

▪ Trim separable fat from meat. Cut meat into 4 or 6 pieces. Spray a *cold* Dutch oven with nonstick spray coating. Add *half* of the steak pieces and brown each piece on both sides. Remove; repeat, browning remaining steak pieces. Drain any fat. Return all meat to Dutch oven.

▪ Add *undrained* tomatoes, onion, carrot, Worcestershire sauce, vinegar, brown sugar, chili powder, oregano, garlic, and bay leaf to Dutch oven. Bring to boiling; reduce heat. Cover; simmer for 2 to 2½ hours or till meat is very tender.

▪ Remove meat from sauce and shred meat. Simmer sauce, uncovered, for 5 to 10 minutes or until slightly thickened. Discard bay leaf. Transfer meat and sauce to 1-, 2-, or 4-serving-size freezer containers. Cover, label, and freeze for up to 6 months.

▪ To reheat, transfer mixture to a saucepan; add 1 tablespoon *water.* Cook over low heat till heated through, stirring occasionally. (Allow 8 to 10 minutes for 1 or 2 servings; 25 to 30 minutes for 4 servings.) Serve on buns. Serves 8.

Nutrition information per serving: 278 calories, 22 g protein, 29 g carbohydrate, 8 g fat, 54 mg cholesterol, 300 mg sodium, 502 mg potassium.

TEX-MEX BEEF SOUP

147 calories

Preparation Time: 25 min. ▪ Cooking Time: 30 min. ▪ Low Fat ▪ Low Cholesterol

	Nonstick spray coating
½	**pound boneless beef round steak, cut into ½-inch cubes**
1	**cup chopped onion**
1	**clove garlic, minced**
2	**cups water**
1	**16-ounce can tomatoes, cut up**
1	**cup chopped carrot**
1	**8-ounce can kidney beans, drained**
½	**cup chopped green pepper**
2	**tablespoons tomato paste**
1	**tablespoon chili powder**
2	**teaspoons instant beef bouillon granules**
¼	**teaspoon pepper**

▪ Spray a large saucepan with nonstick spray coating. Preheat over medium-high heat. Add beef, onion, and garlic. Cook and stir about 3 minutes or till meat is brown.

▪ Stir in water, *undrained* tomatoes, carrot, beans, green pepper, tomato paste, chili powder, bouillon granules, and pepper. Cover and simmer about 30 minutes or till meat is tender. Makes 5 servings.

Nutrition information per serving: 147 calories, 15 g protein, 16 g carbohydrate, 3 g fat, 29 mg cholesterol, 381 mg sodium, 681 mg potassium.

PEPPERY BEEF AND VEGETABLES

316 calories

Preparation Time: 15 min. ▪ Cooking Time: 8 min. ▪ Low Fat ▪ Low Cholesterol

4	**ounces spaghettini**
½	**cup water**
¼	**cup low-sodium** *or* **regular soy sauce**
2	**teaspoons cornstarch**
½	**teaspoon pepper**
⅛	**teaspoon ground red pepper**
	Nonstick spray coating
1	**clove garlic, minced**
1	**cup fresh** *or* **frozen pea pods, halved crosswise**
½	**cup chopped green** *or* **sweet red pepper**
1	**cup sliced fresh mushrooms**
1	**tablespoon cooking oil**
¾	**pound lean boneless beef, cut into thin bite-size strips**

▪ Cook spaghettini according to package directions. Drain well and keep warm.

▪ Meanwhile, for sauce, in a small bowl stir together water, soy sauce, cornstarch, pepper, and red pepper. Set aside.

▪ Spray a *cold* wok or large skillet with nonstick spray coating. Heat over medium-high heat. Add garlic and stir-fry for 30 seconds. Add pea pods and green or red pepper; stir-fry 1 minute. Add mushrooms; stir-fry 1 to 2 minutes more or till vegetables are tender. Remove vegetables from wok.

▪ Add oil to wok. Stir-fry beef in hot oil for 3 to 4 minutes or till done. Push beef to sides of wok. Stir sauce and pour into the center of wok. Cook and stir till thickened and bubbly. Return vegetables to wok; cook and stir all ingredients 1 minute. Toss with spaghettini. Makes 4 servings.

Nutrition information per serving: 316 calories, 27 g protein, 28 g carbohydrate, 10 g fat, 61 mg cholesterol, 678 mg sodium, 429 mg potassium.

DEEP-DISH BEEF PIE

283 calories

Preparation Time: 40 min. ▪ Cooking Time: 1 hr. 20 min. ▪ Low Cholesterol

To flute edges, place thumb flat against inside edge of pie shell. Press the pastry around thumb using thumb and index finger of other hand. Then, press the tines of a fork lightly into the center of each flute.

	Nonstick spray coating
1	**pound lean boneless beef for stew, trimmed of separable fat and cut into ½-inch pieces**
1	**teaspoon cooking oil**
1	**cup chopped onion**
1	**cup chopped celery**
1	**cup sliced carrots**
1	**cup cubed, peeled turnip**
1½	**cups tomato juice**
¾	**teaspoon dried thyme *or* basil, crushed**
¼	**teaspoon salt**
1	**tablespoon all-purpose flour**
2	**cups fresh *or* frozen cut green beans**
	Pastry
1	**teaspoon skim milk**

▪ Spray a large skillet with nonstick coating. Preheat over medium-high heat. Brown *half* the meat in skillet. Remove. Add oil. Brown remaining meat. Return all meat to skillet.

▪ Stir in onion, celery, carrots, turnip, tomato juice, thyme, salt, ⅛ teaspoon *pepper,* and ¼ cup *water.* Cover and simmer 50 to 60 minutes or till meat is nearly tender.

▪ Combine the flour and 2 tablespoons *water.* Stir into skillet mixture. Cook and stir till thickened and bubbly. Stir in green beans. Spoon into a 1½-quart casserole. Cover with Pastry; flute edges. Brush with skim milk. Cut vents for steam.

▪ Bake in a 400° oven for 30 minutes or till pastry is lightly browned and meat and vegetables are tender. Serves 6.

▪ **Pastry:** Combine ¾ cup *all-purpose flour* and ½ teaspoon *baking powder.* Cut in 3 tablespoons *margarine* till mixture resembles coarse crumbs. Sprinkle with 3 tablespoons *cold water,* one tablespoon at a time, stirring with a fork till mixture holds together. Form into a ball. On a floured surface, roll dough into a circle 1 inch larger than the top of the casserole.

Nutrition information per serving: 283 calories, 22 g protein, 26 g carbohydrate, 10 g fat, 48 mg cholesterol, 473 mg sodium, 687 mg potassium.

EASY GREEN CHILI

352 calories

Preparation Time: 15 min. ▪ Cooking Time: 1½ hrs. ▪ Low Fat ▪ Low Cholesterol

¾	pound beef stew meat
1	16-ounce can hominy *or* one 12-ounce can whole kernel corn, drained
1	14½-ounce can tomatoes, cut up
1	large onion, chopped
1	4-ounce can diced green chili peppers, drained
½	cup water
1	teaspoon dried oregano, crushed
1	teaspoon instant beef bouillon granules
2	cloves garlic, minced
1	16-ounce can red kidney beans *or* pinto beans, heated and drained

▪ Trim separable fat from stew meat, then cut into ¾-inch pieces.

▪ In 3-quart saucepan stir together meat, hominy or corn, *undrained* tomatoes, onion, chili peppers, water, oregano, bouillon granules, and garlic. Heat to boiling. Reduce heat. Cover and simmer about 1½ hours or till meat is tender. To serve, ladle mixture into individual bowls and top with hot kidney or pinto beans. Makes 4 servings.

Nutrition information per serving: 352 calories, 28 g protein, 40 g carbohydrate, 10 g fat, 60 mg cholesterol, 878 mg sodium, 895 mg potassium.

BEEF-BARLEY SOUP

232 calories

Preparation Time: 23 min. ▪ Cooking Time: 1¼ hrs. ▪ Low Fat ▪ Low Cholesterol

Freeze leftover soup in 1-cup portions for fast, hot lunches. To reheat, micro-cook on 70% power (medium-high) 5 minutes or till hot. Or, cook, covered, over medium-low heat about 15 minutes.

1½	pounds boneless beef chuck
6	cups water
2	cups sliced celery
2	cups sliced fresh mushrooms
1	cup sliced carrots
1	cup chopped onion
1	teaspoon salt
1	teaspoon dried rosemary, crushed
½	teaspoon pepper
1	clove garlic, minced
1	6-ounce can tomato paste
½	cup quick-cooking barley

■ Trim fat from meat; cut meat into ½-inch cubes. In a Dutch oven combine meat, water, celery, mushrooms, carrots, onion, salt, rosemary, pepper, and garlic. Bring to boiling; reduce heat. Cover and simmer 1 to 1¼ hours or till meat is tender. If necessary, skim fat.

■ Stir in tomato paste and barley. Return to boiling; reduce heat. Cover and simmer about 10 minutes or till barley is done. Makes 8 servings.

Nutrition information per serving: 232 calories, 20 g protein, 25 g carbohydrate, 6 g fat, 51 mg cholesterol, 657 mg sodium, 752 mg potassium.

MEATBALL SANDWICHES

324 calories

Preparation Time: 20 min. ▪ Cooking Time: 10 min. ▪ Low Fat

1	beaten egg
¼	cup skim milk
¼	cup fine dry bread crumbs
¼	cup snipped fresh parsley
3	tablespoons finely chopped onion
4	teaspoons sesame seeds, toasted
1	clove garlic, minced
¼	teaspoon dried mint, crushed
¼	teaspoon salt
¾	pound lean ground beef *or* lamb
	Nonstick spray coating
2	large pita bread rounds, halved
½	cup shredded lettuce
1	medium tomato, chopped
½	cup plain low-fat yogurt

▪ In a medium mixing bowl combine egg, milk, bread crumbs, parsley, onion, *3 teaspoons* of the sesame seeds, the garlic, mint, and salt. Add ground beef or lamb; mix well.

▪ Shape mixture into 24 meatballs.

▪ Spray a large skillet with nonstick spray coating. Preheat over medium-high heat. Add meatballs and brown on all sides. Cover skillet and cook meatballs over low heat for 5 to 10 minutes or till meat is no longer pink.

▪ With a slotted spoon remove meatballs from skillet and drain on paper towels.

▪ To serve, place meatballs in pita bread halves. Add lettuce and tomato. Sprinkle with the remaining *1 teaspoon* of sesame seeds. Serve with yogurt. If desired, serve sandwiches on additional shredded lettuce. Serves 4.

Nutrition information per serving: 324 calories, 26 g protein, 27 g carbohydrate, 12 g fat, 131 mg cholesterol, 273 mg sodium, 433 mg potassium.

SPICY BEEF AND BEAN BURGERS

180 calories

Preparation Time: 15 min. ▪ Cooking Time: 12 min. ▪ Low Fat ▪ Low Cholesterol

1	slightly beaten egg white
½	of a 15-ounce can (¾ cup) pinto beans, drained and mashed
¼	cup soft whole wheat bread crumbs
¼	cup finely chopped celery
1	tablespoon canned diced green chili peppers *or* 1 teaspoon chopped canned jalapeño peppers
⅛	teaspoon garlic powder
1	pound lean ground beef
4	8-inch flour tortillas, halved
8	lettuce leaves
1	cup salsa

▪ In a large mixing bowl combine egg white, beans, bread crumbs, celery, chili peppers, and garlic powder. Add ground beef; mix well.

▪ Shape meat mixture into eight ½-inch-thick oval patties.*

▪ Place patties on the unheated rack of a broiler pan. Broil 4 inches from the heat for 12 to 14 minutes or till meat is no longer pink, turning once.

▪ To serve, place a lettuce leaf and a burger in the center of each tortilla half. Top with *1 tablespoon* of the salsa. Bring ends of tortilla up and over burger. Top with another tablespoon salsa. Makes 8 servings.

*Note: If desired, seal, label, and freeze uncooked meat patties. To use, thaw completely in refrigerator overnight. Cook as directed above.

Nutrition information per serving: 180 calories, 15 g protein, 17 g carbohydrate, 5 g fat, 40 mg cholesterol, 257 mg sodium, 314 mg potassium.

INDIVIDUAL PINEAPPLE MEAT LOAVES

186 calories

Preparation Time: 15 min. ▪ Cooking Time: 30 min. ▪ Low Cholesterol

Serve cool and crispy veggies as a side dish.

1	**beaten egg**
½	**cup quick-cooking rolled oats**
½	**cup finely chopped onion**
¼	**cup finely chopped green pepper**
¼	**teaspoon salt**
1	**pound lean ground beef**
1	**8-ounce can crushed pineapple (juice pack), drained**
2	**tablespoons bottled sweet-and-sour sauce *or* barbecue sauce (optional)**

▪ In a large mixing bowl stir together egg, oats, onion, green pepper, and salt. Add beef and pineapple; mix well.

▪ Divide mixture into 6 equal portions. Shape each portion into a 4x2-inch loaf. Place loaves in a 13x9x2-inch pan.

▪ Bake, uncovered, in a 350° oven for 30 to 35 minutes or till meat is no longer pink. Top each loaf with *1 teaspoon* of the sweet-and-sour or barbecue sauce, if desired. Serves 6.

Nutrition information per serving: 186 calories, 18 g protein, 10 g carbohydrate, 8 g fat, 99 mg cholesterol, 152 mg sodium, 291 mg potassium.

111

BURGERS WITH MUSTARD SAUCE

170 calories

Preparation Time: 15 min. ▪ Cooking Time: 10 min.

1	beaten egg
⅓	cup soft bread crumbs (about ½ slice)
3	tablespoons skim milk
¼	cup finely chopped onion
¼	cup snipped fresh parsley
¼	teaspoon salt
1	pound lean ground beef *or* lamb
2	tablespoons plain low-fat yogurt
2	tablespoons reduced-calorie mayonnaise *or* salad dressing
2	teaspoons Dijon-style mustard
¼	teaspoon dried dillweed
¼	cup chopped seeded cucumber

▪ In a large mixing bowl stir together egg, bread crumbs, milk, onion, parsley, and salt. Add meat and mix well. Shape into six ½-inch-thick patties.

▪ Place meat patties on the unheated rack of a broiler pan. Broil 3 inches from the heat for 5 minutes. Turn and broil 5 to 7 minutes more or till meat is no longer pink.

▪ Meanwhile, for sauce, in a small bowl stir together yogurt, mayonnaise, mustard, and dillweed. Stir in cucumber. Spoon sauce over burgers. Makes 6 servings.

Nutrition information per serving: 170 calories, 17 g protein, 3 g carbohydrate, 9 g fat, 101 mg cholesterol, 237 mg sodium, 253 mg potassium.

ITALIAN-STYLE BURGERS

202 calories

Preparation Time: 15 min. ▪ Cooking Time: 13 min. ▪ Low Cholesterol

¼	**cup fine dry bread crumbs**
3	**tablespoons skim milk**
¼	**cup finely chopped onion**
2	**tablespoons snipped fresh parsley**
1	**tablespoon grated Parmesan cheese**
⅛	**teaspoon garlic powder**
⅛	**teaspoon pepper**
¾	**pound lean ground beef**
1	**medium tomato, sliced**
⅛	**teaspoon dried oregano, crushed**
¼	**cup shredded part-skim mozzarella cheese**

▪ In a medium mixing bowl stir together bread crumbs, milk, onion, parsley, Parmesan cheese, garlic powder, and pepper. Add meat; mix well. Shape into four ¾-inch-thick patties.

▪ Place meat patties on the unheated rack of a broiler pan. Broil 3 inches from the heat for 6 minutes. Turn and broil 6 to 8 minutes more or till meat is no longer pink.

▪ Top each burger with 1 slice of tomato. Sprinkle with oregano, then mozzarella cheese. Broil 1 to 2 minutes more or till cheese is melted. Makes 4 servings.

Nutrition information per serving: 202 calories, 21 g protein, 7 g carbohydrate, 9 g fat, 65 mg cholesterol, 163 mg sodium, 282 mg potassium.

SPAGHETTI WITH MEAT SAUCE

318 calories

Preparation Time: 20 min. ▪ Cooking Time: 35 min. ▪ Low Fat ▪ Low Cholesterol

½	**pound lean ground beef**
1	**cup sliced fresh mushrooms**
½	**cup chopped onion**
½	**cup chopped carrot**
½	**cup chopped green pepper**
¼	**cup chopped celery**
1	**clove garlic, minced**
1	**16-ounce can tomatoes, cut up**
½	**of a 6-ounce can (⅓ cup) tomato paste**
¼	**cup water *or* dry red wine**
½	**teaspoon dried basil, crushed**
¼	**teaspoon dried oregano, crushed**
1	**small bay leaf**
1	**teaspoon cornstarch**
6	**ounces spaghetti**

▪ In a large saucepan cook meat, mushrooms, onion, carrot, green pepper, celery, and garlic till meat is no longer pink and vegetables are tender. Drain off fat.

▪ Stir in *undrained* tomatoes, tomato paste, water or wine, basil, oregano, bay leaf, ¼ teaspoon *salt,* and ⅛ teaspoon *pepper.* Bring to boiling; reduce heat. Cover and simmer for 30 minutes, stirring occasionally. Remove bay leaf.

▪ Combine cornstarch and 1 tablespoon *cold water.* Stir into sauce. Cook and stir till thickened and bubbly. Cook and stir for 2 minutes more.

▪ Meanwhile, cook spaghetti according to package directions. Drain well. Serve sauce over spaghetti. Serves 4.

Nutrition information per serving: 318 calories, 20 g protein, 47 g carbohydrate, 6 g fat, 40 mg cholesterol, 529 mg sodium, 874 mg potassium.

CREAMY BEEF AND ONIONS

343 calories

Preparation Time: 20 min. ▪ Cooking Time: 5 min. ▪ Low Fat ▪ Low Cholesterol

A home-style dish similar to stroganoff.

¾	**pound lean ground beef** *or* **veal**
2	**cups sliced fresh mushrooms**
2	**medium onions, cut into thin wedges**
1	**clove garlic, minced**
1	**10¼-ounce can beef gravy**
⅔	**cup plain low-fat yogurt**
1	**tablespoon Worcestershire sauce**
¼	**teaspoon dried thyme** *or* **sage, crushed**
⅛	**teaspoon pepper**
2	**cups hot cooked rice** *or* **noodles**
2	**tablespoons snipped fresh parsley**

▪ In a large skillet cook meat, mushrooms, onions, and garlic till meat is no longer pink and onion is tender. Drain off fat.

▪ In a mixing bowl stir together beef gravy, yogurt, Worcestershire sauce, thyme or sage, and pepper. Stir into meat mixture. Heat through.

▪ Serve meat mixture over rice or noodles. Sprinkle with parsley. Makes 4 servings.

Nutrition information per serving: 343 calories, 26 g protein, 37 g carbohydrate, 10 g fat, 65 mg cholesterol, 152 mg sodium, 588 mg potassium.

115

SAUCY SPAGHETTI SQUASH OLÉ

314 calories

Preparation Time: 5 min. ▪ Cooking Time: 45 min. ▪ Low Cholesterol

After the squash is cooked, use a fork to scrape the pulp from the shells. It will form spaghetti-like strands.

1	2½- to 3-pound spaghetti squash
1	pound lean ground beef
½	cup chopped onion
1	clove garlic, minced
½	teaspoon cornstarch
1	8-ounce can tomato sauce
⅔	cup tomato juice
1	7-ounce can whole kernel corn with sweet peppers, drained
2	teaspoons chili powder
½	teaspoon dried oregano, crushed
½	cup shredded Monterey Jack cheese

▪ Halve the spaghetti squash lengthwise and remove seeds. Place, cut side down, on a baking sheet. Bake in a 350° oven for 45 to 50 minutes or till tender.

▪ Use a fork to shred and separate the spaghetti squash into strands.

▪ Meanwhile, for sauce, in a large skillet cook beef, onion, and garlic till meat is no longer pink and onion is tender. Drain off fat.

▪ Stir in cornstarch. Stir in tomato sauce, tomato juice, corn, chili powder, and oregano. Cook and stir till slightly thickened and bubbly. Cook and stir 2 minutes more.

▪ To serve, spoon meat mixture over spaghetti squash and top with cheese. Makes 4 servings.

▪ **Microwave directions:** Place squash halves, cut side down, in a baking dish with ¼ cup water. Micro-cook, covered, on 100% power (high) for 15 to 20 minutes or till tender, rearranging once. Continue as above.

Nutrition information per serving: 314 calories, 30 g protein, 17 g carbohydrate, 15 g fat, 92 mg cholesterol, 733 mg sodium, 921 mg potassium.

STUFFED CABBAGE LEAVES

221 calories

Preparation Time: 30 min. ▪ Cooking Time: 20 min. ▪ Low Cholesterol

Place some of the filling near the center of a cabbage leaf. Fold in two opposite sides of the leaf. Starting at an unfolded edge, roll up each leaf, making sure folded sides are included in the roll.

1	**large head cabbage**
1	**pound lean ground beef**
¼	**cup finely chopped onion**
¼	**cup raisins**
2	**tablespoons fine dry bread crumbs**
1	**cup spaghetti sauce**
¼	**teaspoon ground cinnamon**

■ Remove 12 outer leaves from cabbage. Remove any tough center veins from the 12 leaves. Cook *half* of the cabbage leaves in boiling water for 3 minutes to soften. Drain on paper towels. Repeat with remaining leaves.

■ Finely chop enough of the remaining cabbage to make ½ cup. Reserve remaining cabbage for another use.

■ In a large skillet cook ground beef, onion, and the ½ cup chopped cabbage till meat is no longer pink and onion is tender. Drain well. Stir in raisins, bread crumbs, and ¼ *cup* of the spaghetti sauce.

■ Spoon a scant ¼ *cup* of the meat mixture onto each cabbage leaf; fold in sides. Roll up leaf, forming a bundle. Arrange rolls in a 12x7½x2-inch baking dish.

■ For sauce, in a small bowl stir together the remaining spaghetti sauce and cinnamon. Spoon over cabbage rolls.

■ Bake, covered, in a 350° oven for 20 to 25 minutes or till heated through. Spoon sauce over rolls during baking and before serving. Makes 6 servings.

Nutrition information per serving: 221 calories, 18 g protein, 19 g carbohydrate, 9 g fat, 53 mg cholesterol, 271 mg sodium, 643 mg potassium.

SPAGHETTI PIE

262 calories

Preparation Time: 25 min. ▪ Cooking Time: 20 min. ▪ Low Cholesterol

For the spaghetti crust, use two forks, a rubber spatula, or a wooden spoon to firmly press the spaghetti mixture evenly onto the bottom and up the sides of the pie plate. Build the edges high enough to hold all the filling.

4	ounces spaghetti
1	tablespoon margarine
1	beaten egg
¼	cup grated Parmesan cheese
	Nonstick spray coating
1	cup low-fat cottage cheese
½	pound lean ground beef *or* turkey
½	cup chopped onion
½	cup chopped green pepper
1	clove garlic, minced
½	teaspoon fennel seed (optional)
1	8-ounce can tomato sauce
1	teaspoon dried oregano, crushed
½	cup shredded part-skim mozzarella cheese

▪ In a saucepan cook spaghetti in a large amount of boiling unsalted water for 10 to 12 minutes or just till tender. Drain well. Return to saucepan and stir margarine into hot pasta till melted. Stir in egg and Parmesan cheese.

▪ Spray a 9-inch pie plate with nonstick spray coating. Press spaghetti mixture onto the bottom and up the sides of the pie plate, forming a crust. Spread cottage cheese over crust.

▪ In a skillet cook beef or turkey, onion, green pepper, garlic, and fennel seed, if desired, till onion is tender and meat is no longer pink. Drain off fat. Stir in tomato sauce and oregano; heat through. Spread meat mixture over cottage cheese. Sprinkle mozzarella atop meat mixture.

▪ Bake, uncovered, in a 350° oven for 20 to 25 minutes or till bubbly. Makes 6 servings.

Nutrition information per serving: 262 calories, 21 g protein, 21 g carbohydrate, 10 g fat, 84 mg cholesterol, 563 mg sodium, 379 mg potassium.

EGGPLANT BAKE

255 calories

Preparation Time: 25 min. ▪ Cooking Time: 30 min. ▪ Low Cholesterol

1	**small eggplant (about 12 to 14 ounces), peeled and cut into ¼-inch slices**
¾	**pound lean ground beef *or* lamb**
½	**cup chopped onion**
1	**clove garlic, minced**
1	**8-ounce can tomato sauce**
1	**tablespoon margarine**
4	**teaspoons all-purpose flour**
¼	**teaspoon salt**
	Dash pepper
¾	**cup skim milk**
	Nonstick spray coating
3	**tablespoons grated Parmesan cheese**

▪ In a large skillet cook eggplant slices in ½ inch of boiling water, covered, about 6 minutes or till tender. Drain.

▪ In the same skillet cook ground beef, onion, and garlic till beef is no longer pink. Drain off fat. Stir in tomato sauce. Bring to boiling; reduce heat. Simmer, uncovered, about 5 minutes or till of desired consistency. Remove from heat.

▪ Meanwhile, prepare sauce. In a small saucepan melt margarine. Stir in flour, salt, and pepper. Stir in skim milk all at once. Cook and stir till thickened and bubbly. Remove from heat; set aside.

▪ Spray a 10x6x2-inch baking dish with nonstick spray coating. Arrange *half* of the eggplant in dish. Spoon meat mixture atop, then top with remaining eggplant slices. Pour sauce over all ingredients. Sprinkle with Parmesan cheese.

▪ Bake, uncovered, in a 325° oven for 30 minutes or till heated through and top is golden. Makes 4 servings.

Nutrition information per serving: 255 calories, 23 g protein, 14 g carbohydrate, 12 g fat, 64 mg cholesterol, 667 mg sodium, 667 mg potassium.

CURRIED BEEF AND RICE

313 calories

Preparation Time: 15 min. ▪ Cooking Time: 40 min. ▪ Low Fat ▪ Low Cholesterol

1½	cups water
1	large onion, chopped (1 cup)
1	medium carrot, chopped
1	tablespoon instant beef bouillon granules
2 to 3	teaspoons curry powder
1	clove garlic, minced
¾	cup regular brown rice
1½	cups cubed cooked beef (8 ounces)
1	cup frozen peas
1	medium tomato, chopped

▪ In a 2-quart saucepan stir together the water, onion, carrot, bouillon granules, curry powder, and garlic. Heat to boiling, then stir in rice. Cover and simmer for 30 minutes.

▪ Stir beef, peas, and tomato into rice mixture. Cover and simmer about 10 minutes more or till rice and peas are tender. Makes 4 servings.

Nutrition information per serving: 313 calories, 23 g protein, 40 g carbohydrate, 7 g fat, 53 mg cholesterol, 337 mg sodium, 489 mg potassium.

LIVER IN WINE SAUCE

150 calories

Preparation Time: 9 min. ▪ Cooking Time: 9 min. ▪ Low Fat

Substitute turkey breast slices for the liver, if you prefer. For each serving with turkey, calories drop to 117 and cholesterol drops to 53 milligrams.

¾	**pound calf liver**
	Nonstick spray coating
½	**cup chopped onion**
½	**cup chopped green *or* sweet red pepper**
⅓	**cup dry white wine *or* chicken broth**
¼	**teaspoon salt**
	Dash pepper
2	**tablespoons snipped fresh parsley**

▪ Rinse liver; pat dry. Spray a large skillet with nonstick spray coating. Heat skillet over medium-high heat for 1 minute.

▪ Add liver, onion, and green pepper. Cook for 4 to 5 minutes or till vegetables are tender and liver is just pink in the center. Turn liver once.

▪ Stir in wine or chicken broth, salt, and pepper. Heat through. Sprinkle with parsley. Makes 4 servings.

Nutrition information per serving: 150 calories, 17 g protein, 7 g carbohydrate, 4 g fat, 255 mg cholesterol, 198 mg sodium, 323 mg potassium.

PORK AND HAM MAIN DISHES

BROILED CHOPS WITH ITALIAN VEGETABLES *(see page 127)*

PORK ROAST WITH PINEAPPLE CHUTNEY

282 calories

Preparation Time: 15 min. ▪ Cooking Time: 1½ hrs. ▪ Low Cholesterol ▪ Low Sodium

To use a meat thermometer correctly, insert it into the center of the largest muscle or the thickest portion of the meat. The thermometer should not touch any fat or bone, or the bottom of the pan.

1	3-pound pork loin center rib roast, backbone loosened
¼	teaspoon pepper
1	20-ounce can crushed pineapple (juice pack)
½	cup chopped onion
2	tablespoons raisins
2	tablespoons brown sugar
2	tablespoons vinegar
½	teaspoon ground ginger
½	teaspoon ground cinnamon
⅛	teaspoon crushed red pepper (optional)

▪ Trim separable fat from the roast; then rub meat with the pepper. Place roast, rib side down, in a shallow roasting pan. Insert a meat thermometer.
▪ Roast, uncovered, in a 325° oven for 1½ to 2 hours or till thermometer registers 170° (well-done).
▪ Meanwhile, for chutney, in a medium saucepan combine *undrained* pineapple, onion, raisins, brown sugar, vinegar, ginger, cinnamon, and crushed red pepper, if desired. Bring to boiling; reduce heat. Simmer, uncovered, about 30 minutes or till liquid is syrupy. Serve warm with roast. Serves 8.

Nutrition information per serving: 282 calories, 25 g protein, 19 g carbohydrate, 12 g fat, 67 mg cholesterol, 42 mg sodium, 516 mg potassium.

123

APPLE-STUFFED PORK ROAST

199 calories

Preparation Time: 30 min. ▪ Cooking Time: 1 hr. ▪ Low Fat ▪ Low Cholesterol ▪ Low Sodium

To butterfly the roast, make a single lengthwise cut down the center of one narrow edge of the meat, cutting to within ½ inch of the other side. Spread the meat open. At the center of the roast, make one perpendicular slit to the right of the V and one perpendicular slit to the left.

1	small apple, chopped
½	cup soft bread crumbs
¼	cup chopped celery
2	tablespoons raisins
2	tablespoons chopped walnuts
2	tablespoons sliced green onions
	Dash ground nutmeg
2	tablespoons apple juice *or* apple cider
¾	pound pork tenderloin, trimmed of separable fat
½	cup apple juice *or* apple cider
1½	teaspoons cornstarch
⅛	teaspoon ground cinnamon

▪ For stuffing, stir together the chopped apple, bread crumbs, celery, raisins, walnuts, green onions, and nutmeg. Stir in *1 tablespoon* of the apple juice or apple cider.

▪ Butterfly the pork tenderloin (see small photo above).

▪ Cover meat with clear plastic wrap. Pound with a meat mallet to ½-inch thickness. Spread stuffing over meat. Roll up from one of the short sides. Tie with string to secure. Brush with *some* of the remaining 1 tablespoon apple juice.

▪ Place meat on a rack in a shallow roasting pan. Roast, uncovered, in a 350° oven for 1 to 1¼ hours or till meat is no longer pink, brushing with the remainder of the 1 tablespoon apple juice after 30 minutes.

▪ Meanwhile, in a small saucepan stir together the ½ cup apple juice or apple cider, cornstarch, and cinnamon. Cook and stir till thickened and bubbly. Cook and stir for 2 minutes more. Serve with roast. Makes 4 servings.

Nutrition information per serving: 199 calories, 20 g protein, 17 g carbohydrate, 6 g fat, 59 mg cholesterol, 80 mg sodium, 508 mg potassium.

ROAST PORK WITH CABBAGE AND CARROTS   164 calories

Preparation Time: 5 min. ▪ Cooking Time: 45 min. ▪ Low Fat ▪ Low Cholesterol

¾   **pound pork tenderloin, trimmed of
        separable fat**
6   **cups shredded cabbage**
1   **large onion, sliced**
⅔   **cup shredded carrots**
⅓   **cup water**
2   **tablespoons vinegar**
1   **teaspoon dillseed, crushed**
¼   **teaspoon salt**
¼   **teaspoon pepper**

▪ Place pork tenderloin on a rack in a shallow roasting pan. Insert a meat thermometer. Roast in a 325° oven for ¾ to 1 hour or till thermometer registers 170°.

▪ Meanwhile, in a large saucepan combine cabbage, onion, carrots, water, vinegar, dillseed, salt, and pepper. Bring to boiling; reduce heat. Cover and simmer for 8 to 10 minutes or till vegetables are just tender.

▪ Slice pork and serve with vegetables. Makes 4 servings.

Nutrition information per serving: 164 calories, 21 g protein, 13 g carbohydrate, 3 g fat, 59 mg cholesterol, 209 mg sodium, 799 mg potassium.

PORK MEDAILLONS WITH VEGETABLES   154 calories

Preparation Time: 20 min. ▪ Cooking Time: 15 min. ▪ Low Fat ▪ Low Cholesterol

¾	**pound pork tenderloin, trimmed of separable fat**
1	**large onion, cut into thin wedges**
1	**cup celery cut into thin bite-size strips**
1	**cup carrots cut into thin bite-size strips**
2	**cloves garlic, minced**
1	**cup water**
2	**teaspoons instant chicken bouillon granules**
¼	**teaspoon dried tarragon, crushed**
	Dash pepper
1	**tablespoon cornstarch**
1	**tablespoon cold water**
	Nonstick spray coating

▪ Cut pork tenderloin crosswise into ½-inch slices. Place one slice of pork between two pieces of clear plastic wrap. Working from the center to the edges, pound lightly with a meat mallet to ¼-inch thickness. Remove plastic wrap. Repeat with each remaining pork slice; set aside.

▪ In a medium saucepan combine onion, celery, carrots, garlic, the 1 cup water, bouillon granules, tarragon, and pepper. Bring to boiling; reduce heat. Cover and simmer for 10 to 15 minutes or till vegetables are crisp-tender.

▪ Stir together cornstarch and remaining water. Stir into vegetable mixture. Cook and stir till thickened and bubbly; cook and stir 2 minutes more.

▪ Meanwhile, spray a 10-inch skillet with nonstick spray coating. Cook *half* of the pork slices over medium heat for 2 to 3 minutes per side or till no longer pink. Remove from skillet; keep warm. Repeat with remaining pork slices.

▪ To serve, spoon vegetable mixture onto a serving platter. Place pork slices atop vegetables. Makes 4 servings.

Nutrition information per serving: 154 calories, 20 g protein, 10 g carbohydrate, 4 g fat, 59 mg cholesterol, 264 mg sodium, 609 mg potassium.

BROILED CHOPS WITH ITALIAN VEGETABLES   248 calories

Preparation Time: 5 min. ▪ Cooking Time: 12 min. ▪ Low Cholesterol ▪ Low Sodium

1	tablespoon dry white wine *or* orange juice
1	clove garlic, minced
⅛	teaspoon pepper
4	pork loin chops, cut ½ inch thick (1¼ pounds total)
	Nonstick spray coating
2	medium zucchini *or* yellow summer squash, cut into thin strips
1	small green *or* sweet red pepper, cut into strips
1	small onion, sliced
¾	teaspoon dried basil, crushed
½	teaspoon dried oregano, crushed
⅛	teaspoon salt
8	cherry tomatoes, halved

▪ Combine wine, garlic, and pepper; set aside.

▪ Trim separable fat from pork chops. Place on the unheated rack of a broiler pan.

▪ Broil chops 3 to 4 inches from the heat for 6 minutes. Brush with wine mixture. Turn and broil 6 minutes more or till chops are no longer pink. Brush with remaining wine mixture.

▪ Meanwhile, spray a large skillet with nonstick spray coating. Add zucchini or yellow squash, green pepper, onion, basil, oregano, and salt. Cook and stir over medium-high heat for 4 minutes or till vegetables are crisp-tender. Stir in tomato halves; reduce heat. Cover and cook 1 minute more. Serve vegetables with pork chops. Makes 4 servings.

Nutrition information per serving: 248 calories, 26 g protein, 6 g carbohydrate, 13 g fat, 80 mg cholesterol, 129 mg sodium, 663 mg potassium.

PORK CHOPS DIJON

248 calories

Preparation Time: 15 min. ▪ Cooking Time: 15 min. ▪ Low Cholesterol

Keep the ingredients for this dish on hand for an easy last-minute dinner.

3	tablespoons Dijon-style mustard
2	tablespoons low-calorie Italian salad dressing
¼	teaspoon pepper
4	pork loin chops, cut ½ inch thick (1¼ pounds total)
	Nonstick spray coating
1	medium onion, halved and sliced

▪ In a small bowl combine mustard, Italian dressing, and pepper; set aside.

▪ Trim excess fat from chops. Spray a 10-inch skillet with nonstick spray coating. Preheat the skillet over medium-high heat. Add the pork chops and brown on both sides. Remove chops from skillet.

▪ Add onion to skillet. Cook and stir over medium heat for 3 minutes. Push onion aside; return chops to skillet. Spread mustard mixture over chops. Cover and cook over medium-low heat for 15 minutes or till pork is no longer pink. Serve onion over pork chops. Makes 4 servings.

Nutrition information per serving: 248 calories, 25 g protein, 2 g carbohydrate, 14 g fat, 80 mg cholesterol, 390 mg sodium, 421 mg potassium.

PORK-SAUERKRAUT SUPPER

186 calories

Preparation Time: 10 min. ▪ Cooking Time: 1 hr. ▪ Low Fat ▪ Low Cholesterol

1	**16-ounce can sliced potatoes, drained**
1	**14-ounce can sauerkraut with caraway, rinsed and drained**
1	**medium apple, cored and chopped**
1	**tablespoon coarse-grain brown mustard**
½	**cup apple juice** *or* **apple cider**
4	**boneless smoked pork loin chops (10 ounces total)**

▪ Arrange potato slices in an ungreased 12x7½x2-inch baking dish. Stir together sauerkraut, apple, and mustard; spoon over potatoes. Pour apple juice or apple cider over everything in dish. Arrange pork chops in dish.

▪ Bake, covered, in a 350° oven about 1 hour or till heated through. Makes 4 servings.

Nutrition information per serving: 186 calories, 16 g protein, 20 g carbohydrate, 4 g fat, 37 mg cholesterol, 1,527 mg sodium, 503 mg potassium.

CURRIED PORK CHOPS WITH ORANGES

291 calories

Preparation Time: 10 min. ▪ Cooking Time: 35 min. ▪ Low Cholesterol ▪ Low Sodium

2	pork sirloin chops, cut ½ inch thick (1¼ pounds total)
	Nonstick spray coating
½	cup orange juice
1	tablespoon honey
1	to 1½ teaspoons curry powder
2	oranges
2	teaspoons cornstarch
1	tablespoon cold water
1	tablespoon snipped chives *or* parsley

▪ Trim separable fat from pork chops; cut each chop in half.

▪ Spray a large skillet with nonstick spray coating. Preheat over medium-high heat. Add pork chops and brown on both sides. Drain fat.

▪ Add orange juice, honey, and curry powder to skillet. Bring to boiling. Cover and simmer 30 to 40 minutes or till pork chops are tender and no longer pink. Remove pork chops from skillet; keep warm.

▪ Meanwhile, peel oranges. Slice crosswise; then halve circular slices. Set aside.

▪ Stir together cornstarch and water; stir into skillet. Cook and stir till thickened and bubbly. Cook and stir 2 minutes more. Stir in oranges and chives; heat through. Spoon over pork chops. Makes 4 servings.

Nutrition information per serving: 291 calories, 29 g protein, 17 g carbohydrate, 11 g fat, 93 mg cholesterol, 51 mg sodium, 567 mg potassium.

PORK AND PINEAPPLE STIR-FRY

303 calories

Preparation Time: 30 min. ▪ Cooking Time: 10 min. ▪ Low Fat ▪ Low Cholesterol ▪ Low Sodium

¾ **pound lean boneless pork** *or* **turkey breast steaks**

1 **20-ounce can pineapple chunks (juice pack)**

1 **tablespoon cornstarch**

1 **tablespoon Worcestershire sauce**

½ **teaspoon instant chicken bouillon granules**

¼ **teaspoon ground cumin**
   Nonstick spray coating

4 **green onions, bias-sliced into 1-inch pieces (½ cup)**

2 **cups bean sprouts**

1 **cup cherry tomatoes, halved**

4 **cups shredded romaine**

▪ Partially freeze meat. Thinly slice across the grain into bite-size strips. Set aside. Drain pineapple, reserving ¾ cup of juice. Set aside.

▪ For sauce, stir together reserved pineapple juice, cornstarch, Worcestershire sauce, bouillon granules, and cumin. Set aside.

▪ Spray a wok or large skillet with nonstick spray coating. Preheat over medium-high heat. Add green onions and stir-fry for 1½ minutes. Add bean sprouts and stir-fry 1 minute or till vegetables are crisp-tender. Remove from wok.

▪ Add pork to wok and stir-fry for 2 to 3 minutes or till no longer pink. Push pork from center of wok.

▪ Stir sauce and add to center of wok. Cook and stir till thickened and bubbly. Cook and stir for 1 minute more.

▪ Return vegetables to wok. Add tomatoes and pineapple. Stir everything together to coat with sauce. Cook and stir for 1 minute or till heated through. Serve over shredded romaine. Makes 4 servings.

Nutrition information per serving: 303 calories, 26 g protein, 31 g carbohydrate, 9 g fat, 71 mg cholesterol, 134 mg sodium, 725 mg potassium.

COUNTRY-STYLE PORK STEW

231 calories

Preparation Time: 15 min. ▪ Cooking Time: 1¼ hrs. ▪ Low Cholesterol

¾	pound boneless pork shoulder
	Nonstick spray coating
1½	teaspoons instant chicken bouillon granules
1	7½-ounce can tomatoes, cut up
2	small onions, cut into wedges
½	cup sliced celery
1	teaspoon dried oregano, crushed
1	teaspoon ground cumin
2	cloves garlic, minced
1	bay leaf
1	cup yellow summer squash *or* zucchini cut into ½-inch slices
1	9-ounce package frozen cut green beans
1	tablespoon cornstarch

■ Trim fat from pork and cut meat into 1-inch cubes. Spray a Dutch oven or large saucepan with nonstick spray coating. Preheat over medium-high heat. Brown pork in the hot pan; drain fat.

■ Add bouillon granules and 1¼ cups *water*. Stir in the *undrained* tomatoes, onions, celery, oregano, cumin, garlic, and bay leaf. Bring to boiling; reduce heat. Cover and simmer about 1 hour or till pork is tender.

■ Stir in squash and green beans. Return to boiling; reduce heat. Simmer 5 minutes more. Combine cornstarch and 1 tablespoon *cold water*. Stir into pork mixture. Cook and stir till thickened and bubbly. Cook and stir 2 minutes more. Remove bay leaf. Makes 4 servings.

Nutrition information per serving: 231 calories, 18 g protein, 12 g carbohydrate, 12 g fat, 67 mg cholesterol, 303 mg sodium, 597 mg potassium.

SWEET-AND-SOUR PORK KABOBS

250 calories

Preparation Time: 18 min. ▪ Grilling Time: 8 min. ▪ Low Cholesterol

Save your pineapple pieces from falling into the fire by putting them near the middle of the skewers instead of at the ends.

2	medium carrots, bias-sliced into 1-inch pieces
1	8-ounce can pineapple slices (juice pack)
¼	cup red wine vinegar
1	tablespoon cooking oil
1	tablespoon soy sauce
1½	teaspoons cornstarch
1	teaspoon sugar
1	clove garlic, minced
12	ounces lean boneless pork, cut into 1-inch pieces
1	small green pepper, cut into 1-inch squares
1	small sweet red pepper, cut into 1-inch squares

■ In a saucepan cook carrots, covered, in a small amount of boiling water for 8 minutes; drain well. Drain pineapple, reserving juice. Cut pineapple slices into quarters; set aside.

■ For sauce, in a saucepan combine reserved pineapple juice, vinegar, oil, soy sauce, cornstarch, sugar, and garlic. Cook and stir till thickened and bubbly. Cook and stir 1 to 2 minutes more.

■ Thread cooked carrots, pineapple, green and red pepper, and pork on four 12- to 14-inch skewers, leaving ¼ inch between each piece of food.

■ Grill kabobs on an uncovered grill directly over *medium-hot* coals for 8 to 12 minutes or till pork is no longer pink. (*Or,* broil 4 to 5 inches from the heat for 15 to 18 minutes.) Turn kabobs occasionally and brush often with sauce. Serves 4.

Nutrition information per serving: 250 calories, 22 g protein, 18 g carbohydrate, 10 g fat, 62 mg cholesterol, 322 mg sodium, 560 mg potassium.

CREOLE-STYLE PORK

322 calories

Preparation Time: 30 min. ▪ Cooking Time: 10 min. ▪ Low Fat ▪ Low Cholesterol

¾	**pound lean boneless pork**
1	**cup tomato juice**
1	**tablespoon cornstarch**
1	**teaspoon chili powder**
1	**teaspoon lemon juice**
½	**teaspoon sugar**
⅛	**to ¼ teaspoon ground red pepper**
	Nonstick spray coating
1	**cup sliced celery**
2	**cups green beans, cut into 1-inch pieces, *or***
	1 9-ounce package frozen cut green beans, thawed
1	**medium green *or* sweet red pepper, cut into ½-inch squares (⅔ cup)**
1	**to 2 teaspoons cooking oil (optional)**
2	**cups hot cooked rice**

▪ Partially freeze meat. Thinly slice across the grain into bite-size strips.

▪ For sauce, stir together tomato juice, cornstarch, chili powder, lemon juice, sugar, ground red pepper, and ¼ cup *water*. Set aside.

▪ Spray a wok or 12-inch skillet with nonstick spray coating. Preheat over medium-high heat. Add celery and *fresh* green beans, if using. Stir-fry for 2 minutes. Add green pepper and *frozen* thawed beans, if using. Stir-fry about 1½ minutes more or till vegetables are crisp-tender. Remove from wok.

▪ Add oil to hot wok, if necessary. Add pork and stir-fry 2 to 3 minutes or till no longer pink. Push pork from center of wok.

▪ Stir sauce and add to center of wok. Cook and stir till thickened and bubbly. Return vegetables to wok and stir all ingredients together to coat with sauce. Cook and stir for 2 minutes. Serve with rice. Makes 4 servings.

Nutrition information per serving: 322 calories, 22 g protein, 36 g carbohydrate, 10 g fat, 58 mg cholesterol, 291 mg sodium, 570 mg potassium.

PORK AND BROCCOLI STIR-FRY

273 calories

Preparation Time: 30 min. ▪ Cooking Time: 8 min. ▪ Low Cholesterol

Complete your meal with a side dish of rice.

½	pound lean boneless pork
¾	cup chicken broth
1	tablespoon cornstarch
2	tablespoons soy sauce
2	tablespoons dry sherry
⅛	teaspoon crushed red pepper
	Nonstick spray coating
1	medium onion, sliced
1	10-ounce package frozen cut broccoli, thawed and well drained
1	clove garlic, minced
½	teaspoon grated gingerroot
1 to 2	teaspoons cooking oil
½	cup sliced water chestnuts

■ Partially freeze meat. Thinly slice across the grain into bite-size strips.

■ Meanwhile, for sauce, stir together chicken broth, cornstarch, soy sauce, dry sherry, and red pepper. Set aside.

■ Spray a wok or large skillet with nonstick spray coating. Add onion, broccoli, garlic, and gingerroot and stir-fry for 3 minutes or till vegetables are crisp-tender. Remove vegetable mixture from wok.

■ Add oil to hot wok. Add pork and stir-fry for 2 to 3 minutes or till no longer pink. Push pork from center of wok.

■ Stir sauce and add to the center of wok. Cook and stir till thickened and bubbly.

■ Return vegetables to wok. Add water chestnuts and stir all ingredients together to coat with sauce. Cook and stir for 1 to 2 minutes more or till heated through. Makes 3 servings.

Nutrition information per serving: 273 calories, 25 g protein, 18 g carbohydrate, 10 g fat, 63 mg cholesterol, 933 mg sodium, 668 mg potassium.

STUFFED ACORN SQUASH

306 calories

Preparation Time: 20 min. ▪ Cooking Time: 1 hr. 10 min. ▪ Low Fat ▪ Low Cholesterol

	Nonstick spray coating
1	small acorn squash (about 1 pound total)
6	ounces lean ground pork *or* turkey
¼	cup chopped celery
¼	cup chopped onion
¼	teaspoon salt
¼	teaspoon curry powder
	Dash ground cinnamon
½	cup unsweetened applesauce
1	slice raisin bread *or* whole wheat bread, cubed (¾ cup)

▪ Spray a 10x6x2-inch baking dish with nonstick coating. Halve squash; discard seeds. Place squash, cut side down, in baking dish. Bake, uncovered, in a 350° oven 50 minutes.

▪ Meanwhile, for stuffing, in a skillet cook pork, celery, and onion till meat is no longer pink and vegetables are tender. Drain off fat. Stir in salt, curry powder, and cinnamon; cook 1 minute more. Stir in applesauce and bread cubes.

▪ Turn squash cut side up in dish. Place stuffing in squash halves. Bake, uncovered, 20 minutes more. Serves 2.

▪ **Microwave directions:** Place squash, cut side down, in a 10x6x2-inch microwave-safe baking dish. Micro-cook on 100% power (high) for 6½ to 8½ minutes or till tender. Set aside. In a 1-quart casserole cook pork, celery, and onion, covered, on high for 2 to 3 minutes or till pork is no longer pink, stirring twice. Drain. Stir in curry powder, salt, and cinnamon. Cook 30 seconds more. Stir in applesauce and bread cubes. Spoon into squash halves. Cook, uncovered, on high for 3 to 4 minutes or till hot.

Nutrition information per serving: 306 calories, 23 g protein, 38 g carbohydrate, 8 g fat, 63 mg cholesterol, 384 mg sodium, 1,171 mg potassium.

PICADILLO RICE

Preparation Time: 15 min. ▪ Cooking Time: 20 min. ▪ Low Cholesterol

¾	**pound lean ground pork** *or* **beef**
½	**cup chopped onion**
½	**cup chopped green** *or* **sweet red pepper**
1	**16-ounce can tomatoes, cut up**
⅔	**cup water**
2	**tablespoons raisins**
2	**tablespoons chopped pimiento-stuffed olives**
1	**teaspoon chili powder**
1	**teaspoon ground cumin**
¼	**teaspoon salt**
	Dash ground cinnamon (optional)
½	**cup long grain rice**

▪ In a large skillet cook meat, onion, and green pepper till meat is no longer pink and vegetables are tender. Drain well.

▪ Stir in *undrained* tomatoes, water, raisins, olives, chili powder, cumin, salt, and cinnamon. Bring to boiling; stir in rice. Reduce heat. Cover and simmer about 20 minutes or till rice is tender.

▪ If desired, garnish with additional sliced olives. Serves 4.

Nutrition information per serving: 296 calories, 20 g protein, 30 g carbohydrate, 11 g fat, 62 mg cholesterol, 479 mg sodium, 624 mg potassium.

PORK LO MEIN

323 calories

Preparation Time: 20 min. ▪ Cooking Time: 5 min. ▪ Low Fat ▪ Low Cholesterol

¾	pound lean ground pork
2	cups sliced fresh mushrooms
1	cup shredded carrots
½	cup green *or* sweet red pepper cut into bite-size strips
2	cloves garlic, minced
1	tablespoon cornstarch
1	cup chicken broth
1	tablespoon soy sauce
1	teaspoon grated gingerroot
¼	teaspoon crushed red pepper
¼	teaspoon curry powder
4	ounces thin spaghetti, cooked and drained (2 cups cooked)
2	cups bean sprouts
½	cup sliced green onion

▪ In a large skillet cook pork, mushrooms, carrots, green pepper, and garlic till meat is no longer pink and vegetables are tender. Drain off fat.

▪ Stir cornstarch into meat mixture. Stir in chicken broth, soy sauce, gingerroot, crushed red pepper, and curry powder. Cook and stir till thickened and bubbly. Cook and stir for 2 minutes more.

▪ Stir in cooked spaghetti, bean sprouts, and green onion; heat through. If desired, garnish with additional sliced green onion. Makes 4 servings.

Nutrition information per serving: 323 calories, 29 g protein, 34 g carbohydrate, 8 g fat, 62 mg cholesterol, 517 mg sodium, 771 mg potassium.

PORK CASSEROLE WITH BREAD TOPPING

275 calories

Preparation Time: 30 min. ▪ Cooking Time: 20 min. ▪ Low Fat ▪ Low Cholesterol

Complete this meal with a cold, crisp salad.

1	pound lean ground pork *or* turkey
1	cup chopped celery
1	cup chopped onion
1	clove garlic, minced
¼	teaspoon ground cumin
1	10-ounce package frozen whole kernel corn, thawed
1	12-ounce jar salsa
½	cup packaged biscuit mix
⅓	cup cornmeal
⅛	to ¼ teaspoon ground red pepper
½	cup skim milk

■ In a 10-inch skillet cook pork or turkey, celery, onion, garlic, and cumin till vegetables are tender and meat is no longer pink. Drain off fat. Stir in corn and *1 cup* of the salsa. Pour mixture into a 10x6x2-inch baking dish.

■ For topping, in a mixing bowl combine biscuit mix, cornmeal, and red pepper. Stir in milk till almost smooth. Spoon onto meat mixture, forming diagonal lines across the dish.

■ Bake, uncovered, in a 400° oven for 20 to 25 minutes or till topping is lightly browned and a toothpick inserted in topping comes out clean. Meanwhile, heat remaining salsa; pass with casserole. Makes 6 servings.

Nutrition information per serving: 275 calories, 22 g protein, 29 g carbohydrate, 8 g fat, 56 mg cholesterol, 583 mg sodium, 589 mg potassium.

139

PORK JAMBALAYA

299 calories

Preparation Time: 20 min. ▪ Cooking Time: 15 min. ▪ Low Fat ▪ Low Cholesterol

¼	**pound fully cooked smoked turkey sausage**
¾	**cup chopped onion**
1	**cup chopped green *or* sweet red pepper**
1	**cup sliced fresh mushrooms**
1	**clove garlic, minced**
1	**teaspoon chili powder**
¼	**teaspoon ground red pepper**
2¼	**cups water**
1	**16-ounce can tomatoes, cut up**
2	**cups cubed cooked pork**
1	**9-ounce package frozen cut okra**
1	**cup long grain rice**
1	**tablespoon instant chicken bouillon granules**

▪ Halve turkey sausage lengthwise and cut into ¼-inch slices.

▪ In a 12-inch skillet cook sausage, onion, green pepper, mushrooms, and garlic till onion is tender.

▪ Stir in chili powder, ground red pepper, and ¼ teaspoon *pepper.* Cook and stir for 1 minute.

▪ Stir in water, *undrained* tomatoes, pork, okra, *uncooked* rice, and bouillon granules. Bring to boiling; reduce heat. Cover and simmer for 15 to 20 minutes or till rice is tender. Makes 6 servings.

Nutrition information per serving: 299 calories, 21 g protein, 35 g carbohydrate, 8 g fat, 45 mg cholesterol, 522 mg sodium, 667 mg potassium.

BARBECUED PORK

252 calories

Preparation Time: 10 min. ▪ Cooking Time: 18 min. ▪ Low Cholesterol

Serve this as an open-faced sandwich on half of a plain or toasted pita bread round. Or, roll the meat into a flour tortilla.

½	**cup chopped onion**
½	**cup chopped carrot**
⅓	**cup water**
¼	**cup catsup**
2	**tablespoons vinegar**
1	**tablespoon Worcestershire sauce**
1	**teaspoon brown sugar**
1	**teaspoon chili powder**
¼	**teaspoon pepper**
12	**ounces cooked pork, cut into bite-size strips (2 cups)**
½	**cup sliced celery**
1½	**teaspoons cornstarch**
1	**tablespoon water**

▪ In a 2-quart saucepan stir together onion, carrot, the ⅓ cup water, catsup, vinegar, Worcestershire sauce, brown sugar, chili powder, and pepper.

▪ Bring mixture to boiling; reduce heat. Cover and simmer for 10 minutes.

▪ Stir in pork and celery. Simmer, covered, for 5 minutes more or till heated through, stirring once.

▪ Stir together cornstarch and the 1 tablespoon water. Stir into meat mixture. Cook and stir till thickened and bubbly. Cook and stir for 2 minutes more. Makes 4 servings.

Nutrition information per serving: 252 calories, 25 g protein, 11 g carbohydrate, 11 g fat, 77 mg cholesterol, 304 mg sodium, 520 mg potassium.

HAM WITH HONEY-MUSTARD GLAZE

187 calories

Preparation Time: 8 min. ▪ Grilling Time: 13 min. ▪ Low Cholesterol

While your ham is on the grill, toss together a Waldorf salad (easy on the dressing) and pour a glass of skim milk to complete your meal.

2	**fully cooked lean boneless ham slices, cut ¾ inch thick (1 pound total)**
½	**teaspoon finely shredded orange peel**
1	**tablespoon orange juice**
1	**tablespoon Dijon-style mustard**
1	**tablespoon honey**
⅛	**teaspoon ground ginger**

▪ Halve each ham slice, forming four equal portions.

▪ For glaze, in a small bowl combine orange peel, orange juice, mustard, honey, and ginger. Brush over ham slices.

▪ Grill ham on an uncovered grill directly over *medium-hot* coals for 5 minutes. Turn and grill ham 8 to 10 minutes more or till heated through. Brush often with glaze. Serves 4.

▪ **Broiling directions:** Place ham on the unheated rack of a broiler pan. Broil 3 inches from the heat for 6 minutes. Turn and broil 6 to 8 minutes more or till heated through. Brush occasionally with glaze.

Nutrition information per serving: 187 calories, 24 g protein, 6 g carbohydrate, 6 g fat, 60 mg cholesterol, 1,476 mg sodium, 341 mg potassium.

HAM WITH SWEET POTATOES AND APPLES 342 calories

Preparation Time: 15 min. ▪ Cooking Time: 25 min. ▪ Low Fat ▪ Low Cholesterol

1	**1-pound slice fully cooked ham**
1	**18-ounce can sweet potatoes (vacuum packed)**
2	**small apples, cored and cut into thin wedges**
1	**teaspoon finely shredded orange peel**
¾	**cup orange juice**
2	**teaspoons cornstarch**
1	**teaspoon soy sauce**
1	**teaspoon grated gingerroot**
1	**clove garlic, minced**

■ Trim excess fat from ham; cut into 4 equal portions. Cut up any large sweet potatoes. Arrange sweet potatoes and apple wedges in a 12x7½x2-inch baking dish. Arrange ham pieces atop sweet potatoes and apples.

■ In a saucepan combine orange peel, orange juice, cornstarch, soy sauce, gingerroot, and garlic. Cook and stir till thickened and bubbly. Pour over ingredients in baking dish.

■ Bake, covered, in a 375° oven for 15 minutes. Uncover and bake about 10 minutes more till apples are just tender. Makes 4 servings.

Nutrition information per serving: 342 calories, 26 g protein, 44 g carbohydrate, 7 g fat, 60 mg cholesterol, 1,519 mg sodium, 889 mg potassium.

BAKED HAM AND KRAUT ROLLS

236 calories

Preparation Time: 10 min. ▪ Cooking Time: 20 min. ▪ Low Cholesterol

1	**8-ounce can sauerkraut, rinsed and drained**
2	**tablespoons sliced green onions**
½	**teaspoon caraway seed**
6	**thin slices fully cooked ham (6 ounces total)**
¼	**cup reduced-calorie mayonnaise *or* salad dressing**
2	**tablespoons skim milk**
2	**teaspoons prepared mustard**
1	**teaspoon skim milk**

▪ In a medium mixing bowl combine sauerkraut, green onions, and caraway seed. Finely chop *2 slices* of the ham; stir into sauerkraut mixture.

▪ For sauce, in a small mixing bowl stir together mayonnaise or salad dressing, 2 tablespoons milk, and the mustard. Add *¼ cup* of the sauce to the sauerkraut mixture; mix well.

▪ Place *one-fourth* of the sauerkraut mixture on *each* remaining ham slice. Roll up each slice from one side. Place rolls seam side down in a 10x6x2-inch baking dish.

▪ Bake, covered, in a 375° oven about 20 minutes or till heated through. Stir 1 teaspoon milk into remaining sauce. Spoon over ham rolls before serving. Makes 2 servings.

▪ **Microwave directions:** Micro-cook, covered with vented clear plastic wrap, on 100% power (high) for 4 to 6 minutes or till heated through.

Nutrition information per serving: 236 calories, 20 g protein, 7 g carbohydrate, 7 g fat, 57 mg cholesterol, 1,808 mg sodium, 407 mg potassium.

GLAZED HAM WITH SWEET POTATOES

279 calories

Preparation Time: 10 min. ▪ Cooking Time: 25 min. ▪ Low Fat ▪ Low Cholesterol

1	**18-ounce can vacuum-pack sweet potatoes, drained, *or* two medium sweet potatoes, peeled and sliced (12 to 14 ounces total)**
12	**pearl onions, peeled, *or* 12 frozen small whole onions, *or* 3 medium onions, cut into wedges**
¾	**cup orange juice**
2	**tablespoons honey**
1	**tablespoon cold water**
2	**teaspoons cornstarch**
½	**teaspoon finely shredded orange peel**
¼	**teaspoon ground allspice**
¾	**pound fully cooked ham slice, trimmed of separable fat**

■ In a large skillet combine *fresh* sweet potatoes, if using, onions, and orange juice. Bring to boiling; reduce heat. Cover and simmer for 15 to 20 minutes or till vegetables are just tender.

■ Stir together honey, water, cornstarch, orange peel, and allspice; add to skillet. Cook and stir till thickened and bubbly. Add *canned* sweet potatoes, if using, to skillet.

■ Carefully lay ham slice over vegetables in skillet. Cover and simmer for 5 minutes or till ham is heated through. Place ham on platter; spoon vegetables and sauce over ham. Makes 4 servings.

Nutrition information per serving: 279 calories, 20 g protein, 39 g carbohydrate, 5 g fat, 45 mg cholesterol, 1,038 mg sodium, 607 mg potassium.

FETTUCCINE WITH CREAMY HAM SAUCE   344 calories

Preparation Time: 20 min. ▪ Cooking Time: 10 min. ▪ Low Fat ▪ Low Cholesterol

1	12-ounce can evaporated skim milk
2	teaspoons cornstarch
½	teaspoon dry mustard
¼	teaspoon salt
⅛	teaspoon pepper
⅓	cup shredded Swiss cheese (1½ ounces)
1	cup sliced fully cooked ham, cut into thin strips (about 5 ounces)
1	cup cooked broccoli *or* cauliflower cut into bite-size pieces
1	2½-ounce jar sliced mushrooms, drained
6	ounces fettuccine, cooked and drained (3 cups cooked)*
2	tablespoons sliced green onions (optional)

▪ In a medium saucepan stir together milk, cornstarch, mustard, salt, and pepper. Cook and stir over medium heat till thickened and bubbly. Cook and stir 2 minutes more.

▪ Add cheese; stir till melted. Stir in ham, broccoli or cauliflower, and mushrooms. Cook and stir till heated through. Pour over hot pasta. If desired, garnish with sliced green onions. Makes 4 servings.

▪ **Microwave directions:** In a 1½-quart casserole combine milk, cornstarch, mustard, salt, and pepper. Micro-cook on 100% power (high) for 4 to 6 minutes (6 to 8 minutes in low-wattage ovens) or till thickened and bubbly, stirring after every minute. Add cheese, stirring till melted. Add ham, broccoli or cauliflower, and mushrooms. Cook 2 to 3 minutes more (4 to 5 minutes in low-wattage ovens) or till heated through. Serve as directed above.

*****Note:** If desired, omit the fettuccine and serve the ham mixture over 3 cups cooked spaghetti squash. This reduces the calories per serving to 230.

Nutrition information per serving: 344 calories, 24 g protein, 49 g carbohydrate, 5 g fat, 31 mg cholesterol, 766 mg sodium, 619 mg potassium.

ORIENTAL HAM SOUP

142 calories

Preparation Time: 15 min. ▪ Cooking Time: 10 min. ▪ Low Fat ▪ Low Cholesterol

Don't let bok choy be a mystery vegetable. It looks similar to celery, but its stalks are white with dark green leaves. To prepare it, slice the stalks and coarsely shred the leaves.

4	**cups water**
2	**cups sliced bok choy**
¾	**cup carrot cut into thin strips**
¾	**cup chopped onion**
2	**tablespoons soy sauce**
2	**tablespoons dry sherry**
	Dash pepper
8	**ounces fully cooked ham, cut into thin strips (1½ cups)**
½	**cup spinach *or* regular egg noodles**

▪ In a large saucepan or Dutch oven combine water, bok choy, carrot, onion, soy sauce, dry sherry, and pepper. Bring to boiling. Add ham and noodles. Simmer about 10 minutes or till noodles are tender and vegetables are crisp-tender. Makes 4 servings.

Nutrition information per serving: 142 calories, 14 g protein, 11 g carbohydrate, 3 g fat, 35 mg cholesterol, 1,221 mg sodium, 387 mg potassium.

SAVORY HAM AND RICE

229 calories

Preparation Time: 20 min. ▪ Cooking Time: 30 min. ▪ Low Fat ▪ Low Cholesterol

Shorten your preparation time at mealtime by cutting up the vegetables and ham in advance.

1	**cup chopped carrot**
½	**cup chopped onion**
½	**cup chopped green *or* sweet red pepper**
½	**cup water**
1	**10¾-ounce can condensed cream of celery soup**
¾	**cup quick-cooking rice**
8	**ounces fully cooked ham, cut into bite-size pieces (1½ cups)**
¼	**teaspoon ground sage**
⅛	**teaspoon pepper**
	Paprika (optional)

▪ In a medium saucepan combine carrot, onion, green pepper, and water. Bring to boiling; reduce heat. Cover and simmer for 4 to 5 minutes or till crisp-tender. *Do not drain.*

▪ Stir in soup, *uncooked* rice, ham, sage, and pepper. Spoon into a 1½-quart casserole. Sprinkle with paprika, if desired.

▪ Bake, covered, in a 350° oven for 30 to 35 minutes or till rice is tender and mixture is heated through. Serves 4.

Nutrition information per serving: 229 calories, 15 g protein, 27 g carbohydrate, 7 g fat, 38 mg cholesterol, 1,272 mg sodium, 408 mg potassium.

HAM AND CORN TOSTADAS

250 calories

Preparation Time: 15 min. ▪ Cooking Time: 5 min. ▪ Low Cholesterol

1½	**cups chopped fully cooked ham (8 ounces)**
1	**8-ounce can whole kernel corn, drained**
½	**cup salsa**
4	**tostada shells *or* flour tortillas**
1½	**cups shredded lettuce**
½	**cup shredded Monterey Jack cheese *or* Monterey Jack cheese with jalapeño peppers**
¼	**cup plain low-fat yogurt**
2	**tablespoons sliced green onions**

▪ In a medium skillet combine ham, corn, and salsa. Bring to boiling; reduce heat. Cover and simmer for 5 minutes.

▪ Meanwhile, place each tostada shell on a serving plate. Top each with shredded lettuce, ham mixture, and cheese. Garnish with yogurt and green onions. Makes 4 servings.

▪ **Microwave directions:** In a 1-quart casserole combine ham, corn, and salsa. Micro-cook, covered, on 100% power (high) for 5 to 8 minutes or till heated through. Assemble as directed above.

Nutrition information per serving: 250 calories, 19 g protein, 21 g carbohydrate, 10 g fat, 44 mg cholesterol, 1,232 mg sodium, 447 mg potassium.

CABBAGE AND HAM HASH

229 calories

Preparation Time: 20 min. ▪ Cooking Time: 10 min. ▪ Low Fat ▪ Low Cholesterol

½	cup chopped onion
2	cups chopped cabbage
¾	cup shredded carrot
1	tablespoon margarine
12	ounces fully cooked ham, chopped (2¼ cups)
2	cups chopped cooked potatoes
1	teaspoon Worcestershire sauce
⅛	teaspoon pepper

▪ In a 10-inch skillet cook onion, cabbage, and carrot in hot margarine till vegetables are tender.

▪ Stir in ham, potatoes, Worcestershire sauce, and pepper. Spread mixture evenly in skillet. Cook over medium heat for 5 minutes, turning occasionally with spatula. Makes 4 servings.

▪ **Microwave directions:** In a 2-quart casserole combine onion, cabbage, carrot, and margarine. Micro-cook, covered, on 100% power (high) for 5 to 7 minutes (9 to 11 minutes in a low-wattage oven) or till onion is tender, stirring once. Stir in remaining ingredients. Cook, covered, on high for 3 to 4 minutes (4 to 5 minutes in low-wattage ovens) or till heated through, stirring once.

Nutrition information per serving: 229 calories, 19 g protein, 22 g carbohydrate, 7 g fat, 42 mg cholesterol, 1,011 mg sodium, 651 mg potassium.

HAM AND CHEESE FRITTATA

168 calories

Preparation Time: 10 min. ▪ Cooking Time: 12 min.

As the egg mixture sets, run a spatula around the edge of the skillet, lifting the egg mixture to allow uncooked portions to flow underneath.

	Nonstick spray coating
1	cup chopped fully cooked ham (about 5 ounces)
½	cup chopped onion
½	cup chopped green *or* sweet red pepper
6	slightly beaten eggs
¾	cup low-fat cottage cheese
⅛	teaspoon pepper
1	medium tomato, thinly sliced
¼	cup shredded reduced-fat cheddar cheese (1 ounce)

▪ Spray a 10-inch ovenproof skillet with nonstick spray coating. Heat skillet over medium-high heat. Add ham, onion, and green pepper. Cook about 4 minutes or till vegetables are tender and ham is lightly browned.

▪ Meanwhile, in a mixing bowl combine eggs, cottage cheese, and pepper. Pour over ham mixture in skillet.

▪ Cook over medium-low heat. As egg mixture sets, run a spatula around the edge of the skillet, lifting egg mixture to allow uncooked portions to flow underneath. Continue cooking and lifting edges till egg mixture is almost set (surface will be moist).

▪ Place skillet under broiler 5 inches from heat for 1 to 2 minutes or till eggs are set.

▪ Meanwhile, halve tomato slices. Arrange atop frittata. Sprinkle cheddar cheese atop tomato. Broil 1 minute more. Makes 6 servings.

Nutrition information per serving: 168 calories, 16 g protein, 4 g carbohydrate, 9 g fat, 294 mg cholesterol, 501 mg sodium, 239 mg potassium.

HAM AND CHEESE MACARONI

350 calories

Preparation Time: 30 min. ▪ Cooking Time: 30 min. ▪ Low Cholesterol

1	**cup elbow macaroni**
2	**cups broccoli flowerets** *or* **1 10-ounce package frozen cut broccoli, cooked and drained**
1	**cup cubed fully cooked ham** *or* **turkey ham (5 ounces)**
1	**medium green** *or* **sweet red pepper, cut into ¾-inch squares (1 cup)**
1	**cup skim milk**
1	**tablespoon cornstarch**
⅛	**teaspoon pepper**
1	**cup cubed American cheese (4 ounces)**
¾	**cup soft bread crumbs (1 slice)**
1	**tablespoon margarine, melted**

▪ Cook macaroni according to package directions; drain.

▪ In a 2-quart casserole combine macaroni, broccoli, ham, and green or red pepper; set aside.

▪ For sauce, in a small saucepan stir together milk, cornstarch, and pepper. Cook and stir till thickened and bubbly. Add cheese; stir till melted. Stir sauce into mixture in casserole. Combine bread crumbs and margarine; sprinkle atop mixture in casserole.

▪ Bake, uncovered, in a 350° oven for 30 minutes or till bubbly and bread crumbs are lightly browned. Serves 4.

▪ **Microwave directions:** Prepare as above, *except* use a microwave-safe casserole and do not sprinkle bread crumbs over macaroni mixture before cooking. Micro-cook macaroni mixture, covered, on 100% power (high) for 6 to 8 minutes (9 to 10 minutes in a low-wattage oven) or till hot, stirring once. Top with bread crumb mixture. Cook, uncovered, on high 1 minute more.

Nutrition information per serving: 350 calories, 21 g protein, 33 g carbohydrate, 15 g fat, 47 mg cholesterol, 952 mg sodium, 506 mg potassium.

HAM AND POTATO SKILLET

181 calories

Preparation Time: 15 min. ▪ Cooking Time: 20 min. ▪ Low Fat ▪ Low Cholesterol

1	**pound small potatoes**
½	**pound fresh green beans, cut into 1-inch pieces,** *or* **one 9-ounce package frozen cut green beans**
1	**cup water**
1	**8-ounce carton plain low-fat yogurt**
2	**tablespoons all-purpose flour**
2	**teaspoons prepared mustard**
¼	**teaspoon dried dillweed**
⅛	**teaspoon pepper**
1½	**cups cubed fully cooked ham (about 8 ounces)**

■ Slice potatoes; halve any large slices.

■ In a large skillet cook potatoes and *fresh* green beans, if using, in water, covered, about 15 minutes or till potatoes and beans are tender. (If using *frozen* beans, add to potatoes the last 5 minutes of cooking.) Drain well.

■ Meanwhile, in a small saucepan stir together yogurt, flour, mustard, dillweed, and pepper. Cook and stir till thickened and bubbly. Pour over vegetables in skillet. Stir in ham. Heat through. Makes 4 servings.

Nutrition information per serving: 181 calories, 16 g protein, 20 g carbohydrate, 4 g fat, 31 mg cholesterol, 708 mg sodium, 561 mg potassium.

HAM JAMBALAYA

230 calories

Preparation Time: 25 min. ▪ Cooking Time: 20 min. ▪ Low Fat ▪ Low Cholesterol

Jambalaya (jam ba LIE ya) is the Louisiana version of Spanish paella. The name comes from the French word jambon, *meaning ham.*

	Nonstick spray coating
1	cup chopped onion
¾	cup chopped green pepper
½	cup chopped celery
1	clove garlic, minced
2	cups cubed, fully cooked ham (about 10 ounces)
1	14½-ounce can tomatoes, cut up
1¼	cups chicken broth
½	teaspoon dried thyme, crushed
⅛	to ¼ teaspoon ground red pepper
1	bay leaf
¾	cup long grain rice

▪ Spray a large skillet with nonstick spray coating. Add onion, green pepper, celery, and garlic. Cook over medium heat till vegetables are tender.

▪ Add ham, *undrained* tomatoes, chicken broth, thyme, red pepper, and bay leaf. Bring to boiling; stir in rice. Reduce heat; cover and simmer about 20 minutes or till rice is tender. Discard bay leaf. Makes 5 servings.

Nutrition information per serving: 230 calories, 16 g protein, 31 g carbohydrate, 4 g fat, 30 mg cholesterol, 1,020 mg sodium, 538 mg potassium.

VEGETABLE-BEAN SOUP WITH HAM

196 calories

Preparation Time: 1 hr. 10 min. ▪ Cooking Time: 1 hr. 35 min. ▪ Low Fat ▪ Low Cholesterol

¾	cup dry navy beans (5 ounces)
9	cups water
1	cup sliced carrot
1	cup chopped onion
½	cup sliced celery
1	tablespoon instant chicken bouillon granules
1	teaspoon dried basil, crushed
½	teaspoon dried thyme, crushed
¼	teaspoon pepper
2	bay leaves
1	clove garlic, minced
8	ounces fully cooked ham, diced (1½ cups)
1½	cups shredded fresh spinach *or* cabbage

■ Rinse beans. In a large saucepan or Dutch oven combine beans and *4 cups* of the water. Bring to boiling; reduce heat and simmer 2 minutes. Remove from heat; cover and let stand 1 hour. (Or, soak the beans in water overnight in a covered pan.)

■ Drain and rinse beans. Return beans to pan. Add the remaining water, carrot, onion, celery, bouillon granules, basil, thyme, pepper, bay leaves, and garlic. Bring to boiling; reduce heat. Cover and simmer 1½ to 2 hours or till beans are tender. Stir in ham and spinach or cabbage. Simmer 3 to 5 minutes more. Remove bay leaves. Makes 5 servings.

Nutrition information per serving: 196 calories, 17 g protein, 25 g carbohydrate, 3 g fat, 24 mg cholesterol, 808 mg sodium, 749 mg potassium.

SPINACH AND HAM LASAGNA

265 calories

Preparation Time: 30 min. ▪ Cooking Time: 30 min. ▪ Low Fat ▪ Low Cholesterol

6	**lasagna noodles (4 ounces)**
1	**10-ounce package frozen chopped spinach**
2	**cups skim milk**
2	**tablespoons cornstarch**
1	**tablespoon dried minced onion**
1½	**cups diced fully cooked ham (½ pound)**
½	**teaspoon Italian seasoning, crushed**
1	**cup low-fat cottage cheese**
1	**cup shredded mozzarella cheese (4 ounces)**

▪ Cook lasagna noodles in lightly salted boiling water for 10 to 12 minutes or till al dente. Drain. Rinse with cold water; drain again. Set aside.

▪ Meanwhile, cook spinach according to package directions; drain well. Set aside.

▪ For sauce, in a medium saucepan combine milk, cornstarch, and onion. Cook and stir till thickened and bubbly. Cook and stir 2 minutes more.

▪ Spread *2 tablespoons* of the sauce evenly on the bottom of a 10x6x2-inch baking dish. Stir ham and Italian seasoning into remaining sauce.

▪ Arrange 3 lasagna noodles in the dish. Spread with *one-third* of the sauce. Layer spinach atop. Layer another *one-third* of the sauce, the cottage cheese, and *half* of the mozzarella. Place remaining noodles atop. Top with remaining sauce and mozzarella.

▪ Bake in a 375° oven for 30 to 35 minutes or till heated through. Let stand 10 minutes before serving. Serves 6.

Nutrition information per serving: 265 calories, 25 g protein, 25 g carbohydrate, 7 g fat, 53 mg cholesterol, 821 mg sodium, 507 mg potassium.

SWEET-AND-SOUR HAM BALLS

249 calories

Preparation Time: 15 min. ▪ Cooking Time: 30 min. ▪ Low Fat ▪ Low Cholesterol

Rice or noodles is the just-right side dish for these saucy meatballs.

1	**beaten egg**
1	**cup bran flakes cereal**
⅓	**cup skim milk**
¼	**teaspoon ground ginger**
½	**pound ground veal *or* lean ground beef**
½	**pound ground fully cooked ham**
1	**15¼-ounce can pineapple chunks (juice pack)**
1	**cup thinly sliced carrots**
½	**cup chicken broth**
¼	**cup red wine vinegar**
2	**tablespoons cornstarch**
2	**tablespoons honey**
1	**tablespoon soy sauce**
1	**cup fresh *or* frozen pea pods, thawed**

▪ In a large mixing bowl combine egg, bran flakes, milk, and ginger. Let stand 5 minutes. Add meat and mix well. Shape into 24 meatballs.

▪ Arrange meatballs in a 12x7½x2-inch baking dish. Bake, uncovered, in a 350° oven for 30 minutes. Spoon off fat.

▪ Meanwhile, for sauce, drain pineapple, reserving juice. Set both aside. In a large saucepan cook carrots in chicken broth, covered, for 5 minutes or just till tender. *Do not drain.*

▪ Combine vinegar, cornstarch, honey, and soy sauce. Stir into carrot mixture. Stir in reserved pineapple juice. Cook and stir till thickened and bubbly. Stir in pea pods and cook 2 minutes more. Stir in pineapple; heat through. Gently stir in meatballs to coat with sauce. Makes 6 servings.

▪ **Microwave directions:** Place meatballs in a microwave-safe 12x7½x2-inch baking dish. Micro-cook, loosely covered with waxed paper, on 100% power (high) for 5 to 7 minutes, rearranging once. Drain. Prepare sauce as directed above.

Nutrition information per serving: 249 calories, 19 g protein, 30 g carbohydrate, 7 g fat, 95 mg cholesterol, 792 mg sodium, 483 mg potassium.

LAMB AND VEAL
MAIN DISHES

MARINATED LAMB KABOBS *(see page 161)*

BAKED LAMB AND VEGETABLES

256 calories

Preparation Time: 20 min. ▪ Cooking Time: 50 min.

4	**lamb shoulder chops, cut ¾ inch thick (1¾ pounds total)**
1	**large onion, cut into thin wedges (1 cup)**
1	**medium carrot, cut into thin bite-size strips**
1	**medium turnip, cut into thin bite-size strips (¾ cup)**
1	**stalk celery, thinly sliced (½ cup)**
¼	**teaspoon garlic salt**
¼	**teaspoon dried thyme, crushed**
⅛	**teaspoon pepper**
4	**thin slices lemon**

▪ Cut four 12-inch squares of heavy foil. *Or,* cut eight squares of regular foil.

▪ Trim separable fat from meat. Arrange one lamb chop on each square of heavy foil or on a double layer of regular foil. Divide vegetables among lamb chops.

▪ In a mixing bowl stir together garlic salt, thyme, and pepper. Sprinkle evenly over vegetables and chops. Top each with a lemon slice.

▪ Fold foil tightly around chops; place on a baking sheet.

▪ Bake in a 350° oven for 50 minutes or till chops and vegetables are tender. Discard lemon slices before serving. Makes 4 servings.

Nutrition information per serving: 256 calories, 30 g protein, 7 g carbohydrate, 11 g fat, 109 mg cholesterol, 225 mg sodium, 544 mg potassium.

HERBED LAMB WITH APPLES

209 calories

Preparation Time: 16 min. ▪ Marinating Time: several hrs. ▪ Grilling Time: 30 min. ▪ Low Fat ▪ Low Cholesterol

To tightly seal the foil packet of apples, bring up the long edges of the foil and, leaving a little space for steam expansion, seal the foil tightly with a double fold. Then, fold in the short ends to seal.

½	cup apple juice *or* apple cider
¼	teaspoon finely shredded lemon peel
2	tablespoons lemon juice
1	tablespoon honey
1	teaspoon dried rosemary, crushed
1	clove garlic, minced
½	teaspoon salt
¼	teaspoon pepper
1	3½-pound leg of lamb, sirloin half, boned and butterflied
4	small apples, cored and sliced crosswise into ½-inch rings

▪ For marinade, stir together apple juice, lemon peel, lemon juice, honey, rosemary, garlic, salt, and pepper. Set aside.

▪ Place lamb, boned side up, between two pieces of clear plastic wrap. Working from the center to the edges, pound lightly with a meat mallet to 1-inch thickness. Place in a shallow dish. Pour marinade over lamb. Cover and marinate in the refrigerator several hours or overnight. Drain lamb, reserving the marinade.

▪ Place apples on an 18x24-inch piece of heavy foil. Sprinkle with *3 table-spoons* of the reserved marinade. Bring up long edges of foil and, leaving a little space for steam expansion, seal tightly with a double fold. Fold short ends to seal.

▪ Grill lamb and apples on an uncovered grill directly over *medium* coals for 15 minutes. Turn lamb and grill to desired doneness, allowing 15 to 25 minutes more for medium. Brush lamb often with marinade. Grill apples about 15 minutes more or till tender, turning foil packet frequently. Makes 8 servings.

Nutrition information per serving: 209 calories, 25 g protein, 12 g carbohydrate, 6 g fat, 87 mg cholesterol, 198 mg sodium, 367 mg potassium.

MARINATED LAMB KABOBS

125 calories

Preparation Time: 25 min. ▪ Marinating Time: 2 hrs. ▪ Cooking Time: 6 min. ▪ Low Cholesterol ▪ Low Sodium

1	**pound boneless lean leg of lamb, cut 1 inch thick**
⅓	**cup water**
3	**tablespoons lemon juice**
2	**tablespoons snipped fresh mint _or_ 2 teaspoons dried mint, crushed**
1	**tablespoon Dijon-style mustard**
1	**tablespoon cooking oil**
1	**clove garlic, minced**
2	**small zucchini, cut into ½-inch-thick slices**
1	**cup pearl onions _or_ 1 cup frozen small whole onions, thawed**
5	**cherry tomatoes**

▪ Partially freeze lamb. Cut into ¼-inch-thick strips about 3 inches long and 1 inch wide. Place in a plastic bag set in a deep bowl.

▪ For marinade, stir together water, lemon juice, mint, mustard, oil, and garlic. Pour over lamb. Close bag. Marinate in the refrigerator for 2 hours or overnight, turning occasionally. Drain lamb, reserving marinade.

▪ Meanwhile, in a small saucepan cook the zucchini, covered, in a small amount of boiling water for 2 minutes. Drain.

▪ On five 12- to 15-inch skewers, alternately thread lamb accordion-style with onions and zucchini.

▪ Place skewers on the unheated rack of a broiler pan; brush with marinade. Broil 3 inches from the heat for 6 to 8 minutes or to desired doneness, turning occasionally and brushing with marinade.

▪ Add a cherry tomato to the end of each skewer during the last 1 minute of broiling. Makes 5 servings.

Nutrition information per serving: 125 calories, 16 g protein, 4 g carbohydrate, 5 g fat, 53 mg cholesterol, 62 mg sodium, 353 mg potassium.

CURRIED LAMB

307 calories

Preparation Time: 25 min. ▪ Cooking Time: 50 min. ▪ Low Fat ▪ Low Cholesterol

	Nonstick spray coating
1	**pound boneless lean lamb, cut into 1-inch pieces**
¾	**cup chopped onion**
2	**to 3 teaspoons curry powder**
1	**clove garlic, minced**
1	**cup water**
½	**cup apple juice *or* dry red wine**
¾	**cup chopped celery**
¼	**cup mixed dried fruit bits *or* raisins *or* chopped dried apricots**
½	**teaspoon salt**
⅛	**teaspoon pepper**
4	**teaspoons cornstarch**
2	**cups hot cooked rice**

▪ Spray a large *cold* saucepan with nonstick spray coating. Preheat over medium heat. Brown *half* of the meat; remove from saucepan. Add remaining meat, onion, curry powder, and garlic to saucepan; cook till meat is brown and onion is tender. Return all meat to saucepan.

▪ Stir in water and apple juice. Add celery, mixed dried fruit bits, salt, and pepper. Bring to boiling; reduce heat. Cover and simmer for 45 to 60 minutes or till lamb is tender.

▪ Stir cornstarch into 2 tablespoons *water.* Add to mixture in saucepan. Cook and stir till mixture is thickened and bubbly. Cook and stir for 2 minutes more. Serve over hot cooked rice. Makes 4 servings.

Nutrition information per serving: 307 calories, 22 g protein, 42 g carbohydrate, 5 g fat, 66 mg cholesterol, 336 mg sodium, 479 mg potassium.

HERBED LAMB STIR-FRY

220 calories

Preparation Time: 30 min. ▪ Cooking Time: 6 min. ▪ Low Cholesterol ▪ Low Sodium

Savor these flavors inside a pita-bread pocket, too.

¾ **pound lean boneless lamb** *or* **beef top round steak**

¼ **cup sliced green onion**

¼ **cup snipped fresh parsley**

1 **tablespoon lemon juice**

½ **teaspoon dried thyme, crushed,** *or* ¼ **teaspoon dried mint, crushed**

⅛ **teaspoon pepper**

Nonstick spray coating

1 **medium green** *or* **sweet red pepper, cut into bite-size strips**

1 **clove garlic, minced**

1 **tablespoon cooking oil**

2 **6-inch pita bread rounds, split horizontally and quartered**

¼ **cup plain low-fat yogurt**

▪ Partially freeze meat. Thinly slice meat across the grain into bite-size strips.

▪ In a medium mixing bowl combine onion, parsley, lemon juice, thyme or mint, and pepper. Stir in lamb.

▪ Spray a wok or large skillet with nonstick spray coating. Add green pepper and garlic and stir-fry 2 minutes or till pepper is crisp-tender. Remove from wok.

▪ Add oil to hot wok. Add lamb mixture and stir-fry for 2 to 3 minutes or till done. Return peppers to wok. Heat through.

▪ Serve mixture with pita bread. Dollop each serving with some of the yogurt. Makes 4 servings.

Nutrition information per serving: 220 calories, 21 g protein, 13 g carbohydrate, 9 g fat, 65 mg cholesterol, 58 mg sodium, 341 mg potassium.

LENTIL AND LAMB SOUP

197 calories

Preparation Time: 20 min. ▪ Cooking Time: 1 hr. ▪ Low Fat ▪ Low Cholesterol

1	pound lean boneless lamb
	Nonstick spray coating
1	medium onion, chopped (½ cup)
4	cups water
1	14½-ounce can tomatoes, cut up
1	cup coarsely chopped carrots
1	cup sliced celery
1	teaspoon salt
½	teaspoon dried thyme, crushed
¼	teaspoon pepper
1	clove garlic, minced
1	bay leaf
¾	cup lentils

▪ Trim fat from lamb; cut lamb into 1-inch pieces.

▪ Spray a Dutch oven with nonstick spray coating. Heat Dutch oven over medium heat. Brown *half* of the lamb. Remove lamb from Dutch oven. Repeat with remaining lamb and all of the onion. Return first half of lamb to Dutch oven.

▪ Add water, *undrained* tomatoes, carrots, celery, salt, thyme, pepper, garlic, and bay leaf. Bring to boiling; reduce heat. Cover and simmer for 30 minutes.

▪ Rinse lentils; add to lamb mixture. Bring to boiling; reduce heat. Cover and simmer for 30 minutes more or till lamb and lentils are tender. Remove bay leaf. Makes 6 servings.

Nutrition information per serving: 197 calories, 21 g protein, 21 g carbohydrate, 4 g fat, 44 mg cholesterol, 527 mg sodium, 670 mg potassium.

OVEN LAMB STEW

236 calories

Preparation Time: 20 min. ▪ Cooking Time: 1 hr. 25 min. ▪ Low Fat ▪ Low Cholesterol

1½	**pounds lean boneless lamb**
1	**14½-ounce can tomatoes, cut up**
¾	**cup water**
½	**cup dry white wine**
2½	**cups peeled parsnips cut into ½-inch slices (1 pound)**
2	**cups fresh *or* frozen cut green beans**
1	**cup carrots cut into ½-inch slices**
½	**cup chopped onion**
1	**teaspoon dried rosemary, crushed**
½	**teaspoon salt**
⅛	**teaspoon pepper**
1	**clove garlic, minced**
2	**tablespoons cornstarch**
¼	**cup water**
⅓	**cup plain low-fat yogurt**

▪ Trim fat from lamb and cut meat into 1-inch cubes. In an ovenproof Dutch oven combine lamb, *undrained* tomatoes, the ¾ cup water, wine, parsnips, green beans, carrots, onion, rosemary, salt, pepper, and garlic. Bake, covered, in a 350° oven for 1¼ to 1½ hours or till lamb is tender. Remove Dutch oven from the oven to the range top.

▪ Meanwhile, combine cornstarch and the ¼ cup water. Stir into Dutch oven. Cook and stir till thickened and bubbly. Cook and stir 2 minutes more. To serve, dollop some of the yogurt atop each serving. Makes 6 servings.

Nutrition information per serving: 236 calories, 20 g protein, 25 g carbohydrate, 5 g fat, 60 mg cholesterol, 361 mg sodium, 809 mg potassium.

INDIVIDUAL SHEPHERD'S PIES

331 calories

Preparation Time: 12 min. ▪ Cooking Time: 30 min. ▪ Low Cholesterol

	Packaged instant mashed potatoes (enough for 4 servings)
	Skim milk
1	**10-ounce package frozen peas and carrots, thawed**
1½	**cups cubed cooked lamb _or_ beef**
1	**12-ounce jar beef gravy**
½	**teaspoon dried basil, crushed**
1	**tablespoon finely shredded cheddar cheese**

▪ Prepare mashed potatoes according to package directions, _except_ omit butter and substitute skim milk for milk; set potatoes aside.

▪ In a mixing bowl stir together vegetables, lamb, gravy, and basil. Divide among four 12- to 16-ounce casseroles. Top each casserole with mashed potatoes and cheese.

▪ Bake, uncovered, in a 350° oven for 30 to 35 minutes or till mixture is heated through. Makes 4 servings.

▪ **Microwave directions:** Prepare potatoes as directed above. Place _frozen_ vegetables in a 2-quart microwave-safe casserole. Micro-cook, covered, on 100% power (high) for 2 to 4 minutes or till crisp-tender; drain. Stir in lamb, gravy, and basil. Divide among four 12- to 16-ounce microwave-safe casseroles. Top with mashed potatoes and cheese. Micro-cook, uncovered, on 100% power (high) for 9 to 10 minutes or till mixture is heated through, rearranging dishes once.

Nutrition information per serving: 331 calories, 25 g protein, 30 g carbohydrate, 13 g fat, 62 mg cholesterol, 523 mg sodium, 560 mg potassium.

GARLIC-CARAWAY VEAL ROAST

328 calories

Preparation Time: 25 min. ▪ Cooking Time: 2 hrs.

With the fat side of the roast up, cut a number of 1-inch slits randomly around roast. Using your fingers, stuff the sliced garlic into the slits.

1	**3-pound veal rib** *or* **loin roast**
2	**cloves garlic, thinly sliced lengthwise**
1	**teaspoon caraway seed**
	Nonstick spray coating
1	**small onion, sliced and separated into rings**
1	**medium carrot, thinly sliced (½ cup)**
1	**cup chicken broth**
1	**tablespoon all-purpose flour**
½	**teaspoon caraway seed**

■ Trim excess fat from roast. With a sharp knife, make a number of 1-inch slits in roast. Insert garlic slivers into slits. Sprinkle with the 1 teaspoon caraway seed. Place roast on a rack in a shallow roasting pan. Insert meat thermometer into thickest part of meat, not touching bone.

■ Roast, uncovered, in a 325° oven about 2 hours or till thermometer registers 170°. Cover with foil and let stand 15 minutes before carving.

■ Meanwhile, spray a large skillet with nonstick spray coating. Preheat skillet over medium heat. Add onion and carrot. Cook and stir about 5 minutes or till vegetables are tender.

■ Stir together chicken broth, flour, and the ½ teaspoon caraway seed. Add to carrot mixture. Cook and stir till thickened and bubbly. Cook and stir for 1 minute more. Serve with roast. Makes 6 servings.

Nutrition information per serving: 328 calories, 32 g protein, 3 g carbohydrate, 20 g fat, 115 mg cholesterol, 209 mg sodium, 443 mg potassium.

VEAL CHOPS WITH VEGETABLE SAUCE

272 calories

Preparation Time: 10 min. ▪ Cooking Time: 10 min. ▪ Low Cholesterol

The skillet drippings add a rich flavor to the sauce.

4	**boneless veal top loin chops, cut ½ to ¾ inch thick (1¼ to 1½ pounds total)**
1	**tablespoon margarine**
1	**16-ounce package loose-pack frozen broccoli, baby carrots, and water chestnuts**
½	**cup chicken broth**
1	**clove garlic, minced, *or* ⅛ teaspoon bottled minced garlic**
2	**tablespoons white wine Worcestershire sauce**
2	**teaspoons cornstarch**

▪ Trim separable fat from chops. In a 10-inch skillet cook chops over medium heat in hot margarine for 4 to 6 minutes or till veal is of desired doneness, turning once. Transfer to a serving platter; cover with foil to keep warm.

▪ Stir frozen vegetables, broth, and garlic into skillet drippings. Bring to boiling; reduce heat. Cover and simmer for 2 minutes.

▪ Stir together Worcestershire sauce and cornstarch; add to skillet. Cook and stir till thickened and bubbly. Cook and stir for 2 minutes more. Spoon over the veal. Makes 4 servings.

Nutrition information per serving: 272 calories, 25 g protein, 10 g carbohydrate, 14 g fat, 85 mg cholesterol, 236 mg sodium, 533 mg potassium.

VEAL SCALOPPINE

196 calories

Preparation Time: 15 min. ▪ Cooking Time: 15 min. ▪ Low Cholesterol

1	**pound boneless veal leg round steak *or* veal leg sirloin steak, cut ¼ inch thick**
¼	**cup chopped onion**
1	**clove garlic, minced**
1	**7½-ounce can tomatoes, cut up**
2	**tablespoons dry white wine**
2	**teaspoons capers, drained (optional)**
¼	**teaspoon dried oregano, crushed**
⅛	**teaspoon pepper**
	Nonstick spray coating

▪ Cut meat into 8 equal pieces. Place 1 piece of meat between 2 pieces of clear plastic wrap. Using a meat mallet pound meat to about ⅛-inch thickness. Sprinkle meat lightly with salt and pepper. Set aside. Repeat with remaining meat.

▪ For sauce, in a medium saucepan cook onion and garlic, covered, in 2 tablespoons *water* till onion is tender but not brown. Stir in *undrained* tomatoes, wine, capers (if desired), oregano, and pepper. Bring to boiling; reduce heat. Simmer, uncovered, for 10 minutes. Keep warm.

▪ Spray a large skillet with nonstick spray coating. Cook meat, half at a time, over medium-high heat for 1 to 2 minutes per side or to desired doneness. Transfer meat to a serving platter; keep warm. Repeat with remaining veal.

▪ To serve, spoon sauce over veal. Makes 4 servings.

Nutrition information per serving: 196 calories, 22 g protein, 3 g carbohydrate, 9 g fat, 81 mg cholesterol, 141 mg sodium, 389 mg potassium.

VEAL AND POTATOES VINAIGRETTE

333 calories

Preparation Time: 15 min. ▪ Cooking Time: 25 min. ▪ Low Cholesterol

	Nonstick spray coating
3	**medium potatoes, thinly sliced (1 pound)**
1	**small onion, thinly sliced**
1	**pound boneless veal leg round steak, cut ½ inch thick**
1	**tablespoon cooking oil**
1	**tablespoon vinegar *or* lemon juice**
1	**teaspoon honey**
1	**teaspoon cornstarch**
½	**teaspoon instant beef *or* chicken bouillon granules**
¼	**teaspoon dried thyme, crushed**
⅛	**teaspoon salt**
	Dash pepper
	Tomato wedges (optional)

▪ Spray a large skillet with nonstick spray coating. Preheat skillet over medium heat. Add potatoes and onion, spreading evenly. Add 1 cup *water.* Bring to boiling; reduce heat. Cover and cook for 15 minutes or till vegetables are tender. Uncover and cook 3 to 5 minutes more or till lightly browned, turning occasionally with spatula. Transfer vegetables to a serving platter; keep warm.

▪ Meanwhile, cut veal into 8 pieces. Pound each piece to ¼-inch thickness. Add oil to skillet. Cook veal, half at a time, in hot oil over medium-high heat about 1 minute per side or till tender. Remove veal from skillet; arrange atop vegetables.

▪ In a mixing bowl stir together vinegar, honey, cornstarch, bouillon granules, thyme, salt, pepper, and ⅔ cup *water.* Stir into skillet. Cook and stir till thickened and bubbly. Cook and stir 1 minute more. Pour vinegar mixture over meat and vegetables. Serve immediately. If desired, garnish with tomato wedges. Makes 4 servings.

Nutrition information per serving: 333 calories, 25 g protein, 24 g carbohydrate, 15 g fat, 86 mg cholesterol, 249 mg sodium, 892 mg potassium.

STUFFED VEAL ROLLS

225 calories

Preparation Time: 30 min. ▪ Cooking Time: 25 min. ▪ Low Cholesterol

¾	cup chopped green *or* sweet red pepper
½	cup chopped green onion
2	tablespoons water
1	clove garlic, minced
¾	cup soft bread crumbs
1½	pounds boneless veal leg round steak, cut ½ inch thick
3	slices boiled ham, halved (3 ounces total)
	Nonstick spray coating
½	cup chicken broth
¼	teaspoon dried tarragon, crushed
2	teaspoons cornstarch
1	tablespoon water
	Hot cooked couscous (optional)

■ In a small saucepan combine green or sweet red pepper, onion, the 2 tablespoons water, and garlic. Cook over medium-high heat, covered, till vegetables are tender. Stir in soft bread crumbs; set aside.

■ Meanwhile, cut veal into 6 equal pieces. With a meat mallet, pound each piece to ⅛-inch thickness.

■ Lay one half-slice ham over each piece of veal; top with some of the pepper mixture. Fold in sides, then overlap ends, forming bundles. Secure with wooden toothpicks.

■ Spray a large skillet with nonstick spray coating. Preheat skillet over medium heat. Brown veal rolls about 5 minutes, turning once. Add chicken broth and tarragon to the skillet. Cover; simmer 15 minutes or till veal is tender. Remove veal rolls from skillet, reserving juices. Discard toothpicks.

■ Strain juices; return to skillet. Combine cornstarch and the 1 tablespoon water; add to liquid in skillet. Cook and stir till thickened and bubbly. Cook and stir 2 minutes more. Spoon over veal rolls. If desired, serve with couscous. Serves 6.

Nutrition information per serving: 225 calories, 26 g protein, 6 g carbohydrate, 10 g fat, 89 mg cholesterol, 318 mg sodium, 370 mg potassium.

CREAMY VEAL AND MUSHROOMS

339 calories

Preparation Time: 15 min. ▪ Cooking Time: 1¼ hrs. ▪ Low Fat ▪ Low Cholesterol

1¼	**pounds lean boneless veal**
	Nonstick spray coating
1	**14½-ounce can beef broth**
¼	**cup dry white wine *or* water**
½	**teaspoon dried thyme, crushed**
¼	**teaspoon salt**
1	**bay leaf**
8	**ounces pearl onions, peeled, *or* 2 cups frozen small whole onions**
8	**ounces small whole mushrooms (3 cups)**
1	**cup evaporated skim milk**
⅓	**cup all-purpose flour**
⅛	**teaspoon ground nutmeg**
3	**cups hot cooked noodles**
1	**tablespoon lemon juice**

■ Trim separable fat from veal; cut veal into 1-inch pieces. Spray a 3-quart saucepan with nonstick spray coating. Preheat saucepan over medium heat. Brown veal, half at a time, in hot saucepan.

■ Return all veal to saucepan. Add beef broth, wine or water, thyme, salt, and bay leaf. Bring to boiling; reduce heat. Cover and simmer for 45 minutes.

■ Halve any large fresh pearl onions. Stir fresh or frozen onions and mushrooms into veal mixture. Return to boiling; reduce heat. Cover and simmer for 15 minutes more or till onions and mushrooms are tender.

■ Combine evaporated skim milk, flour, and nutmeg. Add to veal mixture. Cook and stir till thickened and bubbly. Cook and stir for 1 more minute. Remove from heat. Discard bay leaf. Stir in noodles and lemon juice. Makes 6 servings.

Nutrition information per serving: 339 calories, 27 g protein, 34 g carbohydrate, 9 g fat, 94 mg cholesterol, 410 mg sodium, 634 mg potassium.

POULTRY
MAIN DISHES

LIME-SAUCED CHICKEN *(see page 177)*

MUSTARD AND HONEY CHICKEN

153 calories

Preparation Time: 6 min. ▪ Cooking Time: 7 min. ▪ Low Fat ▪ Low Cholesterol ▪ Low Sodium

Plan on some extra preparation time if you skin and bone your own chicken breasts.

	Nonstick spray coating
4	**medium (12 ounces total) boned skinless chicken breast halves**
	Salt
2	**teaspoons prepared mustard**
2	**teaspoons honey**

▪ Spray the unheated rack of a broiler pan with nonstick spray coating.
▪ Sprinkle chicken lightly with salt. Arrange chicken on broiler rack.
▪ Broil 4 to 5 inches from the heat for 6 minutes.
▪ Meanwhile, in a small bowl stir together mustard and honey. Brush over chicken.
▪ Broil 1 to 2 minutes more or till chicken is tender and no longer pink. Makes 4 servings.

Nutrition information per serving: 153 calories, 26 g protein, 3 g carbohydrate, 3 g fat, 72 mg cholesterol, 127 mg sodium, 223 mg potassium.

POACHED CHICKEN BREASTS WITH APPLES   182 calories

Preparation Time: 5 min. ▪ Cooking Time: 14 min. ▪ Low Fat ▪ Low Cholesterol ▪ Low Sodium

½	**cup apple juice** *or* **apple cider**
½	**teaspoon instant chicken bouillon granules**
1	**clove garlic, minced**
¼	**teaspoon dried tarragon, crushed**
	Dash pepper
4	**medium (12 ounces total) boned skinless chicken breast halves**
1	**medium apple, cored and thinly sliced**
¼	**cup sliced green onions**
1	**tablespoon water**
1½	**teaspoons cornstarch**

▪ In a 10-inch skillet combine apple juice, bouillon granules, garlic, tarragon, and pepper. Bring to boiling. Add chicken breasts; reduce heat. Cover and simmer for 7 minutes.

▪ Turn chicken over; add apple slices and green onions. Cover and simmer 4 to 5 minutes more or till chicken is tender and no longer pink.

▪ With a slotted spoon remove chicken and apples; keep warm. Reserve cooking liquid.

▪ In a small bowl stir together the water and cornstarch. Stir into liquid in skillet. Cook and stir till thickened and bubbly. Cook and stir for 2 minutes more. Spoon over chicken and apples. Makes 4 servings.

Nutrition information per serving: 182 calories, 27 g protein, 10 g carbohydrate, 3 g fat, 72 mg cholesterol, 111 mg sodium, 316 mg potassium.

CHICKEN ROLL-UPS

217 calories

Advance Preparation Time: 40 min. ▪ Chilling Time: 2 hrs. ▪ Final Preparation Time: 40 min. ▪ Low Fat ▪ Low Cholesterol

	Nonstick spray coating
¾	cup thinly sliced celery
½	cup sliced fresh mushrooms
½	cup thinly sliced carrot
1	small onion, sliced
1	clove garlic, minced
1	7½-ounce can tomatoes
1	8-ounce can tomato sauce
1	teaspoon Italian seasoning, crushed
¾	teaspoon sugar
3	medium chicken breasts
½	cup low-fat ricotta cheese
3	tablespoons grated Parmesan cheese
1	tablespoon snipped fresh parsley
½	cup shredded mozzarella cheese (optional)

▪ For sauce, spray a *cold* large saucepan with nonstick spray coating. Add celery, mushrooms, carrot, onion, and garlic. Cook till onion is tender. Cut up tomatoes. Stir *undrained* tomatoes, tomato sauce, Italian seasoning, and sugar into vegetables. Bring to boiling; reduce heat. Simmer, uncovered, 20 minutes or till mixture is reduced to *2 cups.*

▪ Meanwhile, skin, bone, and cut chicken breasts lengthwise in half. Place each chicken piece between 2 pieces of plastic wrap. Pound with a meat mallet to about ¼-inch thickness.

▪ In a bowl stir together ricotta cheese, Parmesan cheese, and parsley. Spoon about *1½ tablespoons* of the cheese mixture on *each* chicken piece. Fold in long sides of chicken piece, then roll up from short end. Place chicken rolls, seam side down, in an 8x8x2-inch baking dish. Pour sauce over chicken. Cover with foil and refrigerate for 2 to 24 hours.

▪ Before serving, bake, covered, in a 375° oven for 35 to 40 minutes or till chicken is no longer pink. If desired, sprinkle with mozzarella cheese; bake 4 minutes. Transfer to a platter. Serves 6.

Nutrition information per serving: 217 calories, 31 g protein, 9 g carbohydrate, 6 g fat, 81 mg cholesterol, 451 mg sodium, 583 mg potassium.

LIME-SAUCED CHICKEN

170 calories

Preparation Time: 3 min. ▪ Cooking Time: 12 min. ▪ Low Fat ▪ Low Cholesterol ▪ Low Sodium

Be sure to keep the heat at medium while you cook the chicken so it won't stick to the skillet.

	Nonstick spray coating
4	**medium (12 ounces total) boned skinless chicken breast halves**
½	**of a medium lime**
¾	**cup apple juice** *or* **apple cider**
2	**teaspoons cornstarch**
½	**teaspoon instant chicken bouillon granules**

■ Spray a large skillet with nonstick spray coating. Preheat skillet over medium heat. Add chicken. Cook over medium heat for 8 to 10 minutes or till tender and no longer pink, turning to brown evenly. Remove from skillet; keep warm.

■ Meanwhile, remove strips of peel from lime, using a vegetable peeler. Cut peel into thin strips; set aside. Squeeze 1 tablespoon juice from lime.

■ Combine lime juice, apple juice, cornstarch, and bouillon granules; carefully add to skillet. Cook and stir till thickened and bubbly. Cook and stir 2 minutes more.

■ To serve, cut each chicken breast half into 1-inch diagonal pieces. Spoon some sauce over each serving. Garnish with reserved lime peel. Pass remaining sauce. Makes 4 servings.

Nutrition information per serving: 170 calories, 26 g protein, 7 g carbohydrate, 3 g fat, 72 mg cholesterol, 111 mg sodium, 277 mg potassium.

CHICKEN WITH GRAPES

187 calories

Preparation Time: 3 min. ▪ Cooking Time: 12 min. ▪ Low Fat ▪ Low Cholesterol

	Nonstick spray coating
4	**medium (12 ounces total) boned skinless chicken breast halves**
½	**cup apple juice *or* apple cider**
1	**teaspoon instant chicken bouillon granules**
1	**teaspoon cornstarch**
¼	**teaspoon dried mint, crushed (optional)**
1	**cup seedless green *or* red grapes, halved**

▪ Spray a large skillet with nonstick spray coating. Preheat skillet over medium heat. Add chicken. Cook over medium heat for 8 to 10 minutes or till tender and no longer pink, turning to brown evenly. Remove from skillet; keep warm.

▪ Meanwhile combine apple juice, bouillon granules, cornstarch, and, if desired, mint. Add to skillet. Cook and stir till thickened and bubbly. Cook and stir 2 minutes more. Stir in grapes and heat through. Serve over chicken. Serves 4.

Nutrition information per serving: 187 calories, 27 g protein, 11 g carbohydrate, 3 g fat, 72 mg cholesterol, 158 mg sodium, 330 mg potassium.

CHICKEN MARSALA

161 calories

Preparation Time: 11 min. ▪ Cooking Time: 8 min. ▪ Low Fat ▪ Low Cholesterol

Pounding the chicken breasts makes them cook faster and more evenly. Place one piece of chicken, boned side up, between two pieces of clear plastic wrap. Working from the center to edges, pound lightly with a meat mallet to about ¼-inch thickness. Remove plastic wrap. Repeat with the remaining chicken.

4	medium (12 ounces total) boned skinless chicken breast halves
	Nonstick spray coating
1½	cups sliced fresh mushrooms
2	tablespoons sliced green onion
2	tablespoons water
¼	teaspoon salt
¼	cup dry Marsala *or* dry sherry

▪ Place 1 piece of chicken, boned side up, between 2 pieces of clear plastic wrap. Working from the center to the edges, pound lightly with a meat mallet to about ¼-inch thickness. Remove plastic wrap. Repeat with remaining chicken breast halves.

▪ Spray a large skillet with nonstick spray coating. Preheat skillet over medium heat. Add 2 chicken breast halves. Cook over medium heat for 2 to 3 minutes or till tender and no pink remains. Transfer to a platter; keep warm. Repeat with remaining chicken breast halves.

▪ Carefully add mushrooms, green onion, water, and salt to skillet. Cook over medium heat till mushrooms are tender and most of the liquid has evaporated (about 3 minutes). Add Marsala or dry sherry to skillet. Heat through. Spoon vegetables and sauce over chicken. Makes 4 servings.

Nutrition information per serving: 161 calories, 27 g protein, 2 g carbohydrate, 3 g fat, 72 mg cholesterol, 191 mg sodium, 337 mg potassium.

GINGER AND PEACH CHICKEN

321 calories

Preparation Time: 2 min. ▪ Cooking Time: 15 min. ▪ Low Fat ▪ Low Cholesterol

	Nonstick spray coating
4	**medium (12 ounces total) boned skinless chicken breast halves**
1	**8-ounce can peach slices in light syrup**
1	**teaspoon cornstarch**
½	**teaspoon grated gingerroot** *or* **⅛ teaspoon ground ginger**
¼	**teaspoon salt**
½	**of an 8-ounce can (½ cup) sliced water chestnuts, drained**
2	**cups hot cooked rice**
1	**6-ounce package frozen pea pods, cooked and drained**

▪ Spray a large skillet with nonstick spray coating. Preheat skillet over medium heat. Add chicken. Cook over medium heat for 8 to 10 minutes or till tender and no longer pink; turn to brown evenly. Remove from skillet; keep warm.

▪ Meanwhile drain peaches, reserving juice. Add water to juice to equal ½ cup. Stir in cornstarch, gingerroot, and salt. Add to skillet. Cook and stir till thickened and bubbly. Cook and stir 1 minute more. Gently stir in peaches and water chestnuts; heat through.

▪ On a serving platter or 4 individual plates arrange rice, pea pods, and chicken. Spoon sauce over chicken. Serves 4.

Nutrition information per serving: 321 calories, 30 g protein, 41 g carbohydrate, 3 g fat, 72 mg cholesterol, 205 mg sodium, 459 mg potassium.

CHEESY CHICKEN ROLLS

205 calories

Preparation Time: 12 min. ▪ Cooking Time: 20 min. ▪ Low Fat ▪ Low Cholesterol

½	cup shredded low-fat mozzarella cheese
1	2½-ounce jar sliced mushrooms, drained
¼	cup plain low-fat yogurt
1	tablespoon snipped chives
1	tablespoon snipped parsley
1	tablespoon chopped pimiento
4	medium (12 ounces total) boned skinless chicken breast halves
1	tablespoon fine dry bread crumbs
⅛	teaspoon paprika
1	tablespoon plain low-fat yogurt

▪ For filling, in a small bowl combine cheese, mushrooms, the ¼ cup yogurt, chives, parsley, and pimiento.

▪ Place one chicken breast half, boned side up, between two pieces of clear plastic wrap. Working from the center to the edges, pound lightly with a meat mallet to ⅛-inch thickness. Remove plastic wrap. Repeat with remaining chicken. Sprinkle lightly with *salt* and *pepper*.

▪ Spread some of the filling on each chicken breast half. Fold in the sides and roll up. Arrange rolls seam side down in a 10x6x2-inch baking dish.

▪ Combine bread crumbs and paprika. Brush chicken with the 1 tablespoon yogurt; sprinkle with crumb mixture. Bake in a 350° oven for 20 to 25 minutes or till chicken is tender and no longer pink. Makes 4 servings.

Nutrition information per serving: 205 calories, 32 g protein, 4 g carbohydrate, 6 g fat, 82 mg cholesterol, 298 mg sodium, 316 mg potassium.

CHICKEN BREASTS WITH CURRIED STUFFING   223 calories

Preparation Time: 18 min. ▪ Cooking Time: 25 min. ▪ Low Fat ▪ Low Cholesterol

A tempting yogurt sauce lends a bit of tang to this easy-to-stuff chicken dish.

½	**cup shredded carrot**
¼	**cup sliced green onion**
½ to 1	**teaspoon curry powder**
1	**tablespoon margarine**
½	**cup soft bread crumbs**
2	**tablespoons raisins**
1	**tablespoon water**
4	**medium (12 ounces total) boned skinless chicken breast halves**
⅛	**teaspoon salt**
¼	**teaspoon paprika**
¼	**cup plain low-fat yogurt**
2	**teaspoons orange marmalade**

▪ In a small saucepan cook carrot, green onion, and curry powder in margarine till vegetables are tender. Remove from heat and stir in bread crumbs, raisins, and water.

▪ Place one chicken breast half, boned side up, between two pieces of clear plastic wrap. Working from the center to the edges, pound lightly with a meat mallet to ¼-inch thickness. Remove plastic wrap. Repeat with remaining chicken. Sprinkle chicken pieces lightly with salt.

▪ Place *one-fourth* of the stuffing mixture on one half of each chicken breast. Fold the other half of the chicken breast over the filling. Secure with a wooden toothpick. Place chicken in an 8x8x2-inch baking dish. Sprinkle with paprika.

▪ Bake, covered, in a 350° oven about 25 minutes or till chicken is tender and no longer pink.

▪ Meanwhile, combine yogurt and marmalade. To serve, dollop about 1 tablespoon yogurt mixture atop each piece of chicken. Makes 4 servings.

Nutrition information per serving: 223 calories, 28 g protein, 12 g carbohydrate, 6 g fat, 73 mg cholesterol, 209 mg sodium, 363 mg potassium.

CHICKEN WITH MUSTARD RELISH

237 calories

Preparation Time: 10 min. ▪ Grilling Time: 35 min. ▪ Low Fat ▪ Low Cholesterol

2	whole medium chicken breasts (1½ pounds total)
2	teaspoons cooking oil
1	clove garlic, minced
¼	teaspoon chopped shallots *or* green onion
¼	teaspoon dried thyme, crushed
½	medium papaya
1	tablespoon Dijon-style mustard
1	tablespoon plain low-fat yogurt
½	cup finely chopped zucchini *or* yellow summer squash
¼	cup finely chopped red onion
4	radicchio *or* small red cabbage leaves

▪ Skin chicken breasts and halve them lengthwise. Combine oil, garlic, shallots, and thyme. Rub on chicken pieces.

▪ Grill chicken, bone side up, on an uncovered grill directly over *medium* coals for 20 minutes. Turn and grill for 15 to 25 minutes more or till chicken is tender and no longer pink.

▪ Meanwhile, peel, seed, and slice papaya. Set aside. For relish, in a small bowl stir together mustard and yogurt. Stir in zucchini or summer squash, and red onion. Spoon some of the relish into each radicchio leaf.

▪ To serve, place 3 papaya slices on each serving plate. Top with grilled chicken. Serve with relish cups. Serves 4.

Nutrition information per serving: 237 calories, 36 g protein, 6 g carbohydrate, 7 g fat, 97 mg cholesterol, 199 mg sodium, 468 mg potassium.

183

CHICKEN WITH WINE SAUCE

204 calories

Preparation Time: 30 min. ▪ Cooking Time: 35 min. ▪ Low Fat ▪ Low Cholesterol

2	**pounds meaty chicken pieces (breasts, thighs, and drumsticks), skinned**
	Nonstick spray coating
1	**cup sliced fresh mushrooms**
1	**small onion, chopped**
1	**teaspoon dried basil, crushed**
1	**clove garlic, minced**
⅓	**cup chicken broth**
⅓	**cup dry white wine**
¼	**teaspoon salt**
¼	**teaspoon pepper**
1	**tablespoon cornstarch**

▪ Rinse chicken; pat dry; set aside.

▪ Spray a large skillet with nonstick spray coating. Add mushrooms, onion, basil, and garlic. Cook over medium heat till onion is tender.

▪ Stir in chicken broth, wine, salt, and pepper. Arrange chicken in skillet. Bring to boiling; reduce heat. Cover and cook over low heat about 30 minutes or till chicken is tender and no longer pink. Transfer chicken and vegetables to a serving platter; keep warm.

▪ Measure cooking liquid. Add water to equal 1 cup, if necessary. Pour into skillet.

▪ Combine cornstarch and 1 tablespoon *water*. Stir into cooking liquid in skillet. Cook and stir till thickened and bubbly. Cook and stir for 2 minutes more. Serve over chicken. Makes 5 servings.

Nutrition information per serving: 204 calories, 27 g protein, 4 g carbohydrate, 7 g fat, 81 mg cholesterol, 232 mg sodium, 327 mg potassium.

MEDITERRANEAN-STYLE CHICKEN

312 calories

Preparation Time: 20 min. ▪ Cooking Time: 40 min. ▪ Low Fat ▪ Low Cholesterol

1½	to 2 pounds meaty chicken pieces (breasts, thighs, and drumsticks), skinned
	Nonstick spray coating
1	14½-ounce can tomatoes, cut up
¼	cup dry red wine
1	teaspoon sugar
1	teaspoon dried basil, crushed
1	clove garlic, minced
1	bay leaf
1	tablespoon water
2	teaspoons cornstarch
4	ounces spaghetti, cooked
¼	cup sliced pimiento-stuffed olives (optional)

■ Rinse chicken; pat dry.

■ Spray a 10-inch skillet with nonstick spray coating. Preheat over medium heat. Add chicken and brown for 10 to 15 minutes, turning to brown evenly.

■ Add *undrained* tomatoes, wine, sugar, basil, garlic, and bay leaf. Bring to boiling; reduce heat. Cover and simmer about 35 minutes or till chicken is tender. Remove chicken from skillet; keep warm.

■ In a small bowl stir together water and cornstarch. Stir into tomato mixture in skillet. Cook and stir till thickened and bubbly. Cook and stir for 2 minutes more.

■ Serve chicken and sauce over cooked spaghetti. Garnish with olives, if desired. Makes 4 servings.

Nutrition information per serving: 312 calories, 29 g protein, 29 g carbohydrate, 7 g fat, 76 mg cholesterol, 242 mg sodium, 518 mg potassium.

GARLIC-CLOVE CHICKEN

206 calories

Preparation Time: 20 min. ▪ Cooking Time: 45 min. ▪ Low Fat ▪ Low Cholesterol

Cooking garlic without peeling it gives foods a mild garlic flavor. To eat one of the cooked cloves, squeeze it between your thumb and index finger until the clove slips out of its peel.

	Nonstick spray coating
1½	**to 2 pounds meaty chicken pieces (breasts, thighs, and drumsticks), skinned**
25	**cloves garlic (about ½ cup or 2 to 3 bulbs)**
¼	**cup dry white wine**
4	**teaspoons lemon juice**
	Salt
	Ground red pepper

▪ Spray a large skillet with nonstick spray coating. Preheat skillet over medium heat. Add chicken and brown over medium heat for 10 minutes, turning to brown evenly.

▪ Place chicken in an 8x8x2- or 10x6x2-inch baking dish. Add *unpeeled* garlic cloves.

▪ In a small bowl combine wine and lemon juice; pour over chicken. Lightly sprinkle chicken with salt and ground red pepper.

▪ Bake, covered, in a 325° oven 45 to 50 minutes or till chicken is tender. Makes 4 servings.

Nutrition information per serving: 206 calories, 26 g protein, 7 g carbohydrate, 7 g fat, 76 mg cholesterol, 144 mg sodium, 306 mg potassium.

INDIAN-STYLE CHICKEN

325 calories

Preparation Time: 20 min. ▪ Cooking Time: 50 min. ▪ Low Cholesterol

2	large onions, thinly sliced
4	cloves garlic, minced
1	tablespoon olive oil *or* cooking oil
2	cups cooked brown rice
	Nonstick spray coating
2½	pounds meaty chicken pieces (breasts, thighs, and drumsticks), skinned
1	8-ounce carton plain low-fat yogurt
2	tablespoons all-purpose flour
1	teaspoon ground cumin
¼	teaspoon ground ginger
½	cup chopped green *or* sweet red pepper
2	medium tomatoes, seeded and coarsely chopped
	Parsley sprigs

▪ In a large skillet cook onion and garlic in hot oil till onion is tender but not brown. Stir in cooked brown rice.

▪ Spray a 12x7½x2-inch baking dish with nonstick spray coating. Spread rice mixture in baking dish. Arrange chicken pieces atop rice.

▪ In a mixing bowl stir together yogurt, flour, cumin, ginger, and ½ teaspoon *salt.* Stir in chopped green or sweet red pepper. Spoon over chicken in dish.

▪ Bake, covered, in a 350° oven for 50 to 60 minutes or till chicken is tender. Serve with chopped tomatoes. Garnish with parsley. Makes 6 servings.

Nutrition information per serving: 325 calories, 29 g protein, 29 g carbohydrate, 10 g fat, 73 mg cholesterol, 284 mg sodium, 565 mg potassium.

187

SPICY BARBECUED CHICKEN

152 calories

Preparation Time: 10 min. ▪ Grilling Time: 35 min. ▪ Low Cholesterol

½	cup cider vinegar
1	tablespoon Worcestershire sauce *or* white wine Worcestershire sauce
1	tablespoon prepared mustard
1	teaspoon paprika
½	teaspoon pepper
¼	teaspoon celery seed
¼	teaspoon bottled hot pepper sauce
⅛	teaspoon salt
2	pounds meaty chicken pieces (breasts, thighs, and drumsticks), skinned

▪ For sauce, in a small saucepan combine vinegar, Worcestershire sauce, mustard, paprika, pepper, celery seed, hot pepper sauce, and salt. Bring to boiling; reduce heat. Simmer 5 minutes, stirring to dissolve mustard.

▪ Brush chicken pieces with sauce. Grill chicken pieces, bone side up, on an uncovered grill directly over *medium-hot* coals for 20 minutes. Turn and grill 15 to 25 minutes more or till no longer pink, brushing frequently with sauce. Serves 6.

▪ **Broiling directions:** Place chicken pieces, bone side up, on the unheated rack of a broiler pan. Brush with sauce. Broil 4 to 5 inches from the heat about 20 minutes or till lightly browned. Turn chicken pieces skin side up and broil 5 to 15 minutes more or till chicken is no longer pink. Brush occasionally with sauce.

Nutrition information per serving: 152 calories, 22 g protein, 2 g carbohydrate, 6 g fat, 67 mg cholesterol, 168 mg sodium, 219 mg potassium.

PAELLA

Preparation Time: 15 min. ▪ Cooking Time: 40 min. ▪ Low Fat

1½	pounds meaty chicken pieces (breast halves, thighs, and drumsticks)
	Nonstick spray coating
1	cup chopped onion
1	clove garlic, minced
1	14½-ounce can chicken broth
1	7½-ounce can tomatoes, cut up
¼	teaspoon dried thyme, crushed
¼	teaspoon ground saffron
⅛	to ¼ teaspoon ground red pepper
1	cup long grain rice
1	medium green *or* sweet red pepper
½	pound medium shrimp, peeled and deveined
1	cup frozen peas

▪ Rinse chicken; pat dry. Remove and discard skin.

▪ Spray a Dutch oven with nonstick spray coating. Add onion and garlic. Cook over medium heat till onion is tender but not brown.

▪ Add chicken pieces, chicken broth, *undrained* tomatoes, thyme, saffron, and ground red pepper. Bring to boiling; reduce heat. Cover and simmer for 15 minutes.

▪ Stir in rice. Cover and simmer for 15 minutes more or till rice is nearly tender.

▪ Meanwhile, cut green or sweet red pepper into strips. Stir into rice with the shrimp and peas. Cover and simmer for 10 minutes more or till rice and chicken are tender and shrimp turns pink. Makes 6 servings.

Nutrition information per serving: 313 calories, 30 g protein, 34 g carbohydrate, 6 g fat, 108 mg cholesterol, 410 mg sodium, 496 mg potassium.

PINEAPPLE-CHICKEN AND RICE BAKE   280 calories

Advance Preparation Time: 15 min. ▪ Marinating Time: 4 hrs. ▪ Final Preparation Time: 1 hr. 10 min. ▪ Low Fat ▪ Low Cholesterol

A hearty main dish that's ready to serve with little effort.

2	**pounds meaty chicken pieces (breasts, thighs, and drumsticks), skinned**
½	**cup chopped onion**
1	**large red sweet pepper, cut into ¾-inch squares**
1	**8-ounce can pineapple chunks (juice pack)**
¼	**cup frozen orange juice concentrate, thawed**
2	**tablespoons soy sauce**
⅛	**teaspoon ground cloves**
⅔	**cup long grain rice**
1	**cup chicken broth**
	Parsley sprigs *or* paprika

▪ Place chicken pieces, onion, and red pepper into a large plastic bag set in a deep bowl. In a small mixing bowl stir together *undrained* pineapple, orange juice concentrate, soy sauce, and cloves. Pour pineapple mixture over chicken mixture in bag. Seal bag. Marinate the mixture in the refrigerator for 4 to 24 hours, turning bag occasionally.

▪ Before baking, drain chicken, reserving marinade and vegetables. Set chicken aside. Place *uncooked* rice in a 12x7½x2-inch baking dish. Stir chicken broth and the reserved marinade-vegetable mixture into rice. Top with chicken pieces. Cover with foil. Bake in a 375° oven about 1 hour or till chicken and rice are tender. Garnish with parsley or sprinkle with paprika. Makes 6 servings.

Nutrition information per serving: 280 calories, 25 g protein, 30 g carbohydrate, 6 g fat, 67 mg cholesterol, 540 mg sodium, 449 mg potassium.

OVEN-FRIED CHICKEN

168 calories

Preparation Time: 15 min. ▪ Cooking Time: 45 min. ▪ Low Cholesterol ▪ Low Sodium

2	**to 2½ pounds meaty chicken pieces (breasts, thighs, and drumsticks), skinned**
¼	**cup cornflake crumbs**
1	**tablespoon snipped fresh parsley**
⅓	**cup plain low-fat yogurt**
1	**clove garlic, minced**
2	**teaspoons Worcestershire sauce *or* white wine Worcestershire sauce**
	Dash ground red pepper

■ Rinse chicken; pat dry. Place on a rack in a shallow baking pan; set aside.

■ In a small mixing bowl combine cornflake crumbs and parsley; set aside.

■ In another small mixing bowl combine yogurt, garlic, Worcestershire sauce, and pepper.

■ Brush chicken with yogurt mixture, then sprinkle with crumb mixture.

■ Bake, uncovered, in a 375° oven for 45 to 55 minutes or till chicken is tender and no longer pink. Makes 6 servings.

Nutrition information per serving: 168 calories, 23 g protein, 4 g carbohydrate, 6 g fat, 68 mg cholesterol, 137 mg sodium, 224 mg potassium.

CHICKEN AND BARLEY BAKE

257 calories

Preparation Time: 15 min. ▪ Cooking Time: 1 hr. ▪ Low Fat ▪ Low Cholesterol

Spend just a little time getting dinner in the oven, then sit back and relax for an hour.

1	cup chopped onion
¾	cup chopped carrots
¾	cup water
½	cup pearl barley
1½	teaspoons instant chicken bouillon granules
½	teaspoon poultry seasoning
1	clove garlic, minced
4	chicken thighs, skinned (1½ pounds total)
2	tablespoons fresh snipped parsley

▪ In a medium saucepan combine onion, carrots, water, barley, bouillon granules, poultry seasoning, and garlic. Heat mixture to boiling.

▪ Pour *hot* mixture into a 1½-quart casserole. Arrange chicken thighs atop mixture.

▪ Bake, covered, in a 350° oven for 1 hour or till barley and chicken are tender. Sprinkle with parsley. Makes 4 servings.

Nutrition information per serving: 257 calories, 20 g protein, 27 g carbohydrate, 8 g fat, 62 mg cholesterol, 212 mg sodium, 393 mg potassium.

CHICKEN LIVERS IN ITALIAN TOMATO SAUCE 273 calories

Preparation Time: 20 min. ▪ Cooking Time: 10 min. ▪ Low Fat

1	16-ounce can tomatoes, cut up
1	tablespoon cornstarch
1	teaspoon sugar
½	teaspoon Italian seasoning
⅛	to ¼ teaspoon crushed red pepper
	Nonstick spray coating
1	cup thinly bias-sliced carrots
½	cup chopped onion
2	cloves garlic, minced
1	medium green pepper, cut into strips
1	tablespoon cooking oil
½	pound chicken livers, halved
4	ounces spaghetti, cooked and drained

▪ For sauce, stir together *undrained* tomatoes, cornstarch, sugar, Italian seasoning, and red pepper. Set aside.

▪ Spray a wok or large skillet with nonstick spray coating. Stir-fry carrots for 2 minutes. Add onion and garlic; stir-fry for 1 minute. Add green pepper and stir-fry 1 to 3 minutes more or till vegetables are crisp-tender. Remove from wok.

▪ Add oil to hot wok. Stir-fry chicken livers for 2 to 3 minutes or till slightly pink in center. Push livers from center of wok. Stir sauce; add to center of wok. Cook and stir till thickened and bubbly.

▪ Return vegetables to wok; stir all ingredients together to coat with sauce. Cook and stir for 1 minute more or till heated through. Serve immediately over spaghetti. Serves 4.

Nutrition information per serving: 273 calories, 16 g protein, 38 g carbohydrate, 7 g fat, 249 mg cholesterol, 245 mg sodium, 654 mg potassium.

ORIENTAL CHICKEN IN TORTILLAS

310 calories

Preparation Time: 31 min. ▪ Cooking Time: 10 min. ▪ Low Fat

8	**dried mushrooms**
1	**tablespoon soy sauce**
1	**teaspoon cornstarch**
	Nonstick spray coating
2	**beaten eggs**
1	**tablespoon cooking oil**
1	**clove garlic, minced**
9	**ounces boned skinless chicken breast halves, cut into bite-size strips**
1	**cup shredded bok choy *or* cabbage**
½	**of an 8-ounce can (⅓ cup) sliced bamboo shoots, drained and cut into strips**
2	**green onions, sliced**
8	**6-inch flour tortillas**

▪ In a small bowl pour hot water over dried mushrooms to cover. Let stand for 30 minutes; drain well. Cut mushrooms into thin strips, discarding stems. Set aside.

▪ For sauce, in another bowl stir together soy sauce, cornstarch, and ⅓ cup *water*. Set aside.

▪ Spray a *cold* wok or large skillet with nonstick spray coating. Preheat over medium heat. Add eggs. Lift and tilt the wok or skillet to form a thin sheet of egg. Cook, without stirring, till set. Slide egg sheet onto a cutting board. Cut egg into narrow, bite-size strips. Set aside.

▪ Preheat the same wok or skillet over high heat. Add oil. Stir-fry garlic for 30 seconds. Add chicken and stir-fry for 2 to 3 minutes or till no longer pink. Push from center of wok.

▪ Stir sauce and pour into center of wok. Cook and stir till bubbly. Stir in bok choy, bamboo shoots, green onions, mushrooms, and egg strips. Cover; cook 1 minute or till hot.

▪ Spoon some of the chicken mixture into each tortilla. Roll up tortilla and serve immediately. Serves 4.

Nutrition information per serving: 310 calories, 27 g protein, 29 g carbohydrate, 10 g fat, 192 mg cholesterol, 349 mg sodium, 515 mg potassium.

NUTTY CHICKEN FINGERS

Preparation Time: 8 min. ▪ Cooking Time: 7 min. ▪ Low Cholesterol

217 calories

Pecans add a pleasing crunch to moist, tender chicken.

⅓	cup cornflake crumbs
½	cup finely chopped pecans
1	tablespoon dried parsley flakes
⅛	teaspoon salt
⅛	teaspoon garlic powder
12	ounces boned skinless chicken breast halves, cut into 1x3-inch strips
2	tablespoons skim milk

■ In a shallow dish combine cornflake crumbs, pecans, parsley, salt, and garlic powder. Dip chicken in milk, then roll in crumb mixture. Place in a 15x10x1-inch baking pan.

■ Bake in a 400° oven for 7 to 9 minutes or till chicken is tender and no longer pink. Makes 5 servings.

Nutrition information per serving: 217 calories, 23 g protein, 7 g carbohydrate, 10 g fat, 59 mg cholesterol, 178 mg sodium, 245 mg potassium.

CHICKEN FAJITAS

297 calories

Preparation Time: 10 min. ▪ Cooking Time: 10 min. ▪ Low Fat ▪ Low Cholesterol

Plain low-fat yogurt is always a good low-calorie substitute for sour cream.

8	6-inch flour tortillas
	Nonstick spray coating
1	small onion, sliced and separated into rings
2	cloves garlic, minced
1	medium sweet red *or* green pepper, cut into bite-size strips
1	tablespoon cooking oil
9	ounces boned skinless chicken breast halves, cut into bite-size strips
⅓	cup salsa
2	cups shredded lettuce
¼	cup plain low-fat yogurt
1	green onion, thinly sliced

▪ Wrap tortillas in foil. Place in a 300° oven for 10 to 12 minutes or till heated through.

▪ Meanwhile, spray a large skillet with nonstick spray coating. Add onion and garlic; stir-fry for 2 minutes. Add red pepper; stir-fry for 1 to 2 minutes more or till vegetables are crisp-tender. Remove from skillet. Add oil to skillet. Add chicken; stir-fry 3 to 5 minutes or till chicken is tender and no longer pink. Return vegetables to skillet. Add salsa. Cook and stir till heated through.

▪ To serve, divide chicken mixture evenly among tortillas. Top with shredded lettuce. Dollop with yogurt and sprinkle with green onion. Roll up tortillas. Makes 4 servings.

Nutrition information per serving: 297 calories, 24 g protein, 33 g carbohydrate, 7 g fat, 55 mg cholesterol, 197 mg sodium, 373 mg potassium.

FIESTA CHICKEN

248 calories

Preparation Time: 7 min. ▪ Cooking Time: 19 min. ▪ Low Fat ▪ Low Cholesterol

1	8-ounce can tomato sauce
½	cup orange juice
½	cup finely chopped onion
2	tablespoons raisins
2	tablespoons chopped pimiento
½	teaspoon dried oregano, crushed
½	teaspoon chili powder
1	clove garlic, minced
	Several dashes bottled hot pepper sauce
12	ounces boned skinless chicken breast halves, cut into 1-inch pieces
2	teaspoons cornstarch
1	tablespoon water
¼	cup snipped parsley
3	cups hot cooked rice

■ In a large skillet combine tomato sauce, orange juice, onion, raisins, pimiento, oregano, chili powder, garlic, and hot pepper sauce. Bring to boiling; reduce heat. Cover and simmer for 5 minutes.

■ Stir in chicken; return to boiling. Cover and simmer 12 to 15 minutes more or till chicken is tender and no longer pink.

■ Meanwhile combine cornstarch and water. Stir into skillet. Cook and stir till thickened and bubbly. Cook and stir 2 minutes more.

■ Toss parsley with rice. Serve chicken mixture over rice. Makes 6 servings.

Nutrition information per serving: 248 calories, 21 g protein, 35 g carbohydrate, 2 g fat, 49 mg cholesterol, 277 mg sodium, 430 mg potassium.

CHICKEN AND ZUCCHINI IN MUSTARD SAUCE 218 calories

Preparation Time: 15 min. ▪ Cooking Time: 8 min. ▪ Low Cholesterol

½	cup plain low-fat yogurt
2	tablespoons Dijon-style mustard
¼	teaspoon dried tarragon, crushed
	Nonstick spray coating
1	medium carrot, cut into thin strips (½ cup)
1	clove garlic, minced
2	medium zucchini, cut into thin strips (2 cups)
1	tablespoon cooking oil
12	ounces boned skinless chicken breast halves, cut into bite-size pieces
2	cups hot cooked noodles (optional)

▪ For sauce, in a small bowl stir together yogurt, mustard, and tarragon. Set aside.

▪ Spray a wok or large skillet with nonstick spray coating. Heat over medium-high heat. Stir-fry carrot and garlic 1 minute. Add zucchini; stir-fry about 3 minutes more or till vegetables are crisp-tender. Remove from wok.

▪ Add oil to hot wok. Stir-fry chicken for 2 to 3 minutes or till no longer pink. Return vegetables to wok. Add sauce to wok; toss to coat all ingredients with sauce. Cook and stir for 1 minute or till heated through.

▪ If desired, serve with hot cooked noodles. Serves 4.

Nutrition information per serving: 218 calories, 29 g protein, 6 g carbohydrate, 8 g fat, 74 mg cholesterol, 313 mg sodium, 523 mg potassium.

STROGANOFF-STYLE CHICKEN

321 calories

Preparation Time: 7 min. ▪ Cooking Time: 10 min. ▪ Low Fat ▪ Low Cholesterol

6	cups water
5	ounces noodles (about 3 cups)
	Nonstick spray coating
½	cup chopped onion
1	tablespoon cooking oil
12	ounces boned skinless chicken breast halves, cubed
1	8-ounce carton plain low-fat yogurt
2	tablespoons all-purpose flour
1	teaspoon paprika
¼	teaspoon salt
2	4-ounce cans sliced mushrooms

▪ Lightly salt the 6 cups water; bring to boiling. Add noodles; cook according to package directions. Drain well; set aside.

▪ Meanwhile, spray a 10-inch skillet with nonstick spray coating. Cook onion in skillet till nearly tender.

▪ Add oil to skillet. Add chicken and cook for 2 to 3 minutes or till chicken is tender and no longer pink.

▪ In a small bowl stir together yogurt, flour, paprika, and salt.

▪ Add *undrained* mushrooms to skillet. Stir in yogurt mixture. Cook and stir till slightly thickened and bubbly. Cook and stir 1 minute more. Serve over hot noodles. Makes 5 servings.

Nutrition information per serving: 321 calories, 27 g protein, 29 g carbohydrate, 10 g fat, 90 mg cholesterol, 369 mg sodium, 401 mg potassium.

BAKED CURRIED CHICKEN AND RICE

178 calories

Preparation Time: 15 min. ▪ Cooking Time: 45 min. ▪ Low Fat ▪ Low Cholesterol

1	cup water
1	8-ounce can stewed tomatoes
¾	cup quick-cooking brown rice
¼	cup snipped dried apricots
¼	cup raisins
1	tablespoon lemon juice
2	teaspoons curry powder
1	teaspoon instant chicken bouillon granules
½	teaspoon cinnamon
¼	teaspoon salt
2	cloves garlic, minced
1	bay leaf
¾	pound boneless chicken *or* turkey, cut into 1-inch pieces

▪ In a medium saucepan stir together water, *undrained* tomatoes, rice, apricots, raisins, lemon juice, curry powder, bouillon granules, cinnamon, salt, garlic, and bay leaf. Heat to boiling. Stir in chicken or turkey.

▪ Pour the hot chicken mixture into a 1½-quart casserole. Bake, covered, in a 350° oven about 45 minutes or till rice is tender and chicken is no longer pink, stirring occasionally. Remove bay leaf. Makes 5 servings.

Nutrition information per serving: 178 calories, 15 g protein, 25 g carbohydrate, 3 g fat, 36 mg cholesterol, 445 mg sodium, 395 mg potassium.

SOUTHWESTERN CHICKEN

333 calories

Preparation Time: 10 min. ▪ Cooking Time: 27 min. ▪ Low Fat

Nonstick spray coating
1 **cup cubed cooked chicken** *or* **turkey**
1 **8-ounce can whole kernel corn, drained**
1 **4-ounce can chopped green chili peppers, drained**
2 **beaten eggs**
⅔ **cup skim milk**
¾ **cup all-purpose flour**
¼ **teaspoon salt**
⅛ **teaspoon pepper**
½ **cup finely shredded cheddar cheese (2 ounces)**
½ **cup salsa**
½ **cup plain low-fat yogurt**

■ Spray a 9-inch pie plate with nonstick spray coating.

■ In a medium mixing bowl stir together chicken or turkey, corn, and green chili peppers. Spread mixture in pie plate.

■ In the same bowl stir together eggs and milk. Beat in flour, salt, and pepper. Pour over chicken mixture.

■ Bake, uncovered, in a 400° oven for 25 to 30 minutes or till top is set and lightly browned. Sprinkle with cheese and bake for 2 to 3 minutes more or till cheese melts. Serve with salsa and yogurt. Makes 4 servings.

Nutrition information per serving: 333 calories, 22 g protein, 36 g carbohydrate, 11 g fat, 181 mg cholesterol, 1,019 mg sodium, 503 mg potassium.

CHICKEN AND SPINACH CREPES

318 calories

Preparation Time: 1 hr. ▪ Cooking Time: 30 min.

Pour 2 tablespoons of the crepe batter into a preheated 6-inch skillet. Lift and tilt the skillet to swirl the batter and coat the pan with a thin, even layer of batter.

Crepes
2 **cups sliced fresh mushrooms**
½ **cup shredded carrot**
½ **cup sliced leek *or* green onions**
½ **cup water**
¾ **cup evaporated skim milk**
2 **tablespoons cornstarch**
¼ **teaspoon salt**
⅛ **teaspoon pepper**
2 **tablespoons dry sherry**
1 **cup shredded cheddar cheese (4 ounces)**
1 **10-ounce package frozen chopped spinach, thawed and well drained**
2 **cups finely chopped cooked chicken *or* turkey**

■ Prepare crepes. For sauce, combine mushrooms, carrot, leek, and water. Cover; simmer 5 minutes. *Do not drain.* Combine milk, cornstarch, salt, and pepper. Stir into vegetable mixture. Cook and stir till thickened and bubbly. Stir in sherry and *½ cup* of the cheese till melted.

■ For filling, combine spinach, chicken, and *1 cup* sauce. Spoon *¼ cup* filling onto unbrowned side of *each* crepe. Roll up. Arrange crepes, seam side down, in a 13x9x2-inch baking dish. Spoon remaining sauce over crepes. Cover; bake in a 375° oven 25 minutes or till hot. Sprinkle with remaining cheese. Bake, uncovered, 5 minutes more. Serves 6.

■ **Crepes:** Combine ¾ cup *all-purpose flour,* 1 cup *skim milk,* 1 beaten *egg,* and a dash *salt.* Beat till blended. Spray a 6-inch skillet with *nonstick spray coating.* Preheat skillet; then remove skillet from heat. Pour in *2 tablespoons* batter. Lift and tilt skillet to spread batter. Return to heat; brown on one side only. Invert skillet over paper towels; remove crepe. Repeat with remaining batter. Makes 12 crepes.

Nutrition information per serving: 318 calories, 27 g protein, 26 g carbohydrate, 11 g fat, 111 mg cholesterol, 370 mg sodium, 647 mg potassium.

CHICKEN TACOS

283 calories

Preparation Time: 10 min. ▪ Cooking Time: 5 min. ▪ Low Cholesterol

If you have time, warm the taco shells in the oven or microwave.

	Nonstick spray coating
1	cup chopped onion
1	clove garlic, minced
2	cups chopped cooked chicken *or* two 5-ounce cans chunk-style chicken
1	8-ounce can tomato sauce
1	4-ounce can chopped green chili peppers, drained
12	taco shells
2	cups shredded lettuce
1	medium tomato, seeded and chopped
½	cup finely shredded cheddar *or* Monterey Jack cheese (2 ounces)

■ Spray a 10-inch skillet with nonstick spray coating. Add onion and garlic; cook till tender.

■ Stir in chicken, tomato sauce, and green chili peppers; heat through.

■ Divide chicken mixture among taco shells. Top with lettuce, tomato, and cheese. Makes 6 servings.

Nutrition information per serving: 283 calories, 20 g protein, 25 g carbohydrate, 12 g fat, 51 mg cholesterol, 729 mg sodium, 464 mg potassium.

BROCCOLI AND CHICKEN CASSEROLE

290 calories

Preparation Time: 20 min. ▪ Cooking Time: 40 min. ▪ Low Cholesterol

Swiss cheese adds a rich flavor to the creamy sauce.

4	**ounces medium noodles**
2½	**cups chopped cooked chicken *or* turkey**
1	**10-ounce package frozen chopped broccoli, thawed**
½	**cup sliced green onions**
1	**10¾-ounce can condensed cream of mushroom soup**
½	**cup skim milk**
½	**cup shredded Swiss cheese (2 ounces)**
1	**teaspoon dried basil, crushed**
⅛	**teaspoon pepper**
	Paprika

▪ Cook noodles according to package directions. Drain well.

▪ In a 2-quart casserole stir together noodles, chicken or turkey, broccoli, and green onions.

▪ In a medium mixing bowl stir together soup, milk, cheese, basil, and pepper. Stir into noodle mixture.

▪ Bake, covered, in a 350° oven for 40 to 45 minutes or till heated through. Sprinkle with paprika. Makes 6 servings.

Nutrition information per serving: 290 calories, 25 g protein, 22 g carbohydrate, 11 g fat, 61 mg cholesterol, 508 mg sodium, 362 mg potassium.

ORANGE-ROASTED CORNISH GAME HENS

195 calories

Preparation Time: 10 min. ▪ Cooking Time: 45 min. ▪ Low Fat ▪ Low Cholesterol ▪ Low Sodium

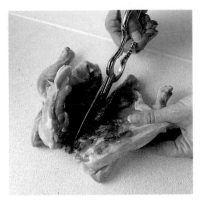

Use kitchen shears to cut a Cornish game hen in half. Begin by cutting through the breastbone, just off center. Then cut through the center of the backbone.

	Nonstick spray coating
1	small onion, finely chopped
1	clove garlic, minced
½	cup chicken broth
1	teaspoon finely shredded orange peel
½	cup orange juice
2	tablespoons honey
4	teaspoons cornstarch
3	1- to 1¼-pound Cornish game hens, split lengthwise
1	medium orange, cut into 6 wedges
	Orange slices (optional)
	Parsley (optional)

▪ Spray a small saucepan with nonstick spray coating. For sauce, cook onion and garlic in the saucepan till onion is tender.

▪ In a small bowl stir together chicken broth, orange peel, orange juice, honey, and cornstarch. Stir into onion mixture in saucepan. Cook and stir till thickened and bubbly. Cook and stir for 2 minutes more. Remove from heat.

▪ Rinse hen halves; pat dry. In a shallow roasting pan place each hen half atop one orange wedge. Baste with some of the sauce.

▪ Roast in a 375° oven for ¾ to 1 hour or till tender and no longer pink. Baste hen halves with sauce after 30 minutes.

▪ Transfer hen halves to a serving platter. If necessary, reheat remaining sauce and serve with hen halves. If desired, garnish with orange slices and parsley. Makes 6 servings.

Nutrition information per serving: 195 calories, 27 g protein, 13 g carbohydrate, 3 g fat, 72 mg cholesterol, 128 mg sodium, 331 mg potassium.

TURKEY WITH CRANBERRY SAUCE

181 calories

Preparation Time: 25 min. ▪ Cooking Time: 2½ hrs. ▪ Low Fat ▪ Low Cholesterol ▪ Low Sodium

Buy cranberries in season and freeze them so you can enjoy this classic combination anytime.

1	2½- to 3-pound turkey breast half with bone, skinned
1½	cups cranberries
½	cup shredded carrot
½	teaspoon finely shredded orange peel
½	cup orange juice
2	tablespoons raisins
2	tablespoons sugar
⅛	teaspoon ground cloves
1	tablespoon water
2	teaspoons cornstarch

▪ Thaw turkey, if frozen. Rinse turkey and pat dry.

▪ Place turkey breast, bone side down, on a rack in a shallow roasting pan. Insert a meat thermometer into the thickest portion of the breast. Cover breast loosely with foil.

▪ Roast in a 325° oven for 2½ to 3 hours or till thermometer registers 165°. Remove foil the last 30 minutes of roasting. Let turkey stand, covered, for 15 minutes before slicing.

▪ Meanwhile, for sauce, in a small saucepan combine cranberries, shredded carrot, orange peel, orange juice, raisins, sugar, and cloves. Bring to boiling; reduce heat. Simmer, uncovered, for 3 to 4 minutes or till cranberry skins pop.

▪ In a small bowl combine water and cornstarch. Stir into cranberries in saucepan. Cook and stir till thickened and bubbly. Cook and stir 2 minutes more.

▪ Serve turkey with cranberry sauce. Makes 8 servings.

Nutrition information per serving: 181 calories, 27 g protein, 10 g carbohydrate, 3 g fat, 62 mg cholesterol, 60 mg sodium, 358 mg potassium.

CORIANDER TURKEY BREAST

129 calories

Preparation Time: 5 min. ▪ Cooking Time: 1¼ hrs. ▪ Low Fat ▪ Low Cholesterol ▪ Low Sodium

To check the coal temperature, hold your hand over the coals where the food will be and count, "One thousand one, one thousand two. . . ." If you have to move your hand away after 2 seconds, the coals are hot; 3 seconds, medium-hot; 4 seconds, medium; 5 seconds, medium-slow; or 6 seconds, slow.

1	2- to 3-pound fresh or frozen turkey breast portion, thawed
2	teaspoons ground coriander
½	teaspoon onion powder
¼	teaspoon chili powder
	Dash ground red pepper
1	tablespoon margarine
1	tablespoon lemon juice

▪ Remove skin and excess fat from turkey breast. In a small saucepan cook coriander, onion powder, chili powder, and red pepper in margarine for 1 minute. Remove from heat and stir in lemon juice. Spread spice mixture on all sides of turkey.

▪ In a covered grill arrange *medium-hot* coals around a drip pan. Test for *medium* heat above the pan. Insert a meat thermometer into the thickest part of turkey breast, but not touching the bone (if present). Place turkey breast on grill rack over drip pan but not over coals. Lower grill hood. Grill 1¼ to 1¾ hours or till thermometer registers 170°. Add more coals as needed. Makes 8 servings.

Nutrition information per serving: 129 calories, 26 g protein, 0 g carbohydrate, 2 g fat, 71 mg cholesterol, 62 mg sodium, 261 mg potassium.

MARINATED TURKEY SLICES

183 calories

Preparation Time: 15 min. ▪ Marinating Time: 2 hrs. ▪ Cooking Time: 12 min. ▪ Low Cholesterol

6	ounces turkey breast slices
¼	teaspoon finely shredded lemon peel
1	tablespoon lemon juice
2	teaspoons cooking oil
½	teaspoon instant chicken bouillon granules
⅛	teaspoon dried thyme, crushed
1	clove garlic, minced
	Dash salt
	Dash pepper
	Nonstick spray coating
1½	cups sliced zucchini *or* yellow summer squash
½	cup sliced fresh mushrooms
1½	teaspoons cornstarch
	Hot cooked rice (optional)

▪ If necessary, cut turkey into 2 equal portions.

▪ For marinade, in a small bowl stir together lemon peel, lemon juice, oil, bouillon granules, thyme, garlic, salt, pepper, and ¼ cup *water*.

▪ Place turkey in a plastic bag set in a bowl. Pour marinade over turkey. Close bag and refrigerate for 2 hours.

▪ Remove turkey from bag, reserving marinade.

▪ Spray an 8-inch skillet with nonstick spray coating. Add turkey slices. Cook over medium heat about 4 minutes or till tender and no longer pink, turning once. Remove turkey from skillet; keep warm.

▪ Add zucchini, mushrooms, and 2 tablespoons *water* to the skillet. Cover and cook for 3 to 4 minutes or till zucchini is crisp-tender.

▪ Meanwhile, stir together the reserved marinade and cornstarch. Add to the vegetables in the skillet. Cook and stir till thickened and bubbly. Cook and stir 1 minute more. Serve the vegetables with turkey slices and, if desired, rice. Serves 2.

Nutrition information per serving: 183 calories, 21 g protein, 8 g carbohydrate, 7 g fat, 44 mg cholesterol, 205 mg sodium, 641 mg potassium.

VEGETABLE-STUFFED TURKEY ROLL   146 calories

Preparation Time: 40 min. ▪ Cooking Time: 1¼ hrs. ▪ Low Fat ▪ Low Cholesterol ▪ Low Sodium

To butterfly the boned turkey breast, begin at one end and cut lengthwise from one side of the breast to within 1 inch of the opposite side.

1	2¼- to 2¾-pound turkey breast half, skinned and boned
	Nonstick spray coating
2	cups sliced fresh mushrooms
½	cup shredded carrot
½	cup thinly sliced celery
¼	cup sliced green onions
½	teaspoon dried thyme, crushed
	Dash pepper
1	tablespoon lemon juice
1	teaspoon instant chicken bouillon granules
1	cup soft bread cubes
1	to 2 tablespoons water

▪ Rinse turkey; pat dry. Butterfly breast. Open meat and lay flat between 2 pieces of clear plastic wrap. With a meat mallet pound turkey to ½-inch thickness (about a 12x10-inch rectangle).

▪ For stuffing, spray a large skillet with nonstick spray coating. Add mushrooms, carrot, celery, green onions, thyme, and pepper. Cook over medium heat till tender. Stir in lemon juice and bouillon granules. Add bread cubes; toss lightly to mix. Stir in enough of the water to moisten. Spoon stuffing over pounded turkey.

▪ Roll up turkey and stuffing starting from a long side. Tuck ends under; tie turkey roll with string. Place on a rack in a shallow baking pan.

▪ Bake in a 350° oven, covered loosely with foil, for 1 hour. Remove foil. Bake 15 to 30 minutes more or till a meat thermometer registers 170°. Remove string. Let stand 10 minutes before slicing. Cut into ½-inch slices to serve. Makes 8 servings.

Nutrition information per serving: 146 calories, 27 g protein, 6 g carbohydrate, 1 g fat, 71 mg cholesterol, 136 mg sodium, 376 mg potassium.

GLAZED TURKEY STEAKS

143 calories

Preparation Time: 4 min. ▪ Grilling Time: 12 min. ▪ Low Fat ▪ Low Cholesterol

2	tablespoons orange marmalade
1	tablespoon lemon *or* lime juice
2	teaspoons soy sauce
1	clove garlic, minced
¼	teaspoon curry powder
4	turkey breast tenderloin steaks (4 ounces each)

■ For glaze, in a small bowl stir together marmalade, lemon or lime juice, soy sauce, garlic, and curry powder. Brush some of the glaze over both sides of turkey steaks.

■ Grill turkey on an uncovered grill directly over *medium* coals for 6 minutes. Turn and brush with glaze. Grill 6 to 9 minutes more or till turkey is tender and no longer pink. Makes 4 servings.

■ **Broiling directions:** Place turkey on unheated rack of a broiler pan. Broil 4 to 5 inches from heat for 3 minutes. Turn and brush with glaze. Broil 3 to 5 minutes more or till no longer pink.

Nutrition information per serving: 143 calories, 26 g protein, 7 g carbohydrate, 1 g fat, 71 mg cholesterol, 217 mg sodium, 272 mg potassium.

TURKEY ROLLS DIVAN

227 calories

Preparation Time: 20 min. ▪ Cooking Time: 30 min. ▪ Low Cholesterol

Arrange the broccoli spears crosswise near one end of the turkey portion. Bring that end of the turkey up and over the broccoli and continue rolling up the turkey.

¾	**pound turkey breast tenderloin**
1	**10¾-ounce can condensed cream of mushroom soup**
¼	**cup skim milk**
2	**tablespoons dry sherry**
⅛	**teaspoon ground nutmeg**
	Dash ground red pepper
8	**broccoli spears, cooked and drained, *or* one 10-ounce package frozen broccoli spears, cooked and drained**
¼	**cup grated Parmesan cheese**

▪ Cut turkey into 4 equal portions. Place one piece of turkey between two pieces of clear plastic wrap. Working from the center to the edges, pound the turkey lightly with a meat mallet till the tenderloin is ¼ inch thick. Remove plastic wrap. Repeat with remaining turkey.

▪ For sauce, in a medium mixing bowl stir together soup, milk, dry sherry, nutmeg, and red pepper. Set aside.

▪ Divide broccoli among turkey slices, placing spears crosswise near one end of each slice. Spoon about *1 tablespoon* of the sauce over *each* portion of broccoli. Roll turkey around broccoli and sauce.

▪ Arrange turkey rolls, seam side down, in a 10x6x2-inch baking dish. Pour remaining sauce over turkey rolls. Sprinkle with Parmesan cheese.

▪ Bake, uncovered, in a 350° oven for 30 minutes or till turkey is no longer pink. Makes 4 servings.

Nutrition information per serving: 227 calories, 25 g protein, 11 g carbohydrate, 8 g fat, 59 mg cholesterol, 790 mg sodium, 388 mg potassium.

211

TURKEY WITH HONEY-MUSTARD SAUCE   113 calories

Preparation Time: 10 min. ▪ Cooking Time: 10 min. ▪ Low Fat ▪ Low Cholesterol ▪ Low Sodium

Add rice and asparagus spears to this main dish for an impressive meal in minutes.

¾	**pound turkey tenderloin steaks, cut about ½ inch thick**
	Nonstick spray coating
¼	**cup chicken broth**
¼	**cup skim milk**
2	**teaspoons all-purpose flour**
2	**teaspoons honey**
½	**teaspoon snipped fresh chives**
	Dash pepper
1	**teaspoon Dijon-style mustard**

▪ Rinse turkey; pat dry.

▪ Spray a large skillet with nonstick spray coating. Preheat skillet over medium heat. Add turkey steaks. Cook for 8 to 10 minutes or till tender and no longer pink, turning once. Remove from skillet; keep warm.

▪ Meanwhile, stir together chicken broth, skim milk, flour, honey, chives, and pepper.

▪ Add broth mixture to skillet. Cook and stir till thickened and bubbly. Cook and stir for 1 minute more. Stir in mustard; heat through. Serve over turkey. Makes 4 servings.

Nutrition information per serving: 113 calories, 20 g protein, 5 g carbohydrate, 1 g fat, 53 mg cholesterol, 127 mg sodium, 230 mg potassium.

SPINACH-STUFFED TURKEY THIGH　　　236 calories

Preparation Time: 45 min. ▪ Cooking Time: 1 hr. 25 min. ▪ Low Cholesterol

To bone thigh, use a sharp knife to make a lengthwise slit through the meat, cutting to the bone. Carefully cut the meat away from the bone on both sides and on the ends, leaving meat in one piece. Remove bone and discard.

1	1½-pound turkey thigh, skinned
2	cups chopped fresh spinach
2	tablespoons chopped onion
1	tablespoon grated Parmesan cheese
1	teaspoon dried basil, crushed
2	teaspoons cornstarch
½	teaspoon instant chicken bouillon granules
2	ounces reduced-calorie cream cheese, cubed
1	tablespoon snipped fresh parsley
1	medium tomato, cut into wedges (optional)

▪ Bone turkey thigh. Place boned thigh meat between 2 pieces of clear plastic wrap. With a meat mallet, pound meat to ½-inch thickness.
▪ In a small saucepan combine spinach and onion. Cook, covered, in a small amount of water for 5 minutes or till onion is tender; drain well. Stir in Parmesan cheese and basil.
▪ Spread spinach mixture evenly over turkey. Roll up, starting at narrowest end. Secure turkey roll with string. Place the roll in a shallow baking pan; cover with foil.
▪ Bake in a 350° oven for 1 hour. Remove foil; bake 25 to 30 minutes more or till tender. Remove roll from pan. Cover and keep warm. Strain juices; add water to equal ⅔ cup.
▪ For sauce, in a small saucepan combine cornstarch and 1 tablespoon *water;* stir in reserved juices and bouillon granules. Cook and stir till thickened and bubbly; cook and stir 2 minutes more. Add cream cheese and parsley; stir till cheese melts. Slice meat to serve; pass sauce with meat. Garnish with tomato wedges, if desired. Makes 4 servings.

Nutrition information per serving: 236 calories, 30 g protein, 3 g carbohydrate, 11 g fat, 96 mg cholesterol, 233 mg sodium, 478 mg potassium.

Turkey Ham and Apple Bake

151 calories

Advance Preparation Time: 15 min. ▪ Chilling Time: 2 hrs. ▪ Final Preparation Time: 40 min. ▪ Low Fat ▪ Low Cholesterol

1	**16-ounce can sauerkraut, drained and rinsed**
2	**medium apples, cored and chopped (about 2 cups)**
½	**cup sliced green onion**
⅓	**cup apple juice *or* apple cider**
1	**tablespoon brown sugar**
1	**teaspoon prepared mustard**
¼	**teaspoon pepper**
1	**pound turkey ham, sliced ½ inch thick**

▪ In a 13x9x2-inch baking dish stir together sauerkraut, apples, onion, apple juice or apple cider, brown sugar, mustard, and pepper. Arrange turkey ham slices on top. Cover with foil and refrigerate 2 to 24 hours.

▪ Before serving, bake, covered, in a 350° oven about 40 minutes or till heated through. Makes 6 servings.

Nutrition information per serving: 151 calories, 15 g protein, 14 g carbohydrate, 4 g fat, 42 mg cholesterol, 1,130 mg sodium, 415 mg potassium.

SPICY PASTA PIE

298 calories

Preparation Time: 35 min. ▪ Cooking Time: 25 min. ▪ Low Cholesterol

4	**ounces broken vermicelli**
1	**pound turkey breakfast sausage**
1	**cup sliced fresh mushrooms**
½	**cup chopped onion**
1	**clove garlic, minced**
1	**7½-ounce can tomatoes, cut up**
½	**of a 6-ounce can (⅓ cup) tomato paste**
1	**teaspoon Italian seasoning**
⅛	**teaspoon crushed red pepper**
	Nonstick spray coating
1	**cup shredded mozzarella cheese (4 ounces)**
2	**tablespoons grated Parmesan *or* Romano cheese**

▪ Cook vermicelli according to package directions. Drain well. Set aside.

▪ Meanwhile, in a large skillet cook turkey sausage, mushrooms, onion, and garlic till sausage is no longer pink and onion is tender. Drain fat, if necessary.

▪ Stir in *undrained* tomatoes, tomato paste, Italian seasoning, and crushed red pepper. Spray a 9-inch quiche dish with nonstick spray coating. Place *half* of the cooked vermicelli in the bottom of the dish. Top with *half* of the mozzarella cheese and *half* of the sausage mixture. Repeat layers.

▪ Cover the dish loosely with foil. Bake in a 350° oven for 25 to 30 minutes or till heated through. Top with Parmesan. Let stand 10 minutes. Cut into wedges to serve. Serves 6.

Nutrition information per serving: 298 calories, 23 g protein, 22 g carbohydrate, 14 g fat, 73 mg cholesterol, 751 mg sodium, 546 mg potassium.

SAUSAGE AND LENTIL CHILI

201 calories

Advance Preparation Time: 1 hr. 50 min. ▪ Final Preparation Time: 10 min. ▪ Low Fat ▪ Low Cholesterol

½	**pound ground turkey sausage**
1½	**pounds beef stew meat, cut into ½-inch pieces**
2	**large onions, chopped**
2	**large green peppers, chopped**
2	**to 3 tablespoons chili powder**
1	**tablespoon instant beef bouillon granules**
1	**teaspoon ground cumin**
1	**teaspoon dried oregano, crushed**
2	**28-ounce cans tomatoes, cut up**
6	**cups water**
1	**cup dry lentils**

▪ In large Dutch oven cook sausage till no longer pink. Remove sausage; drain any fat. Add beef, onions, and green peppers to Dutch oven; cook till onions are tender. Stir in sausage, chili powder, bouillon granules, cumin, and oregano. Cook and stir 1 minute. Stir in *undrained* tomatoes and water. Heat to boiling; reduce heat. Cover and simmer 1 hour or till beef is nearly tender.

▪ Stir lentils into meat mixture. Cover and simmer about 30 minutes more or till beef and lentils are tender. Remove Dutch oven from heat. Pour chili into 1-, 2-, or 4-serving-size freezer containers. Cover and label containers; freeze for up to 6 months.

▪ To reheat on range top, transfer mixture to a saucepan. Cook over medium-low heat till heated through, stirring occasionally. (Allow 10 to 15 minutes for 1 or 2 servings; 30 to 35 minutes for 4 servings.) To reheat in a microwave oven, transfer mixture to a microwave-safe container. Cover and cook on 100% power (high) till heated through, stirring twice. (Allow 8 to 10 minutes for each serving.) Makes 12 servings.

Nutrition information per serving: 201 calories, 23 g protein, 19 g carbohydrate, 4 g fat, 42 mg cholesterol, 525 mg sodium, 786 mg potassium.

TURKEY AND CHEESE WEDGES

268 calories

Preparation Time: 25 min. ▪ Cooking Time: 30 min.

¾	pound ground turkey *or* turkey sausage
1	cup chopped fresh mushrooms
½	cup chopped onion
½	cup chopped green pepper
¼	teaspoon dried oregano, crushed
¼	teaspoon fennel seed, crushed
1	clove garlic, minced
¼	cup grated Parmesan cheese
2	beaten eggs
1	15-ounce container low-fat ricotta cheese
¼	cup snipped fresh parsley
2	medium tomatoes, sliced
2	ounces American *or* mozzarella cheese, shredded

▪ In a large skillet cook turkey, mushrooms, onion, green pepper, oregano, fennel seed, and garlic till turkey is no longer pink and vegetables are tender. Drain off liquid. Stir in Parmesan cheese. Spoon mixture into a 9-inch pie plate.

▪ In a medium mixing bowl stir together eggs, ricotta cheese, parsley, and ¼ teaspoon *pepper.* Spread over turkey mixture.

▪ Bake, uncovered, in a 350° oven for 25 to 30 minutes or till top is set. Arrange tomatoes atop casserole; sprinkle with American cheese. Bake 5 minutes more or till cheese is melted. Let stand 5 minutes before serving. Serves 6.

Nutrition information per serving: 268 calories, 22 g protein, 9 g carbohydrate, 16 g fat, 126 mg cholesterol, 353 mg sodium, 403 mg potassium.

TURKEY AND PEPPER STIR-FRY

259 calories

Preparation Time: 12 min. ▪ Cooking Time: 8 min. ▪ Low Fat ▪ Low Cholesterol

To cook the sauce, push the meat away from the center of the wok. Pour the sauce into the center of the wok and cook and stir till bubbly. By putting the sauce in the center of the wok, it stays near the heat source and cooks quickly. At the same time, the meat stays warm on the sides of the wok.

⅓	**cup water**
2	**tablespoons soy sauce**
2	**teaspoons cornstarch**
	Nonstick spray coating
4	**cups chopped bok choy**
½	**medium green *or* sweet red pepper, cut into thin strips**
¼	**cup finely chopped seeded Anaheim chili pepper *or* 1 tablespoon finely chopped seeded jalapeño pepper***
12	**ounces fully cooked turkey breast, cut into bite-size strips**
¼	**cup sliced water chestnuts**
2	**cups hot cooked rice**

■ For sauce, in a small bowl combine water, soy sauce, and cornstarch; set aside.

■ Spray a wok or large skillet with nonstick spray coating. Stir-fry bok choy, green or sweet red pepper, and Anaheim or jalapeño chili pepper for 2½ to 3 minutes or till peppers are crisp-tender. Remove from wok.

■ Add turkey to wok; stir-fry 2 minutes or till heated through. Push turkey from center of wok. Stir sauce mixture; add to center of wok. Cook and stir till thickened and bubbly.

■ Return vegetables to wok with water chestnuts. Cook and stir all ingredients together for 1 minute more or till heated through. Serve immediately with hot cooked rice. Serves 4.

*Note: Handle fresh, hot chili peppers with care. Wear rubber gloves or plastic bags over your hands to prevent the volatile oils from burning your skin.

Nutrition information per serving: 259 calories, 29 g protein, 31 g carbohydrate, 1 g fat, 70 mg cholesterol, 619 mg sodium, 511 mg potassium.

GARDEN BURGERS

290 calories

Preparation Time: 12 min. ▪ Grilling Time: 16 min. ▪ Low Cholesterol

1	**egg white**
¼	**cup fine dry bread crumbs**
¼	**cup finely shredded carrot**
¼	**cup finely chopped onion**
¼	**cup finely chopped green pepper**
½	**teaspoon salt**
⅛	**teaspoon pepper**
2	**tablespoons grated Parmesan cheese**
1	**pound ground turkey, veal, *or* lean beef**
	Nonstick spray coating
1	**medium tomato, sliced**

▪ In a large bowl combine egg white and bread crumbs. (If using veal or beef, stir in 2 tablespoons *water.*) Stir in carrot, onion, green pepper, salt, and pepper. Add Parmesan cheese and ground meat; mix well. Shape meat mixture into four ¾-inch-thick patties.

▪ Spray a *cold* grill rack with nonstick spray coating. Then, place rack on grill.

▪ Grill burgers on an uncovered grill directly over *medium* coals for 7 minutes. Turn and grill 8 to 11 minutes more or till no pink remains. Place 1 tomato slice atop each burger and grill 1 minute more. Makes 4 servings.

▪ **Broiling directions:** Place burgers on the unheated rack of a broiler pan. Broil 3 to 4 inches from the heat for 7 minutes. Turn and broil 8 to 11 minutes more or till no pink remains. Place 1 tomato slice atop each burger and broil 1 minute more.

Nutrition information per serving: 290 calories, 23 g protein, 8 g carbohydrate, 18 g fat, 79 mg cholesterol, 441 mg sodium, 351 mg potassium.

TURKEY SOUFFLÉ

196 calories

Preparation Time: 20 min. ▪ Cooking Time: 40 min.

	Nonstick spray coating
½	pound ground raw turkey
¼	cup sliced green onion
2	tablespoons cornstarch
¼	teaspoon salt
¼	teaspoon paprika
⅛	teaspoon pepper
¾	cup skim milk
2	tablespoons grated Parmesan cheese
2	tablespoons chopped pimiento
3	egg yolks
3	egg whites

▪ Spray a 10-inch skillet with nonstick spray coating. Add turkey and onion. Cook till turkey is no longer pink. *Do not drain.*

▪ Stir cornstarch, salt, paprika, and pepper into skillet. Add milk all at once. Cook and stir till thickened and bubbly. Cook and stir for 1 minute more. Stir in Parmesan cheese and pimiento.

▪ In a medium mixing bowl beat egg yolks lightly. Gradually add turkey mixture to yolks, stirring constantly.

▪ In a large mixer bowl beat egg whites till stiff peaks form (tips stand straight). Gradually fold in turkey mixture. Pour into an ungreased 1½-quart soufflé dish.

▪ Bake in a 325° oven about 40 minutes or till a knife inserted near the center comes out clean. Serve immediately. Makes 4 servings.

Nutrition information per serving: 196 calories, 18 g protein, 7 g carbohydrate, 11 g fat, 243 mg cholesterol, 294 mg sodium, 271 mg potassium.

TURKEY ENCHILADAS

314 calories

Preparation Time: 25 min. ▪ Cooking Time: 25 min. ▪ Low Fat ▪ Low Cholesterol

12	**6-inch corn tortillas**
	Nonstick spray coating
¾	**pound ground turkey**
½	**cup chopped onion**
½	**cup chopped green pepper**
1	**clove garlic, minced**
2	**tablespoons all-purpose flour**
1	**8-ounce carton plain low-fat yogurt**
1	**14½-ounce can tomatoes**
1	**4-ounce can diced green chili peppers, drained**
1	**teaspoon ground coriander**
½	**teaspoon dried oregano, crushed**
2	**teaspoons cornstarch**
½	**cup shredded Monterey Jack cheese (2 ounces)**

▪ Wrap tortillas in foil. Warm in a 350° oven for 10 minutes.

▪ Spray a large skillet with nonstick spray coating. For filling, add turkey, onion, green pepper, and garlic. Cook over medium heat till turkey is no longer pink and vegetables are tender. Remove from heat.

▪ Meanwhile, in a mixing bowl stir together flour, yogurt, and ¼ teaspoon *salt*. Stir yogurt mixture into turkey mixture.

▪ Divide the filling among tortillas. Roll up tortillas and place seam side down in a 13x9x2-inch baking dish. Bake, covered, in a 350° oven 25 to 30 minutes, or till heated through.

▪ Meanwhile, for sauce, cut up tomatoes. In a small saucepan combine *undrained* tomatoes, green chilies, coriander, oregano, and ¼ teaspoon *salt*. Bring to boiling; reduce heat. Cover and simmer for 20 minutes.

▪ Combine cornstarch and 1 tablespoon *water*. Stir into tomato mixture. Cook and stir till thickened and bubbly; cook and stir 2 minutes more. To serve, pour sauce over tortillas. Sprinkle cheese atop sauce. Serves 6.

Nutrition information per serving: 314 calories, 19 g protein, 38 g carbohydrate, 10 g fat, 46 mg cholesterol, 631 mg sodium, 452 mg potassium.

TURKEY MEATBALLS IN WINE SAUCE   298 calories

Advance Preparation Time: 50 min. ▪ Chilling Time: 2 hrs. ▪ Final Preparation Time: 20 min. ▪ Low Fat ▪ Low Cholesterol

1	egg white
1	cup soft bread crumbs
½	cup finely chopped onion
2	tablespoons skim milk
½	teaspoon salt
¼	teaspoon dried thyme, crushed
	Dash pepper
1	pound ground raw turkey
	Nonstick spray coating
2	cups sliced fresh mushrooms
1	cup water
2	tablespoons cornstarch
1	tablespoon instant chicken bouillon granules
⅓	cup dry white wine
2	tablespoons snipped fresh parsley
2	cups hot cooked noodles

▪ In a medium mixing bowl stir together egg white, soft bread crumbs, ¼ *cup* of the onion, milk, salt, thyme, and pepper. Add turkey; mix well. Shape mixture into 1-inch meatballs.

▪ Spray a 13x9x2-inch baking pan or baking dish with nonstick spray coating. Place meatballs in the baking pan or dish. Bake, uncovered, in a 350° oven for 30 to 35 minutes or till meatballs are no longer pink. Drain any juices; cool meatballs. Then, cover and chill meatballs for 2 to 24 hours.

▪ Before serving, spray a *cold* large skillet with nonstick spray coating. Add mushrooms and remaining ¼ cup onion. Cook till mushrooms and onions are tender. Stir together water, cornstarch, and bouillon granules. Carefully add cornstarch mixture to mushroom mixture in skillet. Cook and stir till thickened and bubbly. Add chilled meatballs and wine; heat through. Stir in parsley. Serve over hot cooked noodles. Makes 5 servings.

Nutrition information per serving: 298 calories, 20 g protein, 30 g carbohydrate, 7 g fat, 71 mg cholesterol, 544 mg sodium, 221 mg potassium.

FISH AND SHELLFISH
MAIN DISHES

STUFFED RED SNAPPER

146 calories

Preparation Time: 15 min. ▪ Cooking Time: 50 min. ▪ Low Fat ▪ Low Cholesterol ▪ Low Sodium

1	3-pound fresh *or* frozen dressed red snapper *or* other fish
	Nonstick spray coating
¾	cup chopped onion
¾	cup chopped celery
1	tablespoon margarine
1½	cups cooked brown *or* long grain rice
1	cup chopped tomato
⅓	cup snipped fresh parsley
½	teaspoon dried thyme, crushed

▪ Thaw fish, if frozen. Rinse fish and pat dry with paper towels. Spray a shallow baking pan with nonstick spray coating. Place fish in pan; set aside.

▪ For stuffing, in a skillet cook onion and celery in margarine till vegetables are tender. Stir in rice, tomato, parsley, and thyme. Spoon stuffing into cavity of fish. Do not pack tightly. Tie or skewer the fish closed. Cover loosely with foil.

▪ Bake in a 350° oven for 50 to 60 minutes or till fish flakes easily when tested with a fork.

▪ Place any remaining stuffing in a casserole and bake, covered, with the fish the last 25 minutes of baking. Serves 8.

Nutrition information per serving: 146 calories, 19 g protein, 12 g carbohydrate, 2 g fat, 31 mg cholesterol, 74 mg sodium, 484 mg potassium.

OVEN-FRIED FISH

167 calories

Preparation Time: 10 min. ▪ Cooking Time: 6 min. per ½-inch thickness of fish ▪ Low Fat ▪ Low Cholesterol

4	**4-ounce fresh *or* frozen cod *or* other fish fillets**
	Nonstick spray coating
3	**tablespoons seasoned fine dry bread crumbs**
3	**tablespoons cornmeal**
¼	**teaspoon celery salt**
	Dash ground red pepper
1	**tablespoon cooking oil**
1	**slightly beaten egg white**

▪ Thaw fish, if frozen. Rinse fish and pat dry with paper towels. Measure thickness of fish. Spray a shallow baking pan with nonstick spray coating; set aside.

▪ Stir together bread crumbs, cornmeal, celery salt, and red pepper. Add oil, tossing to combine. Brush one side of each fish fillet with egg white, then dip in bread crumb mixture. Place fish fillets, crumb side up, in prepared pan.

▪ Bake, uncovered, in a 500° oven 6 to 8 minutes for each ½-inch thickness of fish or till fish flakes easily when tested with a fork. Makes 4 servings.

Nutrition information per serving: 167 calories, 22 g protein, 8 g carbohydrate, 5 g fat, 49 mg cholesterol, 218 mg sodium, 501 mg potassium.

FISH AND PEPPERS

129 calories

Preparation Time: 20 min. ▪ Cooking Time: 4 min. per ½-inch thickness of fish ▪ Low Fat ▪ Low Cholesterol

4	**4-ounce fresh *or* frozen cod *or* other fish fillets**
¾	**cup chicken broth**
1	**medium onion, sliced and separated into rings**
¾	**teaspoon dried oregano *or* marjoram, crushed**
½	**teaspoon finely shredded lemon peel**
1	**tablespoon lemon juice**
1	**clove garlic, minced**
¾	**cup green pepper cut into bite-size strips**
¾	**cup sweet red pepper cut into bite-size strips**
1½	**teaspoons cornstarch**
1	**tablespoon water**
1	**lemon, sliced and halved**

▪ Thaw fish, if frozen. Rinse fish and pat dry with paper towels. Measure thickness of fish; set aside.

▪ In a 10-inch skillet, combine chicken broth, onion, oregano, lemon peel, lemon juice, and garlic. Bring mixture to boiling; reduce heat. Cover and simmer about 3 minutes or till onion is tender.

▪ Arrange fish fillets in onion mixture. Add peppers. Cover and simmer over medium heat 4 to 6 minutes for each ½-inch thickness of fish or till fish flakes easily when tested with a fork. Use a slotted spoon to move fish and vegetable mixture to a serving platter. Keep warm.

▪ Combine cornstarch and water. Add to pan juices. Cook and stir till thickened and bubbly. Cook and stir 2 minutes more. Spoon atop fish and vegetables. Garnish with lemon. Makes 4 servings.

Nutrition information per serving: 129 calories, 22 g protein, 7 g carbohydrate, 1 g fat, 49 mg cholesterol, 207 mg sodium, 669 mg potassium.

CRUNCHY TOPPED FISH WITH POTATO STICKS 346 calories

Preparation Time: 15 min. ▪ Cooking Time: 19 min. ▪ Low Cholesterol

4	**4-ounce fresh *or* frozen catfish *or* other fish fillets, cut ½ to ¾ inch thick**
	Nonstick spray coating
2	**medium baking potatoes (12 ounces total), cut into 3x½x½-inch sticks**
2	**teaspoons cooking oil *or* margarine, melted**
	Garlic salt
¾	**cup herb-seasoned stuffing mix, crushed**
2	**tablespoons margarine, melted**

■ Thaw fish, if frozen. Rinse fish and pat dry with paper towels; set aside.

■ Line a large baking sheet with foil. Spray foil with nonstick spray coating. Arrange potato sticks in a single layer over *half* of the baking sheet. Brush potatoes with oil or the 2 teaspoons melted margarine. Sprinkle with garlic salt. Bake in a 450° oven for 10 minutes.

■ Meanwhile, stir together stuffing mix and the 2 tablespoons melted margarine. Place fish on baking sheet next to potatoes. Sprinkle stuffing mix over fish. Return pan to oven and bake 9 to 12 minutes more or till fish flakes easily when tested with a fork and potatoes are tender. Makes 4 servings.

Nutrition information per serving: 346 calories, 25 g protein, 33 g carbohydrate, 13 g fat, 63 mg cholesterol, 517 mg sodium, 830 mg potassium.

ORANGE ROUGHY WITH TARRAGON SAUCE   226 calories

Preparation Time: 15 min. ▪ Cooking Time: 4 min. per ½-inch thickness of fish ▪ Low Cholesterol

Enhance the flavor of fish with a refreshing new sauce.

4	**4-ounce fresh *or* frozen orange roughy *or* other fish fillets**
¼	**cup reduced-calorie mayonnaise *or* salad dressing**
¼	**cup finely chopped dill pickle**
2	**tablespoons plain low-fat yogurt**
2	**tablespoons snipped fresh parsley**
1	**tablespoon thinly sliced green onion**
¼	**teaspoon dried tarragon, crushed, *or* dry mustard**
	Nonstick spray coating
1	**tablespoon cooking oil**

▪ Thaw fish, if frozen. Rinse fish and pat dry with paper towels; set aside.

▪ For the sauce, in a small bowl stir together mayonnaise, pickle, yogurt, parsley, onion, and tarragon or mustard. Let stand at room temperature while preparing fish.

▪ Spray the unheated rack of a broiler pan with nonstick spray coating. Arrange fish on rack and brush both sides of fillets lightly with oil.

▪ Broil fish 4 inches from the heat till fish flakes easily when tested with a fork. Allow 4 to 6 minutes per ½-inch thickness of fish. If fish is 1 inch or more thick, turn it over halfway through broiling. Serve fish with sauce. Serves 4.

Nutrition information per serving: 226 calories, 17 g protein, 2 g carbohydrate, 16 g fat, 29 mg cholesterol, 379 mg sodium, 441 mg potassium.

POACHED SALMON WITH CAPER SAUCE

219 calories

Preparation Time: 10 min. ▪ Cooking Time: 11 min. ▪ Low Cholesterol

If your supermarket carries salmon steaks larger than 4 ounces each, buy two 8-ounce steaks. After cooking, carefully separate each steak along the backbone and serve each person half of one steak.

4	**4-ounce fresh *or* frozen salmon *or* other fish steaks, cut ¾ inch thick**
1	**cup chicken broth**
¼	**cup dry white wine**
	Dash pepper
4	**lemon slices**
2	**tablespoons water**
2	**teaspoons cornstarch**
2	**teaspoons drained capers**
2	**cups shredded zucchini**

■ Thaw fish, if frozen. Rinse the fish and pat dry with paper towels.

■ In a 10-inch skillet combine chicken broth, wine, and pepper. Bring to boiling; reduce heat. Place fish in skillet; place lemon slices atop fish.

■ Cover and simmer for 8 to 12 minutes or till fish flakes easily when tested with a fork. Remove fish and lemon; keep fish warm. Discard lemon.

■ Gently boil broth mixture, uncovered, till reduced to ¾ cup (about 2 minutes).

■ Stir together water and cornstarch; stir into broth mixture. Stir in capers. Cook and stir till thickened and bubbly. Cook and stir 1 minute more.

■ Divide zucchini among four individual plates. Arrange salmon on zucchini. Spoon sauce over salmon. Serves 4.

Nutrition information per serving: 219 calories, 26 g protein, 2 g carbohydrate, 10 g fat, 70 mg cholesterol, 246 mg sodium, 539 mg potassium.

BULGUR-STUFFED FISH ROLLS

205 calories

Preparation Time: 25 min. ▪ Cooking Time: 20 min. ▪ Low Fat ▪ Low Cholesterol

To make the stuffed fish rolls, place the stuffing near the widest end of the fillet. Lift the wide end of the fillet up and over the stuffing. Then, continue rolling up the stuffing and fillet together.

4	**4-ounce fresh *or* frozen flounder *or* sole fillets**
1¼	**cups water**
½	**cup bulgur**
⅔	**cup finely shredded carrot**
¼	**cup sliced green onion**
¼	**teaspoon finely shredded orange peel**
⅛	**teaspoon salt**
⅛	**teaspoon pepper**
	Nonstick spray coating
2	**tablespoons frozen orange juice concentrate**
1	**tablespoon margarine**
	Dash ground ginger

▪ Thaw fish, if frozen. Rinse fish and pat dry with paper towels.

▪ For stuffing, in a medium saucepan combine water and bulgur. Bring to boiling; reduce heat. Cover and simmer for 12 minutes or till tender. Stir in carrot and onion and cook 5 minutes more. Drain off excess liquid, if necessary. Stir in orange peel, salt, and pepper.

▪ Spoon *¼ cup* of the stuffing onto each fish fillet. Roll fish around filling. Secure with wooden toothpicks, if necessary. Spray an 8x8x2-inch baking dish with nonstick spray coating. Arrange fish rolls, seam side down, in baking dish. Place any remaining stuffing around fish rolls in baking dish.

▪ In a small saucepan heat orange juice concentrate, margarine, and ginger till margarine is melted. Brush mixture over fish rolls.

▪ Bake, uncovered, in a 350° oven 20 to 25 minutes or till fish flakes easily when tested with a fork. Remove toothpicks, if necessary. Serve fish rolls atop extra stuffing. Serves 4.

Nutrition information per serving: 205 calories, 23 g protein, 19 g carbohydrate, 4 g fat, 49 mg cholesterol, 169 mg sodium, 624 mg potassium.

SWORDFISH WITH CUCUMBER SAUCE

124 calories

Preparation Time: 5 min. ▪ Cooking Time: 6 min. ▪ Low Fat ▪ Low Cholesterol ▪ Low Sodium

2	**fresh** *or* **frozen swordfish** *or* **halibut steaks, cut ¾ inch thick (1 pound total)**
⅓	**cup plain low-fat yogurt**
¼	**cup finely chopped cucumber**
1	**teaspoon snipped fresh mint leaves** *or* **dillweed** *or* **¼ teaspoon dried mint, crushed,** *or* **dried dillweed**
	Dash pepper
	Nonstick spray coating

■ Thaw fish, if frozen. For sauce, in a small bowl stir together yogurt, cucumber, mint or dillweed, and pepper. Cover and chill till serving time.

■ Spray a *cold* grill rack with nonstick spray coating. Then place rack over coals. Grill fish steaks over *medium-hot* coals for 4 to 6 minutes or till fish is lightly browned. Turn and grill 2 to 3 minutes more or till fish flakes easily when tested with a fork.

■ Serve fish with cucumber sauce. Makes 4 servings.

■ **Broiling directions:** Spray the unheated rack of a broiler pan with nonstick spray coating. Place fish on rack. Broil 4 inches from the heat for 4 to 6 minutes or till fish is lightly browned. Turn and broil 2 to 3 minutes more or till fish flakes easily when tested with a fork.

Nutrition information per serving: 124 calories, 22 g protein, 2 g carbohydrate, 3 g fat, 33 mg cholesterol, 68 mg sodium, 506 mg potassium.

PARMESAN BAKED FISH

176 calories

Preparation Time: 5 min. ▪ Cooking Time: 12 min. ▪ Low Cholesterol

Cod, salmon, and orange roughy are all good choices for this tasty, easy-to-fix recipe.

4	**4-ounce fresh *or* frozen fish fillets**
	Nonstick spray coating
⅓	**cup reduced-calorie mayonnaise**
2	**tablespoons grated Parmesan cheese**
2	**tablespoons snipped fresh chives *or* sliced green onion**
½	**teaspoon white wine Worcestershire sauce**

▪ Thaw fish, if frozen. Rinse fish and pat dry with paper towels. Spray a 10x6x2-inch baking dish with nonstick spray coating; set aside.

▪ In a small bowl stir together mayonnaise, Parmesan cheese, chives or green onion, and Worcestershire sauce. Spread mayonnaise mixture over fish fillets.

▪ Bake, uncovered, in a 450° oven for 12 to 15 minutes or till fish flakes easily when tested with a fork. Makes 4 servings.

Nutrition information per serving: 176 calories, 22 g protein, 1 g carbohydrate, 9 g fat, 59 mg cholesterol, 238 mg sodium, 477 mg potassium.

POACHED FISH WITH ORANGE SAUCE

151 calories

Preparation Time: 20 min. ▪ Cooking Time: 4 min. per ½-inch thickness of fish ▪ Low Fat ▪ Low Cholesterol

When the fish is completely cooked, it becomes opaque and flakes, as shown. To test for doneness, insert the tines of a fork at a 45-degree angle into the thickest portion of the fish. Then, gently twist the fork and pull up some of the flesh.

4	4-ounce fresh *or* frozen fish fillets
1	medium cucumber
1	teaspoon finely shredded orange peel
1	cup orange juice
1	medium carrot, shredded
¼	teaspoon salt
1	tablespoon cornstarch
1	tablespoon water

■ Thaw fish, if frozen. Rinse fish and pat dry with paper towels. Measure thickness of fish. Set aside.

■ Chop enough of the cucumber to equal ½ cup. Thinly slice the remaining cucumber; set aside.

■ In an ungreased 10-inch skillet stir together the orange peel, orange juice, carrot, and salt. Bring the mixture to boiling. Carefully add fish to skillet. Return the mixture just to boiling; reduce heat. Cover and simmer for 4 to 6 minutes per ½-inch thickness of fish or till the fish flakes easily when tested with a fork.

■ Place cucumber slices on a platter. Use a slotted spatula to transfer fish to platter atop cucumber. Cover with foil to keep warm.

■ For sauce, in a small bowl stir together the cornstarch and water. Stir into the mixture in the skillet. Cook and stir till mixture is thickened and bubbly. Cook and stir for 2 minutes more. Stir in the chopped cucumber. Spoon the sauce over fish. Makes 4 servings.

Nutrition information per serving: 151 calories, 21 g protein, 12 g carbohydrate, 2 g fat, 49 mg cholesterol, 233 mg sodium, 770 mg potassium.

LIME-SAUCED FISH AND CUCUMBERS

161 calories

Preparation Time: 15 min. ▪ Cooking Time: 9 min. ▪ Low Fat ▪ Low Cholesterol ▪ Low Sodium

For a successful stir-fry, remember that firm-fleshed fish stir-fry best. Choose firm-fleshed varieties such as cusk, monkfish, swordfish, or sea bass.

1	**pound fresh *or* frozen skinless, boneless fish**
¼	**cup dry white wine**
¼	**cup chicken broth**
2	**tablespoons lime juice**
2	**teaspoons cornstarch**
1	**teaspoon honey**
¼	**teaspoon ground ginger**
¼	**teaspoon ground coriander**
⅛	**teaspoon pepper**
	Nonstick spray coating
2	**medium cucumbers, seeded, *or* zucchini, cut into 2x½-inch sticks**
1	**medium green *or* sweet red pepper, cut into ¾-inch squares**
1	**teaspoon cooking oil**

▪ Thaw fish, if frozen. Cut into ¾-inch pieces; set aside.

▪ For sauce, stir together wine, chicken broth, lime juice, cornstarch, honey, ginger, coriander, and pepper. Set aside.

▪ Spray a wok or large skillet with nonstick spray coating. Preheat over medium-high heat. Add cucumbers; stir-fry 1½ minutes. Add green or red pepper; stir-fry about 1½ minutes more or till crisp-tender. Remove from wok.

▪ Add *half* of the fish to wok and stir-fry 2 to 3 minutes or till fish flakes easily when tested with a fork. Remove from wok. Add oil to hot wok. Add remaining fish and stir-fry 2 to 3 minutes or till fish flakes easily when tested with a fork. Return all fish to wok. Push fish from center of wok.

▪ Stir sauce and add to center of wok. Cook and stir till thickened and bubbly. Return vegetables to wok; stir ingredients together to coat with sauce. Cook and stir for 1 minute. Serve with lime wedges, if desired. Makes 4 servings.

Nutrition information per serving: 161 calories, 23 g protein, 10 g carbohydrate, 2 g fat, 62 mg cholesterol, 129 mg sodium, 571 mg potassium.

FISH SOUP

Preparation Time: 10 min. ▪ Cooking Time: 15 min. ▪ Low Fat ▪ Low Cholesterol

Cod, haddock, and pike are all good varieties of fish to use in this herbed, tomato-broth soup.

2	cups water
1	16-ounce can tomatoes, cut up
2	cups frozen mixed vegetables
1	cup thinly sliced celery
¾	cup chopped onion
1½	teaspoons instant chicken bouillon granules
1	teaspoon dried oregano, crushed
1	clove garlic, minced
	Several dashes bottled hot pepper sauce
8	ounces fresh *or* frozen fish fillets, cut into 1-inch pieces

▪ In a large saucepan combine water, *undrained* tomatoes, mixed vegetables, celery, onion, bouillon granules, oregano, garlic, and hot pepper sauce. Bring to boiling; reduce heat. Cover and simmer 10 minutes or till vegetables are tender.

▪ Stir in fish. Return just to boiling; reduce heat. Cover and simmer gently about 5 minutes or till fish flakes easily with a fork. Makes 4 servings.

Nutrition information per serving: 159 calories, 16 g protein, 21 g carbohydrate, 2 g fat, 27 mg cholesterol, 441 mg sodium, 796 mg potassium.

TUNA-NOODLE CASSEROLE

285 calories

Preparation Time: 30 min. ▪ Cooking Time: 25 min. ▪ Low Fat ▪ Low Cholesterol

4	ounces medium noodles
1	9¼-ounce can tuna
1	tablespoon margarine
¼	cup fine dry bread crumbs
1	10-ounce package frozen cut green beans
1	cup sliced mushrooms
1	cup chopped onion
¾	cup chopped green *or* sweet red pepper
¼	cup sliced celery
1	teaspoon instant chicken bouillon granules
1	clove garlic, minced
½	teaspoon dried dillweed
1½	cups skim milk
1	tablespoon cornstarch
½	cup shredded process Swiss cheese
¼	cup reduced-calorie mayonnaise

▪ Cook noodles according to package directions; drain and set aside.

▪ Meanwhile, drain and flake tuna; set aside. Melt margarine, then toss with bread crumbs; set aside.

▪ In a large saucepan combine frozen green beans, mushrooms, onion, green or red pepper, celery, bouillon granules, garlic, dillweed, and ½ cup *water*. Bring to boiling; reduce heat. Cover; simmer 5 minutes or till vegetables are tender.

▪ Meanwhile, stir together skim milk and cornstarch. Stir into vegetable mixture. Cook and stir till slightly thickened and bubbly. Remove from heat, then stir in cheese and mayonnaise. Stir in noodles and tuna.

▪ Spoon mixture into a 2-quart casserole. Sprinkle bread crumb mixture atop casserole. Bake, uncovered, in a 350° oven for 25 to 30 minutes or till bread crumbs are golden. Makes 6 servings.

Nutrition information per serving: 285 calories, 22 g protein, 30 g carbohydrate, 9 g fat, 42 mg cholesterol, 252 mg sodium, 510 mg potassium.

FRIED SCALLOPS

127 calories

Preparation Time: 10 min. ▪ Cooking Time: 5 min. ▪ Low Fat ▪ Low Cholesterol

8	**ounces fresh _or_ frozen sea scallops**
1	**tablespoon fine dry bread crumbs**
1	**tablespoon grated Parmesan cheese**
⅛	**teaspoon garlic salt**
⅛	**teaspoon paprika**
	Nonstick spray coating
	Lemon wedges (optional)

▪ Thaw scallops, if frozen. Halve any large scallops.

▪ In a small bowl stir together bread crumbs, Parmesan cheese, garlic salt, and paprika; set aside.

▪ Spray a medium skillet with nonstick spray coating. Heat skillet over medium-high heat. Add scallops. Cook scallops for 5 to 6 minutes or till tender, stirring frequently.

▪ Sprinkle scallops with crumb mixture. Serve immediately. Serve with lemon wedges, if desired. Makes 2 servings.

Nutrition information per serving: 127 calories, 20 g protein, 5 g carbohydrate, 2 g fat, 40 mg cholesterol, 369 mg sodium, 376 mg potassium.

SCALLOPS FLORENTINE

223 calories

Preparation Time: 5 min. ▪ Cooking Time: 10 min. ▪ Low Fat ▪ Low Cholesterol

Put together a simple, yet elegant, meal for guests in no time.

½	**pound fresh *or* frozen scallops**
1	**10-ounce package frozen chopped spinach**
¼	**cup water**
2	**tablespoons dry white wine**
¼	**teaspoon salt**
¼	**teaspoon dried tarragon, crushed**
	Dash pepper
1	**clove garlic, minced**
⅓	**cup canned evaporated skim milk**
4	**teaspoons all-purpose flour**
2	**tablespoons grated Parmesan cheese**

▪ Thaw scallops, if frozen. Cut any large scallops in half.

▪ Cook spinach according to package directions; drain well. Keep warm.

▪ Meanwhile, in a medium skillet combine water, wine, salt, tarragon, pepper, and garlic. Bring to boiling; add scallops. Cover and simmer for 1 to 2 minutes or till scallops are opaque. Remove scallops from skillet with a slotted spoon.

▪ In a small bowl combine milk and flour. Stir into liquid in skillet. Cook and stir till thickened and bubbly. Cook and stir for 1 minute more.

▪ Stir Parmesan cheese into mixture in the skillet. Return scallops to skillet; heat through. Serve scallop mixture over spinach. Makes 2 servings.

Nutrition information per serving: 223 calories, 29 g protein, 18 g carbohydrate, 3 g fat, 44 mg cholesterol, 694 mg sodium, 1,065 mg potassium.

CITRUS SHRIMP AND SCALLOPS

Preparation Time: 10 min. ▪ Marinating Time: 30 min. ▪ Cooking Time: 10 min. ▪ Low Fat

½	**pound fresh *or* frozen scallops**
12	**fresh *or* frozen large shrimp, peeled and deveined (about ½ pound total)**
1	**teaspoon finely shredded orange peel**
½	**cup orange juice**
2	**tablespoons soy sauce**
1	**teaspoon grated gingerroot**
1	**clove garlic, minced**
⅛	**to ¼ teaspoon ground red pepper**
12	**fresh *or* frozen pea pods**
1	**medium orange, cut into 8 wedges**

▪ Halve any large scallops. Place scallops and shrimp in a plastic bag set in a deep bowl. For marinade, combine orange peel, orange juice, soy sauce, gingerroot, garlic, and red pepper. Pour over seafood. Seal bag. Marinate in the refrigerator for 30 minutes. Drain, reserving marinade.

▪ If using fresh pea pods, cook in boiling water about 2 minutes; drain. Or, thaw and drain frozen pea pods.

▪ Wrap one pea pod around each shrimp. Thread pea pods and shrimp onto four 10- to 12-inch skewers alternately with scallops and orange wedges.

▪ Grill kabobs on an uncovered grill directly over *medium-hot* coals for 5 minutes. Turn and brush with marinade. Grill 5 to 7 minutes more or till shrimp turn pink and scallops are opaque. Brush occasionally with marinade. Serves 4.

▪ **Broiling directions:** Place kabobs on the unheated rack of a broiler pan. Broil 4 inches from the heat for 4 minutes. Turn and broil 4 to 6 minutes more or till shrimp turn pink and scallops are opaque. Brush occasionally with marinade.

Nutrition information per serving: 133 calories, 22 g protein, 7 g carbohydrate, 1 g fat, 105 mg cholesterol, 305 mg sodium, 380 mg potassium.

SHRIMP WITH TARRAGON SAUCE

234 calories

Preparation Time: 20 min. ▪ Cooking Time: 15 min. ▪ Low Fat

3	medium potatoes, sliced
¼	cup reduced-calorie mayonnaise *or* salad dressing
¼	cup buttermilk *or* plain low-fat yogurt
2	green onions, sliced
2	tablespoons snipped fresh parsley
¼	teaspoon dried tarragon, crushed
1	clove garlic, minced
2	tablespoons vinegar
1	teaspoon salt
1	pound fresh *or* frozen shrimp, peeled and deveined
4	lettuce leaves
8	cherry tomatoes (optional)

▪ In a saucepan cook potatoes in a small amount of lightly salted boiling water for 10 to 15 minutes or till tender. Drain; set aside.

▪ Meanwhile, for sauce, in a blender container combine mayonnaise or salad dressing, buttermilk or yogurt, green onions, parsley, tarragon, and garlic. Cover and blend till smooth. Set aside.

▪ In a saucepan heat vinegar, salt, and 4 cups *water* to boiling. Add shrimp. Cover and simmer for 1 to 3 minutes or till shrimp turn pink. Drain.

▪ Arrange potato slices and shrimp on lettuce-lined plates.* If necessary, stir some water into the sauce to make of drizzling consistency. Drizzle sauce over potatoes and shrimp. If desired, garnish with cherry tomatoes. Makes 4 servings.

*Note: If desired, chill plates with potatoes and shrimp till serving time. Chill sauce till serving time. Just before serving, drizzle sauce over shrimp and potatoes.

Nutrition information per serving: 234 calories, 21 g protein, 24 g carbohydrate, 6 g fat, 135 mg cholesterol, 767 mg sodium, 857 mg potassium.

PASTA WITH SEAFOOD

230 calories

Preparation Time: 1¼ hrs. ▪ Cooking Time: 10 min. ▪ Low Fat ▪ Low Cholesterol

6	**ounces scallops**
8	**ounces shelled shrimp**
12	**small clams**
6	**ounces spinach spaghetti**
1	**yellow sweet pepper, cut into ¾-inch pieces**
½	**cup chopped onion**
2	**cloves garlic, minced**
½	**teaspoon instant chicken bouillon granules**
1	**teaspoon dried basil, crushed**
½	**teaspoon dried oregano, crushed**
2	**tablespoons cornstarch**
2	**medium tomatoes, seeded and chopped**
2	**tablespoons snipped fresh parsley**
¼	**cup grated Parmesan cheese**

▪ Thaw scallops and shrimp, if frozen. Halve any large scallops. Devein shrimp. Scrub clams under cold running water. Cover clams with salted water, using 3 tablespoons salt to 8 cups cold water. Soak for 15 minutes; drain and rinse. Discard water. Repeat twice. Set aside.

▪ Cook spaghetti according to package directions; drain and keep warm. In a large skillet cook clams, yellow sweet pepper, onion, garlic, bouillon granules, basil, oregano, and ¼ teaspoon *pepper,* covered, in 1 cup *water* about 5 minutes or till vegetables are nearly tender and clams have opened. Remove clams; discard any unopened shells.

▪ Stir together cornstarch and 2 tablespoons *water;* stir into vegetable mixture. Cook and stir till thickened and bubbly. Stir in scallops and shrimp. Cook 3 to 4 minutes more or till scallops are opaque and shrimp turn pink. Stir in tomatoes and clams; heat through. Toss hot spaghetti with seafood mixture and parsley. Serve with Parmesan cheese. Serves 6.

Nutrition information per serving: 230 calories, 20 g protein, 31 g carbohydrate, 2 g fat, 84 mg cholesterol, 296 mg sodium, 475 mg potassium.

SAUTÉED SHRIMP WITH PEPPERS

227 calories

Preparation Time: 15 min. ▪ Cooking Time: 6 min. ▪ Low Fat

Serve the shrimp atop hot cooked rice or orzo. You'll find orzo with the other pastas in your supermarket.

	Nonstick spray coating
1	small sweet red pepper, cut into thin strips
1	small green pepper, cut into thin strips
¼	cup sliced green onions
1	clove garlic, minced
½	pound fresh *or* frozen shrimp, peeled and deveined
½	cup canned sliced water chestnuts
2	tablespoons apricot preserves
1	tablespoon soy sauce
	Dash bottled hot pepper sauce
1	teaspoon toasted sesame seeds

▪ Spray a medium skillet with nonstick spray coating. Heat skillet over medium heat. Add red and green pepper, onion, and garlic; cook for 3 to 4 minutes or till tender.

▪ Add shrimp and water chestnuts. Cook and stir for 3 to 4 minutes or till shrimp turn pink. Remove from heat.

▪ Stir in apricot preserves, soy sauce, and hot pepper sauce. Sprinkle with sesame seeds. Makes 2 servings.

Nutrition information per serving: 227 calories, 20 g protein, 30 g carbohydrate, 3 g fat, 129 mg cholesterol, 653 mg sodium, 627 mg potassium.

LOW-CALORIE SHRIMP CREOLE

290 calories

Preparation Time: 15 min. ▪ Cooking Time: 15 min. ▪ Low Fat

Enjoy the taste of Louisiana home cooking with this Cajun-style dish.

4	cups water
1	pound fresh *or* frozen shelled shrimp
½	cup chopped onion
½	cup chopped green pepper
1	28-ounce can tomatoes, cut up
2	teaspoons instant chicken bouillon granules
1	teaspoon sugar
1	teaspoon dried thyme, crushed
¼	teaspoon bottled hot pepper sauce
2	tablespoons cornstarch
2	cups hot cooked rice
¼	cup snipped parsley

▪ In a large saucepan bring the 4 cups water to boiling; add shrimp. Return to boiling; reduce heat. Simmer for 1 to 3 minutes or till shrimp turn pink; drain and set aside.

▪ In a large skillet combine the onion, green pepper, and ¼ cup *water.* Bring to boiling; reduce heat. Cover and simmer for 3 to 4 minutes or till vegetables are crisp-tender. *Do not drain.*

▪ Stir in *undrained* tomatoes, bouillon granules, sugar, thyme, and bottled hot pepper sauce. Simmer, uncovered, for 8 minutes.

▪ Combine cornstarch and ¼ cup *water;* stir into skillet. Cook and stir over medium heat till thickened and bubbly. Cook and stir for 2 minutes more.

▪ Add shrimp; heat through. Combine rice and parsley. Serve shrimp mixture with rice mixture. Makes 4 servings.

Nutrition information per serving: 290 calories, 26 g protein, 43 g carbohydrate, 2 g fat, 140 mg cholesterol, 680 mg sodium, 830 mg potassium.

CURRIED SHRIMP CREPES

219 calories

Advance Preparation Time: 50 min. ▪ Chilling Time: 2 hrs. ▪ Final Preparation Time: 30 min. ▪ Low Fat

12	ounces frozen, peeled, cooked shrimp *or* frozen crab-flavored, chunk-style fish pieces
12	Crepes *(See recipe page 202)*
	Nonstick spray coating
1	medium onion, chopped
1	clove garlic, minced
2	teaspoons curry powder
1	10¾-ounce can condensed cream of mushroom soup
3	tablespoons skim milk
1	medium apple, chopped

▪ Thaw and drain the frozen shrimp or crab-flavored fish; set aside. Meanwhile, prepare crepes; set aside.

▪ For filling, spray a *cold* medium saucepan with nonstick spray coating. Heat saucepan over medium heat. Add onion and garlic. Cook till onion is tender, stirring often. Add curry powder; cook and stir for 1 minute. Then, stir in condensed soup and milk. Remove from heat. Remove *¾ cup* of the soup mixture; cover and chill. If desired, reserve some shrimp for garnish. Stir remaining shrimp or fish and apple into remaining soup mixture.

▪ To assemble, spoon *¼ cup* of the shrimp or fish mixture onto the unbrowned side of *each* crepe. Roll up. Place filled crepes, seam side down, in a 13x9x2-inch baking dish or 6 individual casseroles. Cover and chill for 2 to 24 hours.

▪ Before serving, stir the reserved soup mixture. Spoon soup mixture on top of filled crepes. Cover and bake in a 350° oven about 30 minutes or till heated through. If desired, garnish with reserved shrimp. Makes 6 servings.

Nutrition information per serving: 219 calories, 17 g protein, 23 g carbohydrate, 6 g fat, 158 mg cholesterol, 598 mg sodium, 303 mg potassium.

SAUCY SHRIMP AND PASTA

Preparation and Cooking Time: 18 min. ▪ Low Fat

4	**ounces thin spaghetti**
1	**14½-ounce can Italian-style stewed tomatoes**
4	**teaspoons cornstarch**
1	**teaspoon dried parsley flakes *or* 1 tablespoon snipped fresh parsley**
½	**teaspoon sugar**
½	**teaspoon dried Italian seasoning**
	Dash ground red pepper
1	**16-ounce package frozen peeled and deveined shrimp**
	Fresh parsley sprigs (optional)

▪ In a 4½-quart Dutch oven bring 4 cups hot water to boiling. Add pasta; cook according to package directions. Drain well.

▪ Meanwhile, in a large saucepan stir together tomatoes, cornstarch, parsley, sugar, Italian seasoning, and red pepper. Cook and stir till thickened and bubbly.

▪ Stir in shrimp. Return to boiling and cook 1 to 3 minutes or till shrimp turn pink.

▪ Serve shrimp mixture over pasta. Garnish with fresh parsley sprigs, if desired. Makes 4 servings.

Nutrition information per serving: 267 calories, 28 g protein, 33 g carbohydrate, 2 g fat, 172 mg cholesterol, 457 mg sodium, 544 mg potassium.

GARLIC-BROILED SHRIMP

170 calories

Preparation Time: 15 min. ▪ Marinating Time: 2 hrs. ▪ Cooking Time: 5 min.

To devein shrimp, use a sharp knife to make a shallow slit along the back from the tail to the head. Look for the black sand vein that runs along the center of the back. If the vein is visible (it will be dark in color), use the tip of knife to remove and discard the vein. Thoroughly rinse and drain the shrimp.

1	**pound fresh *or* frozen extra-large shrimp, peeled and deveined (about 20)**
2	**tablespoons olive oil *or* cooking oil**
2	**tablespoons dry vermouth *or* white wine**
2	**cloves garlic, minced**
	Dash salt
	Dash pepper
2	**medium tomatoes, halved crosswise**

▪ Place shrimp in a plastic bag set in a deep bowl.

▪ For marinade, in a small bowl combine oil, vermouth or white wine, garlic, salt, and pepper. Pour over shrimp in bag. Close bag.

▪ Marinate shrimp in the refrigerator for 2 to 8 hours. Drain shrimp, reserving marinade.

▪ Arrange shrimp on the unheated rack of a broiler pan. Place tomatoes, cut side up, next to shrimp. Brush shrimp and tomatoes with marinade.

▪ Broil 4 to 6 inches from the heat about 5 minutes or till shrimp turn pink, turning shrimp over once. Serves 4.

Nutrition information per serving: 170 calories, 18 g protein, 4 g carbohydrate, 8 g fat, 129 mg cholesterol, 164 mg sodium, 297 mg potassium.

SZECHWAN SHRIMP

155 calories

Preparation Time: 25 min. ▪ Cooking Time: 5 min. ▪ Low Fat

1	**pound fresh *or* frozen shrimp**
2	**tablespoons water**
2	**tablespoons catsup**
1	**tablespoon soy sauce**
1	**tablespoon rice wine *or* dry sherry**
2	**teaspoons cornstarch**
1	**teaspoon honey**
½	**teaspoon crushed red pepper**
1	**teaspoon grated gingerroot *or* ¼ teaspoon ground ginger**
½	**cup sliced green onions**
4	**cloves garlic, minced**
1	**tablespoon peanut oil *or* cooking oil**
	Hot cooked rice (optional)
	Fresh *or* frozen pea pods, cooked (optional)

■ Thaw shrimp, if frozen. Peel and devein shrimp; cut in half lengthwise. Set aside.

■ In a mixing bowl stir together water, catsup, soy sauce, rice wine or dry sherry, cornstarch, honey, crushed red pepper, and *ground* ginger, if using. Set aside.

■ In a large skillet or wok stir-fry green onions, garlic, and *fresh* grated gingerroot, if using, in hot oil for 30 seconds.

■ Add shrimp. Stir-fry 2 to 3 minutes or till shrimp turn pink; push to sides of skillet or wok. Stir catsup mixture; stir into center of skillet. Cook and stir till thickened and bubbly. Cook and stir 2 minutes more. Stir sauce and shrimp together.

■ If desired, serve with hot cooked rice and pea pods. Makes 4 servings.

Nutrition information per serving: 155 calories, 18 g protein, 8 g carbohydrate, 5 g fat, 129 mg cholesterol, 473 mg sodium, 250 mg potassium.

SHRIMP BALL SOUP

196 calories

Preparation Time: 20 min. ▪ Cooking Time: 15 min. ▪ Low Fat ▪ Low Cholesterol

1	slightly beaten egg white
2	tablespoons cornstarch
½	teaspoon ground ginger
8	ounces peeled and deveined shrimp, very finely chopped
6	cups chicken broth
3	tablespoons rice wine *or* dry sherry
¼	teaspoon pepper
1	clove garlic, minced
1	cup fresh pea pods, halved crosswise, *or* ½ of a 6-ounce package frozen pea pods, halved crosswise
¾	cup thinly sliced carrots
4	ounces fresh tofu (bean curd), cubed
3	tablespoons thinly sliced green onion

■ For shrimp balls, in a mixing bowl combine egg white, cornstarch, and ginger. Add shrimp; mix well.

■ In a Dutch oven combine chicken broth, rice wine, pepper, and garlic. Bring to boiling. Add shrimp mixture by rounded teaspoons. Return to boiling; reduce heat. Cover and simmer for 1 minute.

■ Add pea pods, carrots, tofu, and green onion. Return to boiling; reduce heat. Cover and simmer 5 minutes more or till vegetables are crisp-tender. Makes 4 servings.

Nutrition information per serving: 196 calories, 23 g protein, 12 g carbohydrate, 4 g fat, 86 mg cholesterol, 1,255 mg sodium, 574 mg potassium.

CHILLED LOBSTER

149 calories

Preparation Time: 20 min. ▪ Cooking Time: 6 min. ▪ Chilling Time: 2 hrs. ▪ Low Cholesterol

6	**cups water**
1½	**teaspoons salt**
2	**fresh *or* frozen medium rock lobster tails (about 5 ounces each)**
2	**tablespoons reduced-calorie mayonnaise *or* salad dressing**
2	**tablespoons dairy sour cream**
1	**tablespoon snipped fresh parsley**
1	**teaspoon lime juice**
½	**teaspoon curry powder**
	Dash bottled hot pepper sauce

■ In a large saucepan bring water and salt to boiling. Add lobster tails. Return to boiling; reduce heat. Simmer, uncovered, for 6 to 10 minutes or till lobster shells turn bright red and meat is tender. Drain. Cover and chill for 2 to 24 hours.

■ For sauce, in a small mixing bowl stir together mayonnaise or salad dressing, sour cream, parsley, lime juice, curry powder, and hot pepper sauce. Cover and chill till serving time.

■ To serve, place one lobster tail, shell side down, on each serving plate. With scissors, cut the lobster lengthwise. Serve with the sauce. Makes 2 servings.

Nutrition information per serving: 149 calories, 15 g protein, 3 g carbohydrate, 8 g fat, 64 mg cholesterol, 364 mg sodium, 293 mg potassium.

BROILED LOBSTER TAILS

118 calories

Preparation Time: 10 min. ▪ Cooking Time: 9 min. ▪ Low Cholesterol

To butterfly the lobster tail, use kitchen shears or a sharp knife to cut the lobster tail lengthwise through the center of the hard top shell and the meat. Cut to, but not through, the bottom shell. Use your fingers to spread the halves of the tail apart.

4 5-ounce fresh *or* frozen lobster tails
2 tablespoons lemon juice
1 tablespoon margarine, melted
2 tablespoons sliced almonds

▪ Thaw lobster tails, if frozen. Use kitchen shears or a sharp heavy knife to cut lengthwise through the center of the hard top shells and the meat. Cut to, but not through, bottom shell. Spread the halves of tails apart. Place lobster tails, meat side up, on the unheated rack of a broiler pan.

▪ In a small bowl combine lemon juice and margarine. Brush mixture over lobster meat.

▪ Broil 4 inches from the heat for 8 to 10 minutes or till nearly done. Sprinkle with almonds and broil 1 to 2 minutes more or till lobster meat is opaque and almonds are lightly toasted. Makes 4 servings.

Nutrition information per serving: 118 calories, 15 g protein, 2 g carbohydrate, 5 g fat, 51 mg cholesterol, 304 mg sodium, 287 mg potassium.

BAKED CRAB AND BROCCOLI

184 calories

Advance Preparation Time: 20 min. ▪ Chilling Time: 2 hrs. ▪ Final Preparation Time: 20 min. ▪ Low Cholesterol

1	10-ounce package frozen cut broccoli
6	ounces frozen crab-flavored fish pieces, thawed and sliced
2	cups sliced fresh mushrooms
1	clove garlic, minced
1	tablespoon margarine
2	tablespoons all-purpose flour
1	cup skim milk
¼	cup shredded sharp cheddar cheese (1 ounce)
2	tablespoons grated Parmesan cheese
2	tablespoons crushed rich round crackers

▪ Cook broccoli according to package directions; drain. In 4 individual au gratin dishes arrange broccoli and crab-flavored fish pieces. Set dishes aside.

▪ For sauce, in medium saucepan cook mushrooms and garlic in margarine over medium-high heat about 4 minutes or till mushrooms are tender. Stir in flour and ⅛ teaspoon *pepper*. Then, stir in milk. Cook and stir till thickened and bubbly; remove from heat. Stir in cheddar cheese till melted. Spoon sauce on top of broccoli and fish in dishes. Cover dishes with foil and chill for 2 to 24 hours.

▪ Before serving, bake, covered, in a 400° oven for 20 to 25 minutes or till bubbly. Combine Parmesan cheese and cracker crumbs and sprinkle on top of each serving. Serves 4.

Nutrition information per serving: 184 calories, 17 g protein, 13 g carbohydrate, 8 g fat, 34 mg cholesterol, 667 mg sodium, 477 mg potassium.

CRAB AND ASPARAGUS SUPREME

170 calories

Preparation Time: 20 min. ▪ Cooking Time: 10 min. ▪ Low Cholesterol

1	10-ounce package frozen cut asparagus
1	cup sliced fresh mushrooms
¼	cup finely chopped onion
1	tablespoon margarine
1	tablespoon cornstarch
¼	teaspoon salt
⅛	teaspoon ground nutmeg
	Dash pepper
1	cup skim milk
8	ounces fresh *or* frozen crabmeat, drained, *or* frozen crab-flavored, crab-leg-shaped fish pieces, cut into 1-inch pieces
2	tablespoons chopped toasted almonds
2	tablespoons grated Parmesan cheese

■ Cook asparagus according to package directions; drain well. Set aside.

■ In a medium saucepan cook mushrooms and onion in margarine till onion is tender but not brown. Stir in cornstarch, salt, nutmeg, and pepper. Stir in milk all at once. Cook and stir till thickened and bubbly. Cook and stir for 1 minute more. Stir in crab and asparagus.

■ Spoon mixture into four individual casseroles.

■ In a small bowl stir together almonds and Parmesan cheese. Sprinkle atop casseroles.

■ Bake in a 400° oven for 10 minutes or till mixture is heated through and cheese is browned. Makes 4 servings.

Nutrition information per serving: 170 calories, 17 g protein, 11 g carbohydrate, 7 g fat, 27 mg cholesterol, 728 mg sodium, 611 mg potassium.

CRAB CAKES

141 calories

Preparation Time: 10 min. ▪ Cooking Time: 10 min. ▪ Low Fat ▪ Low Cholesterol

1	slightly beaten egg
½	cup plain low-fat yogurt
2	tablespoons reduced-calorie mayonnaise *or* salad dressing
1	tablespoon snipped fresh parsley
2	teaspoons Worcestershire sauce
1	teaspoon prepared mustard
¼	teaspoon paprika
⅛	teaspoon pepper
1	pound crabmeat, drained, flaked, and cartilage removed
¼	cup finely crushed saltine crackers
	Nonstick spray coating
1	medium tomato, sliced
	Lemon wedges (optional)

■ In a medium mixing bowl combine egg, *¼ cup* of the yogurt, mayonnaise or salad dressing, parsley, Worcestershire sauce, mustard, paprika, and pepper. Stir in crabmeat and crushed crackers.

■ Shape crab mixture into five 3-inch patties.

■ Spray a shallow baking pan with nonstick spray coating. Arrange patties in pan. Broil 4 to 6 inches from the heat for 10 to 15 minutes or till lightly browned. Do not turn patties during broiling.

■ Serve crab cakes on tomato slices with remaining yogurt. Garnish with lemon wedges, if desired. Makes 5 servings.

Nutrition information per serving: 141 calories, 18 g protein, 6 g carbohydrate, 4 g fat, 93 mg cholesterol, 822 mg sodium, 284 mg potassium.

CRAB GUMBO

256 calories

Preparation Time: 15 min. ▪ Cooking Time: 12 min. ▪ Low Fat ▪ Low Cholesterol

If you don't have crab on hand, substitute 1 cup diced cooked chicken.

½	**cup chopped green pepper**
½	**cup sliced green onion**
1	**clove garlic, minced**
1	**tablespoon cooking oil**
3	**cups chicken broth**
2	**medium tomatoes, peeled and chopped**
⅛	**teaspoon celery salt**
⅛	**teaspoon dried thyme, crushed**
⅛	**to ¼ teaspoon bottled hot pepper sauce**
½	**of a 10-ounce package (1 cup) frozen sliced okra**
1	**6-ounce can crabmeat**
½	**cup diced turkey ham**
1	**tablespoon filé powder (optional)**
2	**cups hot cooked rice**

■ In a large saucepan cook green pepper, green onion, and garlic in hot oil till vegetables are tender. Stir in chicken broth, tomatoes, celery salt, thyme, and hot pepper sauce. Bring to boiling. Stir in okra; reduce heat. Cover and simmer about 10 minutes or till okra is tender.

■ Meanwhile, drain, flake, and remove cartilage from crabmeat. Stir crabmeat and turkey ham into gumbo. Heat through. Stir in filé powder, if desired.

■ To serve, divide gumbo among four soup bowls. Top each with *one-fourth* of the rice. Makes 4 servings.

Nutrition information per serving: 256 calories, 16 g protein, 33 g carbohydrate, 6 g fat, 42 mg cholesterol, 1,125 mg sodium, 503 mg potassium.

CLAM AND CHEESE CHOWDER

253 calories

Preparation Time: 10 min. ▪ Cooking Time: 10 min. ▪ Low Cholesterol

1¼	cups water
1	teaspoon instant chicken bouillon granules
1	cup shredded carrots
1	cup frozen peas
¼	cup sliced green onions
⅛	teaspoon pepper
1	cup skim milk
2	tablespoons cornstarch
2	6½-ounce cans minced clams
1	cup shredded American cheese (4 ounces)

▪ In a 2-quart saucepan combine water, bouillon granules, carrots, peas, green onions, and pepper. Heat to boiling.

▪ Stir together milk and cornstarch; stir into vegetable mixture. Cook and stir till thickened and bubbly. Cook and stir 1 minute more. Stir in *undrained* clams and the cheese till cheese is melted. Makes 4 servings.

Nutrition information per serving: 253 calories, 22 g protein, 17 g carbohydrate, 10 g fat, 59 mg cholesterol, 630 mg sodium, 597 mg potassium.

LINGUINE WITH CLAM SAUCE

298 calories

Preparation Time: 15 min. ▪ Cooking Time: 15 min. ▪ Low Fat ▪ Low Cholesterol

2	6½-ounce cans minced clams
1	medium green *or* sweet red pepper, chopped
2	green onions, sliced
¼	teaspoon dried basil, crushed
¼	teaspoon crushed red pepper
2	cloves garlic, minced
¼	cup dry white wine
4	teaspoons cornstarch
2	tablespoons snipped fresh parsley
4	ounces linguine, cooked and drained
2	tablespoons grated Parmesan cheese

▪ Drain clams, reserving liquid. In a saucepan combine reserved clam liquid, green or sweet red pepper, onions, basil, crushed red pepper, and garlic. Bring to boiling; reduce heat. Simmer, uncovered, about 5 minutes or till onions are tender.

▪ In a small bowl stir together wine and cornstarch; stir mixture into saucepan. Cook and stir till thickened and bubbly. Cook and stir for 2 minutes more.

▪ Stir in clams and parsley; heat through.

▪ In a large bowl toss linguine with clam mixture. Sprinkle Parmesan cheese atop each serving. Makes 3 servings.

Nutrition information per serving: 298 calories, 36 g protein, 24 g carbohydrate, 4 g fat, 86 mg cholesterol, 218 mg sodium, 917 mg potassium.

OYSTER AND SPINACH CHOWDER

220 calories

Preparation Time: 10 min. ▪ Cooking Time: 20 min. ▪ Low Fat ▪ Low Cholesterol

	Nonstick spray coating
½	**cup chopped onion**
½	**cup shredded carrot**
2½	**cups skim milk**
¼	**cup all-purpose flour**
2	**tablespoons nonfat dry milk powder**
¼	**teaspoon salt**
1	**8-ounce bottle clam juice *or* 1 cup chicken broth**
2	**8-ounce cans whole oysters**
1	**10-ounce package frozen chopped spinach, thawed and well drained**
¼	**teaspoon finely shredded lemon peel (optional)**

▪ Spray a large saucepan with nonstick spray coating. Cook onion and carrot in the saucepan over medium-high heat till onion is tender but not brown.

▪ In a small bowl stir together *1 cup* of the skim milk, the flour, nonfat dry milk powder, and salt; stir into vegetable mixture. Stir in remaining milk and clam juice or chicken broth. Cook and stir over medium heat till thickened and bubbly.

▪ Stir in *undrained* oysters, spinach, and lemon peel, if desired. Heat through, stirring occasionally. To serve, ladle into soup bowls. Makes 4 servings.

Nutrition information per serving: 220 calories, 20 g protein, 28 g carbohydrate, 3 g fat, 60 mg cholesterol, 946 mg sodium, 634 mg potassium.

SEASIDE MUSSELS

238 calories

Preparation Time: 1 hr. ▪ Cooking Time: 15 min. ▪ Low Fat ▪ Low Cholesterol

After washing the mussels, use your fingers to pull out the beard that is visible between the shells of each mussel.

4	**dozen mussels in shells**
½	**cup chopped celery**
½	**cup chopped onion**
2	**cloves garlic, minced**
½	**teaspoon dried thyme, crushed**
1	**bay leaf**
1	**tablespoon olive *or* cooking oil**
1	**cup dry white wine**

▪ Scrub mussels in shells under cold running water. Remove beards (see small photo above).

▪ In an 8- to 10-quart Dutch oven combine 4 quarts *cold water* and ⅓ cup *salt;* add mussels. Soak for 15 minutes; drain and rinse. Discard water. Repeat twice.

▪ In the Dutch oven cook celery, onion, garlic, thyme, and bay leaf in hot olive oil, covered, till onion is tender.

▪ Stir in wine. Cover and simmer for 5 minutes.

▪ Add mussels. Cover and simmer for 3 to 5 minutes or till shells open. Discard any unopened shells and the bay leaf.

▪ Divide mussels and cooking liquid among 4 shallow bowls. Makes 4 servings.

Nutrition information per serving: 238 calories, 21 g protein, 11 g carbohydrate, 7 g fat, 48 mg cholesterol, 331 mg sodium, 365 mg potassium.

MEATLESS MAIN DISHES

SPINACH LASAGNA ROLLS *(see page 267)*

VEGETABLE RICE BAKE

315 calories

Preparation Time: 35 min. ▪ Cooking Time: 30 min.

2	teaspoons instant chicken bouillon granules
⅔	cup long grain rice
½	cup chopped green pepper
2	cups shredded zucchini *or* chopped broccoli
2	beaten eggs
1	cup skim milk
½	teaspoon onion powder
½	teaspoon dried basil, crushed
½	teaspoon dried oregano, crushed
¾	cup shredded low-fat cheddar cheese
½	of an 8-ounce container reduced-calorie soft-style cream cheese
2	tablespoons diced pimiento

▪ In a saucepan combine bouillon granules and 1½ cups *water.* Bring to boiling; add rice. Reduce heat and simmer, covered, for 20 minutes or till tender.

▪ Meanwhile, in a medium saucepan combine green pepper and ½ cup *water.* Bring to boiling; reduce heat. Cover and simmer for 2 minutes. Add shredded zucchini or chopped broccoli. Cover and simmer for 3 to 5 minutes or till crisp-tender; drain well. Set aside.

▪ In a large mixing bowl combine eggs, milk, onion powder, basil, oregano, and ⅛ teaspoon *pepper.*

▪ Stir cheddar cheese and cream cheese into hot rice. Stir rice mixture into egg mixture. Stir in cooked vegetables and pimiento. Spoon into a 10x6x2-inch baking dish.

▪ Bake, uncovered, in a 350° oven for 30 to 35 minutes or till center is set. Let stand 5 minutes before serving. Serves 4.

Nutrition information per serving: 315 calories, 17 g protein, 33 g carbohydrate, 12 g fat, 169 mg cholesterol, 574 mg sodium, 407 mg potassium.

CARROT AND ONION PUFF

218 calories

Preparation Time: 30 min. ▪ Cooking Time: 50 min. ▪ Low Cholesterol

We cut down on the cholesterol by thickening the sauce with oat bran instead of with egg yolks.

1	cup chopped onion
1	cup shredded carrots
1	clove garlic, minced
2	tablespoons water
1½	cups skim milk
½	cup oat bran
2	tablespoons snipped fresh parsley
½	teaspoon salt
⅛	teaspoon ground nutmeg
⅛	teaspoon pepper
1	cup shredded cheddar *or* Monterey Jack cheese (4 ounces)
4	egg whites

▪ In a large saucepan combine onion, carrots, garlic, and water. Bring to boiling; reduce heat. Cover and simmer about 10 minutes or till vegetables are tender, stirring occasionally. *Do not drain.*

▪ Stir in milk, oat bran, parsley, salt, nutmeg, and pepper. Bring to boiling over medium-high heat, stirring constantly. Cook and stir for 2 minutes. Remove from heat. Stir in cheese till melted. Cool slightly.

▪ In a large mixer bowl beat egg whites till stiff peaks form (tips stand straight). Fold in vegetable mixture.

▪ Pour into an ungreased 1½-quart soufflé dish. Bake in a 325° oven about 50 minutes or till top is brown and a knife inserted near the center comes out clean. Serve immediately. Makes 4 servings.

Nutrition information per serving: 218 calories, 17 g protein, 19 g carbohydrate, 10 g fat, 31 mg cholesterol, 551 mg sodium, 460 mg potassium.

CREAMY EGG AND VEGETABLE BAKE

270 calories

Preparation Time: 25 min. ▪ Cooking Time: 25 min. ▪ Low Fat

2	**cups cubed peeled potatoes**
½	**cup chopped onion**
1	**cup frozen mixed vegetables**
1¼	**cups skim milk**
1	**tablespoon cornstarch**
2	**teaspoons instant chicken bouillon granules**
⅛	**teaspoon pepper**
½	**cup shredded low-fat cheddar cheese (2 ounces)**
1	**teaspoon Dijon-style mustard**
	Nonstick spray coating
4	**hard-cooked eggs, sliced**
1	**small tomato, halved and sliced**

▪ In a saucepan cook potatoes and onion, covered, in boiling salted water for 5 minutes. Add mixed vegetables and cook 5 minutes more or till tender; drain well.

▪ Meanwhile, for sauce, in a medium saucepan stir together milk, cornstarch, bouillon granules, and pepper. Cook and stir till thickened and bubbly. Stir in cheese and mustard till cheese is melted.

▪ Spray an 8x1½-inch round baking dish with nonstick spray coating. Spread the vegetables in the bottom of the dish. Top with the egg slices. Pour sauce over all ingredients in dish.

▪ Bake, uncovered, in a 350° oven for 20 minutes. Arrange tomato slices atop. Bake, uncovered, 5 minutes more or till heated through. Makes 4 servings.

Nutrition information per serving: 270 calories, 16 g protein, 32 g carbohydrate, 9 g fat, 284 mg cholesterol, 591 mg sodium, 618 mg potassium.

ASPARAGUS FRITTATA

Preparation Time: 15 min. ▪ Cooking Time: 10 min.

¾	**pound fresh asparagus spears** *or* **one 10-ounce package frozen cut asparagus**
6	**eggs**
¾	**cup low-fat cottage cheese**
2	**teaspoons prepared mustard**
⅛	**teaspoon salt**
	Dash pepper
	Nonstick spray coating
1	**cup sliced fresh mushrooms**
1	**small tomato, cut into wedges**

▪ Cook *fresh* asparagus spears in a small amount of boiling water for 8 to 10 minutes or till crisp-tender; drain. Reserve 3 spears for garnish; cut remaining asparagus into 1-inch pieces. Or, cook *frozen* asparagus according to package directions; drain. Set aside.

▪ Meanwhile, in a medium mixing bowl beat eggs till foamy. Beat in cottage cheese, mustard, salt, and pepper; set aside.

▪ Spray a 10-inch ovenproof skillet with nonstick spray coating. Cook mushrooms over medium heat till just tender. Stir in asparagus pieces. Pour egg mixture over mushrooms and asparagus. (If using fresh asparagus, arrange the 3 reserved spears on top.)

▪ Cook mixture over low heat about 5 minutes or till mixture bubbles slightly and begins to set around the edges.

▪ Bake frittata, uncovered, in a 400° oven about 10 minutes or till set. Garnish each serving with tomato. Serves 4.

Nutrition information per serving: 183 calories, 18 g protein, 7 g carbohydrate, 10 g fat, 416 mg cholesterol, 375 mg sodium, 463 mg potassium.

MEXICAN STRATA

305 calories

Advance Preparation Time: 20 min. ▪ Chilling Time: 2 hrs. ▪ Final Preparation Time: 40 min.

Save even more calories— use reduced-calorie bread and you'll trim off 50 calories per serving.

	Nonstick spray coating
5	**slices white *or* whole wheat bread, cubed (3¾ cups)**
3	**eggs**
1	**cup skim milk**
½	**cup plain low-fat yogurt**
½	**cup shredded Monterey Jack cheese with jalapeño (2 ounces)**
⅓	**cup shredded sharp cheddar cheese**
¾	**cup salsa**
	Parsley sprigs (optional)

■ Spray an 8x1½-inch round baking dish with nonstick spray coating. Spread bread cubes evenly in the baking dish. Set baking dish aside.

■ In medium mixing bowl beat together eggs, skim milk, and yogurt. Stir in Monterey Jack and cheddar cheese. Pour egg mixture over bread cubes in baking dish. Cover and chill for 2 to 24 hours.

■ Before serving, uncover baking dish. Bake in a 325° oven for 35 to 40 minutes or till center is set and top is golden. Let stand for 5 to 10 minutes before cutting. Meanwhile, heat salsa. If desired, spoon some of the salsa on top of the strata; garnish with parsley. Cut into wedges to serve. Pass remaining salsa. Makes 4 servings.

Nutrition information per serving: 305 calories, 17 g protein, 27 g carbohydrate, 14 g fat, 232 mg cholesterol, 762 mg sodium, 391 mg potassium.

TOFU AND CORN QUICHE

212 calories

Preparation Time: 10 min. ▪ Cooking Time: 33 min. ▪ Low Cholesterol

1	teaspoon margarine
2	tablespoons fine dry bread crumbs
12	ounces tofu (fresh bean curd), drained
2	egg whites
1	egg
⅓	cup skim milk
½	teaspoon dried oregano, crushed
⅛	teaspoon garlic powder
¾	cup shredded low-fat cheddar cheese
1	7-ounce can whole kernel corn with sweet peppers, drained
1	tablespoon dried minced onion
1	medium tomato
1	tablespoon snipped fresh parsley (optional)

■ Spread the margarine over the bottom and sides of a 9-inch pie plate. Sprinkle with bread crumbs to coat the dish.

■ Cut up tofu.

■ In a blender container or food processor bowl combine tofu, egg whites, whole egg, milk, oregano, garlic powder, ½ cup of the cheese, ¼ teaspoon *pepper*, and ⅛ teaspoon *salt*.

■ Cover and blend or process till smooth. Stir in corn and dried onion. Pour into prepared pie plate.

■ Bake, uncovered, in a 350° oven for 30 to 35 minutes or till a knife inserted near the center comes out clean.

■ Cut tomato into thin wedges. Arrange wedges atop quiche. Sprinkle with the remaining cheese. Bake for 3 minutes more or till cheese is melted. Garnish with fresh parsley, if desired. Makes 4 servings.

Nutrition information per serving: 212 calories, 18 g protein, 14 g carbohydrate, 10 g fat, 83 mg cholesterol, 411 mg sodium, 254 mg potassium.

BROILED RICE AND VEGETABLE PATTIES   302 calories

Preparation Time: 20 min. ▪ Chilling Time: 1 hr. ▪ Cooking Time: 9 min. ▪ Low Fat ▪ Low Cholesterol

1	**cup finely shredded carrots**
¾	**cup cooked brown rice, cooled**
½	**cup shredded part-skim mozzarella cheese**
⅓	**cup finely chopped onion**
⅓	**cup chopped dry-roasted unsalted peanuts**
¼	**cup fine dry bread crumbs**
1	**tablespoon snipped fresh parsley**
¼	**teaspoon ground ginger**
⅛	**teaspoon ground coriander**
2	**slightly beaten egg whites**
1	**tablespoon reduced-sodium soy sauce**
	Nonstick spray coating
2	**English muffins, split**
½	**cup plain low-fat yogurt**

■ In a large mixing bowl stir together carrots, cooled rice, cheese, onion, peanuts, bread crumbs, parsley, ginger, coriander, and ⅛ teaspoon *pepper*.

■ In a small bowl stir together egg whites and soy sauce. Add to rice mixture; mix well. Cover and chill for 1 hour or till firm enough to handle.

■ Shape chilled rice mixture into four ¾-inch-thick patties. Spray a baking sheet with nonstick spray coating. Place patties on the baking sheet.

■ Broil 4 inches from the heat for 7 minutes. Turn and broil about 2 minutes more or till set.

■ Meanwhile, toast English muffin halves.

■ To serve, place each patty on an English muffin half. Top with 2 tablespoons of yogurt. Makes 4 servings.

Nutrition information per serving: 302 calories, 16 g protein, 39 g carbohydrate, 10 g fat, 10 mg cholesterol, 338 mg sodium, 349 mg potassium.

SPINACH LASAGNA ROLLS

214 calories

Advance Preparation Time: 55 min. ▪ Chilling Time: 2 hrs. ▪ Final Preparation Time: 40 min. ▪ Low Fat ▪ Low Cholesterol

To roll the lasagna noodles, spread a scant ½ cup of the spinach mixture on top of each noodle. Then, roll up each noodle jelly-roll style, starting with one of the short edges. Place the lasagna rolls, seam side down, in the baking dish.

1	10-ounce package frozen chopped spinach
8	lasagna noodles
1	large onion
1	medium green pepper
	Nonstick spray coating
2	cups sliced fresh mushrooms
2	cloves garlic, minced
1	16-ounce can tomatoes
½	teaspoon dried basil
1	8-ounce can tomato sauce
½	teaspoon sugar
2	cups low-fat cottage cheese
½	cup grated Parmesan cheese
1	beaten egg
⅛	teaspoon ground nutmeg

▪ Cook spinach and lasagna noodles separately according to the package directions. Drain and set aside. For the sauce, chop onion and green pepper. Spray a *cold* large saucepan with nonstick spray coating; heat over medium heat. Add onion, green pepper, mushrooms, and garlic. Cook till vegetables are tender. Cut up tomatoes and crush basil. Stir *undrained* tomatoes, basil, tomato sauce, sugar, and ¼ teaspoon *pepper* into the vegetables. Bring to boiling; reduce heat. Simmer, uncovered, 5 minutes or till slightly thickened.

▪ Meanwhile, for filling, in a bowl stir together spinach, cottage cheese, Parmesan cheese, egg, and nutmeg.

▪ Spread a *scant ½ cup* spinach mixture on *each* noodle. Roll up each noodle, jelly-roll style, beginning at a short end. Spoon *1 cup* of sauce mixture into a 12x7½x2-inch baking dish. Place rolls, seam side down, in dish. Spoon on remaining sauce. Cover with plastic wrap; chill 2 to 24 hours.

▪ Before serving, remove plastic wrap. Cover with foil; bake in a 375° oven for 40 to 45 minutes or till bubbly. Serves 8.

Nutrition information per serving: 214 calories, 16 g protein, 28 g carbohydrate, 5 g fat, 44 mg cholesterol, 643 mg sodium, 557 mg potassium.

PASTA PRIMAVERA

297 calories

Preparation Time: 15 min. ▪ Cooking Time: 10 min. ▪ Low Fat ▪ Low Cholesterol

5	**ounces corkscrew macaroni *or* fettuccine**
¼	**cup water**
2	**cups sliced fresh mushrooms**
1	**9-ounce package frozen French-style green beans**
½	**cup coarsely chopped green *or* sweet red pepper**
1	**clove garlic, minced**
1	**12-ounce can evaporated skim milk**
4	**teaspoons cornstarch**
½	**cup shredded provolone *or* mozzarella cheese (2 ounces)**
1	**medium tomato, cut into wedges**

▪ Cook pasta according to package directions; drain well.

▪ Meanwhile, for sauce, in a medium saucepan combine water, mushrooms, frozen green beans, green or red pepper, garlic, ¼ teaspoon *salt,* and ¼ teaspoon *pepper.* Bring to boiling; reduce heat. Cover and simmer for 4 minutes or till vegetables are tender. *Do not drain.*

▪ Stir together milk and cornstarch; stir into vegetable mixture. Cook and stir over medium heat till thickened and bubbly. Cook and stir for 1 minute more. Stir in cheese till melted.

▪ To serve, pour the sauce over pasta. Garnish with tomato wedges. Makes 4 servings.

Nutrition information per serving: 297 calories, 17 g protein, 48 g carbohydrate, 5 g fat, 13 mg cholesterol, 375 mg sodium, 686 mg potassium.

EGGPLANT PARMESAN

249 calories

Preparation Time: 15 min. ▪ Cooking Time: 50 min. ▪ Low Cholesterol

1	beaten egg
¼	cup skim milk
⅛	teaspoon pepper
1	cup crushed saltine crackers (28 crackers)
¼	cup grated Parmesan cheese
2	tablespoons dried parsley flakes
1	medium eggplant, sliced ¼ inch thick (1 pound total)
1	15-ounce can tomato sauce
½	teaspoon dried oregano, crushed
1	clove garlic, minced
	Nonstick spray coating
¾	cup shredded part-skim mozzarella cheese (3 ounces)

▪ In a small bowl combine egg, milk, and pepper. In another bowl stir together cracker crumbs, Parmesan cheese, and dried parsley flakes.

▪ Dip eggplant slices in the milk mixture to coat, then dip both sides in the cracker mixture.

▪ Spray a 12x7½ x2-inch baking dish with nonstick spray coating. Arrange eggplant in dish.

▪ In a bowl stir together tomato sauce, oregano, and garlic; pour over eggplant.

▪ Bake, covered, in a 350° oven for 40 minutes or till eggplant is tender. Sprinkle with mozzarella cheese. Bake, uncovered, 10 minutes more. Makes 4 servings.

Nutrition information per serving: 249 calories, 15 g protein, 28 g carbohydrate, 9 g fat, 85 mg cholesterol, 1,095 mg sodium, 709 mg potassium.

CHEESY PEPPER AND MUSHROOM PIZZA   224 calories

Preparation Time: 55 min. ▪ Cooking Time: 20 min. ▪ Low Fat ▪ Low Cholesterol

1¼	to 1½ cups all-purpose flour
1	package active dry yeast
½	teaspoon sugar
1	teaspoon cooking oil
	Nonstick spray coating
1	tablespoon cornmeal
¾	cup low-fat cottage cheese, drained
1	egg
2	tablespoons grated Parmesan cheese
1	teaspoon dried basil, crushed
1	clove garlic, minced
1	medium green *or* sweet red pepper
1	cup sliced fresh mushrooms
1	cup shredded part-skim mozzarella cheese

▪ For crust, mix ¾ *cup* of the flour, the yeast, sugar, and ¼ teaspoon *salt*. Add oil and ½ cup *warm water* (120° to 130°). Beat with electric mixer on low speed 30 seconds, scraping bowl. Beat on high speed 3 minutes. Stir in as much remaining flour as you can. Then, knead in enough remaining flour to make a moderately stiff dough that is smooth and elastic (5 minutes total). Shape into a ball. Place in a greased bowl; turn once. Cover; let rise in a warm place till double (about 30 minutes). Punch down. Cover; let rest 10 minutes.

▪ On a floured surface roll dough into a 14-inch circle. Place on a pizza pan sprayed with nonstick spray coating and sprinkled with the cornmeal. Build up edges slightly. Bake crust in a 425° oven about 10 minutes or till lightly browned.

▪ In a blender container combine cottage cheese, egg, Parmesan, basil, garlic, and ⅛ teaspoon *pepper*. Cover; blend till smooth. Spread over hot crust. Cut green pepper into rings. Place atop pizza with mushrooms. Sprinkle with mozzarella. Bake in a 425° oven 10 minutes till hot. Serves 6.

Nutrition information per serving: 224 calories, 15 g protein, 26 g carbohydrate, 7 g fat, 60 mg cholesterol, 356 mg sodium, 212 mg potassium.

VEGETARIAN LASAGNA

282 calories

Preparation Time: 40 min. ▪ Cooking Time: 30 min. ▪ Low Cholesterol

8	lasagna noodles
1	10-ounce package frozen chopped broccoli
1	14½-ounce can tomatoes
1	15-ounce can tomato sauce
1	cup chopped celery
1	cup chopped onion
1	cup chopped green *or* sweet red pepper
1½	teaspoons dried basil, crushed*
2	bay leaves
1	clove garlic, minced
1	beaten egg
2	cups low-fat ricotta *or* cottage cheese
¼	cup grated Parmesan cheese
1	cup shredded part-skim mozzarella cheese

▪ Cook noodles and broccoli separately according to their package directions; drain well. Set aside.

▪ For sauce, cut up canned tomatoes. In a large saucepan stir together *undrained* tomatoes, tomato sauce, celery, onion, green pepper, basil, bay leaves, and garlic. Bring to boiling; reduce heat. Simmer, uncovered, 20 to 25 minutes or till sauce is thick, stirring occasionally. Remove bay leaves.

▪ Meanwhile, in a bowl stir together egg, ricotta cheese, Parmesan cheese, and ¼ teaspoon *pepper*. Stir in broccoli.

▪ Spread about ½ *cup* of the sauce in a 13x9x2-inch baking dish. Top with *half* of the noodles, *half* of the broccoli mixture, and *half* of the remaining sauce. Repeat layers, ending with the sauce.

▪ Bake, uncovered, in a 350° oven for 25 minutes; sprinkle with mozzarella. Bake 5 minutes more or till heated through. Let stand 10 minutes before serving. Makes 8 servings.

***Note:** If desired, substitute ½ teaspoon dried *oregano* for ½ teaspoon of the dried basil.

Nutrition information per serving: 282 calories, 18 g protein, 30 g carbohydrate, 10 g fat, 83 mg cholesterol, 646 mg sodium, 620 mg potassium.

271

CHEESE CALZONES

320 calories

Preparation Time: 30 min. ▪ Cooking Time: 15 min. ▪ Low Fat ▪ Low Cholesterol

Spread the filling over one-half of the circle of dough to within ½ inch of the edges. Moisten the edges of dough with water. Bring the other half of the dough up and over the filling. Press the edges together to seal in filling.

1	**16-ounce loaf frozen bread dough, thawed**
½	**cup chopped onion**
1	**tablespoon water**
2	**cloves garlic, minced**
1	**10-ounce package frozen chopped spinach**
1	**teaspoon Italian seasoning**
1	**slightly beaten egg**
1	**15-ounce carton part-skim ricotta cheese**
1	**cup shredded part-skim mozzarella cheese**
¼	**cup grated Parmesan cheese**
	Nonstick spray coating
1	**8-ounce can pizza sauce**

▪ Divide bread dough into 8 equal pieces. Place on a floured surface and cover dough with a towel. Let dough rest while preparing filling.

▪ In a skillet mix onion, water, and garlic. Cover; cook till onion is tender. Add spinach and Italian seasoning. Cover; cook till spinach is thawed, stirring once or twice to break up spinach. Uncover; cook and stir till liquid has evaporated.

▪ Meanwhile, in a medium mixing bowl combine egg, ricotta, mozzarella, and Parmesan cheese.

▪ Roll each portion of dough into a 6-inch circle. Spoon about *2 tablespoons* of the spinach mixture onto one-half of *each* circle. Top spinach mixture with *¼ cup* of the cheese mixture. Moisten edges of dough with a little water. Fold each circle in half, pressing edges together to seal. Flute edges, if desired. Prick tops with the tines of a fork. Place on a baking sheet that has been sprayed with nonstick spray coating.

▪ Bake in a 375° oven for 15 to 20 minutes or till golden. Meanwhile, heat pizza sauce. Serve with calzones. Serves 8.

Nutrition information per serving: 320 calories, 18 g protein, 36 g carbohydrate, 12 g fat, 64 mg cholesterol, 664 mg sodium, 241 mg potassium.

GRILLED THREE-CHEESE SANDWICHES   336 calories

Preparation Time: 15 min. ▪ Cooking Time: 3 min. ▪ Low Fat ▪ Low Cholesterol

1	**cup low-fat cottage cheese, drained**
½	**cup shredded cheddar cheese (2 ounces)**
¼	**cup chopped celery**
2	**tablespoons raisins**
2	**tablespoons grated Parmesan cheese**
6	**slices white *or* whole wheat bread**
	Nonstick spray coating

▪ In a blender container or food processor bowl blend or process cottage cheese till smooth.

▪ In a medium mixing bowl combine cottage cheese, cheddar cheese, celery, raisins, and Parmesan cheese.

▪ Divide cheese mixture among *three* slices of the bread, spreading evenly. Top with the remaining bread.

▪ Spray a griddle or large skillet with nonstick spray coating. Preheat over medium heat. Add sandwiches and cook for 3 to 4 minutes or till cheese is melted, turning once to brown both sides. Makes 3 servings.

Nutrition information per serving: 336 calories, 22 g protein, 37 g carbohydrate, 11 g fat, 31 mg cholesterol, 792 mg sodium, 231 mg potassium.

TOFU AND VEGETABLE STIR-FRY

325 calories

Preparation Time: 15 min. ▪ Cooking Time: 8 min. ▪ Low Fat ▪ No Cholesterol

½	**cup water**
¼	**cup dry sherry**
1	**tablespoon cornstarch**
2	**tablespoons soy sauce**
1	**teaspoon sugar**
1	**teaspoon instant chicken bouillon granules**
¾	**teaspoon ground ginger**
	Nonstick spray coating
1	**cup thinly sliced carrots**
1	**clove garlic, minced**
3	**cups cut-up broccoli**
6	**ounces tofu, cubed**
1	**cup hot cooked brown rice**
1	**tablespoon toasted sesame seeds (optional)**

▪ For sauce, stir together the water, dry sherry, cornstarch, soy sauce, sugar, bouillon granules, and ginger. Set aside.

▪ Spray a wok or large skillet with nonstick spray coating. Preheat over medium-high heat. Add carrots and garlic and stir-fry for 2 minutes. Add broccoli and stir-fry for 3 to 4 minutes more or till all vegetables are crisp-tender. Push vegetables from center of wok.

▪ Stir sauce and add to center of wok. Cook and stir till thickened and bubbly. Add tofu to wok. Stir ingredients together to coat with sauce. Cook and stir for 1 minute.

▪ Serve with hot cooked brown rice. Sprinkle with sesame seeds, if desired. Makes 2 servings.

Nutrition information per serving: 325 calories, 15 g protein, 51 g carbohydrate, 5 g fat, 0 mg cholesterol, 1,279 mg sodium, 810 mg potassium.

TOFU MANICOTTI

285 calories

Preparation Time: 35 min. ▪ Cooking Time: 22 min. ▪ Low Fat ▪ Low Cholesterol

To fill manicotti shells, use a small spoon to fill each shell with about ¼ cup of the filling. The spoon should be smaller in diameter than the shell so you can fill the center without tearing the pasta.

8	manicotti shells
	Nonstick spray coating
½	cup chopped fresh mushrooms
½	cup finely chopped onion
1	tablespoon snipped fresh parsley
1	teaspoon dried Italian seasoning
⅛	teaspoon paprika
10	ounces tofu (fresh bean curd), drained
1	slightly beaten egg white
2	tablespoons grated Parmesan cheese
1¼	cups skim milk
2	tablespoons all-purpose flour
⅛	teaspoon garlic powder
½	cup shredded low-fat cheddar cheese

■ Cook pasta shells according to package directions. Rinse in cold water; drain.

■ Spray a medium skillet with nonstick spray coating. Add mushrooms and onion; cook till tender. Stir in parsley, Italian seasoning, and paprika. Cool slightly.

■ Mash the tofu in a bowl. Stir in egg white, Parmesan cheese, and mushroom and onion mixture. Stuff each manicotti shell with about ¼ *cup* of the tofu mixture. Arrange stuffed shells in a 12x7½x2-inch baking dish.

■ For sauce, in a medium saucepan combine milk, flour, garlic powder, ¼ teaspoon *salt,* and ⅛ teaspoon *pepper.* Cook and stir till thickened and bubbly. Pour sauce over pasta in baking dish.

■ Bake, covered, in a 350° oven for 20 to 25 minutes or till heated through. Spinkle with cheddar cheese. Bake, uncovered, 2 minutes more or till cheese is melted. Serves 4.

Nutrition information per serving: 285 calories, 19 g protein, 36 g carbohydrate, 7 g fat, 13 mg cholesterol, 347 mg sodium, 328 mg potassium.

LENTIL STEW

282 calories

Preparation Time: 10 min. ▪ Cooking Time: 45 min. ▪ Low Fat ▪ No Cholesterol

Lentils are quick to cook and a good source of fiber. A ½-cup serving of cooked lentils contains 4 grams of dietary fiber.

1	cup dry lentils
3½	cups chicken broth
1	14½-ounce can peeled Italian-style tomatoes, cut up
1	cup peeled and chopped potato
½	cup chopped carrot
½	cup chopped celery
½	cup chopped onion
2	tablespoons snipped parsley
1	tablespoon dried basil, crushed
1	clove garlic, minced
	Dash pepper

▪ Rinse and drain lentils. In a large saucepan combine lentils, chicken broth, *undrained* tomatoes, potato, carrot, celery, onion, parsley, basil, garlic, and pepper. Bring to boiling; reduce heat. Cover and simmer for 45 to 50 minutes or till lentils and vegetables are tender, stirring occasionally. Makes 4 servings.

Nutrition information per serving: 282 calories, 19 g protein, 49 g carbohydrate, 2 g fat, 0 mg cholesterol, 873 mg sodium, 1,258 mg potassium.

CURRIED LENTILS AND VEGETABLES

242 calories

Preparation Time: 15 min. ▪ Cooking Time: 30 min. ▪ Low Fat ▪ Low Cholesterol

Add some crunch to your meal with toasted pita bread wedges.

2	cups dry lentils (10 ounces)
4	cups water
1½	cups chopped carrots
1½	cups chopped onions
1	cup chopped celery
1	clove garlic, minced
2 to 3	teaspoons curry powder
1	teaspoon grated fresh gingerroot *or*
	¼ teaspoon ground ginger
1	teaspoon salt
1½	cups plain low-fat yogurt
1	medium tomato, chopped
1	tablespoon snipped fresh parsley *or* cilantro (optional)

▪ Rinse lentils and drain.

▪ In a Dutch oven combine lentils, water, carrots, onions, celery, garlic, curry powder, ginger, and salt. Bring to boiling; reduce heat. Cover and simmer for 30 minutes or till the lentils are tender.

▪ In a medium mixing bowl stir together yogurt, tomato, and parsley, if desired. Serve with lentil mixture. Serves 6.

Nutrition information per serving: 242 calories, 16 g protein, 43 g carbohydrate, 2 g fat, 4 mg cholesterol, 446 mg sodium, 811 mg potassium.

RICE AND BEANS WITH CHEESE

282 calories

Preparation Time: 30 min. ▪ Cooking Time: 23 min. ▪ Low Fat ▪ Low Cholesterol

1⅓	cups water
⅔	cup long grain rice
1	cup shredded carrots
½	cup sliced green onions
1	teaspoon instant chicken bouillon granules
½	teaspoon ground coriander
¼	teaspoon salt
	Dash bottled hot pepper sauce
1	15-ounce can pinto *or* navy beans, drained
1	cup low-fat cottage cheese
1	8-ounce carton plain low-fat yogurt
1	tablespoon snipped fresh parsley
½	cup shredded low-fat cheddar cheese

▪ In a large saucepan combine water, rice, carrots, green onions, bouillon granules, coriander, salt, and bottled hot pepper sauce. Bring to boiling; reduce heat. Cover and simmer for 15 minutes or till rice is tender and the water is absorbed.

▪ Stir in pinto or navy beans, cottage cheese, yogurt, and parsley. Spoon into a 10x6x2-inch baking dish.

▪ Bake, covered, in a 350° oven for 20 to 25 minutes or till heated through. Sprinkle with cheddar cheese. Bake, uncovered, for 3 to 5 minutes more or till cheese melts. Serves 5.

Nutrition information per serving: 282 calories, 19 g protein, 42 g carbohydrate, 4 g fat, 14 mg cholesterol, 489 mg sodium, 548 mg potassium.

TEX-MEX BEANS WITH DUMPLINGS

313 calories

Preparation Time: 20 min. ▪ Cooking Time: 10 min. ▪ Low Fat ▪ No Cholesterol

⅓	cup all-purpose flour
⅓	cup yellow cornmeal
1	teaspoon baking powder
¼	teaspoon salt
1	beaten egg white
¼	cup skim milk
2	tablespoons cooking oil
¾	cup water
1	cup chopped onion
1	clove garlic, minced
1	15-ounce can garbanzo beans, drained
1	15-ounce can red kidney beans, drained
1	15-ounce can tomato sauce
1	4-ounce can diced green chili peppers, drained
2	teaspoons chili powder
¼	teaspoon salt
1½	teaspoons cornstarch

■ In a medium mixing bowl stir together flour, cornmeal, baking powder, and ¼ teaspoon salt; set aside. In a small bowl combine egg white, milk, and oil; set aside.

■ In a 10-inch skillet combine the water, onion, and garlic. Bring to boiling; reduce heat. Cover and simmer 5 minutes or till tender. Stir in garbanzo beans, kidney beans, tomato sauce, green chili peppers, chili powder, and ¼ teaspoon salt.

■ In a small bowl stir together cornstarch and 1 tablespoon *water*. Stir into bean mixture. Cook and stir till slightly thickened and bubbly. Reduce heat.

■ For dumplings, add milk mixture to cornmeal mixture; stir just till combined. Drop dumpling mixture from a tablespoon to make 5 mounds atop the hot bean mixture.

■ Cover and simmer for 10 to 12 minutes or till a toothpick inserted into the center of a dumpling comes out clean. Makes 5 servings.

Nutrition information per serving: 313 calories, 13 g protein, 50 g carbohydrate, 8 g fat, 0 mg cholesterol, 1,023 mg sodium, 839 mg potassium.

MICROWAVE
MAIN DISHES

HERBED POT ROAST

Preparation Time: 5 min. ▪ Cooking Time: 1 hr. 25 min.

1	2½-pound boneless beef chuck roast, cut 2 inches thick
¼	cup dry white wine
2	tablespoons water
1	tablespoon Worcestershire sauce
½	teaspoon dried rosemary *or* oregano, crushed
¼	teaspoon salt
¼	teaspoon pepper
1	clove garlic, minced
2	medium onions, sliced
2	medium green *or* sweet red peppers, cut into bite-size strips
1	tablespoon cornstarch
1	tablespoon water

▪ Trim meat of separable fat. In a 3-quart casserole combine wine, the 2 tablespoons water, Worcestershire sauce, rosemary or oregano, salt, pepper, and garlic. Add meat; turn to coat on all sides.

▪ Cook, covered, on 100% power (high) for 5 minutes. Then cook, covered, on 50% power (medium) for 40 minutes. Turn meat over. Add onions. Cook, covered, on medium for 20 minutes more. Turn meat over again. Add peppers. Cook, covered, on medium for 17 to 20 minutes more or till meat is tender. Remove meat and vegetables; keep warm.

▪ For sauce, skim fat from cooking liquid. Measure liquid. Add water, if necessary, to equal 1 cup total.

▪ In the same casserole stir together cornstarch and the 1 tablespoon water; stir in juices. Cook, uncovered, on 100% power (high) for 3 to 4 minutes or till thickened and bubbly, stirring once. Serve over sliced beef. Makes 8 servings.

Nutrition information per serving: 275 calories, 36 g protein, 5 g carbohydrate, 11 g fat, 107 mg cholesterol, 159 mg sodium, 407 mg potassium.

SPINACH-STUFFED FLANK STEAK

141 calories

Preparation Time: 25 min. ▪ Cooking Time: 21 min. ▪ Low Cholesterol

Using a sharp knife, slice between the wooden picks, cutting the meat roll into 6 equal portions.

1	**10-ounce package frozen chopped spinach**
½	**cup chopped onion**
½	**cup shredded carrot**
1	**clove garlic, minced**
¼	**teaspoon dried basil *or* marjoram, crushed**
1	**to 1¼ pounds beef flank steak**
¼	**teaspoon salt**
¼	**teaspoon pepper**

▪ In a 1½-quart casserole combine spinach, onion, carrot, and garlic. Cook, covered, on 100% power (high) for 6 to 7 minutes or till vegetables are tender, stirring twice. Drain well, squeezing out excess moisture. Stir in basil or marjoram.

▪ Meanwhile, use a sharp knife to score one side of the steak. Place meat, scored side up, between 2 sheets of plastic wrap. Pound meat to ½-inch thickness (about 10x8 inches). Sprinkle with salt and pepper.

▪ Spoon spinach mixture over meat. Roll up from one long side. Secure with wooden picks at even intervals, beginning ¾ inch from one end. Cut between picks into 6 slices.

▪ Place meat rolls, cut side up, in a 12x7½x2-inch baking dish. Flatten slightly with hand. Cover with waxed paper. Cook on 100% power (high) for 5 minutes. Rearrange meat and spoon juices over.

▪ Cook on 50% power (medium) for 10 to 15 minutes or till meat is tender, rearranging once. Remove wooden picks and serve meat with juices. Makes 6 servings.

Nutrition information per serving: 141 calories, 14 g protein, 4 g carbohydrate, 8 g fat, 35 mg cholesterol, 161 mg sodium, 433 mg potassium.

ORIENTAL BEEF AND BROCCOLI

191 calories

Preparation Time: 15 min. ▪ Marinating Time: 10 min. ▪ Cooking Time: 11 min. ▪ Low Fat ▪ Low Cholesterol

¾	pound beef top round steak
1	tablespoon soy sauce
1	tablespoon vinegar
1	tablespoon molasses
1	clove garlic, minced
⅛ to ¼	teaspoon crushed red pepper
1	cup thinly bias-sliced carrots
6	cups fresh broccoli flowerets
1½	teaspoons cornstarch
1	tablespoon water

■ Partially freeze meat. Thinly slice meat across the grain into bite-size strips. Set aside.

■ In a 2-quart casserole stir together soy sauce, vinegar, molasses, garlic, and red pepper. Stir in meat. Cover and let stand at room temperature for 10 minutes.

■ Cook meat mixture, covered, on 100% power (high) for 3 to 5 minutes or till meat is no longer pink, stirring every 2 minutes. With a slotted spoon, remove meat from casserole; set aside. Reserve juices in casserole.

■ Add carrots to juices in casserole. Cook, covered, on high for 1 minute. Add broccoli and cook 4 to 6 minutes more or till vegetables are nearly crisp-tender, stirring every 2 minutes.

■ Stir together cornstarch and water; stir into vegetables. Cook, uncovered, on high for 2 to 3 minutes or till slightly thickened, stirring after every minute. Stir in meat. Cook, covered, on high for 1 minute or till heated through. Serves 4.

Nutrition information per serving: 191 calories, 24 g protein, 14 g carbohydrate, 5 g fat, 53 mg cholesterol, 341 mg sodium, 844 mg potassium.

POLENTA WITH CHUNKY MEAT SAUCE   263 calories

Preparation Time: 50 min. ▪ Cooking Time: 28 min. ▪ Low Fat ▪ Low Cholesterol

1	cup yellow cornmeal
1	cup cold water
1	teaspoon salt
3	cups boiling water
	Nonstick spray coating
1	pound lean ground beef *or* Italian-style turkey sausage
2	green onions, sliced
1	17-ounce can cream-style corn
1	small green pepper, cut into thin strips
1	teaspoon dried Italian seasoning
	Dash pepper
1	2-ounce jar diced pimiento, drained

▪ For polenta, in a 2-quart casserole combine cornmeal, the 1 cup cold water, and salt. Slowly pour boiling water into cornmeal mixture, stirring constantly till the mixture is well blended. Cook, uncovered, on 100% power (high) for 6 to 8 minutes or till very thick, stirring every minute. Spray a 12x7½x2-inch baking dish with nonstick coating. Spread polenta in dish. Cover; cool 45 minutes or chill overnight.

▪ In a 2-quart casserole combine meat and onions. Cook, covered, on high 5 to 7 minutes or till no pink remains, stirring once. Drain; set mixture aside. In the casserole combine corn, green pepper, Italian seasoning, and pepper. Cook, covered, on high 5 to 6 minutes or till green pepper is crisp-tender. Stir in meat mixture and pimiento.

▪ Cut polenta into 24 squares; arrange on platter. Cook, covered with waxed paper, on 70% power (medium-high) 4 to 5 minutes or till heated through. Transfer to serving plates.

▪ Cook meat mixture, covered, on high for 1½ to 2½ minutes or till hot. Serve with polenta slices. Makes 6 servings.

Nutrition information per serving: 263 calories, 19 g protein, 31 g carbohydrate, 8 g fat, 53 mg cholesterol, 625 mg sodium, 381 mg potassium.

TORTILLA PIE

Preparation Time: 20 min. ▪ Cooking Time: 12 min. ▪ Low Cholesterol

½	pound lean ground beef
1	cup finely chopped onion
½	cup finely chopped celery
1	clove garlic, minced
1	8-ounce can red kidney beans, drained
1	cup taco sauce
2	teaspoons chili powder
1	teaspoon ground cumin
	Nonstick spray coating
6	6-inch corn tortillas
1	cup low-fat cottage cheese, drained
1	cup shredded Monterey Jack cheese *or* Monterey Jack cheese with jalapeño peppers

▪ Crumble beef into a 2-quart casserole. Stir in onion, celery, and garlic. Cook, covered, on 100% power (high) for 5 to 7 minutes or till beef is no longer pink and vegetables are tender, stirring once. Drain off fat. Stir in beans, taco sauce, chili powder, and cumin.

▪ Spray a 9-inch pie plate with nonstick spray coating. Line pie plate with tortillas to form a shell. Spoon cottage cheese over tortillas. Top with meat mixture.

▪ Cook, covered with vented clear plastic wrap, on high for 6 to 7 minutes or till heated through, giving the dish a half-turn once. Sprinkle with Monterey Jack cheese. Cook, covered, on high for 1 minute more or till cheese is melted. Let stand for 10 minutes. Makes 6 servings.

Nutrition information per serving: 288 calories, 22 g protein, 26 g carbohydrate, 11 g fat, 46 mg cholesterol, 561 mg sodium, 414 mg potassium.

MEAT LOAF WITH GARDEN SAUCE

208 calories

Preparation Time: 17 min. ▪ Cooking Time: 8 min.

In a 9-inch pie plate, shape the ground meat mixture into a 6-inch ring that's 2 inches wide. A ring shape will cook more evenly in the microwave than the traditional loaf shape.

1	envelope regular vegetable soup mix
1½	cups plain low-fat yogurt
½	teaspoon dried dillweed
1	beaten egg
1	pound lean ground beef
½	cup finely shredded carrot
¼	cup finely chopped celery
¼	cup quick-cooking oats

▪ In a small mixing bowl stir together soup mix, yogurt, and dillweed. Cover and refrigerate mixture till needed.

▪ In a medium mixing bowl stir together egg and ½ *cup* of the yogurt mixture. Stir in ground beef, carrot, celery, and oats till well mixed.

▪ In a 9-inch pie plate shape meat mixture into a ring. (Your ring should be about 6 inches in diameter and 2 inches wide. See small photo above.)

▪ Cook, covered with waxed paper, on 100% power (high) for 8 to 10 minutes (10 to 12 minutes in a low-wattage oven) or till meat is no longer pink, giving dish a quarter-turn every 3 minutes. Serve meat loaf with remaining yogurt mixture. Makes 6 servings.

Nutrition information per serving: 208 calories, 21 g protein, 10 g carbohydrate, 9 g fat, 103 mg cholesterol, 386 mg sodium, 412 mg potassium.

GINGERED PORK

Preparation Time: 35 min. ▪ Marinating Time: 10 min. ▪ Cooking Time: 9 min. ▪ Low Fat ▪ Low Cholesterol

For variety, use ¼ pound of tofu in place of ¼ pound of the pork.

¾	**pound lean boneless pork**
2	**tablespoons soy sauce**
2	**tablespoons dry sherry**
1	**tablespoon grated gingerroot**
1	**clove garlic, minced**
1	**cup sliced fresh mushrooms**
½	**cup green onions cut into 1-inch lengths**
⅓	**cup beef broth**
1	**tablespoon cornstarch**
1	**cup frozen pea pods, thawed and drained**
1	**cup fresh bean sprouts**
2	**cups hot cooked rice**

▪ Partially freeze meat. Thinly slice meat across the grain into bite-size strips. In a 2-quart casserole stir together soy sauce, sherry, gingerroot, and garlic. Stir in meat. Let stand at room temperature for 10 minutes.

▪ Add mushrooms and green onions. Cook, covered, on 100% power (high) for 5 to 7 minutes (6 to 8 minutes in a low-wattage oven) or till pork is no longer pink, stirring every 2 minutes.

▪ Stir together beef broth and cornstarch. Stir into ingredients in casserole. Cook, uncovered, on high for 3 to 4 minutes (4 to 7 minutes in a low-wattage oven) or till sauce is thickened and bubbly, stirring after every minute. Stir in pea pods and bean sprouts. Cook on high for 1 to 2 minutes more or till heated through. Serve over rice. Makes 4 servings.

Nutrition information per serving: 321 calories, 23 g protein, 34 g carbohydrate, 9 g fat, 58 mg cholesterol, 629 mg sodium, 489 mg potassium.

SAUCY CURRIED PORK AND ZUCCHINI

308 calories

Preparation Time: 10 min. ▪ Cooking Time: 29 min. ▪ Low Fat ▪ Low Cholesterol

1	pound lean boneless pork, cut into ½-inch pieces
1	cup chopped onion
2 to 3	teaspoons curry powder
½	teaspoon garlic salt
1	16-ounce can tomatoes, cut up
3	cups zucchini halved lengthwise and sliced
3	tablespoons all-purpose flour
½	cup plain low-fat yogurt
3	cups hot cooked rice

▪ In a 2-quart casserole combine pork, onion, curry, and garlic salt. Cook, covered, on 100% power (high) for 5 to 7 minutes (8 to 10 minutes in a low-wattage oven) or till onion is tender, stirring after 2 minutes. Stir in *undrained* tomatoes.

▪ Cook, covered, on 50% power (medium), or 100% power (high) in low-wattage oven, for 10 minutes. Stir in zucchini. Cook, covered, on medium for 10 to 15 minutes more (8 to 10 minutes on high power in a low-wattage oven) or till pork and zucchini are tender, stirring once.

▪ Stir flour into yogurt; stir into pork mixture. Cook, uncovered, on high for 3 to 4 minutes or till slightly thickened and bubbly, stirring twice. Cook 1 minute more. Serve with hot cooked rice. Makes 6 servings.

Nutrition information per serving: 308 calories, 21 g protein, 36 g carbohydrate, 8 g fat, 53 mg cholesterol, 336 mg sodium, 615 mg potassium.

SPICY STUFFED PEPPERS

266 calories

Preparation Time: 25 min. ▪ Cooking Time: 12 min. ▪ Low Fat ▪ Low Cholesterol

You'll taste just a hint of sweetness in the pleasantly spiced meat filling.

4	**medium green, red,** *or* **yellow sweet peppers**
2	**tablespoons water**
¾	**pound lean ground pork** *or* **beef**
½	**cup finely chopped onion**
½	**cup finely chopped carrot**
1	**clove garlic, minced**
1	**8-ounce can tomato sauce**
½	**cup cooked rice**
¼	**cup raisins**
1	**teaspoon chili powder**
¼	**teaspoon salt**
⅛	**teaspoon ground allspice**
	Few dashes bottled hot pepper sauce

■ Cut tops from peppers; discard seeds and membranes. Chop enough of the tops to make ½ cup; set aside.

■ Place peppers, cut side up, in an 8x8x2-inch baking dish. Add the water and cover with vented clear plastic wrap. Cook on 100% power (high) for 3 to 5 minutes (5 to 7 minutes in low-wattage ovens) or till peppers are barely tender, giving dish a half-turn once. Drain and set aside.

■ Crumble meat into a 2-quart casserole. Stir in the ½ cup chopped green pepper, chopped onion, chopped carrot, and garlic. Cook, covered, on high for 5 to 6 minutes (8 to 9 minutes in low-wattage ovens) or till meat is no longer pink, stirring once. Drain off fat.

■ Stir in tomato sauce, rice, raisins, chili powder, salt, allspice, and hot pepper sauce. Spoon meat mixture into pepper shells. Cover with vented clear plastic wrap.

■ Cook on high for 4 to 5 minutes (5 to 7 minutes in low-wattage ovens) or till filling is hot and peppers are crisp-tender, giving dish a quarter-turn after 2 minutes. Makes 4 servings.

Nutrition information per serving: 266 calories, 23 g protein, 27 g carbohydrate, 8 g fat, 62 mg cholesterol, 545 mg sodium, 884 mg potassium.

CHICKEN WITH ORIENTAL DRESSING 209 calories

Preparation Time: 35 min. ▪ Cooking Time: 23½ min. ▪ Low Cholesterol

To prevent overcooking, cover the drumsticks and wing tips with small pieces of foil. Make sure the foil does not touch itself or the microwave oven.

1	cup sliced fresh mushrooms
¾	cup shredded carrots
3	green onions, bias-sliced into 1-inch lengths (½ cup)
4	slices whole wheat bread, toasted and cut into ½-inch cubes (3 cups)
½	of an 8-ounce can sliced water chestnuts, drained and chopped (½ cup)
2	tablespoons soy sauce
1	tablespoon dry sherry
1	tablespoon cooking oil
¼	teaspoon garlic powder
⅛	teaspoon ground ginger
⅓	to ½ cup chicken broth
1	2½- to 3-pound broiler-fryer chicken

▪ For stuffing, in a 1½-quart casserole cook mushrooms, carrots, green onions, and 2 tablespoons *water,* covered, on 100% power (high) 3 to 4 minutes or till crisp-tender. Add bread cubes and water chestnuts. Combine soy sauce, sherry, oil, garlic powder, and ginger. Toss stuffing with *1 tablespoon* soy mixture and enough broth to moisten. Set aside.

▪ Rinse chicken; pat dry. Pull neck skin to back of bird; twist wing tips under the chicken. Tie legs to tail. Place chicken, breast side down, in a 12x7½x2-inch dish. Brush with some of the remaining soy mixture. Place in microwave oven, allowing 2 to 3 inches between the chicken and the oven walls and ceiling. Cover loosely with waxed paper. Cook on high 10 minutes. Turn chicken breast side up. Brush with remaining soy mixture. To prevent overcooking, shield drumsticks and wing tips with small foil pieces. Cook, covered, on high 8 to 10 minutes or till no longer pink. Cover; let stand 10 minutes.

▪ Meanwhile, cook stuffing, covered, on high for 2½ to 3 minutes or till heated through. Serve with chicken. Serves 6.

Nutrition information per serving: 209 calories, 21 g protein, 14 g carbohydrate, 7 g fat, 55 mg cholesterol, 533 mg sodium, 397 mg potassium.

CHEESE-AND-APPLE-STUFFED CHICKEN

247 calories

Preparation Time: 15 min. ▪ Cooking Time: 6 min. ▪ Low Fat ▪ Low Cholesterol

Whip up this full-flavored dinner for two in less than 30 minutes.

2	**medium (6 to 8 ounces total) boned skinless chicken breast halves**
1	**small apple *or* pear, cored (6 ounces)**
¼	**cup shredded Muenster *or* cheddar cheese (1 ounce)**
¼	**cup apple juice *or* orange juice**
1	**teaspoon cornstarch**
2	**tablespoons sliced green onion**
1	**teaspoon instant chicken bouillon granules**

▪ Rinse chicken; pat dry. Pound chicken to ¼-inch thickness. Chop *half* of the apple; slice the other half. Divide chopped apple and cheese evenly between chicken pieces. Roll up, folding in sides to enclose filling. Secure with wooden toothpicks, if necessary.

▪ Arrange rolls, seam side down, in an 8x8x2-inch baking dish. Add *2 tablespoons* of the fruit juice to dish. Cover with vented microwave-safe plastic wrap.

▪ Cook on 100% power (high) for 2 minutes. Rearrange chicken; add sliced apple. Cover and cook for 2 to 4 minutes more or till chicken is tender and no longer pink. Place chicken and apple slices on serving plates; cover to keep warm.

▪ For sauce, in a 1-cup measure combine cornstarch, remaining fruit juice, green onion, and bouillon granules. Stir in cooking liquid. Cook, uncovered, on high for 2 to 3 minutes or till thickened and bubbly, stirring after every 30 seconds. Spoon sauce over chicken rolls. Makes 2 servings.

Nutrition information per serving: 247 calories, 30 g protein, 14 g carbohydrate, 8 g fat, 86 mg cholesterol, 323 mg sodium, 355 mg potassium.

291

CITRUS CHICKEN

204 calories

Preparation Time: 15 min. ▪ Cooking Time: 7½ min. ▪ Low Fat ▪ Low Cholesterol

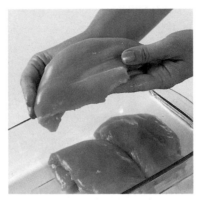

So chicken cooks evenly in the microwave, tuck under any thin portions of the breast halves. This creates an even thickness.

4	**medium (12 to 16 ounces total) boned skinless chicken breast halves**
½	**teaspoon finely shredded lemon *or* lime peel**
1	**tablespoon lemon *or* lime juice**
1	**tablespoon honey**
1	**tablespoon soy sauce**
⅓	**cup orange juice**
2	**teaspoons cornstarch**
2	**medium oranges, peeled and sectioned**

▪ Rinse chicken; pat dry. Arrange chicken in an 8x8x2-inch baking dish, tucking under thin portions of chicken to make an even thickness.

▪ In a mixing bowl combine lemon or lime peel, lemon or lime juice, honey, and soy sauce. Pour over chicken. Cover with vented microwave-safe plastic wrap.

▪ Cook on 100% power (high) for 4 to 6 minutes or till chicken is tender and no longer pink, rearranging and turning chicken over after 3 minutes. Remove chicken from dish, reserving juices in dish. Cover chicken to keep warm.

▪ For sauce, combine orange juice and cornstarch; stir into reserved juices. Cook, uncovered, on high for 3 to 4 minutes or till thickened and bubbly, stirring after every minute till slightly thickened, then every 30 seconds. Stir in orange sections. Cook, uncovered, on high for 30 to 60 seconds more, or till heated through. Spoon atop chicken. Makes 4 servings.

Nutrition information per serving: 204 calories, 27 g protein, 16 g carbohydrate, 3 g fat, 72 mg cholesterol, 321 mg sodium, 391 mg potassium.

CURRIED CHICKEN CASSEROLE

203 calories

Preparation Time: 15 min. ▪ Cooking Time: 13½ min. ▪ Low Fat ▪ Low Cholesterol

1	8-ounce can pineapple chunks (juice pack)
3	cups loose-pack frozen cauliflower, broccoli, and carrots
¼	cup water
8	ounces boned skinless chicken breast halves, cut into bite-size strips
1	8-ounce carton plain low-fat yogurt
2	tablespoons all-purpose flour
2 to 3	teaspoons curry powder
½	teaspoon salt
2	tablespoons chopped salted peanuts

▪ Drain pineapple, reserving juice; set aside.

▪ In a 2-quart casserole combine frozen vegetables and water. Cook, covered, on 100% power (high) for 4 to 6 minutes or till vegetables are nearly thawed, stirring once. Drain.

▪ Stir in chicken and reserved pineapple juice. Cook, covered, on high for 5 to 8 minutes or till chicken is no longer pink, stirring once.

▪ Meanwhile, for sauce, stir together yogurt, flour, curry powder, and salt; stir into casserole. Cook, uncovered, on high for 4 to 7 minutes or till sauce is thickened and bubbly, stirring after every minute. Stir in pineapple chunks. Cook, uncovered, on high for 30 seconds or till heated through. Garnish with peanuts. Makes 4 servings.

Nutrition information per serving: 203 calories, 18 g protein, 23 g carbohydrate, 5 g fat, 37 mg cholesterol, 373 mg sodium, 512 mg potassium.

SOY-GLAZED CHICKEN

207 calories

Preparation Time: 15 min. ▪ Marinating Time: 4 hrs. ▪ Cooking Time: 12 min. ▪ Low Fat ▪ Low Cholesterol

2	**pounds meaty chicken pieces (breast halves, thighs, drumsticks), skinned**
¼	**cup white vinegar** *or* **rice wine vinegar**
2	**tablespoons honey**
2	**tablespoons soy sauce**
4	**cloves garlic, minced**
½	**teaspoon grated fresh gingerroot** *or* **⅛ teaspoon ground ginger**
¼	**teaspoon onion powder**

■ Rinse chicken; pat dry. Place chicken in a plastic bag set in a deep bowl.

■ For marinade, in a mixing bowl combine vinegar, honey, soy sauce, garlic, gingerroot, and onion powder; pour over chicken in bag. Close bag.

■ Marinate in the refrigerator for 4 to 24 hours, turning bag occasionally.

■ Remove chicken from bag, reserving marinade. Arrange chicken in a 12x7½x2-inch baking dish with meaty portions toward edges of the dish. Pour marinade over chicken. Cover with waxed paper.

■ Cook on 100% power (high) for 12 to 14 minutes or till chicken is tender and no longer pink, rearranging and spooning marinade over chicken after 8 minutes. Makes 5 servings.

Nutrition information per serving: 207 calories, 27 g protein, 9 g carbohydrate, 7 g fat, 81 mg cholesterol, 491 mg sodium, 251 mg potassium.

CHICKEN COUNTRY CAPTAIN

331 calories

Preparation Time: 15 min. ▪ Cooking Time: 15 min. ▪ Low Fat ▪ Low Cholesterol

2	pounds meaty chicken pieces (breast halves, thighs, drumsticks), skinned
1	14½-ounce can stewed tomatoes
1	medium green *or* sweet red pepper, chopped
1	clove garlic, minced
2	tablespoons raisins
1	tablespoon quick-cooking tapioca
2 to 3	teaspoons curry powder
½	teaspoon dried thyme, crushed
2	tablespoons toasted slivered almonds (optional)
2½	cups hot cooked rice

▪ Rinse chicken; pat dry. Arrange chicken pieces in a 12x7½x2-inch baking dish with meaty portions toward the edges of the dish.

▪ In a mixing bowl combine *undrained* tomatoes, green or sweet red pepper, garlic, raisins, tapioca, curry, and thyme. Let stand 5 minutes. Pour evenly over chicken. Cover with vented microwave-safe plastic wrap.

▪ Cook on 100% power (high) for 15 to 20 minutes or till chicken is tender and no longer pink, rearranging chicken after 10 minutes. Garnish with almonds, if desired. Serve over rice. Makes 5 servings.

Nutrition information per serving: 331 calories, 30 g protein, 36 g carbohydrate, 7 g fat, 81 mg cholesterol, 289 mg sodium, 537 mg potassium.

CHICKEN WITH MUSHROOMS

239 calories

Preparation Time: 15 min. ▪ Cooking Time: 10 min. ▪ Low Fat ▪ Low Cholesterol

2	cups sliced fresh mushrooms
¼	cup dry white wine *or* chicken broth
1	clove garlic, minced
¼	teaspoon dried basil, crushed
2	cups cubed cooked chicken *or* turkey (11 ounces)
1	14-ounce can artichoke hearts, drained and cut into wedges
1	cup skim milk
3	tablespoons all-purpose flour
⅛	teaspoon salt
	Dash pepper
1	tablespoon snipped fresh parsley

■ In a 2-quart casserole combine mushrooms, wine, garlic, and basil. Cook, covered, on 100% power (high) for 3 to 4 minutes or till mushrooms are tender, stirring once. Stir in chicken and artichoke hearts.

■ In a small bowl stir together milk, flour, salt, and pepper. Stir into casserole. Cook, uncovered, on high for 6 to 9 minutes (12 to 14 minutes in low-wattage ovens) or till thickened and bubbly, stirring after every minute. Cook 1 minute more. Sprinkle with parsley. Makes 4 servings.

Nutrition information per serving: 239 calories, 27 g protein, 19 g carbohydrate, 6 g fat, 64 mg cholesterol, 236 mg sodium, 722 mg potassium.

CHICKEN À LA KING

Preparation Time: 15 min. ▪ Cooking Time: 9 min. ▪ Low Cholesterol

½	**cup chopped carrot**
½	**cup sliced celery**
½	**cup chopped green** *or* **sweet red pepper**
2	**tablespoons water**
1	**10¾-ounce can condensed cream of chicken** *or* **cream of mushroom soup**
½	**cup skim milk**
2	**tablespoons grated Parmesan cheese**
¼	**teaspoon poultry seasoning**
2	**cups cubed cooked chicken** *or* **turkey (11 ounces)**
5	**slices whole wheat bread, toasted,** *or* **5 English muffin halves, toasted**

▪ In a 1½-quart casserole combine carrot, celery, green or sweet red pepper, and water. Cook, covered, on 100% power (high) for 3 to 5 minutes or till vegetables are tender, stirring once.

▪ Stir in soup, milk, Parmesan cheese, and poultry seasoning. Stir in chicken. Cook, covered, on high for 6 to 8 minutes or till bubbly. Serve over toasted bread or English muffin halves. Makes 5 servings.

Nutrition information per serving: 255 calories, 23 g protein, 20 g carbohydrate, 9 g fat, 58 mg cholesterol, 734 mg sodium, 393 mg potassium.

TEX-MEX TURKEY TENDERLOINS

265 calories

Preparation Time: 10 min. ▪ Cooking Time: 12 min. ▪ Low Fat ▪ Low Cholesterol ▪ Low Sodium

4	4-ounce turkey tenderloin steaks, about ½ inch thick
1	teaspoon ground cumin
⅛	teaspoon pepper
1	tablespoon sugar
2	tablespoons vinegar
1½	teaspoons cornstarch
1	large tomato, seeded and chopped
1	cup chopped zucchini
¼	cup sliced green onions
1	4-ounce can diced green chili peppers, drained
2	cups hot cooked rice

▪ Rinse turkey steaks; pat dry. Stir together cumin and pepper; sprinkle on both sides of the turkey steaks.

▪ In a 12x7½x2-inch dish arrange the turkey with meaty portions toward the edges of the dish. Cover with vented microwave-safe plastic wrap. Cook on 100% power (high) for 6 to 7 minutes or till turkey is tender and no longer pink, rearranging once. Cover to keep warm.

▪ For sauce, in a 4-cup measure stir together sugar, vinegar, and cornstarch. Stir in tomato, zucchini, green onions, and chili peppers. Cook, uncovered, on high for 5 to 7 minutes or till mixture is thickened and bubbly, stirring after every minute. Cook on high 1 minute more. Spoon over turkey. Serve with hot cooked rice. Makes 4 servings.

Nutrition information per serving: 265 calories, 29 g protein, 34 g carbohydrate, 1 g fat, 70 mg cholesterol, 50 mg sodium, 513 mg potassium.

BARBECUE-SAUCED TURKEY

209 calories

Preparation Time: 15 min. ▪ Cooking Time: 16½ min. ▪ Low Fat

2	**pounds turkey thighs, skinned**
¼	**cup catsup**
2	**tablespoons dry red wine _or_ water**
1	**tablespoon brown sugar**
1	**tablespoon lemon juice**
2	**teaspoons soy sauce**
1	**teaspoon Worcestershire sauce**
¼	**teaspoon dried thyme, crushed**
¼	**teaspoon liquid smoke flavoring (optional)**
	Dash ground cloves
	Dash garlic powder
1	**tablespoon cornstarch**
1	**tablespoon cold water**

▪ Rinse turkey; pat dry. Place in a 10x6x2-inch baking dish with meaty portions toward edges of the dish.

▪ In a mixing bowl combine catsup, wine or water, brown sugar, lemon juice, soy sauce, Worcestershire sauce, thyme, liquid smoke (if desired), cloves, and garlic powder. Pour over turkey.

▪ Cover dish with vented microwave-safe plastic wrap. Cook on 100% power (high) for 15 to 20 minutes or till turkey is tender and no longer pink, turning turkey over and giving dish a half-turn once. Transfer turkey to a serving platter, reserving cooking liquid.

▪ For sauce, place cooking liquid in a 2-cup measure; skim fat. If necessary, add water to cooking liquid to equal 1 cup. Combine cornstarch and 1 tablespoon cold water. Stir into cooking liquid.

▪ Cook, uncovered, on high for 1½ to 2 minutes or till thickened and bubbly, stirring after every 30 seconds. To serve, slice turkey and spoon sauce atop slices. Makes 4 servings.

Nutrition information per serving: 209 calories, 29 g protein, 10 g carbohydrate, 4 g fat, 112 mg cholesterol, 443 mg sodium, 339 mg potassium.

LEMONY TURKEY MEATBALLS

243 calories

Preparation Time: 20 min. ▪ Cooking Time: 8 min. ▪ Low Fat ▪ Low Cholesterol

1	beaten egg white
1/4	cup whole bran cereal *or* rolled oats
1	teaspoon Worcestershire sauce
1/2	teaspoon finely shredded lemon peel
1	pound ground raw turkey
1	cup chicken broth
1	cup broccoli flowerets
1/2	cup thinly sliced carrot
1	green onion, sliced
1/4	cup plain low-fat yogurt
1	tablespoon cornstarch
1	teaspoon lemon juice
3	cups hot cooked noodles

▪ In a mixing bowl combine egg white, cereal, Worcestershire sauce, and lemon peel. Add turkey; mix well. (Mixture will be soft.) Shape into 24 meatballs.

▪ Arrange meatballs in a 12x7½x2-inch dish. Cover with waxed paper. Cook on 100% power (high) for 4 to 6 minutes or till meatballs are no longer pink, rearranging and turning meatballs over after 3 minutes. Drain off fat.

▪ Meanwhile, for sauce, in a 4-cup measure stir together chicken broth, broccoli, carrot, and green onion. In a small bowl stir together yogurt and cornstarch; stir into vegetable mixture.

▪ Cook sauce, uncovered, on high for 4 to 6 minutes or till thickened and bubbly, stirring after every minute till slightly thickened, then every 30 seconds. Stir in lemon juice; pour sauce over meatballs. Serve over noodles. Serves 6.

Nutrition information per serving: 243 calories, 21 g protein, 25 g carbohydrate, 7 g fat, 76 mg cholesterol, 240 mg sodium, 222 mg potassium.

STUFFED SNAPPER

171 calories

Preparation Time: 30 min. ▪ Cooking Time: 15 min. ▪ Low Fat ▪ Low Cholesterol

1	1½- to 2-pound fresh *or* frozen drawn red snapper *or* rockfish with head and tail removed
1	6-ounce package regular long grain and wild rice mix
1	cup small broccoli flowerets
½	cup chopped onion
½	cup sliced celery
1	tablespoon water
½	teaspoon lemon pepper

■ Thaw fish, if frozen. Prepare rice mix according to package directions, *except* omit butter.

■ For stuffing, in a 1½-quart casserole cook broccoli, onion, celery, and water, covered, on 100% power (high) for 3 to 4 minutes or till onion and celery are crisp-tender. Drain. Stir in the cooked rice and lemon pepper. Set aside.

■ Rinse fish and pat dry with paper towels. Enlarge the fish cavity by cutting from the head end toward the tail. Place in a 12x7½x2-inch baking dish. Loosely spoon some stuffing into cavity. Leave remaining stuffing in casserole; set aside.

■ Cook stuffed fish, covered with vented clear plastic wrap, on high for 10 to 12 minutes or till fish flakes easily when tested with a fork. Give the dish a half-turn after 6 minutes. If necessary, shield the tail end with a small piece of foil. Cover and keep warm.

■ Cook remaining stuffing in casserole, covered, on high for 2 to 3 minutes or till heated through, stirring once. Serve with fish. Makes 6 servings.

Nutrition information per serving: 171 calories, 19 g protein, 20 g carbohydrate, 1 g fat, 28 mg cholesterol, 464 mg sodium, 505 mg potassium.

CREAMY POACHED COD

120 calories

Preparation Time: 10 min. ▪ Cooking Time: 10 min. ▪ Low Fat ▪ Low Cholesterol ▪ Low Sodium

1	pound fresh *or* frozen cod *or* other fish fillets, cut ½ to ¾ inch thick
½	cup finely chopped carrot
½	cup finely chopped onion
1	tablespoon water
½	cup skim milk
1	teaspoon cornstarch
1	teaspoon instant chicken bouillon granules
¼	teaspoon dried dillweed
2	cups hot cooked noodles (optional)

■ Thaw fish, if frozen.

■ Turn under any thin edges of fish. In an 8x8x2-inch baking dish arrange thicker portions of fish fillets toward outer edges of the dish. Cover with vented clear plastic wrap.

■ Cook on 100% power (high) for 4 to 7 minutes (6 to 8 minutes in a low-wattage oven) or till fish flakes easily when tested with a fork, giving dish a half-turn once. Keep warm.

■ In a 2-cup measure combine the carrot, onion, and water. Cook, covered, on high for 4 to 6 minutes or till vegetables are tender, stirring once. Drain.

■ In a small bowl stir together milk, cornstarch, bouillon granules, and dillweed. Stir into vegetables. Cook vegetable mixture, uncovered, on high for 2 to 4 minutes or till thickened and bubbly, stirring twice. Serve vegetables over fish. If desired, serve with hot cooked noodles. Makes 4 servings.

Nutrition information per serving: 120 calories, 22 g protein, 5 g carbohydrate, 1 g fat, 49 mg cholesterol, 129 mg sodium, 599 mg potassium.

FISH STEAKS WITH MUSHROOM SAUCE   132 calories

Preparation Time: 7 min. ▪ Cooking Time: 6 min. ▪ Low Fat ▪ Low Cholesterol

4	**4-ounce fresh *or* frozen halibut *or* other fish steaks, cut ¾ inch thick**
2	**teaspoons cornstarch**
½	**teaspoon instant chicken bouillon granules**
⅛	**teaspoon salt**
½	**cup skim milk**
1	**4-ounce can sliced mushrooms, drained**
¼	**cup shredded carrot**
½	**teaspoon finely shredded lemon peel**
1	**tablespoon snipped fresh parsley**

▪ Thaw fish, if frozen.

▪ Arrange fish steaks in an 8x8x2-inch baking dish. Cover with vented clear plastic wrap. Cook on 100% power (high) for 4 to 8 minutes or till fish flakes easily when tested with a fork. Keep warm while preparing sauce.

▪ In a 2-cup measure stir together cornstarch, bouillon granules, and salt. Stir in milk all at once. Cook, uncovered, on high for 1½ to 3 minutes or till thickened and bubbly, stirring after 1 minute, then every 30 seconds.

▪ Stir in mushrooms and carrot. Cook for 30 to 60 seconds more or till heated through. Stir in lemon peel. Serve over fish steaks. Sprinkle with parsley. Makes 4 servings.

Nutrition information per serving: 132 calories, 22 g protein, 5 g carbohydrate, 2 g fat, 31 mg cholesterol, 286 mg sodium, 546 mg potassium.

SWEET-AND-SOUR FISH

158 calories

Preparation Time: 20 min. ▪ Cooking Time: 8½ min. ▪ Low Fat ▪ Low Cholesterol

1	**pound fresh *or* frozen fish steaks**
1	**medium green *or* sweet red pepper, cut into 1-inch squares (1 cup)**
1	**medium carrot, thinly bias-sliced (½ cup)**
½	**cup chicken broth**
1	**clove garlic, minced**
2	**tablespoons brown sugar**
4	**teaspoons cornstarch**
2	**tablespoons vinegar**
2	**tablespoons soy sauce**
½	**cup seedless grapes, halved**
2	**cups hot cooked rice (optional)**

▪ Thaw fish, if frozen. Cut fish into ¾-inch pieces.

▪ In a 1½-quart casserole cook fish, covered, on 100% power (high) for 3 to 5 minutes or till fish flakes easily when tested with a fork, stirring once. Drain; set aside.

▪ In the casserole combine green or sweet red pepper, carrot, chicken broth, and garlic. Cook, covered, on high for 3 to 5 minutes or till vegetables are just crisp-tender, stirring once. *Do not drain.*

▪ In a small mixing bowl stir together brown sugar, cornstarch, vinegar, and soy sauce. Stir into the vegetable mixture. Cook, uncovered, on high for 1½ to 2 minutes or till thickened and bubbly, stirring every 30 seconds.

▪ Gently stir in fish and grapes. Cook, uncovered, for 1 minute more or till heated through. If desired, serve with hot cooked rice. Makes 4 servings.

Nutrition information per serving: 158 calories, 19 g protein, 18 g carbohydrate, 1 g fat, 41 mg cholesterol, 674 mg sodium, 629 mg potassium.

SPINACH-STUFFED SOLE   178 calories

Preparation Time: 15 min. ▪ Cooking Time: 5 min. ▪ Low Fat ▪ Low Cholesterol

Line each custard cup with one fish fillet by laying the fillet along the sides of the cup. Keep one edge of the fillet near the top of the cup. If necessary, cut the fillet to fit.

4	**fresh *or* frozen sole, flounder, *or* catfish fillets (about ¾ pound total)**
1	**beaten egg white**
1	**cup herb-seasoned croutons**
½	**cup low-fat cottage cheese, drained**
¼	**cup shredded carrot**
2	**tablespoons cocktail sauce**
1	**10-ounce package frozen chopped spinach, thawed and well drained***
	Nonstick spray coating

■ Thaw fish, if frozen.

■ For stuffing, in a mixing bowl stir together egg white, croutons, cottage cheese, carrot, and cocktail sauce. Stir in the drained spinach.

■ Spray four 10-ounce custard cups with nonstick spray coating. Line cups with fish fillets, trimming and piecing as necessary. Spoon stuffing into the center of each cup.

■ Arrange filled cups in the microwave. Cover loosely with waxed paper. Cook on high for 5 to 6 minutes or till fish flakes easily when tested with a fork and stuffing is heated through. Rotate and rearrange the cups once during cooking.

■ To serve, slide the fish and stuffing out of the custard cups onto individual serving plates. Makes 4 servings.

*Note: If desired, thaw spinach in the microwave. In a 1-quart casserole cook frozen spinach, uncovered, on high for 3 to 4 minutes or till thawed, breaking up leaves with a fork after 2 minutes. Drain spinach well, pressing out excess liquid.

Nutrition information per serving: 178 calories, 23 g protein, 12 g carbohydrate, 4 g fat, 41 mg cholesterol, 475 mg sodium, 715 mg potassium.

STEAMED SOLE IN CABBAGE

122 calories

Preparation Time: 20 min. ▪ Cooking Time: 10 min. ▪ Low Fat ▪ Low Cholesterol

1	**pound fresh *or* frozen sole *or* other fish fillets**
8	**medium cabbage leaves *or* Savoy cabbage leaves**
¾	**cup shredded cabbage *or* Savoy cabbage**
½	**cup shredded zucchini**
⅓	**cup finely chopped onion**
¼	**cup shredded carrot**
½	**teaspoon salt**
¼	**teaspoon fines herbes**
⅛	**teaspoon pepper**

▪ Thaw fish, if frozen. Cut fish into 8 portions.

▪ Trim the large center vein from each cabbage leaf, keeping leaf in one piece. Rinse leaves and place in a 12x7½x2-inch baking dish. Cover with vented clear plastic wrap. Cook on 100% power (high) for 3 to 5 minutes or till tender.

▪ In a 1-quart casserole stir together the shredded cabbage, zucchini, onion, and carrot. Cook, covered, on high 3 to 5 minutes or till tender, stirring once. Drain. Stir in salt, fines herbes, and pepper.

▪ Spoon some of the vegetable mixture atop the center of each piece of fish. Bring the ends of the fish up around the filling. Place fish roll near one end of a cabbage leaf. Fold in two sides of the leaf, then roll up beginning from an unfolded end. Secure with toothpicks, if necessary. Place seam side down in the baking dish. Repeat with the remaining fish and cabbage leaves.

▪ Cook, covered, on high 4 to 6 minutes or till fish flakes easily with a fork, giving dish a half-turn once. Serves 4.

Nutrition information per serving: 122 calories, 22 g protein, 4 g carbohydrate, 1 g fat, 54 mg cholesterol, 369 mg sodium, 584 mg potassium.

DEEP-SEA KABOBS   245 calories

Preparation Time: 20 min. ▪ Marinating Time: 2 hrs. ▪ Cooking Time: 7 min. ▪ Low Fat ▪ Low Cholesterol

6	**ounces fresh _or_ frozen skinless and boneless swordfish, salmon, _or_ halibut steaks _or_ fillets, cut ½ inch thick**
1	**large pink grapefruit**
1	**8-ounce can pineapple chunks (juice pack)**
½	**teaspoon dried dillweed**
¼	**teaspoon salt**
⅛	**teaspoon pepper**
1	**small green pepper, cut into ¾-inch squares**
½	**of a 10-ounce package frozen Parisienne carrots, thawed (¾ cup)**
2	**tablespoons water**
	Lettuce leaves (optional)

▪ Thaw fish, if frozen. Cut into ½-inch-wide strips.

▪ Finely shred _1 teaspoon_ grapefruit peel; set aside. Remove remaining peel; discard. Section grapefruit over a bowl to catch juices. Reserve and chill sections. Drain pineapple juices into grapefruit juices. Chill pineapple till needed. Mix grapefruit and pineapple juices, shredded peel, dillweed, salt, and pepper. Add fish. Cover; chill 2 hours, stirring twice.

▪ Drain fish, reserving marinade. In a 1-quart casserole cook green pepper, carrots, and water, covered, on 100% power (high) for 4 to 5 minutes or till crisp-tender. Drain.

▪ On four 12-inch wooden skewers thread fish accordion-style. On four more skewers thread green pepper and carrots. Place all kabobs in a 12x7½x2-inch baking dish. Pour reserved marinade over kabobs. Cover with vented clear plastic wrap. Cook on high 3 to 5 minutes or till fish flakes with a fork, giving dish a half-turn once and brushing juices over kabobs. Serve kabobs with grapefruit and pineapple. Arrange on 2 lettuce-lined plates, if desired. Serves 2.

Nutrition information per serving: 245 calories, 19 g protein, 36 g carbohydrate, 4 g fat, 47 mg cholesterol, 623 mg sodium, 900 mg potassium.

FISH WITH COOL CUCUMBER SAUCE

122 calories

Preparation Time: 10 min. ▪ Cooking Time: 4 min. ▪ Low Fat ▪ Low Cholesterol ▪ Low Sodium

To help the fish cook evenly in the microwave, turn under any thin portions of the fish fillet to create an even thickness of about ½ inch. Then, place the thickest part of the fillet toward the outer edges of the dish.

1	pound fresh *or* frozen fish fillets*
⅓	cup chopped cucumber
2	tablespoons reduced-calorie mayonnaise
2	tablespoons plain low-fat yogurt
1½	teaspoons prepared mustard

▪ Thaw fish, if frozen*.

▪ Turn under any thin edges of fish. In a 12x7½x2-inch baking dish (use an 8x8x2-inch baking dish for low-wattage ovens) arrange fish fillets with thicker portions toward outer edges of the dish. Cover dish with vented clear plastic wrap.

▪ Cook on 100% power (high) for 4 to 7 minutes or till fish flakes easily when tested with a fork, giving dish a half-turn after 3 minutes.

▪ Meanwhile, for sauce, in a small bowl stir together cucumber, mayonnaise, yogurt, and mustard. Serve with fish. Makes 4 servings.

*Note: To thaw fish in the microwave, place in a shallow baking dish. Cover with vented clear plastic wrap. Cook on 30% power (medium-low) for 3½ to 4½ minutes for ½ pound of fish or 6 to 8 minutes for 1 pound. Let stand for 10 minutes. The fish should be pliable and cold on the outside, but still slightly icy in the center of thick areas.

Nutrition information per serving: 122 calories, 21 g protein, 1 g carbohydrate, 3 g fat, 52 mg cholesterol, 132 mg sodium, 503 mg potassium.

CORN-BREAD-COATED FISH

187 calories

Preparation Time: 7 min. ▪ Cooking Time: 4½ min. ▪ Low Fat ▪ Low Cholesterol

Instead of stuffing the fish, eat the stuffing sprinkled on top.

1	**pound fresh *or* frozen fish fillets**
2	**tablespoons buttermilk *or* plain low-fat yogurt**
1	**tablespoon margarine**
½	**cup corn bread stuffing mix, crushed**
⅛	**teaspoon salt**
	Dash to ⅛ teaspoon ground red pepper

▪ Thaw fish, if frozen.

▪ Turn under any thin edges of fish. In a 12x7½x2-inch baking dish (use an 8x8x2-inch baking dish for low-wattage ovens) arrange thicker portions of fish fillets toward outer edges of the dish. Brush fish with buttermilk or yogurt.

▪ In a small mixing bowl cook margarine on 100% power (high) about 30 seconds or till melted. Stir in stuffing mix, salt, and red pepper.

▪ Spoon stuffing mixture over fish fillets. Cook fish, uncovered, on high for 4 to 7 minutes (7 to 9 minutes for low-wattage ovens) or till fish flakes easily when tested with a fork. Give the dish a half-turn after 3 minutes. Serves 4.

Nutrition information per serving: 187 calories, 23 g protein, 13 g carbohydrate, 4 g fat, 50 mg cholesterol, 399 mg sodium, 513 mg potassium.

FISH WITH VEGETABLES AND RICE

144 calories

Preparation Time: 15 min. ▪ Cooking Time: 11 min. ▪ Low Fat ▪ Low Cholesterol

4	3-ounce fresh *or* frozen fish fillets
1	cup sliced celery
¼	cup sliced green onion
⅓	cup chopped green *or* sweet red pepper
2	tablespoons water
⅛	teaspoon dried tarragon, crushed
1	cup chicken broth
1	cup quick-cooking rice
¼	cup grated Parmesan cheese

■ Thaw fish, if frozen.

■ In a 2-quart casserole combine celery, green onion, green or sweet red pepper, water, and tarragon. Cook, covered, on 100% power (high) for 3 to 5 minutes or till tender, stirring once.

■ Stir in chicken broth. Cook, uncovered, on high for 4 to 6 minutes or till mixture boils.

■ Stir in rice. Cover and let stand for 5 minutes.

■ Stir in cheese. Spread rice mixture evenly in an 8x8x2-inch baking dish. Arrange fish atop rice.

■ Cook, covered with vented clear plastic wrap, on high for 4 to 7 minutes or till fish flakes easily when tested with a fork. Makes 4 servings.

Nutrition information per serving: 144 calories, 20 g protein, 8 g carbohydrate, 3 g fat, 42 mg cholesterol, 383 mg sodium, 538 mg potassium.

SALMON CUPS WITH CREAMED PEAS

199 calories

Preparation Time: 15 min. ▪ Cooking Time: 7 min.

Create an eye-catching presentation by using elegant individual casserole dishes. Or, after the salmon cooks, let it stand 1 to 2 minutes. Then unmold onto plates and fill with peas.

1	beaten egg
¼	cup finely chopped onion
2	tablespoons fine dry bread crumbs
1	6¾-ounce can skinless and boneless salmon *or* tuna, drained
1	cup fresh *or* frozen peas
2	tablespoons water
¼	cup plain low-fat yogurt
2	teaspoons cornstarch
½	teaspoon instant chicken bouillon granules
½	teaspoon finely shredded lemon peel
⅓	cup skim milk

▪ In a medium mixing bowl stir together the egg, onion, and bread crumbs. Add salmon or tuna; mix well. Divide mixture among three 6-ounce custard cups. Press mixture onto the bottom of the cups and 1½ inches up the sides. Set aside.

▪ In a 1-quart casserole combine peas and water. Cook, covered, on 100% power (high) for 3 to 5 minutes or till tender, stirring once. Drain in a colander. Set aside.

▪ In the casserole stir together the yogurt, cornstarch, bouillon granules, and lemon peel. Stir in milk all at once.

▪ Cook, uncovered, on high for 2 to 5 minutes or till thickened and bubbly, stirring after 1 minute, then every 30 seconds. Stir in peas. Keep warm while cooking salmon.

▪ Cook salmon cups, covered with vented clear plastic wrap, on high for 2 to 4 minutes or till set.

▪ To serve, spoon peas into salmon cups. Makes 3 servings.

Nutrition information per serving: 199 calories, 19 g protein, 15 g carbohydrate, 7 g fat, 118 mg cholesterol, 494 mg sodium, 424 mg potassium.

SCALLOPS AND BROCCOLI WITH PASTA

278 calories

Preparation Time: 10 min. ▪ Cooking Time: 11½ min. ▪ Low Fat ▪ Low Cholesterol

¾	pound fresh *or* frozen scallops *or* peeled and deveined shrimp
1	10-ounce package frozen cut broccoli
½	cup sliced green onions
2	tablespoons dry white wine
1	teaspoon dried fines herbes
½	teaspoon lemon pepper
¼	teaspoon garlic powder
4	teaspoons cornstarch
2	teaspoons instant chicken bouillon granules
1	2-ounce jar sliced pimiento, drained and chopped
6	ounces spaghetti *or* fettuccine, cooked and drained

▪ Thaw scallops or shrimp, if frozen. Halve large scallops.

▪ In a 1½-quart casserole combine broccoli and 2 tablespoons *water*. Cook, covered, on 100% power (high) for 6 to 8 minutes or till tender, stirring once. Drain in a colander.

▪ In the casserole mix scallops or shrimp, green onions, wine, fines herbes, lemon pepper, and garlic powder.

▪ Cook, covered, on high for 2 to 4 minutes or till scallops are opaque or shrimp are pink, stirring once. Remove scallops or shrimp from casserole, reserving cooking liquid.

▪ Measure reserved liquid; add water to equal 1 cup. In the casserole combine cornstarch and 2 tablespoons *water*. Stir in cooking liquid mixture and bouillon granules.

▪ Cook, uncovered, on high for 2½ to 5 minutes or till thickened and bubbly, stirring after every minute till mixture starts to thicken, then every 30 seconds. Stir in broccoli, scallops or shrimp, and pimiento.

▪ Cook, uncovered, on high for 1 to 2 minutes or till heated through. Serve over hot cooked pasta. Makes 4 servings.

Nutrition information per serving: 278 calories, 22 g protein, 42 g carbohydrate, 1 g fat, 28 mg cholesterol, 421 mg sodium, 561 mg potassium.

LEMONY SHRIMP AND ASPARAGUS

241 calories

Preparation Time: 8 min. ▪ Cooking Time: 12 min. ▪ Low Fat

¾	**pound fresh *or* frozen peeled and deveined shrimp**
¾	**pound fresh asparagus, cut into 2-inch pieces, *or* one 10-ounce package frozen cut asparagus**
1	**clove garlic, minced**
2	**tablespoons water**
1	**medium green *or* sweet red pepper, cut into thin strips**
2	**tablespoons soy sauce**
½	**teaspoon finely shredded lemon peel**
1	**tablespoon lemon juice**
1	**teaspoon cornstarch**
2	**cups hot cooked rice**
	Lemon wedges (optional)

▪ Thaw shrimp, if frozen.

▪ In a 1½-quart casserole combine the asparagus, garlic, and water.

▪ Cook, covered, on 100% power (high) for 4 to 5 minutes or till asparagus is just crisp-tender. Stir in shrimp and green or sweet red pepper.

▪ Cook, covered, on high for 5 to 7 minutes (7 to 9 minutes in a low-wattage oven) or till shrimp are pink and asparagus is tender, stirring once. Remove shrimp and vegetables with a slotted spoon, reserving liquid in casserole.

▪ Meanwhile, in a bowl combine the soy sauce, lemon peel, lemon juice, and cornstarch. Stir into liquid in casserole.

▪ Cook, uncovered, on high for 2 to 4 minutes or till thickened and bubbly, stirring after every minute till mixture begins to thicken, then every 30 seconds.

▪ Stir shrimp and vegetables into casserole. Cook, uncovered, on high for 1 to 2 minutes or till heated through. Serve with rice and lemon wedges, if desired. Makes 4 servings.

Nutrition information per serving: 241 calories, 23 g protein, 33 g carbohydrate, 2 g fat, 129 mg cholesterol, 643 mg sodium, 555 mg potassium.

SEAFOOD ENCHILADAS

281 calories

Preparation Time: 10 min. ▪ Cooking Time: 5 min. ▪ Low Fat ▪ Low Cholesterol

Mexican flavors blend well with a rich, creamy filling.

4	**ounces frozen crab-flavored fish pieces** *or* **crabmeat**
⅔	**cup skim milk**
2	**tablespoons all-purpose flour** **Dash salt**
¼	**cup shredded cheddar cheese (1 ounce)**
½	**of a 4-ounce can (2 tablespoons) chopped green chili peppers**
4	**6-inch flour tortillas**
2	**tablespoons salsa**

▪ Thaw crab-flavored fish pieces or crabmeat, if frozen. Cut into bite-size pieces; set aside.

▪ In a 2-cup measure stir together skim milk, flour, and salt. Cook, uncovered, on 100% power (high) for 1½ to 2½ minutes (2½ to 3½ minutes in a low-wattage oven) or till thickened and bubbly, stirring every 30 seconds. Stir in cheese till melted. Stir in crab and green chili peppers.

▪ Divide crab mixture among tortillas, spreading down the center. Roll up tortillas.

▪ Place filled tortillas, seam side down, in 2 individual au gratin dishes. Cover with vented clear plastic wrap.

▪ Cook on 70% power (medium-high) for 3 to 4 minutes (2 to 3 minutes on high power in a low-wattage oven) or till heated through.

▪ Top tortillas with salsa. Cook, covered, on medium-high (high power in a low-wattage oven) about 30 seconds or till salsa is hot. Makes 2 servings.

Nutrition information per serving: 281 calories, 16 g protein, 39 g carbohydrate, 7 g fat, 28 mg cholesterol, 910 mg sodium, 263 mg potassium.

CREAMY CRAB AND PASTA CASSEROLES 250 calories

Preparation Time: 10 min. ▪ Cooking Time: 10 min. ▪ Low Fat ▪ Low Cholesterol

3	**ounces spinach noodles**
	Crumb Topping
½	**cup chopped celery**
¼	**cup finely chopped green *or* sweet red pepper**
2	**tablespoons thinly sliced green onions**
1	**cup skim milk**
2	**tablespoons all-purpose flour**
1	**teaspoon Worcestershire sauce**
½	**teaspoon dried thyme, crushed**
	Several dashes bottled hot pepper sauce
12	**ounces crabmeat, drained and cartilage removed**
2	**tablespoons finely chopped pimiento**

▪ Cook noodles according to package directions; drain.

▪ Meanwhile, prepare Crumb Topping. Set aside.

▪ In a 1-quart casserole combine celery, green pepper, green onions, and 1 tablespoon *water*. Cook, covered, on 100% power (high) for 3 minutes or till tender; drain.

▪ Stir together milk, flour, Worcestershire sauce, thyme, hot pepper sauce, and ⅛ teaspoon *salt*. Stir into vegetables in casserole. Cook, uncovered, on high for 2 to 3 minutes or till thickened and bubbly, stirring every 30 seconds. Stir in crabmeat and pimiento.

▪ Divide noodles among four 8- to 10-ounce casseroles. Layer crabmeat mixture and Crumb Topping atop noodles. Cook, uncovered, on high for 5 minutes or till bubbly, rearranging dishes after 3 minutes. Serves 4.

▪ **Crumb Topping:** In a small bowl stir together 2 tablespoons grated *Parmesan cheese,* 2 tablespoons *fine dry bread crumbs,* and 1 tablespoon *margarine,* melted.

Nutrition information per serving: 250 calories, 23 g protein, 26 g carbohydrate, 6 g fat, 60 mg cholesterol, 950 mg sodium, 400 mg potassium.

SIDE DISHES

VEGETABLE AND PASTA TOSS *(see page 319)*

TWICE-BAKED POTATOES

98 calories

Preparation Time: 10 min. ■ Cooking Time: 65 min. ■ Low Fat ■ Low Cholesterol

Put a large star tip on the end of a pastry bag. Fold back the top of the bag several inches. Spoon the potato filling into the bag. Unfold the top and twist closed. Hold the twist between your thumb and your forefinger. Gently squeeze the bag to release the filling while guiding the bag with your other hand.

4	small baking potatoes (5 to 6 ounces each)
2	ounces reduced-calorie cream cheese, cubed and softened
2	tablespoons snipped chives
¼	teaspoon dried basil, crushed
⅛	teaspoon salt
	Dash pepper
3	to 4 tablespoons skim milk
	Paprika

■ Prick potatoes with a fork. Bake in a 375° oven for 45 to 50 minutes or till tender. Cool slightly. Cut potatoes in half lengthwise. Gently scoop out each potato half, leaving a thin shell. Set shells aside.

■ Put pulp into a small mixer bowl. Add cream cheese, chives, basil, salt, and pepper; beat till smooth. Add milk, a tablespoon at a time, beating till potato mixture is fluffy.

■ Pipe or spoon potato mixture into shells. Sprinkle with paprika. Place on a baking sheet. Cover loosely with foil.

■ Bake in a 375° oven for 10 minutes. Uncover potatoes and bake 10 minutes more or till heated through. Serves 8.

■ **Microwave directions:** Micro-cook pricked potatoes on 100% power (high) for 10 to 12 minutes or till tender. Halve potatoes and prepare filling as above. Place filled potato shells on a 12-inch microwave-safe platter. Cover with vented clear plastic wrap. Cook on high for 1 to 2 minutes or till heated through.

Nutrition information per serving: 98 calories, 3 g protein, 18 g carbohydrate, 2 g fat, 5 mg cholesterol, 70 mg sodium, 318 mg potassium.

FLUFFY DILLED CARROTS AND POTATOES

86 calories

Preparation Time: 15 min. ▪ Cooking Time: 27 min. ▪ Low Fat ▪ No Cholesterol

Save on cleanup time by mashing the vegetables in the saucepan they cook in.

1½	cups sliced carrots
¾	cup peeled and sliced potato *or* parsnip
1	to 2 tablespoons skim milk
2	teaspoons margarine
¼	teaspoon salt
¼	teaspoon dried dillweed
⅛	to ¼ teaspoon onion powder
	Dash pepper

▪ In a saucepan bring 2 inches of water to boiling. Add carrots and potato or parsnip. Return to boiling; reduce heat. Cover and simmer about 25 minutes or till very tender. Drain.

▪ With an electric mixer on low speed or a potato masher, beat or mash vegetables. Add milk, margarine, salt, dillweed, onion powder, and pepper; beat or mash till nearly smooth.

▪ If necessary, reheat mixture over low heat, stirring constantly. Makes 3 servings.

▪ **Microwave directions:** In a 1½-quart microwave-safe casserole combine carrots, potato or parsnip, and ½ cup water. Micro-cook, covered, on 100% power (high) for 10 to 12 minutes (12 to 14 minutes in low-wattage oven) or till very tender, stirring once. Drain. Mash vegetables and season as above. If necessary, return mixture to casserole and cook, covered, on high for 1 to 2 minutes or till heated through.

Nutrition information per serving: 86 calories, 2 g protein, 15 g carbohydrate, 3 g fat, 0 mg cholesterol, 238 mg sodium, 453 mg potassium.

VEGETABLE AND PASTA TOSS

78 calories

Preparation Time: 15 min. ▪ Cooking Time: 8 min. ▪ Chilling Time: 2 hrs. ▪ Low Fat ▪ No Cholesterol

¾	**cup corkscrew pasta** *or* **elbow macaroni**
1	**cup broccoli flowerets**
1	**cup cauliflower flowerets**
1	**9-ounce package frozen artichoke hearts, thawed and halved**
½	**cup thinly sliced carrot**
¼	**cup sliced green onions**
½	**cup reduced-calorie Italian salad dressing**

▪ Cook pasta according to package directions. Add broccoli and cauliflower to boiling pasta for the last minute of cooking; drain. Rinse with cold water; drain well.

▪ In a large mixing bowl combine pasta mixture, artichoke halves, carrot, and green onions.

▪ Add the Italian dressing; toss to coat.

▪ Cover and refrigerate for 2 to 24 hours. Makes 6 servings.

Nutrition information per serving: 78 calories, 3 g protein, 15 g carbohydrate, 1 g fat, 0 mg cholesterol, 314 mg sodium, 287 mg potassium.

STIR-FRIED ORIENTAL VEGETABLES

41 calories

Preparation Time: 15 min. ▪ Cooking Time: 5½ min. ▪ Low Fat ▪ No Cholesterol

1	**tablespoon molasses** *or* **brown sugar**
1	**tablespoon soy sauce**
1	**tablespoon vinegar**
	Nonstick spray coating
1	**teaspoon grated fresh gingerroot**
1	**cup green onions bias-sliced into ¼-inch lengths**
6	**ounces fresh pea pods** *or* **one 6-ounce package frozen pea pods**
2	**cups shredded Chinese cabbage** *or* **cabbage**
1	**cup thin bite-size strips green** *or* **sweet red pepper**
1	**cup fresh bean sprouts**

▪ For sauce, stir together molasses or brown sugar, soy sauce, and vinegar. Set aside.

▪ Spray a wok or large skillet with nonstick spray coating. Preheat over medium-high heat. Stir-fry gingerroot for 30 seconds.

▪ Add onions and stir-fry for 1 minute. Add pea pods and cabbage; stir-fry for 2 minutes. Add green or sweet red pepper and bean sprouts; stir-fry for 1 minute more or till vegetables are crisp-tender.

▪ Pour sauce over vegetables; toss to coat. Heat through. Serve immediately. Makes 6 servings.

Nutrition information per serving: 41 calories, 2 g protein, 9 g carbohydrate, 0 g fat, 0 mg cholesterol, 196 mg sodium, 273 mg potassium.

TOMATO AND ZUCCHINI SALAD

46 calories

Preparation Time: 15 min. ▪ Low Cholesterol

1	**large tomato, coarsely chopped**
1	**small zucchini, thinly sliced**
2	**tablespoons sliced green onions**
1	**teaspoon snipped fresh basil leaves**
	or ¼ **teaspoon dried basil, crushed**
2	**tablespoons reduced-calorie Italian salad**
	dressing
2	**lettuce leaves**
2	**tablespoons crumbled feta cheese** *or* **shredded**
	part-skim mozzarella cheese

▪ In a medium mixing bowl combine tomato, zucchini, green onions, basil, and Italian salad dressing. Toss lightly to mix.

▪ Line 2 salad plates with lettuce. Divide tomato mixture between plates. Sprinkle each serving with *half* of the cheese. Makes 2 servings.

Nutrition information per serving: 46 calories, 2 g protein, 6 g carbohydrate, 2 g fat, 6 mg cholesterol, 285 mg sodium, 302 mg potassium.

BAKED STUFFED TOMATOES

86 calories

Preparation Time: 20 min. ▪ Cooking Time: 10 min. ▪ No Cholesterol

4	**medium tomatoes**
2	**cloves garlic, minced**
1	**tablespoon margarine**
½	**cup chopped green pepper**
1	**tablespoon snipped fresh basil** *or* **1 teaspoon dried basil, crushed**
¾	**cup croutons**
2	**tablespoons snipped fresh parsley**

▪ Cut a ½-inch slice from the top of each tomato; discard tops. Scoop out pulp; discard seeds. Coarsely chop pulp (should have about 1 cup). Set aside.

▪ In a medium skillet cook garlic in margarine for 30 seconds. Stir in tomato pulp, green pepper, and basil. Cook for 2 minutes or till green pepper is crisp-tender. Stir in croutons and parsley.

▪ Spoon crouton mixture into tomatoes. Arrange stuffed tomatoes in a 9-inch pie plate.

▪ Bake, uncovered, in a 350° oven for 10 to 15 minutes or till heated through. Makes 4 servings.

Nutrition information per serving: 86 calories, 2 g protein, 10 g carbohydrate, 4 g fat, 0 mg cholesterol, 146 mg sodium, 254 mg potassium.

TOMATOES AND ZUCCHINI

46 calories

Preparation Time: 15 min. ▪ Cooking Time: 15 min. ▪ Low Fat ▪ Low Cholesterol

	Nonstick spray coating
1	large onion, thinly sliced
1	clove garlic, minced
1	14½-ounce can tomatoes, cut up
2	medium zucchini, thinly sliced
1	medium green pepper, chopped
½	teaspoon dried basil, crushed
¼	teaspoon pepper
2	tablespoons grated Parmesan cheese

▪ Spray a large skillet with nonstick spray coating. Cook onion and garlic in skillet till onion is tender but not brown, stirring occasionally.

▪ Stir in *undrained* tomatoes, zucchini, green pepper, basil, and pepper. Cover and simmer for 10 minutes or till zucchini is tender, stirring occasionally. Uncover and simmer about 5 minutes or till most of the liquid evaporates.

▪ Pour into 6 individual serving bowls. Sprinkle with Parmesan cheese. Makes 6 servings.

Nutrition information per serving: 46 calories, 3 g protein, 8 g carbohydrate, 1 g fat, 2 mg cholesterol, 153 mg sodium, 351 mg potassium.

GARLIC AND PEPPER STIR-FRY

67 calories

Preparation Time: 12 min. ▪ Cooking Time: 8 min. ▪ No Cholesterol ▪ Low Sodium

1	**tablespoon cooking oil**
2	**to 3 cloves garlic, minced**
2	**medium carrots, bias-sliced**
½	**of a medium sweet red pepper, cut into strips**
½	**of a medium green pepper, cut into strips**
½	**of a medium yellow pepper, cut into strips**
1	**small onion, sliced and separated into rings**
1	**cup sliced fresh mushrooms**

▪ Preheat a wok or large skillet over high heat; add oil. Add garlic and stir-fry for 1 minute.

▪ Add carrots and stir-fry for 2 minutes.

▪ Add peppers and onion and stir-fry for 2 minutes.

▪ Add mushrooms and stir-fry about 2 minutes more or till vegetables are crisp-tender. Makes 4 servings.

Nutrition information per serving: 67 calories, 1 g protein, 8 g carbohydrate, 4 g fat, 0 mg cholesterol, 15 mg sodium, 291 mg potassium.

MARINATED CUCUMBERS

52 calories

Preparation Time: 15 min. ▪ Chilling Time: 2 hrs. ▪ No Cholesterol ▪ Low Sodium

A tangy side dish perfect to serve with poached or broiled fish.

¼	**cup water**
1	**tablespoon sugar**
3	**tablespoons vinegar**
2	**teaspoons salad oil**
½	**teaspoon dried basil, crushed**
⅛	**teaspoon pepper**
	Several dashes bottled hot pepper sauce
2	**medium cucumbers, thinly sliced (about 3 cups)**
1	**small onion, thinly sliced**
½	**cup sliced radishes**
4	**lettuce leaves (optional)**

▪ In a medium mixing bowl stir together water, sugar, vinegar, oil, basil, pepper, and hot pepper sauce.

▪ Add cucumbers and onion; toss to coat. Cover and refrigerate for 2 to 24 hours.

▪ Before serving, toss radishes with cucumbers and onion. Serve on lettuce-lined plates, if desired. Makes 4 servings.

Nutrition information per serving: 52 calories, 1 g protein, 8 g carbohydrate, 2 g fat, 0 mg cholesterol, 7 mg sodium, 201 mg potassium.

WILTED GREENS WITH PASTA

66 calories

Preparation Time: 15 min. ▪ Cooking Time: 12 min. ▪ Low Fat ▪ No Cholesterol

½ **cup tiny ring macaroni (anelli)** *or* **tiny shell macaroni** *or* **other tiny pasta**

4 **cups torn fresh spinach** *or* **romaine**

¼ **cup sliced green onions**

2 **cloves garlic, minced**

2 **teaspoons cooking oil**

2 **tablespoons lemon juice**

1 **tablespoon soy sauce**

1 **teaspoon honey**

Dash ground red pepper

▪ Cook pasta according to package directions; drain well. Keep warm.
▪ Meanwhile, in a large serving bowl combine spinach and green onions.
▪ For dressing, in a small skillet cook garlic in hot oil for 1 minute. Add lemon juice, soy sauce, honey, and ground red pepper. Heat just to boiling.
▪ Pour hot dressing over greens. Add hot pasta; toss to mix well. Makes 6 servings.

Nutrition information per serving: 66 calories, 3 g protein, 11 g carbohydrate, 2 g fat, 0 mg cholesterol, 201 mg sodium, 256 mg potassium.

LEMONY BROWN RICE AND VEGETABLES   107 calories

Preparation Time: 5 min. ▪ Cooking Time: 50 min. ▪ Low Fat ▪ No Cholesterol

Long grain rice is featured in this photo. (See Note below.)

1½	cups chicken broth
½	cup brown rice*
¼	teaspoon ground cumin
⅛	teaspoon pepper
1	small green *or* sweet red pepper, chopped
¼	cup sliced green onion
1	cup frozen peas
2	tablespoons snipped fresh parsley
1	teaspoon finely shredded lemon peel

▪ In a saucepan heat broth to boiling. Stir in rice, cumin, and pepper. Cover and simmer for 30 minutes. Stir in chopped green or sweet red pepper and green onion; return to boiling. Cover and simmer about 15 minutes more or till rice is tender. Stir in peas, parsley, and lemon peel; heat through. Makes 5 servings.

*Note: If desired, substitute *long grain rice* for the brown rice. Decrease broth to *1¼ cups* and cook rice, cumin, and pepper, covered, for 10 minutes. Add green or sweet red pepper and green onion. Cook, covered, for 10 minutes more or till rice is tender. Continue as directed above.

Nutrition information per serving: 107 calories, 5 g protein, 20 g carbohydrate, 1 g fat, 0 mg cholesterol, 268 mg sodium, 199 mg potassium.

SPANISH RICE

Preparation Time: 10 min. ▪ Cooking Time: 25 min. ▪ Low Fat ▪ No Cholesterol

1	cup water
¾	cup chopped green pepper
½	cup chopped onion
½	cup chopped celery
½	teaspoon salt
1	14½-ounce can tomatoes, cut up
¾	cup long grain rice
1	teaspoon chili powder
⅛	teaspoon pepper
	Dash bottled hot pepper sauce

▪ In a medium saucepan combine water, green pepper, onion, celery, and salt. Bring to boiling; reduce heat. Cover and simmer for 5 minutes.

▪ Stir in *undrained* tomatoes, rice, chili powder, pepper, and hot pepper sauce. Return to boiling; reduce heat. Cover and simmer about 20 minutes or till rice is tender and liquid is absorbed. Makes 6 servings.

Nutrition information per serving: 109 calories, 3 g protein, 24 g carbohydrate, 0 g fat, 0 mg cholesterol, 292 mg sodium, 248 mg potassium.

SAVORY RISOTTO

130 calories

Preparation Time: 15 min. ▪ Cooking Time: 20 min. ▪ Low Fat ▪ Low Cholesterol

1	cup chopped fresh mushrooms
¾	cup long grain rice
½	cup chopped onion
1	tablespoon margarine
2	cups chicken *or* beef broth
2	tablespoons dry white wine
1	tablespoon grated Parmesan cheese

▪ In a medium saucepan cook mushrooms, rice, and onion in margarine over medium-low heat for 8 to 10 minutes or till onion is tender and rice is lightly toasted.

▪ Carefully add broth and wine to skillet. Bring to boiling; reduce heat. Cover and simmer for 15 to 20 minutes or till rice is tender.

▪ Stir in cheese. Cover and let stand for 5 minutes before serving. Makes 6 servings.

Nutrition information per serving: 130 calories, 4 g protein, 21 g carbohydrate, 3 g fat, 1 mg cholesterol, 302 mg sodium, 162 mg potassium.

ROSY WHITE AND WILD RICE

107 calories

Preparation Time: 5 min. ▪ Cooking Time: 50 min. ▪ Low Fat ▪ No Cholesterol

If you like brown rice, substitute it for the long grain rice. Add it to the boiling water with the wild rice. They'll cook in the same amount of time.

2	cups water
¼	teaspoon salt
⅓	cup wild rice, rinsed and drained
½	cup long grain rice
1	14½-ounce can stewed tomatoes, cut up
½	teaspoon dried basil, crushed
½	teaspoon dried thyme, crushed
⅛	teaspoon pepper
1	clove garlic, minced
⅓	cup plain low-fat yogurt (optional)

▪ In a medium saucepan heat water and salt to boiling. Add wild rice; reduce heat. Cover and simmer for 20 minutes.

▪ Stir in long grain rice. Return to boiling; reduce heat. Cover and simmer for 15 to 20 minutes more or till all rice is tender.

▪ Meanwhile, in a small saucepan combine *undrained* tomatoes, basil, thyme, pepper, and garlic. Bring to boiling; reduce heat. Simmer, uncovered, for 15 minutes or till mixture is very thick. Remove from heat.

▪ Add tomato mixture to rice; mix well. Serve at once. Garnish each serving with yogurt, if desired. Makes 6 servings.

Nutrition information per serving: 107 calories, 3 g protein, 24 g carbohydrate, 0 g fat, 0 mg cholesterol, 260 mg sodium, 205 mg potassium.

PEPPER-RICE TIMBALES

99 calories

Preparation Time: 10 min. ▪ Cooking Time: 20 min. ▪ Low Fat ▪ No Cholesterol

To mold the rice, pack the hot rice into ramekins or custard cups that have been sprayed with nonstick spray coating. Immediately invert ramekins over a serving plate to release the rice.

2½	cups water
2	teaspoons instant chicken bouillon granules
1	cup long grain rice
1	medium sweet red pepper, finely chopped
2	teaspoons cooking oil
	Nonstick spray coating
	Green pepper strips (optional)

▪ In a large saucepan combine water and bouillon granules. Bring to boiling, stirring to dissolve granules. Add rice; reduce heat. Cover and simmer for 20 to 25 minutes or till all the liquid is absorbed.

▪ Meanwhile, in a skillet, cook the sweet red pepper in hot cooking oil till edges are lightly browned. Add the cooked peppers to rice; mix well.

▪ Spray four 5-ounce ramekins or custard cups with nonstick spray coating. Immediately divide *half* of the rice mixture among ramekins; pack rice firmly into ramekins. Invert each ramckin to unmold. Repeat with remaining rice. Serve immediately. Garnish with green pepper strips, if desired. Makes 8 servings.

Nutrition information per serving: 99 calories, 2 g protein, 19 g carbohydrate, 1 g fat, 0 mg cholesterol, 94 mg sodium, 52 mg potassium.

HERBED COUSCOUS AND VEGETABLES

108 calories

Preparation Time: 10 min. ▪ Cooking Time: 8 min. ▪ Low Fat ▪ No Cholesterol

1	cup sliced fresh mushrooms
1	tablespoon margarine
1	cup water
1	tablespoon snipped fresh parsley
½	teaspoon dried basil, crushed
¼	teaspoon salt
⅛	teaspoon dried oregano, crushed
	Dash pepper
⅔	cup couscous
1	medium tomato, peeled, seeded, and chopped

▪ In a medium saucepan cook mushrooms in hot margarine till tender.
▪ Carefully add water to saucepan. Stir in parsley, basil, salt, oregano, and pepper. Bring to boiling; remove from heat. Stir in couscous.
▪ Let stand, covered, for 5 minutes. Stir in tomato. Makes 4 servings.

Nutrition information per serving: 108 calories, 3 g protein, 17 g carbohydrate, 3 g fat, 0 mg cholesterol, 170 mg sodium, 125 mg potassium.

BULGUR PILAF

126 calories

Preparation Time: 5 min. ▪ Cooking Time: 15 min. ▪ Low Fat ▪ No Cholesterol

1	14½-ounce can tomatoes, cut up
¼	cup sliced green onions
1	teaspoon instant chicken bouillon granules
½	teaspoon dried thyme, crushed
1	cup bulgur
¼	cup raisins

▪ Drain tomatoes, reserving juice. Add enough water to juice to equal 2 cups. Set tomatoes aside.

▪ In a medium saucepan combine tomato juice-water mixture, green onions, bouillon granules, and thyme.

▪ Bring mixture to boiling; add bulgur. Cover and simmer for 12 minutes. Stir in tomatoes and raisins. Cover and simmer for 3 to 5 minutes more or till bulgur is tender and all the liquid is absorbed. Makes 6 servings.

Nutrition information per serving: 126 calories, 4 g protein, 28 g carbohydrate, 1 g fat, 0 mg cholesterol, 176 mg sodium, 289 mg potassium.

333

CHEESY POLENTA SQUARES

91 calories

Preparation Time: 50 min. ▪ Cooking Time: 25 min. ▪ Low Fat ▪ Low Cholesterol

	Nonstick spray coating
1½	**cups skim milk**
½	**cup cornmeal**
½	**cup cold water**
¼	**teaspoon salt**
¼	**cup plain low-fat yogurt**
¼	**cup grated Parmesan cheese**
	Dash ground red pepper
	Canned pizza sauce (optional)

▪ Spray an 8x8x2-inch baking pan with nonstick spray coating. In a 2-quart saucepan heat milk to simmering.

▪ Meanwhile, in a mixing bowl stir together cornmeal, cold water, and salt. Gradually add cornmeal mixture to simmering milk, stirring constantly.

▪ Cook and stir till mixture returns to simmering; reduce heat. Cook, uncovered, over low heat about 10 minutes or till thick, stirring frequently.

▪ Spread cornmeal mixture in prepared baking pan. Let stand, uncovered, for 30 to 40 minutes or till firm.

▪ Meanwhile, in a small bowl combine yogurt, Parmesan cheese, and ground red pepper. Set aside.

▪ Cut polenta into 12 portions. Transfer to an oval baking dish or 15x10x1-inch baking pan that has been sprayed with nonstick spray coating. Spoon yogurt mixture over polenta.

▪ Bake, uncovered, in a 425° oven for 10 to 12 minutes till tops are golden and polenta is heated through. Serve with pizza sauce, if desired. Makes 6 servings.

Nutrition information per serving: 91 calories, 5 g protein, 13 g carbohydrate, 2 g fat, 5 mg cholesterol, 200 mg sodium, 143 mg potassium.

SPAGHETTI WITH COTTAGE CHEESE PESTO   153 calories

Preparation Time: 15 min. ▪ Low Fat ▪ Low Cholesterol

Use fresh herbs for a full-flavored pesto.

1	**10-ounce package frozen chopped spinach, thawed and well drained**
½	**cup hot water**
⅓	**cup low-fat cottage cheese**
⅓	**cup snipped fresh basil *or* 2 tablespoons dried basil, crushed**
2	**tablespoons grated Parmesan cheese**
1	**tablespoon olive oil *or* cooking oil**
2	**cloves garlic, minced**
4	**ounces spaghetti *or* fusilli, cooked and drained**

▪ For pesto, in a blender container or food processor bowl combine spinach, water, cottage cheese, basil, Parmesan cheese, oil, and garlic.

▪ Cover and blend or process till smooth.

▪ Spoon *half* of the pesto (about ½ cup) over the hot pasta. Toss to mix well. Serve immediately.

▪ Seal, label, and freeze the remaining pesto. To serve, thaw the pesto in the refrigerator. Place in a small saucepan and heat over low heat. Toss pesto with another 4 ounces spaghetti or fusilli, cooked and drained. Makes two 4-serving portions of pesto.

Nutrition information per serving: 153 calories, 7 g protein, 25 g carbohydrate, 3 g fat, 2 mg cholesterol, 95 mg sodium, 287 mg potassium.

MACARONI AND TOMATOES

97 calories

Preparation Time: 5 min. ▪ Cooking Time: 15 min. ▪ Low Fat ▪ Low Cholesterol

4	**ounces elbow macaroni (1 cup)**
1	**8-ounce can stewed tomatoes**
1	**cup sliced fresh mushrooms**
¼	**teaspoon dried oregano, crushed**
	Dash pepper
¼	**cup shredded low-fat cheddar cheese (1 ounce)**

▪ In a large saucepan cook macaroni in boiling water for 6 to 8 minutes or till nearly tender. Drain well; return macaroni to the saucepan.

▪ Add *undrained* tomatoes, the mushrooms, oregano, and pepper. Cover and simmer for 5 minutes or till macaroni is tender and most of the liquid is absorbed.

▪ Pour into a serving bowl; sprinkle with cheese. Makes 6 servings.

Nutrition information per serving: 97 calories, 4 g protein, 17 g carbohydrate, 1 g fat, 3 mg cholesterol, 132 mg sodium, 175 mg potassium.

CARAWAY NOODLES WITH CABBAGE

83 calories

Preparation Time: 10 min. ▪ Cooking Time: 10 min. ▪ Low Fat ▪ Low Cholesterol

6	cups water
¼	teaspoon salt
2	ounces medium noodles
¼	cup chopped onion
1	cup shredded cabbage
½	cup plain low-fat yogurt
½	teaspoon caraway seed
	Dash pepper

▪ In a large saucepan bring water and salt to boiling. Add noodles and onion. Reduce heat slightly and boil gently, uncovered, for 5 minutes.

▪ Add cabbage to boiling water and cook for 3 to 5 minutes more or till noodles and cabbage are tender. Drain well. Return noodles and cabbage to saucepan.

▪ Stir in yogurt, caraway seed, and pepper. Heat through, but *do not boil.* Makes 4 servings.

Nutrition information per serving: 83 calories, 4 g protein, 14 g carbohydrate, 1 g fat, 15 mg cholesterol, 159 mg sodium, 154 mg potassium.

PASTA WITH ONION SAUCE

132 calories

Preparation Time: 10 min. ▪ Cooking Time: 15 min. ▪ Low Fat ▪ Low Cholesterol

Combine this creamy pasta side dish with cooked carrots and broiled or grilled beef or chicken for a complete meal.

3	ounces linguine *or* fettuccine
1½	cups fresh broccoli flowerets
	Nonstick spray coating
1	medium onion, sliced and separated into rings
¾	cup skim milk
2	teaspoons cornstarch
1	teaspoon instant chicken bouillon granules
	Dash pepper
	Dash ground nutmeg
2	tablespoons dry white wine
2	ounces shredded part-skim mozzarella cheese

▪ Cook linguine or fettuccine according to package directions, adding the broccoli for the last 5 minutes of cooking. Drain well.

▪ Meanwhile, spray a large skillet with nonstick spray coating. Add onion to the skillet. Cook, covered, over medium-low heat about 10 minutes or till tender, stirring occasionally.

▪ In a small bowl stir together milk, cornstarch, bouillon granules, pepper, and nutmeg. Add to onion in skillet. Cook and stir over medium heat till thickened and bubbly. Cook and stir for 2 minutes more. Stir in wine and cheese till cheese is melted. Pour cheese mixture over pasta and broccoli; toss to coat. Makes 5 servings.

Nutrition information per serving: 132 calories, 7 g protein, 19 g carbohydrate, 3 g fat, 7 mg cholesterol, 161 mg sodium, 220 mg potassium.

WHITE BEAN AND PEPPER SALAD

74 calories

Preparation Time: 15 min. ▪ Chilling Time: 2 hrs. ▪ Low Fat ▪ No Cholesterol ▪ Low Sodium

2	tablespoons lemon juice
1½	teaspoons olive *or* salad oil
½	teaspoon sugar
¼	teaspoon dried dillweed *or* fennel seed, crushed
⅛	teaspoon pepper
1	clove garlic, minced
1	15-ounce can white kidney beans, drained and rinsed
½	cup chopped green *or* sweet red pepper
½	cup chopped cucumber
¼	cup sliced green onions

■ In a medium mixing bowl stir together lemon juice, oil, sugar, dillweed or fennel seed, pepper, and garlic.

■ Add beans, green or sweet red pepper, cucumber, and green onions. Toss to coat.

■ Cover and refrigerate for 2 to 24 hours. Makes 6 servings.

Nutrition information per serving: 74 calories, 4 g protein, 12 g carbohydrate, 1 g fat, 0 mg cholesterol, 2 mg sodium, 237 mg potassium.

ORIENTAL BEAN SALAD

54 calories

Preparation Time: 15 min. ▪ Chilling Time: 4 hrs. ▪ Low Fat ▪ No Cholesterol

Cut preparation time by using a 16-ounce can of cut wax or green beans instead of cooking fresh or frozen beans.

1	**tablespoon lime** *or* **lemon juice**
1	**tablespoon soy sauce**
1	**tablespoon snipped fresh cilantro** *or* **parsley**
1	**teaspoon sugar**
1	**teaspoon sesame oil**
	Dash garlic powder
	Dash crushed red pepper (optional)
2	**cups cooked cut wax** *or* **green beans**
1	**cup fresh bean sprouts**
1	**medium green** *or* **sweet red pepper, cut into ½-inch pieces**
1	**teaspoon toasted sesame seeds**

▪ In a large mixing bowl stir together lime or lemon juice, soy sauce, cilantro or parsley, sugar, sesame oil, garlic powder, and, if desired, crushed red pepper.

▪ Add cooked wax or green beans, bean sprouts, and green or sweet red pepper; toss to coat.

▪ Cover and refrigerate for 4 to 24 hours.

▪ To serve, sprinkle with toasted sesame seeds. Serves 4.

Nutrition information per serving: 54 calories, 3 g protein, 9 g carbohydrate, 1 g fat, 0 mg cholesterol, 262 mg sodium, 290 mg potassium.

CURRIED BARLEY

Preparation Time: 10 min. ▪ Cooking Time: 15 min. ▪ Low Fat ▪ No Cholesterol

2	cups water
⅔	cup quick-cooking barley
½	cup chopped carrot
½	cup chopped onion
1	teaspoon instant chicken bouillon granules
1	teaspoon curry powder
⅛	teaspoon salt
1	tablespoon toasted sliced almonds

■ In a medium saucepan stir together water, barley, carrot, onion, bouillon granules, curry powder, and salt.
■ Bring to boiling; reduce heat. Cover and simmer about 15 minutes or till barley is tender. Stir in almonds. Makes 4 servings.

Nutrition information per serving: 144 calories, 5 g protein, 29 g carbohydrate, 1 g fat, 0 mg cholesterol, 162 mg sodium, 100 mg potassium.

CORN CHOWDER

121 calories

Preparation Time: 10 min. ▪ Cooking Time: 15 min. ▪ Low Fat ▪ Low Cholesterol

1	**14½-ounce can chicken broth**
1	**cup chopped onion**
⅛	**teaspoon pepper**
1	**12-ounce can evaporated skim milk**
¼	**cup all-purpose flour**
1	**12-ounce can whole kernel corn with sweet peppers**
1	**tablespoon snipped fresh parsley (optional)**

■ In a medium saucepan combine broth, onion, and pepper. Bring to boiling; reduce heat. Cover and simmer for 5 minutes or till onion is tender.
■ In a small bowl stir together milk and flour. Stir into broth mixture. Cook and stir till thickened and bubbly. Stir in corn.* Heat through. If desired, sprinkle with parsley. Makes 6 servings.
*Note: If desired, when adding the corn, add one 6-ounce can *minced clams,* undrained, or 1 cup chopped cooked *chicken.* Makes 3 main-dish servings (330 calories for each serving).

Nutrition information per serving: 121 calories, 8 g protein, 21 g carbohydrate, 1 g fat, 2 mg cholesterol, 431 mg sodium, 394 mg potassium.

ITALIAN TOMATO AND RICE SOUP

66 calories

Preparation Time: 5 min. ▪ Cooking Time: 20 min. ▪ Low Fat ▪ No Cholesterol

1	**12-ounce jar chunky salsa**
1	**cup sodium-reduced tomato juice**
⅓	**cup quick-cooking brown rice**
1	**tablespoon dried minced onion**
1	**teaspoon Italian seasoning, crushed**
½	**teaspoon instant chicken bouillon granules**
⅛	**teaspoon dried minced garlic**
⅛	**teaspoon pepper**
1	**16-ounce package loose-pack frozen zucchini, carrots, cauliflower, lima beans, and Italian beans**
⅓	**cup finely shredded *or* grated Parmesan cheese (optional)**

■ In a large saucepan combine the salsa, tomato juice, brown rice, onion, Italian seasoning, bouillon granules, garlic, pepper, and 2 cups *water*. Bring to boiling; reduce heat. Cover and simmer for 10 minutes.

■ Meanwhile, place frozen vegetables in a colander. Run cold water over vegetables till thawed. Stir vegetables into the rice mixture. Return to boiling; reduce heat. Cover and simmer for 5 to 10 minutes or till rice and vegetables are tender.

■ Top each serving with cheese, if desired. Makes 6 servings.

Nutrition information per serving: 66 calories, 2 g protein, 15 g carbohydrate, 0 g fat, 0 mg cholesterol, 438 mg sodium, 422 mg potassium.

CHEESE AND VEGETABLE SOUP

94 calories

Preparation Time: 15 min. ▪ Cooking Time: 15 min. ▪ Low Fat ▪ Low Cholesterol

1	cup chicken broth
½	cup chopped peeled potato
¼	cup chopped celery
¼	cup chopped carrot
¼	cup chopped green *or* sweet red pepper
1	cup skim milk
2	tablespoons all-purpose flour
¼	cup shredded American cheese
	Dash ground nutmeg

■ In a medium saucepan combine chicken broth, potato, celery, carrot, and green or sweet red pepper. Bring to boiling; reduce heat. Cover and simmer for 10 to 12 minutes or till vegetables are tender.

■ In a small bowl stir together milk and flour; stir into saucepan. Cook and stir till thickened and bubbly. Cook and stir for 1 minute more. Stir in cheese till melted; stir in nutmeg. Makes 4 servings.

■ **Microwave directions:** In a 1½- or 2-quart microwave-safe casserole combine chicken broth, potato, celery, carrot, and green or sweet red pepper. Micro-cook, covered, on 100% power (high) for 8 to 10 minutes or till vegetables are tender. In a small bowl stir together milk and flour; stir into casserole. Micro-cook, uncovered, on high for 3 to 4 minutes, stirring after every minute till mixture begins to thicken. Then, stir every 30 seconds till thickened and bubbly; micro-cook 1 minute more. Stir in cheese till melted; stir in nutmeg.

Nutrition information per serving: 94 calories, 6 g protein, 11 g carbohydrate, 3 g fat, 8 mg cholesterol, 337 mg sodium, 335 mg potassium.

TORTELLINI SOUP

Preparation Time: 5 min. ▪ Cooking Time: 10 min. ▪ Low Fat ▪ Low Cholesterol

3	**cups water**
1	**7½-ounce can tomatoes, cut up**
1	**tablespoon instant beef bouillon granules**
½	**teaspoon dried basil, crushed**
¼	**teaspoon dried oregano, crushed**
1	**cup loose-pack frozen broccoli, cauliflower, and carrots**
½	**cup frozen cheese tortellini**
1	**tablespoon snipped fresh parsley**

▪ In a medium saucepan combine the water, *undrained* tomatoes, bouillon granules, basil, and oregano. Bring to boiling. Stir in frozen vegetables and tortellini.

▪ Return to boiling; reduce heat. Simmer, uncovered, for 7 minutes or till tortellini are tender. Stir in parsley. Makes 4 servings.

Nutrition information per serving: 68 calories, 4 g protein, 12 g carbohydrate, 1 g fat, 8 mg cholesterol, 417 mg sodium, 237 mg potassium.

RICH TOMATO SOUP

86 calories

Preparation Time: 10 min. ▪ Cooking Time: 10 min. ▪ Low Cholesterol

½	**cup chopped onion**
¾	**cup chopped green *or* sweet red pepper**
1	**tablespoon margarine**
1½	**teaspoons fresh snipped basil *or* ½ teaspoon dried basil, crushed**
⅛	**teaspoon ground red pepper (optional)**
2	**cups tomato juice**
1	**cup buttermilk**
	Fresh basil leaves *or* lime slices (optional)

▪ In a small saucepan cook onion and green or sweet red pepper in margarine till very tender. Stir in basil and ground red pepper, if desired. Cook and stir for 1 minute more. Remove from heat.

▪ In a blender container combine cooked vegetable mixture, tomato juice, and buttermilk. Cover and blend till smooth.

▪ Return mixture to saucepan and heat through. Or, chill thoroughly. Garnish each serving with fresh basil leaves or lime slices, if desired. Makes 4 servings.

Nutrition information per serving: 86 calories, 3 g protein, 11 g carbohydrate, 4 g fat, 2 mg cholesterol, 538 mg sodium, 458 mg potassium.

APPLE-CHEESE MOLD

33 calories

Preparation Time: 15 min. ▪ Chilling Time: 2½ hrs. ▪ Low Cholesterol

Serve this refreshing fruit salad with a steaming bowl of chili.

1	**4-serving-size package low-calorie lemon-flavored gelatin**
1	**cup boiling water**
¾	**cup cold water**
⅔	**cup finely chopped red apple**
⅓	**cup shredded low-fat cheddar cheese**
¼	**cup chopped celery**

▪ In a medium mixing bowl dissolve gelatin in boiling water. Stir in cold water. Chill till partially set (the consistency of unbeaten egg whites).

▪ Fold apple, cheese, and celery into gelatin.

▪ Pour gelatin mixture into a 3-cup mold. *Or,* pour into 6 individual molds or 6-ounce custard cups.

▪ Cover and chill till firm. Unmold onto a serving plate or salad plates. Makes 6 servings.

Nutrition information per serving: 33 calories, 2 g protein, 4 g carbohydrate, 1 g fat, 4 mg cholesterol, 116 mg sodium, 34 mg potassium.

CURRIED FRUIT SALAD

102 calories

Preparation Time: 20 min. ▪ Low Fat ▪ Low Cholesterol ▪ Low Sodium

⅓	cup plain low-fat yogurt
1	teaspoon honey *or* sugar
½	teaspoon curry powder
4	lettuce leaves
1	cup seedless grapes, halved
1	medium kiwi fruit, peeled and sliced
1	large orange, sectioned
1	medium apple, sliced
1	tablespoon chopped peanuts (optional)

▪ For dressing, in a small mixing bowl stir together yogurt, honey or sugar, and curry powder.

▪ Line 4 salad plates with lettuce leaves.

▪ Arrange grapes, kiwi fruit, orange sections, and apple slices on lettuce; drizzle with dressing. Sprinkle peanuts atop fruit and dressing, if desired. Makes 4 servings.

Nutrition information per serving: 102 calories, 2 g protein, 24 g carbohydrate, 1 g fat, 1 mg cholesterol, 17 mg sodium, 333 mg potassium.

FRUIT AND PASTA SALAD

65 calories

Preparation Time: 15 min. ▪ Chilling Time: 2 hrs. ▪ Low Fat ▪ Low Cholesterol ▪ Low Sodium

1	**medium orange**
¼	**cup plain low-fat yogurt**
1	**teaspoon sugar**
	Dash salt
¼	**cup tiny bow tie pasta, cooked and drained**
2	**medium apples, cored and chopped**
2	**tablespoons sliced green onions**

▪ Finely shred enough orange peel to make ½ teaspoon; set aside. Remove the remaining peel from orange and section orange over a bowl to catch juice. Measure 2 tablespoons of the juice.

▪ In a medium mixing bowl stir together orange peel, the 2 tablespoons juice, the yogurt, sugar, and salt. Mix well. Add cooked pasta, chopped apples, and sliced green onions; toss to coat. Gently stir in orange sections.

▪ Cover and chill for 2 to 24 hours. Makes 6 servings.

Nutrition information per serving: 65 calories, 1 g protein, 18 g carbohydrate, 0 g fat, 1 mg cholesterol, 30 mg sodium, 150 mg potassium.

CREAMY SALAD DRESSING

17 calories

Preparation Time: 5 min. ▪ Low Cholesterol ▪ Low Sodium

Serve 1 tablespoon of the dressing with ¾ cup of your macaroni salad or coleslaw.

¼	**cup plain low-fat yogurt**
2	**tablespoons reduced-calorie mayonnaise** *or* **salad dressing**
2	**tablespoons skim milk**
1	**tablespoon snipped fresh parsley** *or* **chives**
	Dash salt

▪ In a small mixing bowl combine yogurt, mayonnaise, skim milk, parsley or chives, and salt.* Makes 8 servings (1 tablespoon each).

***Note:** If desired, add any of the following to the dressing: 1 teaspoon *prepared horseradish;* ¼ teaspoon dried *basil, oregano,* or *thyme,* crushed; ¼ teaspoon dried *dillweed; or* ⅛ teaspoon *celery seed.*

Nutrition information per serving: 17 calories, 1 g protein, 1 g carbohydrate, 1 g fat, 2 mg cholesterol, 45 mg sodium, 27 mg potassium.

TOFU SALAD DRESSING

26 calories

Preparation Time: 10 min. ▪ Chilling Time: 2 hrs. ▪ Low Cholesterol ▪ Low Sodium

Transform this dressing into a vegetable dip by reducing the buttermilk to 2 to 4 tablespoons.

4	ounces soft tofu (fresh bean curd), cubed
⅓	cup buttermilk
2	tablespoons vinegar
½	teaspoon Italian seasoning, crushed
¼	teaspoon dry mustard
1	small clove garlic, minced
	Dash salt
	Dash pepper
¼	teaspoon celery seed

■ In a blender container or food processor bowl combine tofu, buttermilk, vinegar, Italian seasoning, dry mustard, garlic, salt, and pepper.
■ Cover and blend or process till smooth.
■ Transfer to a covered container. Stir in celery seed.
■ Cover and chill at least 2 hours. Makes 5 servings (2 tablespoons each).

Nutrition information per serving: 26 calories, 2 g protein, 2 g carbohydrate, 1 g fat, 1 mg cholesterol, 45 mg sodium, 47 mg potassium.

SPICY CITRUS DRESSING

39 calories

Preparation Time: 10 min. ▪ No Cholesterol ▪ No Sodium

Drizzle this dressing over fruit and salad greens or over mixed fruit.

¼	cup lemon *or* lime juice
1	tablespoon salad oil
2	tablespoons honey
¼	teaspoon ground cinnamon, allspice, *or* cardamom
⅛	teaspoon paprika

▪ In a screw-top jar combine lemon or lime juice; oil; honey; cinnamon, allspice, or cardamom; and paprika.*

▪ Cover and shake well.

▪ Chill till serving time. Shake before serving. Makes 7 servings (1 tablespoon each).

*Note: If desired, add any one of the following to the dressing: ½ teaspoon *poppy seed* or *sesame seed;* dash *bottled hot pepper sauce;* or 1 teaspoon finely chopped *crystallized ginger.*

Nutrition information per serving: 39 calories, 0 g protein, 6 g carbohydrate, 2 g fat, 0 mg cholesterol, 0 mg sodium, 16 mg potassium.

MICROWAVE
SIDE DISHES

BROCCOLI RICE *(see page 356)*

NEW POTATO SALAD

93 calories

Preparation Time: 10 min. ▪ Cooking Time: 13 min. ▪ Chilling Time: 4 hrs. ▪ Low Fat ▪ Low Cholesterol

¾	pound fresh green beans, cut into 1-inch pieces*
½	cup water
¾	pound tiny whole new potatoes, quartered
3	tablespoons reduced-calorie mayonnaise *or* salad dressing
3	tablespoons plain low-fat yogurt
2	tablespoons skim milk
½	teaspoon onion salt
¼	teaspoon dried dillweed
1	small tomato, coarsely chopped

■ In a 2-quart casserole combine beans and the water. Cook, covered, on 100% power (high) for 5 minutes.

■ Add potatoes. Cook, covered, on high for 8 to 10 minutes (10 to 12 minutes in low-wattage ovens) or till beans and potatoes are tender, stirring once. Drain in a colander; set aside.

■ In the same casserole stir together mayonnaise or salad dressing, yogurt, milk, onion salt, and dillweed. Stir in beans and potatoes. Cover and chill for 4 hours or till thoroughly chilled. Stir in chopped tomato. Makes 6 servings.

*Note: If desired, substitute one 9-ounce package *frozen cut green beans* for the fresh green beans. Combine the beans, the water, and potatoes in a 2-quart casserole. Cook, covered, on high for 9 to 11 minutes (13 to 15 minutes in low-wattage ovens) or till tender, stirring twice. Continue as directed.

Nutrition information per serving: 93 calories, 3 g protein, 16 g carbohydrate, 2 g fat, 3 mg cholesterol, 192 mg sodium, 475 mg potassium.

CREAMY PEAS AND ONIONS

127 calories

Preparation Time: 5 min. ▪ Cooking Time: 9 min. ▪ Low Fat ▪ No Cholesterol

2	**10-ounce packages frozen peas with pearl onions**
2	**tablespoons water**
¼	**cup reduced-calorie soft-style cream cheese**
2	**tablespoons skim milk**
¼	**teaspoon cracked black pepper**
⅛	**teaspoon garlic powder**

▪ In a 1½-quart casserole combine frozen vegetables and water.

▪ Cook, covered, on 100% power (high) for 7 to 9 minutes (11 to 14 minutes in low-wattage ovens) or till just tender. Drain well.

▪ Stir in the cream cheese, milk, pepper, and garlic powder.

▪ Cook, covered, on high for 2 to 3 minutes or till heated through, stirring once. Makes 5 servings.

Nutrition information per serving: 127 calories, 6 g protein, 17 g carbohydrate, 4 g fat, 0 mg cholesterol, 561 mg sodium, 230 mg potassium.

355

BROCCOLI RICE

75 calories

Preparation Time: 8 min. ▪ Cooking Time: 3 min. ▪ Low Fat ▪ No Cholesterol

¼	**cup quick-cooking rice**
¼	**cup water**
1	**teaspoon margarine**
½	**teaspoon instant chicken bouillon granules**
1	**cup coarsely chopped broccoli**
2	**tablespoons chopped green *or* sweet red pepper (optional)**

▪ In a 1-quart casserole combine rice, water, margarine, and bouillon granules. Add broccoli and green or sweet red pepper, if desired.

▪ Cook, covered, on 100% power (high) for 3 to 5 minutes or till broccoli is crisp-tender. Let stand, covered, for 3 to 5 minutes or till liquid is absorbed. Stir before serving. Makes 2 servings.

Nutrition information per serving: 75 calories, 2 g protein, 12 g carbohydrate, 2 g fat, 0 mg cholesterol, 127 mg sodium, 145 mg potassium.

LEMON-TARRAGON VEGETABLES

35 calories

Preparation Time: 15 min. ▪ Cooking Time: 9 min. ▪ Low Fat ▪ No Cholesterol

A fresh-tasting vegetable combo that's great with grilled meat or poultry.

½	teaspoon finely shredded lemon peel
1	tablespoon lemon juice
¼	teaspoon dried tarragon, crushed
⅛	teaspoon salt
1	medium onion, cut into thin wedges
8	ounces large whole fresh mushrooms, halved *or* quartered
2	small yellow summer squash, halved lengthwise and cut into ½-inch-thick slices (2 cups total)
¾	cup bias-sliced celery
2	tablespoons sliced pimiento

▪ In a 2-quart casserole combine lemon peel, juice, tarragon, and salt.

▪ Add onion. Cook, covered, on 100% power (high) for 3 minutes.

▪ Add mushrooms, squash, celery, and pimiento; toss gently to coat with lemon mixture.

▪ Cook, covered, on high for 6 to 9 minutes (10 to 12 minutes in low-wattage ovens) or till vegetables are tender, stirring once. Serve with a slotted spoon. Makes 4 servings.

Nutrition information per serving: 35 calories, 2 g protein, 7 g carbohydrate, 0 g fat, 0 mg cholesterol, 78 mg sodium, 426 mg potassium.

CARROTS WITH ONIONS

62 calories

Preparation Time: 10 min. ▪ Cooking Time: 6 min. ▪ Low Fat ▪ No Cholesterol

1	pound carrots, thinly sliced (3 cups)
1	small onion, sliced and separated into rings
3	tablespoons water
½	teaspoon dried thyme, crushed
¼	teaspoon salt
¼	teaspoon garlic powder
	Dash pepper
1	teaspoon margarine

▪ In a 1½-quart casserole combine carrots, onion, water, thyme, salt, garlic powder, and pepper.
▪ Cook on 100% power (high) for 6 to 8 minutes (10 to 12 minutes in low-wattage ovens) or till carrots are crisp-tender, stirring once.
▪ Add margarine; toss to coat vegetables. Makes 4 servings.

Nutrition information per serving: 62 calories, 1 g protein, 13 g carbohydrate, 1 g fat, 0 mg cholesterol, 185 mg sodium, 387 mg potassium.

MUSTARD-SAUCED CORN

89 calories

Preparation Time: 8 min. ▪ Cooking Time: 7 min. ▪ Low Fat ▪ No Cholesterol

1	**10-ounce package frozen whole kernel corn**
1	**medium green *or* sweet red pepper, chopped (¾ cup)**
¼	**cup chopped onion**
1	**tablespoon water**
2	**teaspoons margarine**
2	**teaspoons prepared mustard *or* Dijon-style mustard**
	Dash salt
	Dash pepper

▪ In a 1-quart casserole combine corn, green or sweet red pepper, onion, and water.

▪ Cook, covered, on 100% power (high) for 6 to 8 minutes (10 to 12 minutes in low-wattage ovens) or till corn and onion are tender, stirring once.

▪ Stir in margarine, mustard, salt, and pepper. Cook, covered, on high for 1 minute more. Stir to mix well. Serves 4.

Nutrition information per serving: 89 calories, 3 g protein, 17 g carbohydrate, 3 g fat, 0 mg cholesterol, 89 mg sodium, 205 mg potassium.

SPAGHETTI SQUASH PRONTO

52 calories

Preparation Time: 5 min. ▪ Cooking Time: 10 min. ▪ No Cholesterol ▪ Low Sodium

To remove the pulp from the shell of the cooked spaghetti squash, insert a fork into the pulp. Twist the fork slightly and the pulp will separate into spaghettilike strands. Then, rake the squash strands out of the shell.

1	2½-pound spaghetti squash
2	teaspoons margarine, melted
1	teaspoon white wine Worcestershire sauce *or* Worcestershire sauce
½	teaspoon dried dillweed
	Dash pepper

▪ Cut spaghetti squash in half lengthwise. Reserve 1 squash half for another use. Remove seeds from remaining squash half.

▪ Place squash, cut side down, in a shallow baking dish. Cook, uncovered, on 100% power (high) for 10 to 14 minutes or till pulp can just be pierced with a fork, giving dish a half-turn twice.

▪ Meanwhile, combine margarine, Worcestershire sauce, dillweed, and pepper.

▪ To serve, use a fork to shred and separate squash pulp into strands. Rake the squash from the shell and place in a serving dish; toss with margarine mixture. Makes 4 servings.

Nutrition information per serving: 52 calories, 1 g protein, 7 g carbohydrate, 2 g fat, 0 mg cholesterol, 54 mg sodium, 114 mg potassium.

CAULIFLOWER AMANDINE

42 calories

Preparation Time: 15 min. ▪ Cooking Time: 10 min. ▪ Low Fat ▪ No Cholesterol

4	**cups cauliflower flowerets (1 pound)**
1	**medium green *or* sweet red pepper, cut into ¾-inch pieces (1 cup)**
¼	**cup finely chopped onion**
¾	**cup chicken broth**
2	**teaspoons cornstarch**
1	**tablespoon lemon juice**
2	**tablespoons toasted sliced almonds**

▪ In a 3-quart casserole combine cauliflower, green or sweet red pepper, onion, and ¼ *cup* of the broth. Cook, covered, on 100% power (high) for 7 to 9 minutes (9 to 11 minutes in low-wattage ovens) or till cauliflower is tender, stirring once.

▪ Combine remaining chicken broth and the cornstarch. Stir into cauliflower mixture. Cook on high for 2 to 3 minutes (3 to 4 minutes in low-wattage ovens) or till thickened and bubbly, stirring every 30 seconds.

▪ Stir in lemon juice. Cook on high for 1 minute more or till heated through. Sprinkle with almonds. Makes 6 servings.

Nutrition information per serving: 42 calories, 2 g protein, 6 g carbohydrate, 1 g fat, 0 mg cholesterol, 108 mg sodium, 315 mg potassium.

ASPARAGUS WITH ORANGE MAYONNAISE

30 calories

Preparation Time: 15 min. ▪ Cooking Time: 7 min. ▪ Low Fat ▪ Low Cholesterol ▪ Low Sodium

Arrange asparagus spears in the baking dish with the tips facing the center. This prevents the delicate tips from overcooking before the firm stems are done.

1	pound asparagus
2	tablespoons water
2	tablespoons plain low-fat yogurt
1	tablespoon reduced-calorie mayonnaise
½	teaspoon finely shredded orange peel
1	tablespoon orange juice
	Dash ground red pepper
	Orange slices (optional)

■ Wash asparagus; break off woody bases.

■ Arrange asparagus in a shallow baking dish with the tips facing the center; add the water. Cover with vented clear plastic wrap.

■ Cook on 100% power (high) for 7 to 9 minutes (8 to 10 minutes in low-wattage ovens) or till asparagus is tender, rearranging once. Drain.

■ Meanwhile, in a small bowl combine yogurt, mayonnaise, orange peel, orange juice, and red pepper. Spoon over hot asparagus. If desired, garnish with orange slices. Serves 6.

Nutrition information per serving: 30 calories, 2 g protein, 4 g carbohydrate, 1 g fat, 1 mg cholesterol, 19 mg sodium, 208 mg potassium.

SAUCY CARAWAY CABBAGE

60 calories

Preparation Time: 10 min. ▪ Cooking Time: 13 min. ▪ Low Fat ▪ Low Cholesterol

¾	**cup skim milk**
¼	**cup shredded Swiss cheese**
1	**⅞-ounce envelope mushroom sauce mix**
¼	**teaspoon caraway seeds**
⅛	**teaspoon pepper**
5	**cups shredded cabbage (1 pound)***
½	**cup sliced green onions**

▪ For sauce, in a 2-quart casserole stir together milk, cheese, sauce mix, caraway seeds, and pepper. Cook, covered, on 100% power (high) for 3 to 4 minutes (5 to 6 minutes in low-wattage ovens) or till bubbly.

▪ Stir in cabbage and green onions. Cook, covered, on high for 10 to 12 minutes (14 to 16 minutes in low-wattage ovens) or till cabbage is crisp-tender, stirring twice. Serves 6.

***Note:** If desired, substitute 4 cups cauliflower flowerets for the cabbage. Cook sauce as directed above. Stir in cauliflower and onions. Cook, covered, on high for 7 to 10 minutes (10 to 12 minutes in low-wattage ovens) or till cauliflower is crisp-tender, stirring twice.

Nutrition information per serving: 60 calories, 4 g protein, 8 g carbohydrate, 2 g fat, 5 mg cholesterol, 304 mg sodium, 241 mg potassium.

SPINACH WITH PARMESAN CHEESE

44 calories

Preparation Time: 5 min. ▪ Cooking Time: 7½ min. ▪ Low Fat ▪ Low Cholesterol

2	green onions, sliced
1	clove garlic, minced
2	tablespoons water
1	pound fresh spinach leaves, washed and trimmed (12 cups)*
1	tablespoon grated Parmesan cheese
1	teaspoon lemon juice

▪ In a 3-quart casserole combine onions, garlic, and water. Cook on 100% power (high) for 30 to 60 seconds or till onions are tender.

▪ Add spinach. Cook, covered, on high for 7 to 9 minutes or till spinach is tender, stirring once. Drain well.

▪ Sprinkle with Parmesan cheese and lemon juice. (This recipe not recommended for low-wattage ovens.) Makes 3 to 4 servings.

*Note: If desired, substitute one 10-ounce package frozen chopped spinach for fresh spinach. Use a 1½-quart casserole and decrease the second cooking time to 6 to 8 minutes.

Nutrition information per serving: 44 calories, 5 g protein, 6 g carbohydrate, 1 g fat, 2 mg cholesterol, 146 mg sodium, 793 mg potassium.

MEXICAN LENTILS AND VEGETABLES

82 calories

Preparation Time: 35 min. ▪ Cooking Time: 24 min. ▪ Low Fat ▪ No Cholesterol

Pep up plain poultry, meat, or fish with this spicy dish.

½	**cup dry lentils**
1½	**cups hot water**
1	**medium carrot, chopped**
1	**small onion, chopped**
1	**clove garlic, minced**
1	**teaspoon chili powder**
1	**8-ounce can tomatoes, drained and cut up**
1	**4-ounce can diced green chili peppers, drained**
1	**medium green *or* sweet red pepper, chopped**
1	**tablespoon snipped fresh cilantro *or* parsley**
2	**tablespoons lime *or* lemon juice**
½	**teaspoon salt**

▪ Rinse lentils; drain.

▪ In a 2-quart casserole combine lentils, hot water, carrot, onion, garlic, and chili powder.

▪ Cook, covered, on 100% power (high) for 4 minutes or till boiling. Cook on 50% power (medium) for 20 minutes more or till lentils are just tender.

▪ Stir in drained tomatoes, green chili peppers, green or sweet red pepper, cilantro or parsley, lime or lemon juice, and salt. Cover and let stand for 30 minutes. Serve warm. Makes 6 servings.

Nutrition information per serving: 82 calories, 6 g protein, 16 g carbohydrate, 0 g fat, 0 mg cholesterol, 193 mg sodium, 369 mg potassium.

SAUCY PRUNES AND PEACHES

110 calories

Preparation Time: 10 min. ▪ Cooking Time: 9 min. ▪ Low Fat ▪ No Cholesterol ▪ Low Sodium

Add some pizzazz to your morning bowl of oats with this warm, spiced fruit.

1	cup orange juice
2	tablespoons sugar
¼	teaspoon ground cinnamon
⅛	teaspoon ground cloves
½	cup halved, pitted prunes
4	medium peaches, peeled, pitted, and sliced, *or* nectarines, pitted and sliced

▪ In a 1½-quart casserole combine orange juice, sugar, cinnamon, and cloves. Add prunes.

▪ Cook, covered, on 100% power (high) for 5 minutes or till prunes are softened.

▪ Add peaches or nectarines. Cook, covered, on high for 4 to 6 minutes or till peaches or nectarines are tender and heated through, stirring once. Makes 5 servings.

Nutrition information per serving: 110 calories, 1 g protein, 28 g carbohydrate, 0 g fat, 0 mg cholesterol, 1 mg sodium, 353 mg potassium.

MAPLE FRUIT COMPOTE

86 calories

Preparation Time: 10 min. ▪ Cooking Time: 4 min. ▪ Low Fat ▪ No Cholesterol ▪ Low Sodium

Serve this compote as a fruit sauce for ham or on its own for dessert.

¼	cup apple juice
2	tablespoons maple-flavored syrup
¼	teaspoon ground cinnamon
⅛	teaspoon ground nutmeg
2	medium apples, cored and cut into bite-size pieces
1	small pear, cored and cut into ½-inch cubes
1	teaspoon vanilla

▪ In a 1½-quart casserole stir together apple juice, maple-flavored syrup, cinnamon, and nutmeg. Add apples and pear.

▪ Cook, covered, on 100% power (high) for 4 to 5 minutes (7 to 9 minutes in low-wattage ovens) or till fruit is tender, stirring once. Stir in vanilla. Makes 4 servings.

Nutrition information per serving: 86 calories, 0 g protein, 22 g carbohydrate, 0 g fat, 0 mg cholesterol, 2 mg sodium, 143 mg potassium.

BREADS AND DESSERTS

BLUEBERRY GEMS *(see page 380)*

SPICY WHEAT AND OAT BREAD

89 calories

Preparation Time: 2¼ hrs. ▪ Cooking Time: 30 min. ▪ Low Fat ▪ No Cholesterol ▪ Low Sodium

1½	**to 2 cups all-purpose flour**
1	**package active dry yeast**
½	**teaspoon salt**
½	**teaspoon ground cinnamon**
¼	**teaspoon ground allspice**
⅛	**teaspoon ground ginger**
1	**cup water (120° to 130°)**
2	**tablespoons molasses, honey, *or* maple-flavored syrup**
1½	**teaspoons cooking oil**
1	**cup whole wheat flour**
½	**cup quick-cooking rolled oats**
	Nonstick spray coating
	Skim milk
	Rolled oats

■ In a small mixer bowl mix *1¼ cups* of the all-purpose flour, the yeast, salt, and all the spices. Add the water, molasses, and oil. Beat with an electric mixer on low speed for 30 seconds, scraping bowl constantly. Beat on high speed for 3 minutes. Stir in whole wheat flour, the ½ cup oats, and as much of the remaining all-purpose flour as you can.

■ On a lightly floured surface knead in enough remaining flour to make a moderately stiff dough that is smooth and elastic (6 to 8 minutes). Shape into a ball. Place in a bowl sprayed with nonstick coating; turn once. Cover; let rise in a warm place till double (about 1 hour). Punch down; turn out onto a floured surface. Cover; let rest 10 minutes.

■ Spray an 8x4x2-inch loaf pan with nonstick spray coating. Shape dough into a loaf; place in pan. Cover; let rise in a warm place till nearly double (about 30 to 45 minutes). Brush with skim milk and sprinkle lightly with additional oats.

■ Bake in a 375° oven for 30 to 35 minutes or till done. Remove from pan; cool. Makes 1 loaf (16 servings).

Nutrition information per serving: 89 calories, 3 g protein, 18 g carbohydrate, 1 g fat, 0 mg cholesterol, 68 mg sodium, 85 mg potassium.

CORNMEAL AND WHEAT GERM BRAIDS   108 calories

Preparation Time: 2 hrs. ▪ Cooking Time: 30 min. ▪ Low Fat ▪ No Cholesterol ▪ Low Sodium

3¾	to 4¼ cups all-purpose flour
2	packages active dry yeast
1¾	cups skim milk
3	tablespoons sugar
3	tablespoons cooking oil
½	teaspoon salt
¾	cup cornmeal
½	cup toasted wheat germ
	Nonstick spray coating

▪ In a large mixer bowl combine *2 cups* of the flour and the yeast. Heat milk, sugar, oil, and salt just till warm (120° to 130°). Add to flour mixture. Beat with an electric mixer on low speed 30 seconds, scraping bowl. Beat on high speed 3 minutes. Stir in cornmeal and wheat germ. Stir in as much of the remaining flour as you can. Turn out onto a lightly floured surface. Knead in enough of the remaining flour to make a moderately stiff dough that is smooth and elastic (6 to 8 minutes). Shape into a ball. Place in a bowl sprayed with nonstick coating; turn once. Cover; let rise in a warm place till double (about 1 hour). Punch down; divide into 6 portions. Cover; let rest 10 minutes. Roll each portion into a 10-inch rope.

▪ For each loaf, braid 3 ropes together and tuck ends under. Spray two 8x4x2-inch loaf pans with nonstick spray coating. Place braids in pans. Cover; let rise till nearly double (about 30 minutes). Bake in a 375° oven about 30 minutes or till done. To prevent overbrowning, cover loaves with foil the last 5 minutes of baking. Remove from pans; cool. Serves 28.

Nutrition information per serving: 108 calories, 3 g protein, 19 g carbohydrate, 2 g fat, 0 mg cholesterol, 47 mg sodium, 74 mg potassium.

BREAD KNOTS

Preparation Time: 65 min. ▪ Cooking Time: 10 min. ▪ Low Fat ▪ No Cholesterol ▪ Low Sodium

Skip the knot-tying step and you've got tradition- al, soft and chewy bread- sticks. Bake as directed.

1 to 1⅓ cups all-purpose flour
1 package quick-rise active dry yeast
1 teaspoon caraway seed *or* ½ to 1 teaspoon coarsely ground pepper
½ teaspoon salt
¾ cup hot water (125° to 130°)
1 tablespoon cooking oil
1 cup whole wheat flour
Nonstick spray coating
Milk

▪ In a small mixer bowl combine *¾ cup* of the all-purpose flour, the yeast, caraway seed or pepper, and salt. Add water and oil. Beat with electric mixer on low speed for 30 seconds, scraping bowl constantly. Beat on high speed 3 minutes. Stir in the whole wheat flour and as much of the remain- ing all-purpose flour as you can.

▪ On a floured surface knead in enough of the remaining all-purpose flour to make a stiff dough that is smooth and elastic (5 to 8 minutes). Shape into a ball. Cover; let rest 15 minutes.

▪ Divide dough into 4 portions. Divide each portion into 6 pieces. Roll each piece into an 8- to 10-inch rope. Tie each piece into a loose knot, leaving 2 long ends. Tuck top end under roll. Bring bottom end up and tuck into center of roll.

▪ Place 1 inch apart on baking sheets sprayed with nonstick spray coating. Cover; let rise till nearly double (20 minutes). Brush lightly with milk. If desired, sprinkle with additional caraway seed. Bake in a 375° oven 10 to 12 minutes or till golden brown. Cool. Makes 24 rolls (24 servings).

Nutrition information per serving: 42 calories, 1 g protein, 8 g carbohydrate, 1 g fat, 0 mg cholesterol, 45 mg sodium, 31 mg potassium.

DILL ROLLS

88 calories

Preparation Time: 1¾ hrs. ▪ Cooking Time: 15 min. ▪ Low Fat ▪ Low Cholesterol

These batter-bread rolls have a crust similar to French bread.

1½	**cups all-purpose flour**
1	**package active dry yeast**
1	**cup low-fat cottage cheese**
¼	**cup water**
1	**tablespoon sugar**
2	**teaspoons dillseed** *or* **caraway seed**
½	**teaspoon salt**
1	**egg**
	Nonstick spray coating

▪ In a small mixer bowl combine *1 cup* of the flour and the yeast.

▪ In a small saucepan heat and stir cottage cheese, water, sugar, dillseed or caraway seed, and salt till warm (120° to 130°). Add to flour mixture along with egg.

▪ Beat with an electric mixer on low speed for 30 seconds, scraping bowl constantly. Beat on high speed for 3 minutes.

▪ Add remaining flour; beat at low speed about 2 minutes or till nearly smooth.

▪ Cover batter and let rise in a warm place till double (about 45 minutes). Stir batter down with a wooden spoon. Let rest for 5 minutes.

▪ Spray 12 muffin cups with nonstick spray coating. Spoon batter evenly into cups. Cover loosely with plastic wrap; let batter rise till nearly double (about 30 minutes).

▪ Bake in a 375° oven for 15 to 18 minutes or till golden. Serve warm. Makes 12 rolls (12 servings).

Nutrition information per serving: 88 calories, 5 g protein, 14 g carbohydrate, 1 g fat, 24 mg cholesterol, 171 mg sodium, 54 mg potassium.

CORN BREAD

91 calories

Preparation Time: 10 min. ▪ Cooking Time: 20 min. ▪ Low Fat ▪ No Cholesterol

1	cup all-purpose flour
¾	cup cornmeal
1	tablespoon sugar
1	tablespoon baking powder
½	teaspoon salt
2	egg whites
1	cup skim milk
1	tablespoon cooking oil
	Nonstick spray coating

■ In a medium mixing bowl stir together flour, cornmeal, sugar, baking powder, and salt.

■ In a small mixing bowl beat egg whites, milk, and oil*. Stir into dry ingredients just till mixed.

■ Spray a 9x9x2-inch baking pan with nonstick spray coating. Pour batter into pan. Bake in a 400° oven for 20 to 25 minutes or till a toothpick inserted near the center comes out clean. Makes 12 servings.

*Note: If desired, stir one 4-ounce can *chopped green chili peppers,* drained, into milk mixture.

Nutrition information per serving: 91 calories, 3 g protein, 16 g carbohydrate, 2 g fat, 0 mg cholesterol, 183 mg sodium, 71 mg potassium.

IRISH SODA BREAD

82 calories

Preparation Time: 15 min. ▪ Cooking Time: 30 min. ▪ Low Fat ▪ No Cholesterol

Irish Soda Bread

Whole Wheat Raisin Soda Bread

2	cups all-purpose flour
1	teaspoon baking powder
½	teaspoon baking soda
¼	teaspoon salt
3	tablespoons margarine
1	slightly beaten egg white
¾	cup buttermilk
	Nonstick spray coating

▪ In a medium mixing bowl stir together flour, baking powder, soda, and salt. Cut in margarine till mixture resembles coarse crumbs. Make a well in the center of the mixture.

▪ In a small mixing bowl combine egg white and buttermilk. Add all at once to dry mixture. Stir just till moistened.

▪ On a lightly floured surface knead dough 10 to 12 strokes till nearly smooth. Shape into a 7-inch round loaf.

▪ Spray a baking sheet with nonstick spray coating. Place bread dough on baking sheet. With a sharp knife, make 2 slashes in the top to form an X.

▪ Bake in a 375° oven about 30 minutes or till golden. Serve warm. Makes 1 loaf (16 servings).

▪ **Whole Wheat Raisin Soda Bread:** Prepare as above, *except* substitute 1 cup of *whole wheat flour* for 1 cup of the all-purpose flour. Add ¼ cup *raisins* to flour mixture before adding liquid ingredients. (86 calories per serving)

Nutrition information per serving: 82 calories, 2 g protein, 12 g carbohydrate, 2 g fat, 0 mg cholesterol, 127 mg sodium, 36 mg potassium.

BOSTON BROWN BREAD

70 calories

Preparation Time: 10 min. ▪ Cooking Time: 2 hrs.* ▪ Low Fat ▪ No Cholesterol

½ cup whole wheat *or* rye flour
¼ cup all-purpose flour
¼ cup cornmeal
½ teaspoon baking powder
¼ teaspoon baking soda
¼ teaspoon salt
½ cup buttermilk
¼ cup molasses
1 beaten egg white
1 teaspoon cooking oil
¼ cup raisins
   Nonstick spray coating

▪ In a medium mixing bowl stir together flours, cornmeal, baking powder, soda, and salt. Stir in buttermilk, molasses, egg white, and oil just till blended. Stir in raisins.

▪ Spray a 4- or 4½-cup ovenproof mold, bowl, or 7½x3½x2-inch loaf pan with nonstick spray coating. Pour batter into mold or pan. Cover tightly with foil.

▪ Place mold or pan on a rack set in a large Dutch oven. Pour *hot* water into Dutch oven around the mold or pan to a depth of 1 inch.

▪ Bring water to boiling; reduce heat. Cover and simmer for 2 to 2½ hours or till a wooden pick inserted near the center comes out clean. Add boiling water to the Dutch oven as needed.

▪ Remove mold from Dutch oven. Cool 10 minutes on a wire rack. Remove bread from pan. Serve warm. Serves 12.

*Note: If desired, bake the bread. Do not cover mold or pan with foil and bake in a 350° oven about 45 to 50 minutes.

Nutrition information per serving: 70 calories, 2 g protein, 14 g carbohydrate, 1 g fat, 0 mg cholesterol, 98 mg sodium, 142 mg potassium.

APPLE-SPICE LOAF

110 calories

Preparation Time: 15 min. ▪ Cooking Time: 45 min. ▪ Low Fat ▪ No Cholesterol ▪ Low Sodium

1½	cups all-purpose flour
½	teaspoon baking soda
½	teaspoon ground cinnamon
¼	teaspoon baking powder
¼	teaspoon ground nutmeg
2	beaten egg whites
¾	cup brown sugar
¾	cup shredded peeled apple
3	tablespoons cooking oil
½	teaspoon finely shredded orange peel
	Nonstick spray coating

■ In a small mixing bowl stir together flour, soda, cinnamon, baking powder, and nutmeg.

■ In a large mixing bowl stir together egg whites, brown sugar, apple, oil, and orange peel. Stir flour mixture into apple mixture just till combined.

■ Spray an 8x4x2-inch loaf pan with nonstick spray coating. Pour batter into prepared pan.

■ Bake in a 350° oven for 45 to 50 minutes or till a toothpick inserted near the center comes out clean. Cool bread in pan for 10 minutes. Remove from pan and cool thoroughly on a wire rack. Makes 1 loaf (16 servings).

Nutrition information per serving: 110 calories, 2 g protein, 20 g carbohydrate, 3 g fat, 0 mg cholesterol, 49 mg sodium, 59 mg potassium.

BANANA BREAD

125 calories

Preparation Time: 10 min. ▪ Cooking Time: 45 min. ▪ Low Fat ▪ No Cholesterol

Stick with this moist and tender variation of quick bread. It's lower in calories, fat, and cholesterol than the traditional version.

1½	cups all-purpose flour
1¼	teaspoons baking powder
½	teaspoon baking soda
½	teaspoon ground cinnamon
⅛	teaspoon salt
2	slightly beaten egg whites
1	cup mashed banana
¾	cup sugar
¼	cup cooking oil
	Nonstick spray coating

▪ In a medium mixing bowl stir together flour, baking powder, baking soda, cinnamon, and salt.

▪ In a large mixing bowl stir together egg whites, banana, sugar, and oil. Stir flour mixture into banana mixture just till moistened.

▪ Spray an 8x4x2-inch loaf pan with nonstick spray coating. Spread batter in prepared pan. Bake in a 350° oven for 45 to 50 minutes or till a toothpick inserted near the center comes out clean.

▪ Cool bread in the pan for 10 minutes. Remove from pan and cool thoroughly on a wire rack. For easier slicing, wrap the bread in plastic wrap and store overnight. Makes 1 loaf (16 servings).

Nutrition information per serving: 125 calories, 2 g protein, 22 g carbohydrate, 4 g fat, 0 mg cholesterol, 81 mg sodium, 73 mg potassium.

BUTTERMILK BISCUITS

91 calories

Preparation Time: 10 min. ▪ Cooking Time: 10 min. ▪ No Cholesterol

Sweeten the warm biscuits with Orange Spread.

1	**cup all-purpose flour***
1	**teaspoon baking powder**
⅛	**teaspoon baking soda**
⅛	**teaspoon salt**
⅓	**cup buttermilk *or* sour milk**
2	**tablespoons cooking oil**
	Orange Spread (optional)

■ In a medium bowl combine flour, baking powder, baking soda, and salt.
■ In a small bowl stir together buttermilk and oil. Pour over flour mixture; stir till well mixed.
■ On a lightly floured surface, knead dough gently for 10 to 12 strokes. Roll or pat dough to ½-inch thickness. Cut with a 2-inch biscuit cutter, dipping cutter in flour between cuts. Transfer biscuits to an ungreased baking sheet.
■ Bake in a 450° oven for 10 to 12 minutes or till golden. Serve warm with Orange Spread. Makes 8 biscuits (8 servings).
*Note: If desired, substitute ¼ cup whole wheat flour or oat bran for ¼ cup of the all-purpose flour.
Orange Spread: In a small mixer bowl beat one-half of an 8-ounce package *reduced-calorie cream cheese* and 2 tablespoons *orange marmalade* or *peach* or *apricot preserves* till creamy. Beat in ¼ cup *reduced-calorie soft margarine* till smooth. Makes 12 servings (59 calories per 1-tablespoon serving).

Nutrition information per serving: 91 calories, 2 g protein, 12 g carbohydrate, 4 g fat, 0 mg cholesterol, 99 mg sodium, 31 mg potassium.

TWO-BRAN REFRIGERATOR MUFFINS

115 calories

Preparation Time: 12 min. ▪ Cooking Time: 20 min. ▪ Low Fat ▪ No Cholesterol

⅔ cup whole bran cereal
⅓ cup oat bran
⅔ cup boiling water
½ cup skim milk
2 beaten egg whites
2 tablespoons cooking oil
1½ cups all-purpose flour
¼ cup packed brown sugar
1½ teaspoons baking powder
1 teaspoon cinnamon
¼ teaspoon salt
Nonstick spray coating

▪ In a medium mixing bowl stir together whole bran cereal and oat bran. Stir in the boiling water. Stir in milk, egg whites, and oil. Set aside.

▪ In a small bowl stir together flour, brown sugar, baking powder, cinnamon, and salt. Add all at once to cereal mixture, stirring just till moistened.

▪ Bake immediately or store batter in a tightly covered container in the refrigerator for up to 1 week.

▪ To bake, spray muffin cups with nonstick spray coating. Stir muffin batter and fill muffin cups two-thirds full. Bake in a 400° oven about 20 minutes or till a toothpick inserted near the center comes out clean. Remove from pans; serve warm. Makes 12 muffins (12 servings).

Nutrition information per serving: 115 calories, 3 g protein, 21 g carbohydrate, 3 g fat, 0 mg cholesterol, 131 mg sodium, 109 mg potassium.

BLUEBERRY GEMS

37 calories

Preparation Time: 10 min. ▪ Cooking Time: 17 min. ▪ Low Fat ▪ No Cholesterol ▪ Low Sodium

The smaller size of these muffins makes them perfect for serving at a brunch.

1½	cups all-purpose flour
¼	cup sugar
1½	teaspoons baking powder
¼	teaspoon salt
2	egg whites
⅔	cup orange juice
2	tablespoons cooking oil
1	teaspoon vanilla
1	cup fresh *or* frozen blueberries
	Nonstick spray coating

■ In a medium mixing bowl combine flour, sugar, baking powder, and salt. In a small mixing bowl beat egg whites, orange juice, oil, and vanilla. Add to dry ingredients, stirring just till moistened. Fold in blueberries.

■ Spray 1¾-inch muffin cups* with nonstick spray coating. Fill muffin cups half full.

■ Bake in a 400° oven about 17 minutes or till golden. Cool slightly before serving. Makes 36 muffins.

*Note: If desired, bake the muffin batter in 2½-inch muffin cups about 20 minutes or till golden. Makes 12 muffins.

Nutrition information per 1¾-inch muffin: 37 calories, 1 g protein, 6 g carbohydrate, 1 g fat,0 mg cholesterol, 31 mg sodium, 20 mg potassium.

ITALIAN ONION FLATBREAD

77 calories

Preparation Time: 2 hrs. ▪ Cooking Time: 36 min. ▪ Low Fat ▪ No Cholesterol ▪ Low Sodium

For variety, sprinkle the bread with a combination of poppy and sesame seed.

1¼	**cups water**
¼	**cup dried minced onion**
2½	**to 3 cups all-purpose flour**
1	**package active dry yeast**
½	**teaspoon salt**
1	**tablespoon olive oil** *or* **cooking oil**
	Nonstick spray coating
1	**teaspoon poppy seed** *or* **sesame seed**

■ In a saucepan combine the water and dried onion; let stand 10 minutes. Heat to 120° to 130°. In a small mixer bowl combine *1 cup* flour, the yeast, and salt. Add onion mixture and oil to flour mixture. Beat with electric mixer at low speed for 30 seconds. Beat on high speed 3 minutes. Stir in as much of the remaining flour as you can. On a lightly floured surface knead in enough remaining flour to make a stiff dough that is smooth and elastic (8 to 10 minutes). Shape into a ball. Place in a bowl sprayed with nonstick coating; turn once. Cover; let rise in warm place till double (about 1 hour).
■ Punch dough down. On a lightly floured surface divide dough into thirds. Cover; let rest 10 minutes. Roll each portion of dough into a 12-inch circle. Wrap dough around rolling pin; unroll onto a baking sheet sprayed with nonstick coating. Brush dough with water and sprinkle with poppy or sesame seed. Cover; let rise till nearly double (35 to 40 minutes). Bake, one at a time, in a 400° oven 12 to 15 minutes. To serve, break into pieces. Makes 3 rounds (18 servings).

Nutrition information per serving: 77 calories, 2 g protein, 14 g carbohydrate, 1 g fat, 0 mg cholesterol, 61 mg sodium, 40 mg potassium.

PEACH TART

132 calories

Preparation Time: 30 min. ▪ Cooking Time: 10 min. ▪ Chilling Time: 2 hrs. ▪ Low Cholesterol

1	**cup all-purpose flour**
¼	**teaspoon salt**
¼	**cup chilled margarine**
2 to 4	**tablespoons cold water**
½	**of an 8-ounce package reduced-calorie cream cheese, softened**
2	**tablespoons sugar**
½	**teaspoon vanilla**
4 *or* **5**	**medium peaches** *or* **nectarines, peeled, pitted, and sliced**
½	**cup low-calorie apple jelly**

▪ For pastry, in a mixing bowl combine the flour and salt. Cut in the chilled margarine till pieces are the size of small peas.

▪ Sprinkle *1 tablespoon* of the cold water over part of the mixture. Toss with a fork. Push to the side of the bowl. Repeat till all of the mixture is moistened. Form into a ball.

▪ On a lightly floured surface roll pastry into a 12-inch circle.

▪ Wrap pastry around the rolling pin. Ease into an 11-inch flan pan. *Do not stretch.* Press pastry ½ inch up the sides of the pan. If necessary, trim pastry even with the top of the pan. Prick bottom of crust well with tines of a fork.

▪ Bake in 450° oven for 10 to 12 minutes or till golden. Cool on wire rack.

▪ Meanwhile, in a small mixing bowl stir together cream cheese, sugar, and vanilla till smooth. Spread atop cooled crust. Arrange peach slices in circles atop cheese mixture.

▪ In a small saucepan heat apple jelly till melted. Spoon atop peaches. Chill at least 2 hours. Makes 12 servings.

Nutrition information per serving: 132 calories, 2 g protein, 17 g carbohydrate, 6 g fat, 7 mg cholesterol, 144 mg sodium, 100 mg potassium.

LEMON TORTE WITH RASPBERRIES

80 calories

Preparation Time: 20 min. ▪ Chilling Time: 5 hrs. ▪ Low Fat ▪ No Cholesterol

	Nonstick spray coating
1	4-serving-size package low-calorie lemon-flavored gelatin
½	cup boiling water
½	of a 6-ounce can (⅓ cup) frozen lemonade concentrate, thawed
1	12-ounce can evaporated skim milk
2	cups cubed angel food cake
2	cups fresh raspberries
1	tablespoon sugar

■ Spray the bottom only of an 8-inch springform pan with nonstick spray coating; set aside.

■ In a large bowl dissolve lemon gelatin in the boiling water. Stir in thawed lemonade concentrate and evaporated skim milk. Cover and chill in the refrigerator for 1 to 1½ hours or till mixture mounds when spooned.

■ After chilling, beat gelatin mixture with an electric mixer on medium to high speed for 5 to 6 minutes or till fluffy.

■ Arrange angel food cake cubes in the bottom of the springform pan. Pour gelatin mixture over cake cubes. Cover and chill in the refrigerator for 4 hours or till firm.

■ Meanwhile, in a small bowl stir together raspberries and sugar. Cover and chill at least 2 hours.

■ To serve, cut torte into wedges and spoon raspberries on top. Makes 12 servings.

Nutrition information per serving: 80 calories, 4 g protein, 17 g carbohydrate, 0 g fat, 0 mg cholesterol, 70 mg sodium, 190 mg potassium.

FLAN

87 calories

Preparation Time: 20 min. ▪ Cooking Time: 25 min. ▪ Low Fat

This caramel custard is a popular Spanish dessert.

¼	cup sugar
3	eggs
1	cup skim milk
½	cup evaporated skim milk *or* skim milk
2	tablespoons sugar
1	teaspoon vanilla
	Dash salt

▪ In a small saucepan cook the ¼ cup sugar over medium-high heat till sugar begins to melt; shake pan occasionally. Reduce heat to low and cook till sugar is melted and golden brown (about 5 minutes more), stirring occasionally.

▪ Quickly pour caramelized sugar into an 8x1½-inch round baking pan, tilting pan to coat bottom.

▪ In a mixing bowl beat eggs. Stir in skim milk and evaporated skim milk, the 2 tablespoons sugar, the vanilla, and salt. Pour into caramel-coated pan.

▪ Set the round pan in a large baking pan set on an oven rack. Pour hot water into the large baking pan around the round pan to a depth of 1 inch.

▪ Bake, uncovered, in a 325° oven for 25 to 30 minutes or till a knife inserted near the center of the custard comes out clean. Cover and chill thoroughly.

▪ Loosen flan from sides of pan. Carefully invert onto a serving plate. Makes 8 servings.

Nutrition information per serving: 87 calories, 5 g protein, 13 g carbohydrate, 2 g fat, 81 mg cholesterol, 74 mg sodium, 126 mg potassium.

CHOCOLATE-CINNAMON ANGEL CAKE **117 calories**

Preparation Time: 1½ hrs. ▪ Cooking Time: 40 min. ▪ Low Fat ▪ No Cholesterol ▪ Low Sodium

To fold the flour mixture into the beaten egg whites, cut down through the mixture with a rubber scraper, then across the bottom, and up and over the top.

1½	cups egg whites (10 to 12 large eggs)
1	cup sifted cake flour *or* sifted all-purpose flour
1½	cups sifted powdered sugar
3	tablespoons unsweetened cocoa powder
½	teaspoon ground cinnamon
1½	teaspoons cream of tartar
1	teaspoon vanilla
1	cup sugar

▪ Bring egg whites to room temperature (about 1 hour).

▪ Meanwhile, sift flour, powdered sugar, cocoa powder, and cinnamon together three times. Set aside.

▪ In a large mixer bowl beat the egg whites, cream of tartar, and vanilla with an electric mixer on medium speed till soft peaks form (tips curl).

▪ Gradually add the sugar, *2 tablespoons* at a time, beating on high speed till stiff peaks form (tips stand straight). Transfer to a larger bowl, if necessary.

▪ Sift about *one-fourth* of the flour mixture over the beaten egg whites; fold in gently. Repeat, folding in the remaining flour mixture by fourths.

▪ Pour into an ungreased 10-inch tube pan.

▪ Bake on the lowest rack in a 350° oven for 40 to 45 minutes or till top springs back when lightly touched.

▪ *Immediately* invert cake (leave in pan); cool thoroughly. Loosen sides of cake from pan; remove cake. Slice into 16 wedges. Makes 16 servings.

Nutrition information per serving: 117 calories, 3 g protein, 27 g carbohydrate, 0 g fat, 0 mg cholesterol, 39 mg sodium, 41 mg potassium.

GINGERBREAD CUPCAKES

137 calories

Preparation Time: 10 min. ▪ Cooking Time: 15 min. ▪ No Cholesterol

The crackly tops and flavor of these cupcakes will remind you of gingersnap cookies.

1	cup all-purpose flour
½	teaspoon baking powder
½	teaspoon ground ginger
½	teaspoon ground cinnamon
¼	teaspoon baking soda
	Dash salt
1	slightly beaten egg white
⅓	cup molasses
⅓	cup water
3	tablespoons cooking oil
	Sifted powdered sugar (optional)

■ Line eight 2½-inch muffin cups with paper bake cups; set aside.

■ In a medium mixing bowl stir together flour, baking powder, ginger, cinnamon, soda, and salt.

■ In a small mixing bowl stir together the egg white, molasses, water, and oil. Stir molasses mixture into flour mixture just till blended.

■ Spoon mixture into prepared muffin cups.

■ Bake in a 350° oven for 15 to 20 minutes or till cupcakes spring back when pressed lightly in center. If desired, sprinkle with powdered sugar. Serve warm or cool. Makes 8 cupcakes (8 servings).

Nutrition information per serving: 137 calories, 2 g protein, 20 g carbohydrate, 5 g fat, 0 mg cholesterol, 82 mg sodium, 168 mg potassium.

BREAD PUDDING

Preparation Time: 10 min. ▪ Cooking Time: 35 min. ▪ Low Fat

Save about 20 calories per serving by using reduced-calorie raisin bread.

	Nonstick spray coating
2	**eggs**
2	**egg whites**
1½	**cups skim milk**
2	**tablespoons honey**
1	**teaspoon vanilla**
4	**slices raisin bread, cubed (3 cups)**

▪ Spray an 8-inch round baking dish with nonstick spray coating.

▪ In a large mixing bowl beat eggs and egg whites till foamy. Beat in milk, honey, and vanilla. Stir in bread cubes. Pour into the prepared baking dish.

▪ Bake in a 325° oven for 35 to 40 minutes or till a knife inserted near the center comes out clean.

▪ To serve, spoon warm pudding into dessert dishes. Makes 6 servings.

Nutrition information per serving: 128 calories, 7 g protein, 20 g carbohydrate, 3 g fat, 93 mg cholesterol, 145 mg sodium, 188 mg potassium.

BISCOTTI

39 calories

Preparation Time: 1¼ hrs. ▪ Cooking Time: 30 min. ▪ Low Fat ▪ Low Cholesterol ▪ Low Sodium

When Biscotti logs are complete-ly cool, use a serrated knife to cut them into ½-inch slices.

	Nonstick spray coating
2	**cups all-purpose flour**
2	**teaspoons baking powder**
2	**teaspoons aniseed, crushed**
1	**teaspoon finely shredded lemon peel**
¼	**cup margarine**
½	**cup sugar**
2	**eggs**

▪ Spray a large baking sheet with nonstick spray coating; set aside.

▪ In a mixing bowl stir together flour, baking powder, aniseed, and lemon peel. Set aside.

▪ In a small mixer bowl beat margarine with an electric mixer on medium speed till softened. Add sugar; beat till fluffy. Add eggs; beat well. Stir in flour mixture.

▪ On waxed paper shape dough into two 12-inch-long logs. Place on pre-pared baking sheet; flatten logs slightly.

▪ Bake in a 375° oven for 15 to 20 minutes or till lightly browned. Cool completely on wire racks (about 1 hour).

▪ Cut each log into ½-inch slices. Arrange slices, one cut side down, on the baking sheet.

▪ Bake in a 300° oven for 10 minutes. Turn over; bake 5 to 10 minutes longer or till crisp and dry. Cool completely on wire racks. Makes 48 cookies (48 servings).

Nutrition information per serving: 39 calories, 1 g protein, 6 g carbohydrate, 1 g fat, 11 mg cholesterol, 27 mg sodium, 10 mg potassium.

MOCHA SOUFFLÉ

103 calories

Preparation Time: 1½ hrs. ▪ Cooking Time: 20 min. ▪ Low Fat ▪ Low Cholesterol

6	**egg whites**
¼	**cup sugar**
2	**tablespoons cornstarch**
3	**tablespoons unsweetened cocoa powder**
2	**teaspoons instant coffee crystals**
1	**cup canned evaporated skim milk**
1	**tablespoon orange- or coffee-flavored liqueur**
1½	**teaspoons vanilla**
½	**teaspoon cream of tartar**

▪ Bring egg whites to room temperature (about 1 hour).

▪ Meanwhile, in a saucepan combine the sugar, cornstarch, cocoa powder, and coffee crystals. Stir in milk all at once. Cook and stir over medium heat till bubbly; cook and stir for 2 minutes more. Remove from heat.

▪ Stir in liqueur and vanilla. Pour into a large bowl. Cover surface of mixture with clear plastic wrap. Set aside.

▪ In a large mixer bowl beat egg whites and cream of tartar till stiff peaks form (tips stand straight). Fold about *one-fourth* of the egg whites into the chocolate mixture to lighten. Fold in remaining egg whites.

▪ Gently pour mixture into an ungreased 2- to 2½-quart soufflé dish.

▪ Bake in a 375° oven 20 to 25 minutes or till a knife inserted near the center comes out clean. Serve immediately. Makes 6 servings.

Nutrition information per serving: 103 calories, 7 g protein, 17 g carbohydrate, 1 g fat, 1 mg cholesterol, 115 mg sodium, 248 mg potassium.

PAVLOVA

114 calories

Preparation Time: 1¼ hrs. ▪ Cooking Time: 35 min. ▪ Low Fat ▪ No Cholesterol

This chewy meringue dessert was named after a Russian ballerina who performed in Australia and New Zealand in the early 1900s. Expect the shell under the fruit to have a soft, marshmallowlike texture.

2	egg whites
1	teaspoon white vinegar *or* ¼ teaspoon cream of tartar
⅛	teaspoon salt
½	cup sugar
2½	cups sliced *or* cut up fresh fruit (strawberries, kiwi fruit, pineapple, *and/or* papaya)
⅓	cup thawed frozen whipped dessert topping

■ Line a baking sheet with foil. Draw six 3-inch circles on the foil. Set aside.

■ In a small mixer bowl combine egg whites, vinegar, and salt. Beat with an electric mixer on medium speed till soft peaks form (tips curl).

■ Gradually add the ½ cup sugar, 1 tablespoon at a time, beating on high speed till very stiff peaks form (tips stand straight) and sugar is almost dissolved (about 4 minutes).

■ Use the back of a spoon to spread the meringue over the circles on the foil, building the sides up.

■ Bake in a 300° oven for 35 minutes. Turn off oven. Let meringue shells dry in oven, with door closed, for at least 1 hour. Remove from foil.

■ To serve, spoon fruit into meringue shells. Top with whipped topping. Makes 6 servings.

Nutrition information per serving: 114 calories, 2 g protein, 25 g carbohydrate, 1 g fat, 0 mg cholesterol, 64 mg sodium, 174 mg potassium.

MERINGUE SHELLS WITH FRESH FRUIT   141 calories

Preparation Time: 1½ hrs. ▪ Cooking Time: 35 min. ▪ Low Fat ▪ Low Cholesterol ▪ Low Sodium

Using the back of a spoon, spread the meringue mixture over each circle on the brown paper. Build up the sides to form a shell. Or, use a pastry bag to pipe the mixture onto the baking sheet.

2	egg whites (at room temperature)
½	teaspoon vanilla
⅛	teaspoon cream of tartar
½	cup sugar
1	8-ounce carton fruit-flavored low-fat yogurt
2	cups sliced strawberries
1	kiwi fruit, peeled and sliced

▪ Line a large baking sheet with plain brown paper or parchment paper. Draw six 3- to 4-inch circles on the paper; set aside.

▪ For meringue, in a small mixer bowl beat egg whites, vanilla, and cream of tartar with electric mixer on medium speed till soft peaks form. Add sugar, *1 tablespoon* at a time, beating on high speed till very stiff peaks form and sugar is almost dissolved (about 7 minutes).

▪ Spread or pipe meringue over circles on paper, building up sides to form shells. Bake in a 300° oven for 35 minutes.

▪ Turn off oven; let meringue dry in oven with door closed for 1 hour. *Do not open oven.* Lift meringues off paper.

▪ To serve, spoon yogurt into shells. Arrange fruit atop yogurt. Makes 6 servings.

Nutrition information per serving: 141 calories, 3 g protein, 32 g carbohydrate, 1 g fat, 2 mg cholesterol, 40 mg sodium, 272 mg potassium.

PUMPKIN CUSTARDS

103 calories

Preparation Time: 10 min. ▪ Cooking Time: 35 min. ▪ Low Fat ▪ Low Cholesterol

A petite crustless pumpkin pie in a dish.

2	egg whites
1	cup canned pumpkin
¾	cup evaporated skim milk
3	tablespoons sugar
½	teaspoon ground cinnamon
⅛	teaspoon ground ginger
⅛	teaspoon ground allspice
	Dash salt
	Whipped dessert topping (optional)

■ In a medium mixing bowl beat egg whites till foamy. Stir in canned pumpkin, evaporated skim milk, sugar, cinnamon, ginger, allspice, and salt.
■ Place four 6-ounce custard cups or ramekins in a shallow baking pan. Pour pumpkin mixture into cups.
■ Place the baking pan containing the cups on oven rack. Pour *boiling* water around custard cups in baking pan to a depth of 1 inch.
■ Bake in a 325° oven for 35 to 40 minutes or till a knife inserted near the centers comes out clean. Remove custard cups from water. Serve warm or chilled. If desired, garnish with whipped dessert topping. Makes 4 servings.

Nutrition information per serving: 103 calories, 6 g protein, 20 g carbohydrate, 0 g fat, 2 mg cholesterol, 117 mg sodium, 311 mg potassium.

APRICOT CUSTARDS

120 calories

Preparation Time: 10 min. ▪ Cooking Time: 30 min. ▪ Low Fat

1	**8-ounce can unpeeled apricot halves (water pack), drained**
1	**beaten egg**
½	**cup skim milk**
1	**tablespoon sugar**
¼	**teaspoon vanilla**
	Few drops rum flavoring *or* almond extract
	Dash ground cardamom *or* ground nutmeg

■ If desired, slice 2 apricot halves for garnish; set aside. Chop remaining apricot halves. Place chopped apricots on paper towels to drain thoroughly.

■ Place two 6-ounce custard cups or soufflé dishes in a shallow baking pan. Divide chopped apricot halves between custard cups or soufflé dishes.

■ In a small mixing bowl combine the egg, milk, sugar, vanilla, and rum flavoring or almond extract. Pour the egg mixture atop fruit. Sprinkle with cardamom or nutmeg.

■ Place the baking pan containing the cups on oven rack. Pour *boiling* water around custard cups in baking pan to a depth of 1 inch.

■ Bake in a 325° oven for 30 to 35 minutes or till a knife inserted near the centers comes out clean. Remove custard cups from water. Serve warm. If desired, garnish with the reserved apricot pieces. Makes 2 servings.

Nutrition information per serving: 120 calories, 6 g protein, 17 g carbohydrate, 3 g fat, 140 mg cholesterol, 70 mg sodium, 350 mg potassium.

RASPBERRY WHIP

97 calories

Preparation Time: 10 min. ▪ Chilling Time: 1¼ hrs. ▪ Low Fat ▪ Low Cholesterol

Chill the gelatin mixture until it's the consistency of unbeaten egg whites. This way when other ingredients are added to the gelatin, they will stay evenly distributed.

1	**cup fresh *or* frozen raspberries**
1	**3-ounce package raspberry-flavored gelatin***
1	**cup boiling water**
⅔	**cup cold water**
1	**8-ounce carton vanilla low-fat yogurt**

■ Thaw raspberries, if frozen; drain.

■ In a small mixing bowl dissolve gelatin in the boiling water. Add the cold water. Cover and chill about 45 minutes or till partially set (the consistency of unbeaten egg whites).

■ Add yogurt. Beat with an electric mixer on medium speed for 1 to 2 minutes or till light and foamy. If necessary, chill mixture till it mounds when spooned.

■ Meanwhile, divide *half* of the raspberries among 6 dessert dishes. Spoon gelatin mixture on top. Garnish with remaining raspberries. Chill 30 minutes or till firm. Makes 6 servings.

*Note: If desired, substitute one 4-serving-size package low-calorie raspberry-flavored gelatin for the regular gelatin. This reduces the calorie count to 50 calories per serving.

Nutrition information per serving: 97 calories, 3 g protein, 20 g carbohydrate, 1 g fat, 2 mg cholesterol, 72 mg sodium, 150 mg potassium.

CHOCOLATE-CHEESE DESSERT

145 calories

Preparation Time: 20 min. ▪ Chilling Time: 4½ hrs. ▪ Low Cholesterol

To save time, pour the chocolate-cheese mixture into dessert dishes immediately after mixing.

1	envelope unflavored gelatin
½	cup *cold* water
¾	cup low-fat cottage cheese
½	of an 8-ounce package reduced-calorie cream cheese, cut up
⅓	cup sugar
3	tablespoons unsweetened cocoa powder
1	cup skim milk
1	teaspoon vanilla

▪ In a small saucepan stir together the gelatin and cold water; let stand 5 minutes. Heat and stir over low heat till gelatin dissolves.

▪ Meanwhile, in a blender container or food processor bowl combine cottage cheese, cream cheese, sugar, and cocoa powder. (If using the blender, add 2 or 3 tablespoons of the milk to make blending easier.)

▪ Cover and blend or process till smooth (1 to 2 minutes). Stop to scrape sides, if necessary.

▪ Add milk, vanilla, and warm gelatin mixture. Cover and blend or process till combined.

▪ Chill mixture, stirring occasionally, till mixture mounds when spooned (about 30 minutes). Spoon mixture into 6 dessert dishes. Cover and chill in the refrigerator 4 hours or till firm. Makes 6 servings.

Nutrition information per serving: 145 calories, 8 g protein, 15 g carbohydrate, 6 g fat, 19 mg cholesterol, 230 mg sodium, 130 mg potassium.

MINT-CHOCOLATE CHIP ICE MILK

96 calories

Preparation Time: 2 hrs. ▪ Low Fat ▪ Low Cholesterol

¾	**cup sugar**
1	**envelope unflavored gelatin**
1	**12-ounce can evaporated skim milk**
1	**egg white**
1	**egg**
2½	**cups skim milk**
2	**tablespoons white crème de menthe**
2	**teaspoons vanilla**
	Several drops green food coloring (optional)
1½	**squares (1½ ounces) semisweet chocolate, chopped**

▪ In a large saucepan stir together the sugar and gelatin. Stir in evaporated skim milk. Cook and stir over medium-low heat till sugar and gelatin dissolve and mixture almost boils; remove from heat.

▪ In a small bowl slightly beat egg white and egg. Stir about ½ *cup* of the hot gelatin mixture into the eggs; return all to saucepan.

▪ Cook and stir over low heat 2 minutes more. *Do not boil.*

▪ Stir in 2½ cups skim milk, crème de menthe, and vanilla. Cover and chill in the refrigerator for 1 hour.

▪ Stir food coloring into cooled milk mixture, if desired. Stir in semisweet chocolate.

▪ Freeze mixture in a 4- to 5-quart ice cream freezer according to manufacturer's directions. Makes 16 (½-cup) servings.

Nutrition information per serving: 96 calories, 4 g protein, 17 g carbohydrate, 1 g fat, 19 mg cholesterol, 55 mg sodium, 159 mg potassium.

WATERMELON SHERBET

83 calories

Preparation Time: 25 min. ▪ Freezing Time: 8 hrs. ▪ Low Fat ▪ No Cholesterol ▪ Low Sodium

4	**cups cubed, seeded watermelon**
½	**cup sugar**
1	**envelope unflavored gelatin**
⅓	**cup cranberry juice cocktail**

▪ Place watermelon cubes in a blender container or food processor bowl. Cover and blend or process till smooth. (There should be 3 cups of the mixture.) Stir in sugar.

▪ In a small saucepan combine gelatin and cranberry juice cocktail. Let stand for 5 minutes. Stir mixture over low heat till gelatin is dissolved.

▪ Stir the gelatin mixture into the melon mixture. Pour into an 8x8x2-inch baking pan.

▪ Cover and freeze for 2 hours or till firm.

▪ Break up frozen mixture and place in a chilled mixer bowl. Beat with an electric mixer on medium to high speed or till mixture is fluffy.

▪ Return to pan. Cover and freeze for 6 hours or till firm. Makes 8 (½-cup) servings.

Nutrition information per serving: 83 calories, 1 g protein, 20 g carbohydrate, 0 g fat, 0 mg cholesterol, 3 mg sodium, 96 mg potassium.

FRUITY YOGURT ICE

111 calories

Preparation Time: 15 min. ▪ Freezing Time: 9 hrs. ▪ Low Fat ▪ Low Cholesterol ▪ Low Sodium

Both the raspberry and peach versions of this tangy, refreshing dessert are shown here.

1	**15-** *or* **16-ounce can red raspberries, peach slices, blueberries,** *or* **apricot halves**
2	**8-ounce cartons vanilla low-fat yogurt**
1	**tablespoon honey**

▪ Place *undrained* raspberries, peaches, blueberries, or apricot halves in a blender container or food processor bowl. Blend or process till smooth. If using raspberries, strain them to remove seeds.
▪ In a medium mixing bowl stir together blended fruit, yogurt, and honey. Pour into an 8x8x2-inch pan.
▪ Cover and freeze for 3 to 4 hours or till firm.
▪ Break frozen mixture into chunks with a wooden spoon and place in a chilled large mixer bowl.
▪ Beat with an electric mixer on medium speed till fluffy. Return to pan.
▪ Cover and freeze for 6 hours more or till firm.
▪ To serve, let mixture stand at room temperature for 5 minutes; then scoop into dessert dishes. Serves 8.

Nutrition information per serving: 111 calories, 3 g protein, 24 g carbohydrate, 1 g fat, 3 mg cholesterol, 38 mg sodium, 186 mg potassium.

COFFEE ICE

Preparation Time: 15 min. ▪ Freezing Time: 4 hrs. ▪ Low Fat ▪ No Cholesterol ▪ Low Sodium

Italian ices, such as this one, are typically served with mounds of whipped cream. If you like, serve this version with a lower-calorie dessert topping.

¼	cup sugar
2	tablespoons instant espresso coffee powder
½	cup boiling water
1	cup cold water
5	strawberries (optional)

■ In a small bowl combine sugar and coffee powder. Add boiling water; stir till dissolved. Stir in cold water.
■ Pour mixture into a 9x5x3-inch loaf pan. Freeze about 2 hours or till firm.
■ Break frozen mixture into small chunks; place in a small chilled mixer bowl. Beat with electric mixer on low speed till fluffy.
■ Freeze mixture for 2 hours or till firm.
■ To serve, scrape or scoop ice into small dessert dishes. If desired, garnish each serving with a strawberry. Makes 5 (½-cup) servings.

Nutrition information per serving: 44 calories, 0 g protein, 11 g carbohydrate, 0 g fat, 0 mg cholesterol, 1 mg sodium, 77 mg potassium.

PEACHY CHERRY SAUCE

105 calories

Preparation Time: 8 min. ▪ Cooking Time: 10 min. ▪ Low Fat ▪ Low Cholesterol ▪ Low Sodium

¼	**cup reduced-calorie orange marmalade**
¼	**cup orange juice**
2	**teaspoons cornstarch**
1	**teaspoon margarine**
¼	**teaspoon ground cardamom** *or* **cinnamon**
2	**cups sliced, peeled peaches** *or* **sliced nectarines** *or* **frozen unsweetened peach slices**
1	**cup pitted dark sweet cherries** *or* **frozen unsweetened pitted dark sweet cherries**
½	**cup frozen yogurt** *or* **ice milk**

▪ In a medium saucepan combine marmalade, orange juice, cornstarch, margarine, and cardamom. Cook and stir till thickened and bubbly. Stir in fresh or frozen peaches and cherries. Cover and cook over medium heat for 10 to 12 minutes or till fruits are just tender, stirring once. Cool slightly.

▪ To serve, spoon sauce into dessert dishes. Top each serving with a small spoonful of the frozen yogurt. Serves 5.

Nutrition information per serving: 105 calories, 2 g protein, 21 g carbohydrate, 2 g fat, 1 mg cholesterol, 41 mg sodium, 270 mg potassium.

RUM-SAUCED BANANAS

151 calories

Preparation Time: 5 min. ▪ Cooking Time: 2½ min. ▪ Low Fat ▪ Low Cholesterol ▪ Low Sodium

¼	**cup apple juice**
4	**teaspoons brown sugar**
1	**teaspoon margarine**
	Dash ground nutmeg
2	**large bananas, peeled and sliced (1¾ cups)**
1	**tablespoon rum**
1	**cup vanilla- *or* coffee-flavored ice milk**

▪ In a 1-quart microwave-safe casserole combine apple juice, brown sugar, margarine, and nutmeg. Micro-cook, uncovered, on 100% power (high) for 1 minute.

▪ Add bananas, tossing to coat. Cook on 100% power (high) for 1½ to 2 minutes or till bananas are heated through; spoon sauce over bananas once.

▪ Pour rum over bananas in casserole. Carefully ignite with a long match. Serve banana mixture over ice milk. Makes 4 servings.

Nutrition information per serving: 151 calories, 2 g protein, 29 g carbohydrate, 3 g fat, 5 mg cholesterol, 41 mg sodium, 372 mg potassium.

SWEET AND SPICY PEACHES   65 calories

Preparation Time: 10 min. ▪ Cooking Time: 2 min. ▪ Low Fat ▪ Low Cholesterol ▪ Low Sodium

2	tablespoons brown sugar
1	tablespoon lime *or* lemon juice
½	teaspoon vanilla
¼	teaspoon ground allspice
3	medium peaches, peeled, pitted, and sliced
¼	cup plain low-fat yogurt

▪ In a 1-quart microwave-safe casserole combine sugar, lime or lemon juice, vanilla, and allspice. Add peaches.

▪ Micro-cook, covered, on 100% power (high) for 2 to 5 minutes (5 to 7 minutes in low-wattage ovens) or till the peaches are tender and heated through, stirring once.

▪ To serve, top each serving with yogurt. Serves 4.

Nutrition information per serving: 65 calories, 1 g protein, 15 g carbohydrate, 0 g fat, 1 mg cholesterol, 13 mg sodium, 193 mg potassium.

SAUCY RHUBARB AND STRAWBERRIES

61 calories

Preparation Time: 10 min. ▪ Cooking Time: 8 min. ▪ Chilling Time: 1½ hrs. ▪ Low Fat ▪ No Cholesterol ▪ Low Sodium

¼	**cup sugar**
¼	**cup orange juice**
2	**cups rhubarb cut into ½-inch slices** *or* **frozen sliced rhubarb (8 ounces)**
2	**teaspoons cornstarch**
1	**tablespoon water**
1	**cup sliced strawberries**

■ In a small saucepan combine sugar and orange juice. Bring to boiling; add fresh or frozen rhubarb. Return to boiling; reduce heat. Cover and simmer for 5 to 7 minutes or till rhubarb is nearly tender. Drain rhubarb, reserving syrup.

■ If necessary, add water to reserved syrup to make ⅔ cup. Pour syrup into saucepan. Stir together cornstarch and the water; stir into syrup. Cook and stir till thickened and bubbly. Cook and stir for 2 minutes more. Remove saucepan from the heat.

■ Gently stir in rhubarb and strawberries. Cover and chill thoroughly (about 1½ hours). Makes 6 servings.

Nutrition information per serving: 61 calories, 1 g protein, 15 g carbohydrate, 0 g fat, 0 mg cholesterol, 2 mg sodium, 200 mg potassium.

DRIED FRUIT ROYALE

92 calories

Preparation Time: 8 min. ▪ Cooking Time: 23 min. ▪ Chilling Time: 4 hrs. ▪ Low Fat ▪ No Cholesterol ▪ Low Sodium

Served warm, this variation of a fruit soup is a delicious accompaniment to pork.

1	**8-ounce can pineapple tidbits (juice pack)**
1	**cup mixed dried fruit**
1	**cup water**
4	**inches stick cinnamon**
	Dash ground cloves *or* 2 whole cloves
1	**tablespoon honey**
⅓	**cup vanilla low-fat yogurt (optional)**

▪ Drain pineapple, reserving juice. Cut up any large pieces of dried fruit.

▪ In a medium saucepan stir together reserved pineapple juice, water, cinnamon, and cloves. Bring to boiling and add dried fruit; reduce heat. Cover and simmer for 15 to 20 minutes or till fruit is tender. Remove cinnamon and whole cloves, if using. Stir in honey and pineapple tidbits. Serve warm or cover and chill 4 hours or overnight.

▪ To serve, spoon into individual serving dishes. Dollop each serving with some of the vanilla yogurt, if desired. Serves 6.

Nutrition information per serving: 92 calories, 1 g protein, 24 g carbohydrate, 0 g fat, 0 mg cholesterol, 5 mg sodium, 239 mg potassium.

FRESH FRUIT WITH CREAMY SAUCE

82 calories

Preparation Time: 15 min. ▪ Low Fat ▪ Low Cholesterol

½	**cup low-fat cream-style cottage cheese**
½	**cup unsweetened applesauce**
1	**tablespoon honey**
1	**cup sliced nectarines *or* sliced, peeled peaches *or* orange sections *or* sliced strawberries**
1	**cup sliced apple *or* pear**
½	**cup seedless grapes**
1	**small banana, sliced**
	Ground cinnamon *or* ground nutmeg

▪ For sauce, in a blender container or food processor bowl combine cottage cheese, applesauce, and honey. Cover and blend or process till smooth.

▪ In a large bowl stir together nectarine slices, apple slices, grapes, and banana slices. Divide fruit among 6 dessert dishes. Spoon some of the sauce over each serving and sprinkle with cinnamon or nutmeg. Serves 6.

Nutrition information per serving: 82 calories, 3 g protein, 17 g carbohydrate, 1 g fat, 2 mg cholesterol, 77 mg sodium, 190 mg potassium.

SPICY FRUIT CUP

78 calories

Preparation Time: 12 min. ▪ Chilling Time: 1 hr. ▪ Low Fat ▪ No Cholesterol ▪ Low Sodium

1	**8-ounce can pineapple chunks (juice pack)**
½	**cup orange juice**
2	**tablespoons dry white wine**
⅛	**teaspoon ground cinnamon**
	Dash ground nutmeg
2	**medium oranges, peeled and sectioned**
1	**medium pear, cored and sliced**
1	**cup strawberries, halved**

▪ In a mixing bowl combine the *undrained* pineapple, orange juice, wine, cinnamon, and nutmeg. Carefully stir in the orange sections, pear slices, and strawberries. Cover and chill for 1 hour. Makes 6 servings.

Nutrition information per serving: 78 calories, 1 g protein, 19 g carbohydrate, 0 g fat, 0 mg cholesterol, 1 mg sodium, 240 mg potassium.

SWEET-TOPPED RASPBERRIES

91 calories

Preparation Time: 8 min. ▪ Low Cholesterol ▪ Low Sodium

½	teaspoon finely shredded orange peel
2	tablespoons orange juice
2	cups raspberries, blueberries, *or* sliced strawberries
⅔	cup thawed frozen nondairy whipped dessert topping
⅓	cup vanilla low-fat yogurt

▪In a medium bowl stir together orange peel and orange juice. Add raspberries; toss to coat. For topping, in a small bowl stir together dessert topping and yogurt.

▪Divide raspberry mixture among 4 dessert dishes. Spoon some of the topping over each serving. Sprinkle with additional finely shredded orange peel, if desired. Serve at once. Makes 4 servings.

Nutrition information per serving: 91 calories, 2 g protein, 14 g carbohydrate, 4 g fat, 1 mg cholesterol, 17 mg sodium, 155 mg potassium.

CALICO FRUIT

88 calories

Preparation Time: 10 min. ▪ Low Fat ▪ No Cholesterol ▪ Low Sodium

Turn this fruit combination into a salad by serving it on a lettuce leaf.

⅓	cup fresh *or* frozen blueberries
1	6-ounce can apricot nectar (¾ cup)
1	tablespoon honey
½	teaspoon vanilla
1	16-ounce can unpeeled apricot halves (water pack), drained
1	large apple, sliced (1 cup)
1	cup seedless grapes

▪ Thaw frozen blueberries and drain, if using. Chill thawed blueberries till serving time.

▪ In a small bowl stir together apricot nectar, honey, and vanilla.

▪ In a large bowl combine apricots, apple, grapes, and *fresh* blueberries, if using. Pour honey mixture over fruit; toss gently to coat. Cover and chill up to 4 hours. Just before serving, stir in thawed *frozen* blueberries, if using. Makes 6 servings.

Nutrition information per serving: 88 calories, 1 g protein, 22 g carbohydrate, 0 g fat, 0 mg cholesterol, 4 mg sodium, 270 mg potassium.

PINEAPPLE FLAMBÉ

122 calories

Preparation Time: 15 min. ▪ Low Fat ▪ Low Cholesterol ▪ Low Sodium

To flame the dessert, use rum that is at least 70 proof. Pour the rum into a small saucepan and heat over low heat or over the flame of a candle till just warm. If desired, pour the heated rum into a large ladle. Using a long match, carefully ignite the rum and pour over the pineapple.

½	teaspoon finely shredded orange peel
¼	cup orange juice
2	teaspoons cornstarch
½	teaspoon ground ginger
1	20-ounce can crushed pineapple (juice pack)
2	tablespoons light rum
1½	cups vanilla ice milk *or* frozen yogurt

▪ In a 10-inch skillet stir together orange peel, orange juice, cornstarch, and ginger. Stir in *undrained* pineapple. Cook and stir till slightly thickened and bubbly.

▪ In a small saucepan heat rum over low heat just till warm. Carefully ignite rum and pour over pineapple mixture. Serve immediately over ice milk. Makes 6 servings.

Nutrition information per serving: 122 calories, 2 g protein, 24 g carbohydrate, 1 g fat, 5 mg cholesterol, 27 mg sodium, 204 mg potassium.

BAKED APPLES WITH CHEESE TOPPING 139 calories

Preparation Time: 10 min. ▪ Cooking Time: 40 min. ▪ Low Fat ▪ Low Cholesterol

4	**small apples, cored (about 4 ounces each)**
¼	**cup snipped pitted whole dates *or* raisins**
¼	**cup water**
2	**ounces Neufchâtel cheese**
½	**teaspoon vanilla**
3	**to 4 teaspoons skim milk**
	Ground nutmeg *or* ground cinnamon

▪ Cut off a strip of peel from the top of each apple. Arrange apples in a 9-inch pie plate. Fill apples with dates or raisins. Add water to pie plate. Bake, covered, in a 350° oven for 40 minutes or till apples are tender. Cool slightly.

▪ Meanwhile, for topping, stir together cheese and vanilla. Stir in enough skim milk to make of desired consistency.

▪ To serve, dollop apples with some of the topping. Sprinkle lightly with nutmeg or cinnamon. Makes 4 servings.

▪ **Microwave directions:** Prepare as above, *except* arrange apples in a microwave-safe 9-inch pie plate. Add water to pie plate. Cover with vented clear plastic wrap. Micro-cook on 100% power (high) for 3 to 7 minutes (7 to 10 minutes in a low-wattage oven) or till tender, rearranging once.

Nutrition information per serving: 139 calories, 2 g protein, 27 g carbohydrate, 4 g fat, 11 mg cholesterol, 63 mg sodium, 239 mg potassium.

BANANA POPS

Preparation Time: 8 min. ▪ Freezing Time: 3 hrs. ▪ Low Fat ▪ No Cholesterol ▪ Low Sodium

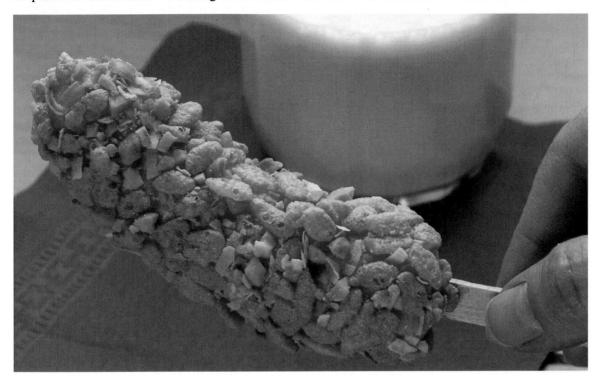

Eating breakfast on the run? A Banana Pop, bran muffin, and a glass of skim milk will fill the bill.

2	medium bananas, peeled and halved crosswise
¼	cup crisp rice cereal
1	tablespoon toasted chopped coconut
1	tablespoon finely chopped peanuts
¼	teaspoon ground nutmeg, ground cinnamon, *or* apple pie spice
2	teaspoons maple-flavored syrup

▪ Insert a wooden stick* into the cut end of each banana half. Place on a baking sheet. Freeze 1 hour or till bananas are firm.

▪ Meanwhile, in a shallow dish mix cereal, coconut, peanuts, and nutmeg. Brush frozen bananas with syrup, then roll in cereal mixture to coat.

▪ Wrap each pop individually in plastic wrap; return to freezer. Freeze 2 hours more or till completely frozen. Serves 4.

*Note: If desired, substitute plastic forks or knives for the wooden sticks.

Nutrition information per serving: 93 calories, 1 g protein, 19 g carbohydrate, 2 g fat, 0 mg cholesterol, 23 mg sodium, 266 mg potassium.

CHOCOLATE PEARS

76 calories

Preparation Time: 10 min. ▪ Cooking Time: 30 min. ▪ Low Fat ▪ No Cholesterol ▪ No Sodium

2	**medium pears, peeled, halved, and cored**
1	**tablespoon lemon *or* lime juice**
1	**teaspoon vanilla**
2	**tablespoons semisweet chocolate pieces**

▪ Arrange pear halves, cut side up, in a 9-inch pie plate. Stir together lemon juice and vanilla, and brush over pears.

▪ Bake, covered, in a 375° oven for 30 to 35 minutes or till pears are tender. Uncover pears and sprinkle with chocolate pieces. Spoon any liquid in the pie plate over pears. Serve warm. Makes 4 servings.

▪ **Microwave directions:** Prepare pears as above. Place in a microwave-safe 9-inch pie plate. Cover with waxed paper. Micro-cook on 100% power (high) for 4 to 6 minutes (7 to 9 minutes in a low-wattage oven) or till pears are tender.

Nutrition information per serving: 76 calories, 1 g protein, 16 g carbohydrate, 2 g fat, 0 mg cholesterol, 0 mg sodium, 124 mg potassium.

CRUMB-TOPPED PEACHES

95 calories

Preparation Time: 10 min. ▪ Cooking Time: 5 min. ▪ Low Cholesterol ▪ Low Sodium

½ cup white grape juice *or* apple juice *or* apple cider

2 large peaches, peeled, halved, and pitted*

2 teaspoons margarine

3 vanilla wafers, crushed

2 tablespoons sliced almonds

▪ In a medium skillet heat juice or cider to boiling; add peach halves. Cover and simmer 5 to 6 minutes or till tender, turning over once. Place one fruit half in each dessert dish. Drizzle juice around fruit.

▪ Meanwhile, in a small skillet melt margarine. Stir in crushed wafers and almonds. Stir over medium-low heat till almonds are lightly toasted. Sprinkle over fruit. Makes 4 servings.

*Note: If desired, substitute four canned juice-pack peach halves, drained, for the fresh peaches. Simmer peaches in the juice or cider for 3 to 4 minutes or till peaches are heated through. Continue as directed.

Nutrition information per serving: 95 calories, 1 g protein, 13 g carbohydrate, 5 g fat, 1 mg cholesterol, 31 mg sodium, 173 mg potassium.

APPLE PHYLLO TRIANGLES

118 calories

Preparation Time: 15 min. ▪ Cooking Time: 15 min. ▪ No Cholesterol

To shape the phyllo strips into triangles, fold the end of the phyllo nearest the filling over the filling at a 45-degree angle. Repeat folding phyllo at this angle to enclose the filling, using the entire strip.

1	**medium baking apple, peeled and chopped (1 cup)**
2	**tablespoons raisins**
1	**tablespoon sugar**
1	**teaspoon all-purpose flour**
1	**teaspoon lemon juice**
½	**teaspoon ground cinnamon**
3	**sheets phyllo dough**
2	**tablespoons margarine, melted**
	Nonstick spray coating

▪ For filling, in a small mixing bowl combine apple, raisins, sugar, flour, lemon juice, and cinnamon. Set aside.

▪ Lightly brush *1 sheet* of the phyllo dough with *some* of the melted margarine. Place another sheet of phyllo dough on top of the first sheet, then brush with margarine. Top with the third sheet of phyllo. *Do not brush with margarine.*

▪ Cut the stack of phyllo sheets lengthwise into four strips.

▪ For each triangle, spoon *one-fourth* of the filling about 1 inch from one end of *each* strip.

▪ Fold the end over the filling at a 45-degree angle. Continue folding to form a triangle that encloses the filling, using the entire strip. Repeat with remaining strips of phyllo and filling.

▪ Place triangles on a baking sheet sprayed with nonstick spray coating. Brush the tops of the triangles with the remaining margarine.

▪ Bake in a 375° oven about 15 minutes or till golden. Serve warm or cool. Makes 4 servings.

Nutrition information per serving: 118 calories, 1 g protein, 16 g carbohydrate, 6 g fat, 0 mg cholesterol, 109 mg sodium, 85 mg potassium.

SNACKS AND BEVERAGES

MARINATED ZUCCHINI AND MUSHROOMS *(see page 421)*

COTTAGE CHEESE-DILL DIP

27 calories

Preparation Time: 15 min. ▪ Chilling Time: 1 hr. ▪ Low Cholesterol

Use a green, yellow, or sweet red pepper shell for an attractive serving bowl.

1	cup low-fat cottage cheese
2	tablespoons sliced green onion
2	tablespoons snipped fresh parsley
1	teaspoon dried dillweed
1	teaspoon Worcestershire sauce
⅛	teaspoon pepper
	Dash garlic powder

▪ In blender container or food processor bowl place the cottage cheese, green onion, snipped parsley, dillweed, Worcestershire sauce, pepper, and garlic powder. Cover and blend or process till smooth. Chill, covered, for at least 1 hour before serving.

▪ Serve with an assortment of sliced raw vegetables or crackers. Makes 8 (2-tablespoon) servings.

Nutrition information per serving: 27 calories, 4 g protein, 1 g carbohydrate, 1 g fat, 2 mg cholesterol, 122 mg sodium, 41 mg potassium.

LAYERED BEAN DIP

75 calories

Preparation Time: 25 min. ▪ Chilling Time: 4 hrs. ▪ Low Fat ▪ Low Cholesterol

1	**15-ounce can pinto *or* red kidney beans, drained**
¼	**cup salsa**
1	**4-ounce can chopped green chili peppers, drained**
4	**ounces bottled roasted red bell pepper, drained and chopped (about ½ cup), *or* one 4-ounce jar pimiento, drained and chopped**
1	**cup low-fat cottage cheese**
1	**cup chopped tomato**
¼	**cup shredded low-fat cheddar cheese**
	Tortilla Crisps *or* assorted sliced raw vegetables

■ In a blender container or food processor bowl place beans and salsa. Cover and blend or process till smooth. Spread mixture evenly in a 9-inch pie plate. Sprinkle with green chilies and roasted red pepper or pimiento.

■ Wash blender container or food processor bowl. Place cottage cheese in the blender container or food processor bowl. Cover and blend or process till smooth. Then, carefully spread cottage cheese on top of bean mixture in pie plate. Cover and chill for at least 4 hours before serving.

■ Before serving, sprinkle tomato and cheddar cheese on top of cottage cheese layer. Serve with Tortilla Crisps or sliced vegetables. Makes 18 (¼-cup) servings.

■ **Tortilla Crisps:** Cut twelve 6-inch *flour* or *corn tortillas each* into 6 wedges. Place wedges in a single layer on an ungreased baking sheet. Bake in a 350° oven for 5 to 10 minutes or till crisp. Serve 4 crisps per serving.

Nutrition information per serving: 75 calories, 4 g protein, 13 g carbohydrate, 1 g fat, 2 mg cholesterol, 90 mg sodium, 133 mg potassium.

FRESH FRUIT DIP

87 calories

Preparation Time: 10 min. ▪ Low Fat ▪ Low Cholesterol ▪ Low Sodium

Serve as a snack or as a delicious dessert.

1	**8-ounce carton plain low-fat yogurt**
¼	**cup unsweetened applesauce**
1	**tablespoon powdered sugar**
½	**teaspoon vanilla**
⅛	**teaspoon ground cinnamon, nutmeg, *or* ginger**
3	**cups assorted sliced fresh fruit (such as pineapple chunks, strawberries, apple slices, and peach slices)**

■ In a small bowl stir together yogurt, applesauce, powdered sugar, vanilla, and cinnamon, nutmeg, or ginger.

■ To serve, spear fruit with toothpicks, then dip into yogurt mixture. Makes 6 (3-tablespoon) servings.

Nutrition information per serving: 87 calories, 3 g protein, 18 g carbohydrate, 1 g fat, 2 mg cholesterol, 28 mg sodium, 274 mg potassium.

GARLIC-SPINACH DIP

23 calories

Preparation Time: 20 min. ▪ Cooking Time: 4 min. ▪ Low Cholesterol ▪ Low Sodium

To make toasted pita wedges, split pita pockets and cut each half into wedges. Bake the wedges on an ungreased baking sheet in a 350° oven for 8 to 10 minutes.

1	10-ounce package frozen chopped spinach
10	cloves garlic, 1 clove elephant garlic, *or* 2 tablespoons bottled minced garlic
¼	cup skim milk
⅛	teaspoon salt
	Dash bottled hot pepper sauce
1	8-ounce package Neufchâtel cheese, softened
	Chopped tomato *or* shredded Monterey Jack cheese (optional)

▪ In a saucepan cook frozen spinach according to package directions, then drain well.

▪ Place garlic in a blender container or food processor bowl. Cover and blend or process for 5 to 10 seconds or till minced. Add the cooked spinach, milk, salt, and hot pepper sauce. Cover and blend or process till well combined. Add Neufchâtel cheese; cover and blend or process till smooth.

▪ Transfer spinach mixture to the saucepan. Cook and stir over medium-low heat for 4 to 5 minutes or till mixture is heated through.

▪ To serve, transfer dip to a small serving bowl. If desired, sprinkle with chopped tomato or Monterey Jack cheese. Serve with toasted pita wedges or Tortilla Crisps (see recipe, page 417). Makes 32 (1-tablespoon) servings.

Nutrition information per serving: 23 calories, 1 g protein, 1 g carbohydrate, 2 g fat, 5 mg cholesterol, 44 mg sodium, 43 mg potassium.

COTTAGE CHEESE AND APPLE SNACKS

106 calories

Preparation Time: 15 min. ▪ Low Cholesterol

To keep the apple or pear slices from turning brown, brush them with a little lemon juice.

1	cup low-fat cottage cheese
2	tablespoons peanut butter
¼	teaspoon ground cinnamon *or* apple pie spice
1	to 2 teaspoons skim milk
3	medium apples *or* pears, cored and sliced

■ For dip, in blender container or food processor bowl place the cottage cheese, peanut butter, and cinnamon or apple pie spice. Cover and blend or process till smooth. If necessary, stir in enough milk to make dip of desired consistency.

■ Serve the dip immediately or cover and chill it for up to 24 hours. Serve dip with the apple or pear slices. Makes 6 (2-tablespoon) servings.

Nutrition information per serving: 106 calories, 7 g protein, 13 g carbohydrate, 4 g fat, 3 mg cholesterol, 178 mg sodium, 156 mg potassium.

MARINATED ZUCCHINI AND MUSHROOMS   23 calories

Preparation Time: 20 min. ▪ Marinating Time: 8 hrs. ▪ No Cholesterol ▪ Low Sodium

Make appetizer kabobs by threading the vegetables onto small wooden skewers.

8	**ounces small whole fresh mushrooms (3 cups)**
2	**small zucchini *and/or* yellow summer squash, bias-sliced into ½-inch-thick slices (2 cups)**
1	**small sweet red pepper, cut into square pieces (½ cup)**
¼	**cup lemon juice**
2	**tablespoons olive oil *or* vegetable oil**
1	**tablespoon sugar**
¼	**teaspoon salt**
¼	**teaspoon dried tarragon *or* oregano, crushed**
¼	**teaspoon pepper**
1	**clove garlic, minced**

■ Place mushrooms, zucchini and/or yellow summer squash, and red pepper in a plastic bag set in a deep bowl.

■ For marinade, in small mixing bowl stir together lemon juice, oil, sugar, salt, tarragon or oregano, pepper, and garlic. Mix well. Pour marinade over vegetables in bag. Seal bag. Marinate vegetables in the refrigerator for 8 hours or overnight, turning bag occasionally.

■ To serve, pour vegetables and marinade into serving dish. Serve with toothpicks. Makes about 8 (⅔-cup) servings.

Nutrition information per serving: 23 calories, 1 g protein, 3 g carbohydrate, 1 g fat, 0 mg cholesterol, 19 mg sodium, 188 mg potassium.

OVEN-FRIED VEGETABLES

51 calories

Preparation Time: 10 min. ▪ Cooking Time: 9 min. ▪ Low Cholesterol

Mock french-fried vegetables without the fat.

	Nonstick spray coating
¼	cup fine dry bread crumbs
1	tablespoon grated Parmesan cheese
⅛	teaspoon paprika
2	cups ¼-inch-thick zucchini slices, onion rings, *or* cauliflower flowerets
2	tablespoons reduced-calorie Italian salad dressing

■ Spray a *cold* baking sheet with nonstick spray coating. Set aside.

■ In a 9-inch pie plate stir together bread crumbs, Parmesan cheese, and paprika till well mixed. In a medium mixing bowl place zucchini, onion rings, or cauliflower. Drizzle vegetables with salad dressing; toss till coated. Then, roll vegetables in crumb mixture till coated. Place the coated vegetables in a single layer on the prepared baking sheet.

■ Bake vegetables in a 450° oven for 9 to 11 minutes or till golden. Makes 4 (½-cup) servings.

Nutrition information per serving: 51 calories, 2 g protein, 7 g carbohydrate, 2 g fat, 2 mg cholesterol, 79 mg sodium, 175 mg potassium.

STUFFED MUSHROOMS

30 calories

Preparation Time: 20 min. ▪ Cooking Time: 10 min. ▪ Low Fat ▪ Low Cholesterol

1	**10-ounce package frozen chopped spinach**
	Nonstick spray coating
1½	**pounds large fresh mushrooms (about 20)**
¼	**cup chopped onion**
2	**cloves garlic, minced**
1	**tablespoon margarine**
¼	**cup grated Parmesan cheese**
¼	**cup fine dry bread crumbs**
¼	**cup finely chopped pimiento**
½	**teaspoon dried basil, crushed**
½	**teaspoon dried oregano, crushed**
¼	**teaspoon salt**
	Dash pepper

■ Thaw spinach, then drain well by squeezing excess liquid from it. Meanwhile, spray a *cold* 15x10x1-inch baking pan with nonstick coating. Set baking pan aside.

■ Remove stems from mushrooms. Set tops aside. Chop enough mushroom stems to make *2 cups.* In a 10-inch skillet cook chopped mushroom stems, onion, and garlic in margarine till onion is tender but not browned. Add thawed spinach. Cook over low heat till most of the liquid is evaporated.

■ Stir Parmesan cheese, bread crumbs, pimiento, basil, oregano, salt, and pepper into spinach mixture. Spoon mixture into mushroom tops.

■ Place stuffed mushroom tops in the prepared baking pan. Bake in a 425° oven for 10 to 15 minutes or till mushrooms are tender. Makes about 20 servings.

Nutrition information per serving: 30 calories, 2 g protein, 4 g carbohydrate, 1 g fat, 1 mg cholesterol, 78 mg sodium, 187 mg potassium.

SWEET AND SPICY POPCORN

76 calories

Preparation Time: 10 min. ▪ Cooking Time: 15 min. ▪ Low Fat ▪ No Cholesterol ▪ Low Sodium

	Nonstick spray coating
6	cups popped popcorn (using no oil)
2	tablespoons sugar
2	teaspoons water
¼	teaspoon ground cinnamon
⅛	teaspoon ground nutmeg
⅛	teaspoon ground ginger

▪ Spray a *cold* 13x9x2-inch baking pan with nonstick spray coating. Place popcorn in the baking pan.

▪ In a small mixing bowl stir together sugar, water, cinnamon, nutmeg, and ginger. Add spice mixture to popcorn in baking pan. Toss popcorn till coated. Bake in a 350° oven for 15 minutes, stirring once or twice.

▪ Transfer popcorn from baking pan to a large piece of foil. Cool popcorn completely. If desired, store in a tightly covered container. Makes 6 (¾-cup) servings.

Nutrition information per serving: 76 calories, 2 g protein, 16 g carbohydrate, 1 g fat, 0 mg cholesterol, 1 mg sodium, 40 mg potassium.

CURRIED SNACK MIX

74 calories

Preparation Time: 10 min. ▪ Cooking Time: 20 min. ▪ Low Fat ▪ No Cholesterol

3	**plain rice cakes, broken into bite-size pieces**
1	**cup bite-size square corn cereal _or_ oyster crackers**
¾	**cup pretzel sticks, halved (1 ounce)**
1	**tablespoon margarine, melted**
1	**teaspoon Worcestershire sauce**
½ to ¾	**teaspoon curry powder**

▪ In a 13x9x2-inch baking pan stir together broken rice cakes, corn cereal or oyster crackers, and pretzels.

▪ In a custard cup stir together melted margarine, Worcestershire sauce, and curry powder. Drizzle mixture over cereal mixture. Toss cereal mixture till coated. Bake in a 300° oven for 20 minutes, stirring twice. If desired, store cooled mixture in a tightly covered container. Makes 6 (½-cup) servings.

Nutrition information per serving: 74 calories, 1 g protein, 12 g carbohydrate, 2 g fat, 0 mg cholesterol, 176 mg sodium, 24 mg potassium.

PEANUT BUTTER AND OATMEAL COOKIES 69 calories

Preparation Time: 20 min. ▪ Cooking Time: 8 min. ▪ No Cholesterol

1	cup all-purpose flour
½	teaspoon baking soda
½	cup margarine
½	cup peanut butter
⅓	cup sugar
⅓	cup packed brown sugar
2	egg whites
½	teaspoon vanilla
1	cup rolled oats

▪ In a bowl stir together flour and baking soda. Set flour mixture aside. In a large mixing bowl beat margarine with electric mixer on medium to high speed about 30 seconds or till softened.

▪ Add peanut butter, sugar, and brown sugar to margarine. Beat till thoroughly combined, scraping sides of bowl occasionally. Add egg whites and vanilla. Beat till well combined. Add flour mixture, then beat on low speed till combined. Stir in oats.

▪ Drop dough from a rounded teaspoon 2 inches apart on an ungreased cookie sheet. Bake in a 375° oven for 8 to 10 minutes or till edges are golden. Remove cookies from cookie sheet and cool on a wire rack. Makes about 36.

Nutrition information per cookie: 69 calories, 2 g protein, 9 g carbohydrate, 3 g fat, 0 mg cholesterol, 51 mg sodium, 47 mg potassium.

SPICY COFFEE

Preparation Time: 10 min. ▪ Cooking Time: 5 min. ▪ Low Fat ▪ No Cholesterol ▪ Low Sodium

4	**cups brewed coffee**
2	**inches stick cinnamon**
½	**teaspoon whole allspice**
2	**2x½-inch strips orange peel**
	Stick cinnamon (optional)

▪ In a medium saucepan combine coffee, 2 inches stick cinnamon, allspice, and orange peel. Bring to boiling; reduce heat. Cover and simmer for 5 minutes.

▪ Remove solids from coffee with a slotted spoon. Pour coffee into coffee cups. If desired, garnish with cinnamon sticks. Makes 6 (5-ounce) servings.

▪ **Iced Spicy Coffee:** Prepare Spicy Coffee as above, *except* thoroughly chill coffee after simmering. To serve, pour coffee over ice in tall glasses.

Nutrition information per serving: 3 calories, 0 g protein, 0 g carbohydrate, 0 g fat, 0 mg cholesterol, 3 mg sodium, 85 mg potassium.

ORANGE AND SPICE TEA

41 calories

Preparation Time: 10 min. ▪ Cooking Time: 5 min. ▪ Low Fat ▪ No Cholesterol ▪ Low Sodium

2	cups water
3	inches stick cinnamon, broken
6	whole cloves
2	tea bags
1	cup orange juice
1	tablespoon brown sugar

▪ In a saucepan combine water, cinnamon, and cloves. Bring to boiling; remove from heat.

▪ Add tea bags; let stand for 5 minutes. Remove tea bags.

▪ Stir in orange juice and sugar; heat through.

▪ Pour mixture through a wire strainer into 4 mugs. Makes 4 (6-ounce) servings.

Nutrition information per serving: 41 calories, 0 g protein, 10 g carbohydrate, 0 g fat, 0 mg cholesterol, 2 mg sodium, 130 mg potassium.

BANANA NOG

90 calories

Freezing Time: 30 min. ▪ Preparation Time: 5 min. ▪ Low Fat ▪ Low Cholesterol ▪ Low Sodium

Freeze the banana when you bring it home from the store so it's ready to go into the blender whenever you're ready for a cool drink.

1	small banana
1	cup skim milk
1	cup ice milk
¼	teaspoon vanilla extract
	Ground nutmeg

▪ Peel and cut up banana. Place in freezer container or bag; freeze till firm.
▪ In a blender container combine milk, ice milk, banana, and vanilla extract. Cover and blend till smooth. Sprinkle each serving with nutmeg. Makes 4 (6-ounce) servings.
▪ **Tropical Banana Nog:** Prepare Banana Nog as above, *except* add ¼ teaspoon *coconut extract* and omit nutmeg. Garnish each serving with ½ teaspoon toasted *coconut.* (Add 5 calories per serving.)
▪ **Orange-Banana Nog:** Prepare Banana Nog as above, *except* substitute *orange juice* for the milk. (Add 6 calories per serving.)

Nutrition information per serving: 90 calories, 4 g protein, 16 g carbohydrate, 2 g fat, 6 mg cholesterol, 58 mg sodium, 262 mg potassium.

CRANBERRY PUNCH

74 calories

Preparation Time: 25 min. ▪ Freezing Time: 6 hrs. ▪ Low Fat ▪ No Cholesterol ▪ Low Sodium

To decorate the ice ring, arrange three whole cranberries in a cluster atop each orange slice. Add the lemon leaves where desired.

2	**24-ounce bottles unsweetened white grape juice**
2	**12-ounce cans frozen cranberry juice cocktail concentrate, thawed**
3	**16-ounce bottles low-calorie lemon-lime carbonated beverage**
	Ice Ring

▪ In a large punch bowl combine white grape juice and cranberry juice cocktail concentrate. Just before serving, stir in lemon-lime carbonated beverage. Add Ice Ring. Makes 30 (4-ounce) servings.

▪ **Ice Ring:** Fill a 6-cup ring mold *half* full of water; freeze till firm (about 4 hours). Cut 3 *orange slices* in half; arrange atop frozen ice layer. Garnish with *whole cranberries* and *lemon leaves.* Add enough water to just cover the oranges, cranberries, and lemon leaves. Freeze till firm (about 2 hours).

Nutrition information per serving: 74 calories, 0 g protein, 19 g carbohydrate, 0 g fat, 0 mg cholesterol, 10 mg sodium, 79 mg potassium.

TROPICAL PUNCH

65 calories

Preparation Time: 5 min. ▪ Cooking Time: 10 min. ▪ Chilling Time: 4 hrs. ▪ Low Fat ▪ No Cholesterol ▪ Low Sodium

2	**cups water**
¼	**cup sugar**
1	**1-inch piece fresh gingerroot** *or* **3 inches stick cinnamon**
1	**6-ounce can frozen pineapple** *or* **orange juice concentrate**
⅓	**cup lime juice**
2	**cups carbonated water, chilled**
	Ice
4	**lime slices, halved**

▪In a medium saucepan combine water, sugar, and gingerroot or cinnamon. Bring to boiling; reduce heat. Cover and simmer for 10 minutes. Remove from heat. Remove and discard gingerroot or cinnamon stick.

▪Stir in pineapple juice or orange juice concentrate and lime juice. Pour into a pitcher. Cover and chill 4 hours or till thoroughly chilled.

▪Just before serving, stir in carbonated water. Serve over ice. Garnish with lime slices. Makes 8 (5-ounce) servings.

Nutrition information per serving: 65 calories, 0 g protein, 17 g carbohydrate, 0 g fat, 0 mg cholesterol, 13 mg sodium, 113 mg potassium.

HOT COCOA

95 calories

Preparation Time: 5 min. ▪ Cooking Time: 6 min. ▪ Low Fat ▪ Low Cholesterol

2	**tablespoons sugar**
2	**tablespoons unsweetened cocoa powder**
3	**cups skim milk**
½	**teaspoon vanilla**

▪ In a medium saucepan stir together sugar and cocoa powder. Gradually stir in milk till smooth. Heat over medium heat till warm. Remove from heat; stir in vanilla. Makes 4 (6-ounce) servings.

▪ **Hot Mocha:** Prepare Hot Cocoa as above, *except* stir in 2 teaspoons *instant coffee crystals* with the cocoa powder.

▪ **Peppermint Cocoa:** Prepare Hot Cocoa as above, *except* stir in 6 drops *peppermint extract* with vanilla.

▪ **Almond Cocoa:** Prepare Hot Cocoa as above, *except* stir in 10 drops *almond extract* with vanilla.

▪ **Microwave directions:** In a 4-cup microwave-safe measure combine sugar and cocoa powder. Gradually stir in milk till smooth. Cook, uncovered, on 100% power (high) for 6 to 8 minutes or till warm, stirring after every 2 minutes. Stir in vanilla.

Nutrition information per serving: 95 calories, 7 g protein, 16 g carbohydrate, 1 g fat, 3 mg cholesterol, 114 mg sodium, 321 mg potassium.

PEACH-BERRY PUNCH

65 calories

Preparation Time: 15 min. ▪ Low Fat ▪ No Cholesterol ▪ Low Sodium

To sieve raspberries, place thawed raspberries in a wire strainer. Press the berries firmly with the back of a large spoon till berries are crushed and only the seeds are left in the strainer.

1	10-ounce package frozen raspberries, thawed
2¼	cups unsweetened pineapple juice, chilled
1	cup peach *or* apricot nectar, chilled
¼	cup lemon juice
2	cups carbonated water, chilled
12	frozen unsweetened peach slices

▪ Sieve raspberries; discard seeds.

▪ In a punch bowl stir together sieved raspberries, pineapple juice, peach or apricot nectar, lemon juice, and carbonated water. Float frozen peach slices in bowl. Makes 12 (4-ounce) servings.

▪ **Peach Melba Cream Punch:** Add 1 cup *vanilla ice milk* or *frozen yogurt* to punch bowl before adding raspberries. Stir in remaining ingredients till ice milk or yogurt is melted. (Add 15 calories for each serving.)

Nutrition information per serving: 65 calories, 0 g protein, 16 g carbohydrate, 0 g fat, 0 mg cholesterol, 10 mg sodium, 113 mg potassium.

EASY CHOCOLATE SHAKES

90 calories

Preparation Time: 5 min. ▪ Low Fat ▪ Low Cholesterol

Pudding mix replaces ice cream to thicken this easy-to-fix shake.

4	**cups cold skim milk**
1	**package reduced-calorie instant chocolate pudding mix (4-serving size)**
	Few drops mint *or* rum extract (optional)
½	**cup ice cubes**

▪ In a blender container combine milk, pudding mix, and mint or rum extract, if desired.

▪ Cover and blend till smooth. Add ice cubes; cover and blend till combined. Let stand 3 minutes to thicken slightly. Makes 5 (8-ounce) servings.

Nutrition information per serving: 90 calories, 7 g protein, 15 g carbohydrate, 0 g fat, 4 mg cholesterol, 135 mg sodium, 324 mg potassium.

PEPPY TOMATO SIPPER

Preparation Time: 5 min. ▪ Low Fat ▪ No Cholesterol

2	**cups tomato juice *or* vegetable juice cocktail**
2	**tablespoons lime *or* lemon juice**
1	**teaspoon Worcestershire sauce**
½	**teaspoon prepared horseradish**
	Few drops bottled hot pepper sauce
	Ice cubes
	Celery sticks for garnish (optional)

▪In a small pitcher stir together tomato juice or vegetable juice cocktail, lime juice or lemon juice, Worcestershire sauce, horseradish, and hot pepper sauce.

▪Pour mixture over ice in glasses. If desired, garnish with celery sticks. Makes 2 (8-ounce) servings.

▪**Peppy Tomato Slush:** Prepare Peppy Tomato Sipper as above, *except* omit ice cubes. Pour tomato mixture into an 8x8x2-inch baking dish. Cover and freeze for 1 to 2 hours or till slushy. Spoon into glasses.

Nutrition information per serving: 48 calories, 2 g protein, 12 g carbohydrate, 0 g fat, 0 mg cholesterol, 910 mg sodium, 556 mg potassium.

BREAKFAST AND BRUNCH CHOICES

NO-FRY FRENCH TOAST *(see page 445)*

MEXICALI EGGS

Preparation Time: 25 min.

To add the eggs to the sauce, break one egg at a time into a custard cup or small bowl. Then, holding the lip of the dish as close to the sauce as possible, carefully slide the egg into the simmering tomato sauce. Be careful not to break the yolks as you slip them into the skillet. Space eggs evenly in the sauce.

4	6-inch flour tortillas
4	slices Canadian-style bacon, diced (4 ounces)
1	7½-ounce can whole tomatoes, cut up
⅓	cup chopped onion
¼	cup diced green chili peppers, drained
1	clove garlic, minced
⅛	teaspoon salt
4	eggs
¼	cup shredded cheddar cheese (1 ounce)

■ Brush one side of each tortilla with water to soften. Press each tortilla, brushed side up, into a 10-ounce custard cup or individual casserole. Bake in a 400° oven for 5 to 7 minutes or till crisp. Sprinkle bacon in tortilla cups.

■ Meanwhile, for sauce, in a medium skillet combine *undrained* tomatoes, onion, green chili peppers, garlic, and salt. Bring to boiling; reduce heat. Cover and simmer 5 minutes.

■ Break one egg into a saucer or custard cup, then pour into simmering sauce (see small photo above). Repeat with remaining eggs. Cover and simmer about 5 minutes more or till eggs are just set.

■ Spoon some of the sauce and one egg into each tortilla cup. Sprinkle with cheese. Let stand 1 to 2 minutes or till cheese begins to melt. Makes 4 servings.

Nutrition information per serving: 242 calories, 17 g protein, 19 g carbohydrate, 11 g fat, 299 mg cholesterol, 843 mg sodium, 338 mg potassium.

SALMON-FILLED PUFFY OMELET   209 calories

Preparation Time: 13 min. ▪ Cooking Time: 7 min.

3	eggs, separated
	Dash salt
	Dash pepper
	Nonstick spray coating
1	ounce Neufchâtel cheese, cut up
2	ounces thinly sliced smoked salmon, smoked turkey, *or* ham, chopped
1	tablespoon snipped fresh parsley

▪ Preheat oven to 350°. In a small mixing bowl with electric mixer, beat egg whites with salt and pepper till stiff peaks form (tips stand straight). In another bowl, lightly beat yolks with a fork. Fold whites into yolks.

▪ Spray a 10-inch ovenproof skillet with nonstick spray coating. Heat skillet over medium-high heat. Spread egg mixture in pan. Cook 3 to 5 minutes or till bottom is golden. Place skillet in hot oven. Bake 3 minutes or till nearly dry. Sprinkle with cheese, salmon, and parsley. Bake 1 minute more or till cheese is melted.

▪ To serve, fold omelet in half. Makes 2 servings.

Nutrition information per serving: 209 calories, 17 g protein, 1 g carbohydrate, 15 g fat, 434 mg cholesterol, 1,994 mg sodium, 169 mg potassium.

HAM AND FRUIT STRATA

283 calories

Preparation Time: 25 min. ▪ Chilling Time: 4 hrs. ▪ Cooking Time: 45 min.

2½	cups cubed firm-textured bread (about 3½ slices)
4	ounces cubed fully cooked ham (¾ cup)
1	8-ounce can pear halves *or* slices (juice pack), drained and chopped
½	cup shredded cheddar cheese (2 ounces)
3	slightly beaten eggs
1½	cups skim milk
⅛	teaspoon ground nutmeg

▪ In an 8x8x2-inch baking dish layer bread, ham, chopped pears, and shredded cheese.

▪ Combine eggs, milk, and nutmeg, and pour evenly into dish. Cover and chill 4 to 24 hours.

▪ Bake, uncovered, in a 325° oven about 45 minutes or till center is just set and top is golden. Cool 10 minutes before cutting into squares. Garnish with additional pear slices, if desired. Makes 4 servings.

Nutrition information per serving: 283 calories, 20 g protein, 24 g carbohydrate, 12 g fat, 238 mg cholesterol, 671 mg sodium, 356 mg potassium.

BRUNCH TURNOVERS

285 calories

Preparation Time: 18 min. ▪ Cooking Time: 20 min. ▪ Low Fat ▪ Low Cholesterol

To seal the turnovers, press the edges of the pastry together firmly with the tines of a fork. This gives the turnovers an attractive appearance and it prevents leaking.

1	**cup finely chopped cooked chicken *or* turkey (6 ounces)**
½	**of a 10-ounce package frozen chopped spinach *or* broccoli, thawed and well drained**
⅓	**cup shredded low-fat mozzarella cheese**
3	**tablespoons sliced green onion**
½	**teaspoon dried oregano, crushed**
⅛	**teaspoon garlic salt**
	Dash pepper
¾	**cup packaged biscuit mix**
½	**cup whole wheat flour**
⅓	**cup skim milk**
½	**cup pizza sauce**

▪ For filling, in a mixing bowl combine chicken, spinach or broccoli (cut up any large pieces of broccoli), cheese, onion, oregano, garlic salt, and pepper. Set aside.

▪ In a mixing bowl, stir together biscuit mix and flour. Stir in milk just till moistened. Turn dough out onto a lightly floured surface and knead 10 to 12 strokes. Divide dough into 4 equal pieces. Roll each piece into a 7-inch circle.

▪ Spoon *one-fourth* of the filling onto one half of *each* circle of dough. Fold the other half of the dough over the filling and seal edges with the tines of a fork. Place turnovers on an ungreased baking sheet.

▪ Bake in a 400° oven about 20 minutes or till golden. Meanwhile, in a small saucepan, heat pizza sauce till hot. Serve with hot turnovers. Makes 4 servings.

Nutrition information per serving: 285 calories, 21 g protein, 32 g carbohydrate, 8 g fat, 43 mg cholesterol, 631 mg sodium, 363 mg potassium.

TURKEY AND APPLE BREAKFAST SAUSAGE 101 calories

Preparation Time: 12 min. ▪ Cooking Time: 10 min. ▪ Low Cholesterol ▪ Low Sodium

½ **pound ground turkey**
2 **tablespoons soft bread crumbs**
½ **cup shredded apple**
¼ **teaspoon leaf sage, crushed**
¼ **teaspoon pepper**
⅛ **teaspoon salt**
⅛ **teaspoon paprika**
Dash ground nutmeg
Nonstick spray coating

▪ In a large bowl, combine turkey, bread crumbs, apple, sage, pepper, salt, paprika, and nutmeg. Shape mixture into four ½-inch-thick patties.
▪ Spray the unheated rack of broiler pan with nonstick spray coating. Arrange patties on rack. Broil 4 to 5 inches from the heat about 10 minutes or till no pink remains; turn once. (Or, spray a large skillet with nonstick spray coating. Cook sausage over medium heat for 8 to 10 minutes or till no pink remains.) Makes 4 servings.

Nutrition information per serving: 101 calories, 10 g protein, 3 g carbohydrate, 5 g fat, 35 mg cholesterol, 116 mg sodium, 135 mg potassium.

FEATHERY PANCAKES

152 calories

Preparation Time: 13 min. ▪ Cooking Time: 8 min. ▪ Low Fat ▪ Low Cholesterol

If you decide to splurge and have a third pancake, add 62 calories to your total calories for the meal.

½	**cup whole wheat flour**
½	**cup all-purpose flour**
1	**tablespoon sugar**
2	**teaspoons baking powder**
¼	**teaspoon salt**
¾	**cup skim milk**
1	**teaspoon cooking oil**
2	**egg whites**
	Nonstick spray coating
	Strawberry Sauce

▪ In a mixing bowl combine flours, sugar, baking powder, and salt. Stir in milk and oil. In another bowl, beat egg whites till stiff (tips stand straight). Fold egg whites into flour mixture.

▪ Spray a griddle with nonstick spray coating. Preheat griddle over medium heat. For each pancake pour about ¼ cup batter onto the hot griddle. Cook over medium heat till pancakes are golden brown (1 to 2 minutes per side); turn to second sides when pancakes have bubbly surfaces and slightly dry edges. Serve pancakes with Strawberry Sauce. Makes 5 servings (2 pancakes each).

▪ **Strawberry Sauce:** In a blender container or food processor bowl combine 2 cups *fresh* or *thawed frozen unsweetened strawberries,* 1 tablespoon *sugar,* and 1 teaspoon *vanilla.* Cover and blend or process till smooth. In a small saucepan, heat sauce till warm. Serve over pancakes. Makes 1 cup (5 servings).

Nutrition information per serving: 152 calories, 6 g protein, 29 g carbohydrate, 2 g fat, 1 mg cholesterol, 267 mg sodium, 237 mg potassium.

CORNMEAL PANCAKES WITH APPLESAUCE   254 calories

Preparation Time: 8 min. ▪ Cooking Time: 8 min. ▪ Low Fat

1	cup all-purpose flour
¾	cup cornmeal
1	tablespoon sugar
1½	teaspoons baking powder
½	teaspoon apple pie spice
¼	teaspoon salt
2	slightly beaten eggs
1	cup skim milk
1	teaspoon cooking oil
	Nonstick spray coating
¾	cup unsweetened applesauce

■ In a medium mixing bowl stir together flour, cornmeal, sugar, baking powder, apple pie spice, and salt. In a small mixing bowl combine eggs, milk, and oil. Add all at once to flour mixture and stir just till blended but still slightly lumpy.

■ Spray a griddle with nonstick spray coating. Preheat griddle over medium heat. For each pancake pour about ¼ cup batter onto hot griddle. Cook over medium heat till pancakes are golden brown (1 to 2 minutes per side). Turn the pancakes to second sides when they have bubbly surfaces and slightly dry edges.

■ Meanwhile, in a small saucepan heat applesauce till warm. Serve with pancakes. Makes 5 servings (2 pancakes each).

Nutrition information per serving: 254 calories, 8 g protein, 45 g carbohydrate, 4 g fat, 111 mg cholesterol, 261 mg sodium, 201 mg potassium.

BREAKFAST BLINTZES

257 calories

Preparation Time: 55 min. ▪ Low Fat ▪ Low Cholesterol ▪ Low Sodium

To enclose the filling, fold 2 op-posite edges of the crepe to the middle so they overlap. Then, fold the remaining edges of the crepe to the middle so you have a square or rectangular packet.

1	cup all-purpose flour
1½	cups skim milk
1	egg
	Nonstick spray coating
½	teaspoon shortening
1	16-ounce carton dry cottage cheese
1	egg white
1	tablespoon sugar
½	teaspoon finely shredded orange peel
2	tablespoons orange juice
⅛	teaspoon ground cinnamon
	Strawberry Sauce (see page 442)

▪ For crepes, combine flour, milk, and the 1 egg. Beat with rotary beater till blended. Spray a 6-inch skillet or crepe pan with nonstick spray coating. Preheat skillet over medium heat. Remove from heat and pour in about 2 tablespoons batter. Lift and tilt skillet to spread batter. Return skillet to heat and brown crepe on one side only. Remove from pan. Repeat with remaining batter to make 15 crepes total. Brush skillet as needed with shortening between cooking of crepes.

▪ For filling, in a blender container or food processor bowl combine cottage cheese, egg white, sugar, orange peel, orange juice, and cinnamon. Blend or process till smooth. Spoon about *2 tablespoons* cheese mixture onto the unbrowned side of *each* crepe. Fold 2 opposite edges of crepe over top of filling. Fold in remaining edges, forming a square packet. Repeat with remaining filling and crepes.

▪ Spray a shallow baking pan with nonstick coating. Arrange blintzes in pan. Bake in a 350° oven 15 to 20 minutes or till heated through. Serve with Strawberry Sauce. Serves 5.

Nutrition information per serving: 257 calories, 23 g protein, 34 g carbohydrate, 3 g fat, 62 mg cholesterol, 74 mg sodium, 308 mg potassium.

NO-FRY FRENCH TOAST

282 calories

Preparation Time: 10 min. ▪ Cooking Time: 11 min. ▪ Low Fat ▪ Low Cholesterol

Give each slice of bread just a quick dip in the egg mixture so you have enough for all 8 slices.

	Nonstick spray coating
1	**slightly beaten egg**
1	**slightly beaten egg white**
¾	**cup skim milk**
1	**teaspoon vanilla**
8	**½-inch-thick slices French bread**
¼	**teaspoon finely shredded orange peel**
⅔	**cup orange juice**
1	**tablespoon honey**
1½	**teaspoons cornstarch**
⅛	**teaspoon ground cinnamon**

▪ Spray a large baking sheet with nonstick spray coating. In a shallow bowl combine egg, egg white, milk, and vanilla. Dip bread slices in egg mixture just long enough to coat both sides. Place on baking sheet.

▪ Bake in a 450° oven about 6 minutes or till bread is lightly browned. Turn bread over and bake 5 to 8 minutes more or till golden.

▪ Meanwhile, for syrup, in a small saucepan stir together orange peel, orange juice, honey, cornstarch, and cinnamon. Cook and stir till thickened and bubbly. Cook and stir 2 minutes more. Serve toast with warm orange syrup. Serves 4.

Nutrition information per serving: 282 calories, 11 g protein, 51 g carbohydrate, 4 g fat, 72 mg cholesterol, 460 mg sodium, 248 mg potassium.

BRAN MUFFINS

142 calories

Preparation Time: 10 min. ▪ Cooking Time: 15 min. ▪ Low Cholesterol

For just 43 more calories, you can enjoy your muffin with 2 tablespoons of low-fat ricotta cheese.

1	**cup whole bran cereal**
1	**cup skim milk**
¼	**cup sugar**
1	**slightly beaten egg**
¼	**cup cooking oil**
½	**teaspoon finely shredded lemon peel**
1	**cup all-purpose flour**
½	**cup whole wheat flour**
2	**teaspoons baking powder**
¼	**teaspoon salt**
	Nonstick spray coating

■ In a medium mixing bowl combine cereal and milk. Let stand 3 minutes. Stir in sugar, egg, oil, and lemon peel. In a large bowl stir together flours, baking powder, and salt. Add cereal mixture to dry ingredients and stir just till moistened. Bake immediately or cover and refrigerate up to 4 days.

■ To bake, spray 12 muffin pan cups with nonstick spray coating. Fill each cup about *two-thirds* full with batter. Bake in a 400° oven for 15 to 20 minutes or till a toothpick inserted near the center comes out clean. Makes 12 servings (12 muffins).

■ **Berry Variation:** Prepare muffin batter as above, *except* stir ¾ cup blueberries or raspberries into the batter.

Nutrition information per serving: 142 calories, 4 g protein, 22 g carbohydrate, 5 g fat, 23 mg cholesterol, 164 mg sodium, 134 mg potassium.

PEACH SHORTCAKE

118 calories

Preparation Time: 10 min. ▪ Cooking Time: 20 min. ▪ Low Cholesterol

1	cup all-purpose flour
1	tablespoon sugar
1	teaspoon baking powder
½	teaspoon ground cinnamon
¼	cup margarine
1	slightly beaten egg white
¼	cup skim milk
¼	teaspoon vanilla
	Nonstick spray coating
3	medium peaches, peeled, pitted, and sliced, *or* one 16-ounce can peach slices (juice pack), drained
½	cup vanilla low-fat yogurt

■ In a medium mixing bowl stir together flour, sugar, baking powder, and cinnamon. Cut in margarine till mixture resembles coarse crumbs. Make a well in center. Combine egg white, milk, and vanilla; add all at once to flour mixture. Stir till dough clings together.

■ Spray a 9-inch pie plate with nonstick spray coating. With floured fingers, press batter evenly in pie plate. Bake in a 350° oven for 20 to 25 minutes or till golden. Cool slightly.

■ Meanwhile, chop 2 peach slices and stir into the yogurt. Arrange remaining peach slices over top of shortcake. Spoon yogurt mixture over all. Serve warm. Makes 10 servings.

Nutrition information per serving: 118 calories, 3 g protein, 16 g carbohydrate, 5 g fat, 1 mg cholesterol, 100 mg sodium, 108 mg potassium.

BREAKFAST RICE CEREAL

155 calories

Preparation Time: 8 min. ▪ Cooking Time: 14 min. ▪ Low Fat ▪ Low Cholesterol ▪ Low Sodium

Start your day with a fruity, hot rice cereal.

1½	cups water
⅛	teaspoon salt
1	cup quick-cooking brown rice
⅓	cup mixed dried fruit bits
¾	cup skim milk
	Dash ground nutmeg
2	to 3 tablespoons brown sugar

▪ In a 2-quart saucepan bring water and salt to boiling; add rice and dried fruit bits. Cover and simmer 12 to 14 minutes or till rice is tender and liquid is absorbed. Stir in milk and nutmeg. Heat through. Serve with brown sugar. Serves 4.

Nutrition information per serving: 155 calories, 4 g protein, 34 g carbohydrate, 1 g fat, 1 mg cholesterol, 97 mg sodium, 249 mg potassium.

GRANOLA

Preparation Time: 12 min. ▪ Cooking Time: 45 min. ▪ Low Fat ▪ No Cholesterol ▪ Low Sodium

If you like your granola for breakfast, pour ⅓ cup milk over ½ cup of granola. Then, tally up another 28 calories per serving.

3	**cups regular rolled oats**
1	**cup shredded unpeeled apple**
½	**cup wheat germ**
¼	**cup honey**
¼	**cup water**
1	**teaspoon ground cinnamon**
1	**teaspoon vanilla** *or* **½ teaspoon almond extract**
	Nonstick spray coating

▪ In a large bowl combine oats, apple, and wheat germ; mix well. In a small saucepan stir together honey, water, and cinnamon. Heat to boiling; remove from heat. Stir in vanilla or almond extract. Pour over oat mixture; mix well.

▪ Spray a 15x10x1-inch baking pan with nonstick spray coating. Spread oat mixture evenly in pan. Bake in a 325° oven about 45 minutes or till golden brown, stirring occasionally. Spread onto foil to cool. Store in an airtight container in the refrigerator up to 2 weeks. Makes eight ½-cup servings.

Nutrition information per serving: 179 calories, 6 g protein, 34 g carbohydrate, 3 g fat, 0 mg cholesterol, 2 mg sodium, 177 mg potassium.

FRUITY OATMEAL

133 calories

Preparation Time: 12 min. ▪ Cooking Time: 5 min. ▪ Low Fat ▪ No Cholesterol

2	cups water
¼	teaspoon salt
1	cup rolled oats
1	cup chopped peeled peaches *or* chopped apple
¼	cup raisins *or* snipped pitted whole dates
⅛	teaspoon ground cinnamon
½	cup skim milk

■ In a medium saucepan bring water and salt to boiling. Stir in oats, peaches or apple, raisins, and cinnamon. Reduce heat and simmer, uncovered, for 5 minutes, stirring occasionally. Remove from heat. Cover and let stand for 2 minutes.

■ Divide oat mixture among 4 bowls. Pour 2 tablespoons milk over each serving. Makes 4 servings.

Nutrition information per serving: 133 calories, 5 g protein, 27 g carbohydrate, 1 g fat, 0 mg cholesterol, 151 mg sodium, 272 mg potassium.

TAKE-ALONG LUNCHES

GARBANZO BEAN AND VEGETABLE SALAD *(see page 459)*

ZIPPY TUNA SANDWICH

228 calories

Preparation Time: 10 min. ▪ Chilling Time: overnight ▪ Low Fat

For a tuna-fruit combo, substitute drained crushed pineapple for the dill pickle.

1	**6½-ounce can tuna (water pack), drained and broken into chunks**
1	**hard-cooked egg, chopped**
¼	**cup finely chopped dill pickle**
¼	**cup finely chopped celery**
2	**tablespoons reduced-calorie mayonnaise**
1	**teaspoon prepared mustard**
3	**lettuce leaves**
3	**small pita bread rounds, halved**

■ In a small mixing bowl combine tuna, egg, pickle, celery, mayonnaise, and mustard; mix gently.

■ Divide among 3 small airtight containers. Chill overnight. Store up to 3 days in the refrigerator. Makes 3 servings.

■ For each serving, pack 1 lettuce leaf and 2 pita bread halves in separate small clear plastic bags. Carry with 1 container of the tuna mixture in an insulated lunch box with a frozen ice pack.

■ To serve, place some lettuce and tuna mixture into each pita bread half.

Nutrition information per serving: 228 calories, 23 g protein, 18 g carbohydrate, 6 g fat, 134 mg cholesterol, 849 mg sodium, 272 mg potassium.

MUFFULETTAS

321 calories

Preparation Time: 25 min. ▪ Chilling Time: overnight ▪ Low Cholesterol

To hollow out the rolls, cut the top third off the roll. Use the tines of a fork to mark a line around the inside edges of the roll, leaving about a ½-inch shell. Remove the bread from the center of the roll with your fingers or the fork.

1	tablespoon wine vinegar
1	teaspoon olive *or* salad oil
¼	teaspoon dried oregano, crushed
2	ounces cooked turkey, cut into bite-size strips
1	ounce sliced turkey salami luncheon meat, cut into bite-size strips
1	ounce sliced provolone cheese, cut into bite-size pieces
½	cup chopped fresh mushrooms
¼	cup chopped green *or* sweet red pepper
2	tablespoons sliced green onions
2	French-style rolls (about 6 inches long)

▪ In a small bowl combine vinegar, oil, and oregano.

▪ Add turkey, turkey salami, cheese, mushrooms, green or sweet red pepper, and green onions. Toss to mix well.

▪ Divide between 2 small airtight containers. Chill overnight. Store up to 3 days in the refrigerator. Makes 2 servings.

▪ For each serving, cut the top off 1 roll. Scoop out the center, reserving the crumbs for another use.

▪ Pack the roll in a small clear plastic bag. Carry with 1 container of the turkey mixture in an insulated lunch box with a frozen ice pack.

▪ To serve, spoon the turkey mixture into the bottom of roll. Add roll top.

Nutrition information per serving: 321 calories, 20 g protein, 34 g carbohydrate, 11 g fat, 45 mg cholesterol, 616 mg sodium, 305 mg potassium.

CURRIED CHICKEN BUNDLES

240 calories

Preparation Time: 20 min. ▪ Cooking Time: 12 min. ▪ Chilling Time: overnight ▪ Low Fat ▪ Low Cholesterol

It's easy to quickly reheat the chilled sandwiches. Just pop them into the microwave for 30 to 60 seconds on 100% (high) power.

2 cups chopped cooked chicken *or* turkey (10 ounces)
½ cup chopped celery
⅓ cup part-skim ricotta cheese
¼ cup shredded carrot
1 tablespoon apricot preserves *or* chutney
1 teaspoon curry powder
¼ teaspoon ground cinnamon
Dash salt
1 10-ounce package refrigerated pizza dough

▪ In a medium bowl combine chicken, celery, ricotta cheese, carrot, preserves or chutney, curry powder, cinnamon, and salt. Set aside.

▪ Unroll pizza dough; cut into 6 squares. Divide chicken mixture among squares. Bring the corners of dough to the center over filling, stretching as necessary. Pinch the open edges together to seal. Place bundles on an ungreased baking sheet.

▪ Bake in a 375° oven for 12 to 15 minutes or till golden. Cool for 30 minutes on a wire rack.

▪ Pack each bundle in a small clear plastic bag or freezer bag. Chill overnight. Store up to 3 days in the refrigerator or 1 month in the freezer. Makes 6 servings.

▪ For each serving, pack 1 chilled or frozen sandwich in an insulated lunch box with a frozen ice pack.

Nutrition information per serving: 240 calories, 19 g protein, 26 g carbohydrate, 6 g fat, 46 mg cholesterol, 300 mg sodium, 211 mg potassium.

LAYERED PICNIC PÂTÉ

196 calories

Preparation Time: 45 min. ▪ Cooking Time: 1¼ hrs. ▪ Chilling Time: overnight

Place the beans, eggs, and carrot sticks end to end atop the meat in the pan to form a pattern. When the pâté is sliced, each piece should show the layers of vegetables and egg.

1	slightly beaten egg
½	cup skim milk
¾	cup soft bread crumbs
¼	cup finely chopped onion
2	tablespoons snipped fresh parsley
½	teaspoon dried oregano, crushed
¼	teaspoon dried thyme, crushed
¼	teaspoon dried sage, crushed
12	ounces ground veal
12	ounces lean ground beef *or* pork
4	ounces fresh whole green beans, cooked
2	hard-cooked eggs, quartered lengthwise
1	medium carrot, cut into 3-inch sticks and cooked

▪ In a mixing bowl combine egg and milk. Stir in bread crumbs, onion, parsley, oregano, thyme, sage, ¾ teaspoon *salt,* and ⅛ teaspoon *pepper.* Add veal and beef; mix well.

▪ Pat *one-fourth* of the meat mixture into an 8x4x2-inch loaf pan. Arrange green beans atop meat. Top with another *one-fourth* of the meat mixture. Arrange hard-cooked eggs atop meat. Top with another *one-fourth* of the meat mixture, the carrot strips, and remaining meat mixture.

▪ Bake in a 350° oven for 1¼ to 1½ hours. Remove fat with a baster or spoon as it accumulates during cooking.

▪ Cool in pan for 10 minutes. Drain off any remaining fat. Cover with foil. To weight pâté, place canned vegetables or other heavy object on loaf in pan. Chill overnight. Remove weight. Remove pâté from pan; cut into 8 slices. Serve with Dijon-style mustard, if desired. Makes 8 servings.

▪ Pack each serving in a clear plastic bag or freezer bag. Store up to 3 days in refrigerator or 1 month in freezer. Carry in an insulated lunch box with a frozen ice pack.

Nutrition information per serving: 196 calories, 20 g protein, 6 g carbohydrate, 10 g fat, 162 mg cholesterol, 299 mg sodium, 328 mg potassium.

FRUITY COTTAGE CHEESE SALAD

217 calories

Preparation Time: 7 min. ▪ Chilling Time: overnight ▪ Low Fat ▪ Low Cholesterol

½	**cup low-fat cottage cheese**
1	**small apple, chopped**
	(½ cup)
2	**tablespoons mixed dried fruit bits** *or* **raisins**
2	**teaspoons reduced-calorie mayonnaise** *or* **salad dressing**
	Dash ground cinnamon, ground nutmeg, *or* **apple pie spice**
1	**lettuce leaf**

▪ In an airtight container stir together cottage cheese, apple, dried fruit bits, mayonnaise, and cinnamon. Chill overnight. Makes 1 serving.

▪ Pack 1 lettuce leaf in a small clear plastic bag. Carry with the container of the cottage cheese mixture in an insulated lunch box with a frozen ice pack.

▪ Serve cottage cheese mixture atop lettuce leaf.

Nutrition information per serving: 217 calories, 16 g protein, 27 g carbohydrate, 5 g fat, 13 mg cholesterol, 519 mg sodium, 368 mg potassium.

LUNCH BOX CHICKEN SALAD

256 calories

Preparation Time: 35 min. ▪ Chilling Time: overnight ▪ Low Fat ▪ Low Cholesterol

When you're in a hurry, use canned green beans—they're already cooked!

½	**cup plain low-fat yogurt**
2	**tablespoons orange juice**
1	**teaspoon honey** *or* **sugar**
4	**teaspoons Dijon-style mustard**
	Dash pepper
⅔	**cup elbow macaroni, cooked**
1	**cup cooked cut green beans**
5	**ounces cooked chicken** *or* **ham, cut into bite-size strips (1 cup)***
½	**cup shredded carrot**
2	**tablespoons sliced green onions**

▪ For dressing, in a large mixing bowl stir together yogurt, orange juice, honey or sugar, mustard, and pepper.

▪ Add cooked macaroni, green beans, chicken or ham, carrot, and green onions. Toss to mix well.

▪ Divide among 3 small airtight containers. Chill overnight. Store up to 3 days in the refrigerator. Makes 3 servings.

▪ Carry in an insulated lunch box with a frozen ice pack.

*Note: If desired, substitute one 6½-ounce can *tuna* (water pack), drained and broken into chunks, for chicken or ham.

Nutrition information per serving: 256 calories, 20 g protein, 31 g carbohydrate, 5 g fat, 44 mg cholesterol, 275 mg sodium, 502 mg potassium.

CHICKEN AND RICE SALAD

306 calories

Preparation Time: 45 min. ■ Chilling Time: *overnight* ■ Low Cholesterol

1⅓	cups water
⅔	cup brown rice *or* long grain rice
⅓	cup skim milk
¼	cup reduced-calorie mayonnaise *or* salad dressing
2	tablespoons lemon juice
½	cup chopped celery
½	cup chopped seeded cucumber
2	tablespoons sliced green onions
2	tablespoons snipped fresh parsley
2	5½-ounce cans chunk-style chicken *or* two 6½-ounce cans tuna (water pack)
1	small tomato, seeded and chopped (½ cup)

■ In a saucepan combine the water and rice. Bring to boiling; reduce heat. Cover and simmer 35 minutes for brown rice (15 minutes for long grain rice) or till rice is tender and water is absorbed. Remove from heat. Let stand, covered, 5 minutes.

■ Meanwhile, in a large mixing bowl combine milk, mayonnaise, lemon juice, and ⅛ teaspoon *pepper.* Stir in celery, cucumber, green onions, parsley, and cooked rice. Mix well.

■ Drain chicken or tuna; break into chunks. Gently stir into rice mixture.

■ Divide mixture among 4 small airtight containers. Sprinkle with tomato. Chill overnight. Store up to 3 days in the refrigerator. Makes 4 servings.

■ Carry in an insulated lunch box with a frozen ice pack.

Nutrition information per serving: 306 calories, 21 g protein, 29 g carbohydrate, 11 g fat, 54 mg cholesterol, 502 mg sodium, 339 mg potassium.

GARBANZO BEAN AND VEGETABLE SALAD   224 calories

Preparation Time: 20 min. ▪ Chilling Time: overnight ▪ Low Cholesterol

Pack some crunchy crackers or breadsticks to eat with your salad.

1	tablespoon lemon juice
1	clove garlic, minced
1	tablespoon snipped fresh basil *or* 1 teaspoon dried basil, crushed
⅛	teaspoon pepper
1	15-ounce can garbanzo beans, rinsed and drained
1½	cups coarsely chopped broccoli*
1	7½-ounce can tomatoes, cut up
1	cup cubed part-skim mozzarella cheese
½	cup sliced carrots

▪ In a large mixing bowl combine lemon juice, garlic, basil, and pepper.

▪ Stir in garbanzo beans, broccoli, *undrained* tomatoes, cheese, and carrots. Toss to mix well.

▪ Divide mixture among 4 small airtight containers. Chill overnight. Store up to 3 days in the refrigerator. Makes 4 servings.

▪ Carry in an insulated lunch box with a frozen ice pack.

*Note: If desired, cook broccoli in boiling water for 1 minute; drain. Add to salad as directed above.

Nutrition information per serving: 224 calories, 16 g protein, 24 g carbohydrate, 7 g fat, 18 mg cholesterol, 286 mg sodium, 515 mg potassium.

SHRIMP AND FRUIT SALAD

204 calories

Preparation Time: 25 min. ▪ Marinating Time: 2 hrs. ▪ Chilling Time: overnight ▪ Low Fat

Try a slice of cantaloupe with this refreshing seafood salad.

12	**ounces fresh *or* frozen peeled and deveined shrimp**
1	**15¼-ounce can pineapple chunks (juice pack)**
1	**medium orange, peeled and sectioned**
1	**tablespoon snipped fresh mint *or* 1 teaspoon dried mint, crushed**
	Dash salt
	Dash pepper
½	**cup sliced celery**
½	**cup lemon low-fat yogurt**

▪ In a large saucepan cook shrimp in boiling water about 3 minutes or till shrimp turn pink; drain. Rinse shrimp under cold water; drain well.

▪ Drain pineapple chunks, reserving juice. Combine pineapple chunks and orange sections; cover and chill.

▪ For marinade, in a medium bowl combine *¼ cup* of the reserved pineapple juice, the mint, salt, and pepper.

▪ Stir in cooked shrimp and the celery. Cover and marinate in the refrigerator for 2 hours. Drain off marinade; discard marinade.

▪ Stir pineapple chunks and orange sections into shrimp mixture.

▪ In a small bowl combine *2 tablespoons* of the remaining pineapple juice and the yogurt. Toss with the shrimp mixture.

▪ Divide mixture among 4 small airtight containers. Chill overnight. Store up to 2 days in the refrigerator. Serves 4.

▪ Carry in an insulated lunch box with a frozen ice pack.

Nutrition information per serving: 204 calories, 19 g protein, 28 g carbohydrate, 2 g fat, 130 mg cholesterol, 191 mg sodium, 456 mg potassium.

HEARTY ITALIAN-STYLE SOUP

238 calories

Preparation Time: 20 min. ▪ Cooking Time: 25 min. ▪ Low Fat ▪ Low Cholesterol

2	14½-ounce cans beef broth
2	cups shredded cabbage
1	14½-ounce can tomatoes, cut up
2	medium potatoes, cubed
½	cup chopped carrot
½	cup chopped celery
½	cup chopped onion
¼	cup snipped fresh parsley
1	teaspoon dried Italian seasoning, crushed
¼	teaspoon garlic salt
¼	teaspoon pepper
1	15-ounce can white kidney beans, drained
1½	cups chopped cooked beef *or* chicken (8 ounces)

▪ In a large saucepan or Dutch oven combine broth, cabbage, *undrained* tomatoes, potatoes, carrot, celery, onion, parsley, Italian seasoning, garlic salt, and pepper. Bring to boiling; reduce heat. Cover and simmer about 20 minutes or till vegetables are tender.

▪ Stir in beans and beef or chicken.

▪ Divide among 6 airtight containers or freezer containers. Store up to 3 days in the refrigerator or 1 month in the freezer. Makes 6 servings.

▪ For each serving, boil soup from one container, covered, for 3 minutes before packing in a preheated insulated vacuum bottle. (To preheat the vacuum bottle, fill the bottle with *hot* water. Cover with the lid; let stand for 5 minutes. Pour out the water and immediately fill with the hot soup.)

Nutrition information per serving: 238 calories, 16 g protein, 26 g carbohydrate, 8 g fat, 33 mg cholesterol, 676 mg sodium, 926 mg potassium.

GAZPACHO

50 calories

Preparation Time: 10 min. ▪ Chilling Time: overnight ▪ Low Fat ▪ No Cholesterol

Enjoy this soup with a slice of Layered Picnic Pâté. (See recipe, page 455.)

1	**6-ounce can vegetable juice cocktail *or* tomato juice**
¼	**cup chopped cucumber**
¼	**cup chopped green pepper**
1	**tablespoon sliced green onion**
1	**teaspoon lemon juice**
	Dash pepper
	Dash bottled hot pepper sauce

▪ In a small airtight container combine vegetable juice cocktail, cucumber, green pepper, green onion, lemon juice, pepper, and bottled hot pepper sauce. Chill overnight. Makes 1 side-dish serving.

▪ Carry cold in a prechilled insulated vacuum bottle. *Or,* boil soup, covered, for 3 minutes before packing in a preheated insulated vacuum bottle.

▪ To prechill (or preheat) the vacuum bottle, fill the bottle with cold (or hot) water. Cover with the lid; let stand for 5 minutes. Pour out the water and immediately fill with the cold (or hot) soup.

Nutrition information per serving: 50 calories, 2 g protein, 12 g carbohydrate, 0 g fat, 0 mg cholesterol, 624 mg sodium, 479 mg potassium.

STRAWBERRY-YOGURT PUDDING

79 calories

Preparation Time: 15 min. ▪ Chilling Time: overnight ▪ Low Fat ▪ Low Cholesterol

Treat your family to this simple-to-prepare dessert. Then, pack up the left-over servings to carry with lunch the next day.

1	**4-serving-size package reduced-calorie instant chocolate** *or* **vanilla pudding mix**
1	**cup skim milk**
2	**8-ounce cartons plain low-fat yogurt**
2	**cups sliced strawberries**

▪ In a medium mixing bowl beat pudding mix and milk with an electric mixer or rotary beater till smooth.

▪ Stir in yogurt. Gently stir in strawberries.

▪ Divide among 8 airtight containers. Chill overnight. Store up to 3 days in the refrigerator. Makes 8 servings.

▪ Carry in an insulated lunch box with a frozen ice pack.

Nutrition information per serving: 79 calories, 4 g protein, 13 g carbohydrate, 1 g fat, 4 mg cholesterol, 221 mg sodium, 291 mg potassium.

APRICOT-OATMEAL BARS

70 calories

Preparation Time: 15 min. ▪ Cooking Time: 20 min. ▪ Low Fat ▪ No Cholesterol

1	cup all-purpose flour
½	cup whole wheat flour
½	teaspoon salt
½	teaspoon baking soda
½	teaspoon ground cinnamon
1	beaten egg
¼	cup packed brown sugar
½	cup plain low-fat yogurt
⅓	cup water
¼	cup molasses
¼	cup cooking oil
1	cup quick-cooking rolled oats
¾	cup snipped dried apricots
½	cup raisins
¾	cup sifted powdered sugar
1	to 2 tablespoons orange juice *or* milk

▪ In a large mixing bowl combine the all-purpose flour, whole wheat flour, salt, baking soda, and cinnamon.

▪ In a medium mixing bowl combine egg, brown sugar, yogurt, water, molasses, and oil. Stir into flour mixture; mix well.

▪ Stir in oats, apricots, and raisins. Spread in a 13x9x2-inch baking pan.

▪ Bake in a 350° oven for 20 to 25 minutes or till a toothpick inserted near the center comes out clean. Cool.

▪ For glaze, stir together powdered sugar and enough orange juice or milk to make of drizzling consistency. Drizzle over bars. Makes 36 bars (36 servings).

Nutrition information per serving: 70 calories, 1 g protein, 14 g carbohydrate, 2 g fat, 0 mg cholesterol, 50 mg sodium, 105 mg potassium.

PUMPKIN-RAISIN DROPS

42 calories

Preparation Time: 15 min. ▪ Cooking Time: 12 min. ▪ Low Fat ▪ Low Cholesterol ▪ Low Sodium

Brighten the cookie tops with a sprinkle of powdered sugar.

1	beaten egg
¾	cup canned pumpkin
⅓	cup brown sugar
1	tablespoon cooking oil
1	teaspoon vanilla
¾	cup all-purpose flour
1	teaspoon pumpkin pie spice
¼	teaspoon baking soda
⅛	teaspoon salt
¼	cup raisins
	Nonstick spray coating

▪ In a medium mixing bowl stir together egg, pumpkin, brown sugar, oil, and vanilla.

▪ In a small mixing bowl stir together flour, pumpkin pie spice, baking soda, and salt. Add dry ingredients to pumpkin mixture. Stir in raisins.

▪ Spray a baking sheet with nonstick spray coating. Drop the dough by rounded teaspoonfuls 1 inch apart onto the cookie sheet.

▪ Bake in a 350° oven for 12 to 14 minutes or till done. Cool on a wire rack. Makes 24 cookies (24 servings).

Nutrition information per serving: 42 calories, 1 g protein, 8 g carbohydrate, 1 g fat, 11 mg cholesterol, 27 mg sodium, 44 mg potassium.

CALORIE TALLY

TOFU SALAD DRESSING *(see page 351)*

Keeping track of your daily calorie intake? Use this handy chart to find the per-serving calorie count for more than 265 foods.

A-B

APPLE; fresh; 1 medium _____ 80
APPLESAUCE, canned
    sweetened; ½ cup _____ 98
    unsweetened; ½ cup _____ 53
APRICOTS
    canned, in syrup; ½ cup _____ 108
    fresh; 3 medium _____ 50
ASPARAGUS, cooked, drained; 4 spears ___ 15
AVOCADO, peeled; ½ avocado _____ 170
BACON
    Canadian-style, cooked; 2 slices _____ 85
    crisp strips, medium thickness; 3 slices ___ 110
BANANA; 1 medium _____ 105
BEANS
    baked, with tomato sauce and pork,
        canned; ½ cup _____ 155
    garbanzo, cooked, drained; ½ cup _____ 135
    green snap, cooked, drained; ½ cup _____ 23
    navy, dry, cooked, drained; ½ cup _____ 113
    red kidney, canned; ½ cup _____ 115
BEEF, corned, canned; 3 ounces _____ 185
BEEF CUTS, cooked
    flank steak, lean only; 3 ounces _____ 207
    ground beef, lean; 3 ounces _____ 234
    ground beef, regular; 3 ounces _____ 260
    pot roast, chuck, lean only; 3 ounces ___ 196
    rib roast, lean only; 3 ounces _____ 204
    round steak, lean only; 3 ounces _____ 165
    sirloin steak, lean only; 3 ounces _____ 177
BEEF LIVER, braised; 3 ounces _____ 137
BEETS, cooked, diced; ½ cup _____ 28
BEVERAGES
    beer; 12 ounces _____ 150
    cola; 12 ounces _____ 160
    ginger ale; 12 ounces _____ 125
    gin, rum, vodka (80 proof); 1½ ounces ___ 95
    table wine, white; 3½ ounces _____ 80
BLUEBERRIES
    fresh; ½ cup _____ 40
    frozen, sweetened; ½ cup _____ 93

BREADS
    bagel; 1 (3½-inch diameter) _____ 200
    bun, frankfurter or hamburger; 1 _____ 119
    English muffin, plain; 1 _____ 140
    French; 1 slice (1 inch thick) _____ 100
    pita; 1 (6½-inch diameter) _____ 165
    raisin; 1 slice _____ 65
    white; 1 slice _____ 65
    whole wheat; 1 slice _____ 70
BROCCOLI
    cooked, drained; 1 medium stalk _____ 50
    frozen chopped, cooked, drained; ½ cup ___ 25
BRUSSELS SPROUTS, cooked, drained;
    ½ cup _____ 30
BUTTER; 1 tablespoon _____ 100

C

CABBAGE
    common varieties, raw, shredded; 1 cup ___ 15
    red, raw, shredded; 1 cup _____ 20
CAKES, baked from mixes
    angel food, no icing; 1/12 cake _____ 125
    devil's food or yellow, 2 layers, 9-inch-
        diameter, chocolate frosting; 1/16 cake ___ 235
CANDIES
    caramel; 1 ounce _____ 115
    gumdrops; 1 ounce _____ 100
    hard; 1 ounce _____ 110
    milk-chocolate bar; 1 ounce _____ 145
CANTALOUPE; ½ of a 5-inch-diameter
    melon _____ 95
CARROTS
    cooked, drained, sliced; ½ cup _____ 35
    raw; 1 large _____ 30
CATSUP; 1 tablespoon _____ 15
CAULIFLOWER
    cooked, drained; ½ cup _____ 15
    raw, whole flowerets; 1 cup _____ 25
CELERY, raw, chopped; ½ cup _____ 10
CEREALS, ready to eat
    bran flakes; about ¾ cup _____ 90
    cornflakes; about 1¼ cups _____ 110
    granola; about ⅓ cup _____ 125
    wheat flakes; about 1 cup _____ 100

CHEESES

American, process; 1 ounce _____ 105
blue; 1 ounce _____ 100
Camembert; 1 ounce _____ 86
cheddar; 1 ounce _____ 115
cottage, cream-style, large curd; 1 cup _____ 235
cottage, low fat (2% fat); 1 cup _____ 205
cream cheese; 1 ounce _____ 100
cream cheese, reduced calorie; 1 ounce _____ 60
Monterey Jack; 1 ounce _____ 106
mozzarella, part skim milk; 1 ounce _____ 72
Neufchâtel; 1 ounce _____ 74
Parmesan, grated; 1 tablespoon _____ 25
ricotta, part skim milk; 1 cup _____ 340
Swiss, natural; 1 ounce _____ 105

CHERRIES

canned, in syrup, sweet; ½ cup _____ 107
canned, water pack, tart, pitted; ½ cup _____ 45
fresh, sweet, whole; 10 cherries _____ 50

CHICKEN

breast, skinned, roasted; ½ breast _____ 142
canned, with broth; 5 ounces _____ 234
dark meat, skinned, roasted; 1 cup _____ 286
light meat, skinned, roasted; 1 cup _____ 242

CHOCOLATE

bitter; 1 ounce _____ 145
semisweet; 1 ounce _____ 143
sweet plain; 1 ounce _____ 150
syrup, fudge-type; 2 tablespoons _____ 125
syrup, thin-type; 2 tablespoons _____ 85

CLAMS, canned; 3 ounces _____ 85
COCONUT, sweetened, shredded; ¼ cup _____ 118

COOKIES

chocolate chip; 1 (2¼-inch-diameter) _____ 45
cream sandwich, chocolate; 1 _____ 49
sugar; 1 (2½-inch-diameter) _____ 59
vanilla wafer; 3 (1¾-inch-diameter) _____ 56

CORN

canned, cream-style; ½ cup _____ 93
canned, vacuum pack, whole kernel;
½ cup _____ 83
sweet, cooked; 1 ear (5x1¾ inches) _____ 85

CORNSTARCH; 1 tablespoon _____ 29
CRABMEAT, canned; ½ cup _____ 68
CRACKERS
cheese; 1 (1-inch square) _____ 5

CRACKERS, continued

graham; 2 (2½-inch square) _____ 60
saltine; 2 (2-inch square) _____ 25

CREAM

half-and-half; 1 tablespoon _____ 20
whipping; 1 tablespoon _____ 50

CUCUMBER; 6 large slices _____ 5

D-L

DATES, fresh or dried, pitted; 10 _____ 230
DOUGHNUTS
cake, plain; 1 (3¼x1 inch) _____ 210
yeast; 1 (3¾x1¼ inches) _____ 235

EGG

fried; 1 large _____ 95
poached, or hard or soft cooked; 1 large _____ 80
scrambled, plain; made with 1 large egg _____ 110
white; 1 large _____ 15
yolk; 1 large _____ 65

EGGNOG; 1 cup _____ 340
EGGPLANT, cooked, diced; ½ cup _____ 13
FISH
haddock, breaded, fried; 3 ounces _____ 175
halibut, broiled; 3 ounces _____ 140
herring, pickled; 3 ounces _____ 190
salmon, broiled or baked; 3 ounces _____ 140
salmon, canned, pink; 3 ounces _____ 120
sardines, canned, in oil, drained;
3 ounces _____ 175
tuna, canned, in oil, drained; 3 ounces _____ 165
tuna, canned, in water, drained; 3 ounces _____ 135

FLOUR

all-purpose; 1 cup _____ 455
whole wheat; 1 cup _____ 400

FRANKFURTER, cooked; 1 _____ 145
GRAPEFRUIT
fresh; ½ medium _____ 40
juice, canned, sweetened; 1 cup _____ 115
juice, fresh; 1 cup _____ 95

GRAPES, green, seedless; 10 _____ 35
HAM, fully cooked, lean only; 2.4 ounces _____ 105
HONEYDEW MELON; 1/10 of a
6½-inch-diameter melon _____ 45

ICE CREAM, vanilla

    ice milk; 1 cup (about 4% fat) ———— 185

    regular; 1 cup (about 11% fat) ———— 270

    soft serve; 1 cup ———————————— 223

JAM; 1 tablespoon ———————————— 55

JELLY; 1 tablespoon ————————————— 50

KALE, cooked, drained; ½ cup ————— 20

KIWI FRUIT; 1 ——————————————— 45

KOHLRABI, cooked, drained, diced; ½ cup —— 25

LAMB, cooked

    loin chop, lean only; 2.3 ounces ———— 140

    roast leg, lean only; 2.6 ounces ———— 140

LEMONADE, frozen concentrate,

    sweetened, reconstituted; 1 cup ———— 106

LETTUCE

    Boston; ¼ of a medium head ————— 5

    iceberg; ¼ of a medium compact head ——— 20

LIMEADE, frozen concentrate,

    sweetened, reconstituted; 1 cup ———— 100

LOBSTER, cooked; ½ cup —————————— 69

LUNCHEON MEATS

    bologna; 1 slice (1 ounce) ———————— 90

    salami, cooked; 1 slice (1 ounce) ———— 73

M-R

MAPLE SYRUP; 1 tablespoon —————— 50

MARGARINE, soft or regular; 1 tablespoon — 100

MAYONNAISE; 1 tablespoon —————— 100

MILK

    buttermilk; 1 cup ————————————— 100

    chocolate drink (2% fat); 1 cup ———— 180

    condensed, sweetened, undiluted; 1 cup — 980

    dried nonfat, instant; 1 cup ————— 245

    evaporated, skim, undiluted; 1 cup——— 200

    evaporated, whole, undiluted; 1 cup ——— 340

    low fat (2% fat); 1 cup ————————— 120

    skim; 1 cup ———————————————— 85

    whole; 1 cup —————————————— 150

MOLASSES, light; 2 tablespoons ————— 85

MUFFINS

    blueberry; 1 ——————————————— 135

    bran; 1 ————————————————— 125

    corn; 1 ————————————————— 145

MUSHROOMS

    canned, drained; ⅓ cup ———————— 12

    raw, sliced; 1 cup ——————————— 20

NUTS

    almonds; 1 ounce ——————————— 165

    cashews, roasted in oil; 1 ounce ———— 165

    peanuts, roasted in oil, shelled; 1 ounce —— 165

    pecans; 1 ounce ———————————— 190

    walnuts; 1 ounce ——————————— 170

OIL; 1 tablespoon ———————————— 125

OLIVES

    green; 4 medium or ripe; 3 small ———— 15

ONIONS

    green, without tops; 6 small ————— 10

    mature, raw, chopped; ½ cup ———— 28

ORANGES

    fresh; 1 medium ——————————— 60

    juice, canned, unsweetened; 1 cup ——— 105

    juice, fresh; 1 cup —————————— 110

    juice, frozen concentrate, reconstituted;

      1 cup ———————————————— 110

OYSTERS, raw; ½ cup (6 to 10 medium) —— 80

PANCAKE; 1 (4-inch-diameter) ————— 60

PEACHES

    canned, in juice; ½ cup ———————— 55

    canned, in syrup; ½ cup ——————— 95

    fresh; 1 medium ——————————— 35

PEANUT BUTTER; 1 tablespoon ———— 95

PEA PODS, cooked, drained; ½ cup ———— 33

PEARS

    canned, in juice; 2 halves ——————— 63

    canned, in syrup; ½ cup ———————— 95

    fresh; 1 medium ——————————— 100

PEAS, green, cooked; ½ cup ——————— 63

PEPPERONI; 1 slice (⅛ inch thick) ———— 27

PEPPERS, green, sweet, chopped; ¾ cup —— 20

PICKLES

    dill; 1 medium ———————————— 5

    sweet; 1 small ————————————— 20

PIES; ⅛ of a 9-inch pie

    apple ———————————————— 303

    blueberry —————————————— 286

    cherry ——————————————— 308

    lemon meringue ———————————— 268

    pumpkin —————————————— 240

PINEAPPLE

    canned, in juice; ½ cup ———————— 75

    fresh, diced; ½ cup —————————— 38

    juice, canned, unsweetened; 1 cup ——— 140

PLUMS
canned, in juice; ½ cup _____ 73
fresh; 1 (2-inch diameter) _____ 36
POPCORN
plain, air-popped; 1 cup _____ 30
plain, popped in oil; 1 cup _____ 55
PORK, cooked
chop, loin center cut, lean only;
2½ ounces _____ 165
sausage, links; 3 ounces _____ 150
POTATO CHIPS; 10 medium _____ 105
POTATOES
baked; 1 (about 8 ounces) _____ 220
boiled; 1 (about 5 ounces) _____ 120
mashed with milk; ½ cup _____ 80
sweet, baked; 1 medium _____ 115
PRUNE JUICE, canned; 1 cup _____ 180
PRUNES, dried, uncooked, pitted; 5 large _____ 115
PUDDINGS, cooked
chocolate; ½ cup _____ 150
vanilla; ½ cup _____ 145
PUMPKIN, canned; 1 cup _____ 85
RAISINS; 1 cup (not packed) _____ 435
RASPBERRIES
fresh; ½ cup _____ 30
frozen, sweetened; ½ cup _____ 128
RHUBARB
cooked, sweetened; ½ cup _____ 140
raw, diced; 1 cup _____ 26
RICE
brown, cooked; ½ cup _____ 115
white, cooked; ½ cup _____ 113
white, quick cooking, cooked; ½ cup _____ 93
ROLLS
cloverleaf; 1 (2½-inch diameter) _____ 85
hard; 1 (3¾-inch diameter) _____ 155
sweet; 1 medium _____ 220

S-Z

SALAD DRESSINGS
blue cheese; 1 tablespoon _____ 75
French; 1 tablespoon _____ 85
Italian; 1 tablespoon _____ 80
mayonnaise; 1 tablespoon _____ 100

SALAD DRESSINGS, continued
mayonnaise-type; 1 tablespoon _____ 60
Thousand Island; 1 tablespoon _____ 60
SHERBET, orange; ½ cup _____ 135
SHORTENING; 1 tablespoon _____ 115
SHRIMP, canned; 3 ounces _____ 100
SOUPS, condensed, canned (diluted with water unless specified otherwise)
beef bouillon, broth, consommé; 1 cup _____ 15
chicken noodle; 1 cup _____ 75
cream of chicken, diluted with milk; 1 cup _____ 190
cream of mushroom, diluted with milk; 1 cup _____ 205
tomato; 1 cup _____ 85
tomato, diluted with milk; 1 cup _____ 160
SOUR CREAM, dairy; ½ cup _____ 248
SPINACH
canned, drained; ½ cup _____ 25
frozen, cooked, drained; ½ cup _____ 28
raw, torn; 1 cup _____ 10
SQUASH
summer, cooked, drained, sliced; ½ cup _____ 18
winter, baked, cubed; ½ cup _____ 40
STRAWBERRIES
fresh, whole; ½ cup _____ 23
frozen, sweetened, sliced; ½ cup _____ 123
SUGARS
brown, packed; ½ cup _____ 410
granulated; 1 tablespoon _____ 45
powdered; ½ cup _____ 193
TOMATOES
canned; ½ cup _____ 25
fresh; 1 medium _____ 25
juice, canned; 1 cup _____ 40
paste, canned; 1 cup _____ 220
sauce; 1 cup _____ 75
TURKEY, roasted, light and dark; 1 cup _____ 240
TURNIPS, cooked, diced; ½ cup _____ 15
VEAL, cooked, cutlet; 3 ounces _____ 185
WAFFLE; 1 section (4½ x 4½ x ⅝ inches) _____ 140
WATERMELON; 1 wedge (8x4 inches) _____ 155
YOGURT
low fat, fruit flavored; 8 ounces _____ 230
low fat, plain; 8 ounces _____ 145

INDEX

A-B

Acorn Squash, Stuffed, 136
Almond Cocoa, 432
Antipasto Salad, 85
Apples
  Apple and Oat Bran
    Muffins, 40
  Apple-Cheese Mold, 347
  Apple Phyllo
    Triangles, 414
  Apple-Spice Loaf, 376
  Apple-Stuffed Pork
    Roast, 124
  Baked Apples with Cheese
    Topping, 410
  Deep-Dish Apple Pie, 68
  Herbed Lamb with
    Apples, 160
  Hot Ham and Apple
    Slaw, 77
  Poached Chicken Breasts
    with Apples, 175
  Turkey and Apple
    Breakfast Sausage, 441
  Turkey Ham and Apple
    Bake, 214
Apricot Custards, 393
Apricot-Oatmeal Bars, 464
Asparagus
  Asparagus Frittata, 263
  Asparagus with Orange
    Mayonnaise, 362
  Crab and Asparagus
    Supreme, 252
  Lemony Herbed
    Asparagus, 32
  Lemony Shrimp and
    Asparagus, 313
Baked Apples with Cheese
  Topping, 410
Baked Crab and
  Broccoli, 251
Baked Curried Chicken and
  Rice, 200
Baked Ham and Kraut
  Rolls, 144
Baked Lamb and
  Vegetables, 159
Baked Stuffed Tomatoes, 322

Bananas
  Banana Bread, 377
  Banana Nog, 429
  Banana Pops, 411
  Orange-Banana Nog, 429
  Rum-Sauced Bananas, 401
  Tropical Banana Nog, 429
Barbecue Recipes
  Barbecue Beef
    Sandwiches, 103
  Barbecued Pork, 141
  Barbecue-Sauced
    Turkey, 299
  Chicken with Mustard
    Relish, 183
  Coriander Turkey
    Breast, 207
  Deviled Steak, 92
  Glazed Turkey Steaks, 210
  Grilled Flank Steak, 89
  Ham with Honey-Mustard
    Glaze, 142
  Spicy Barbecued
    Chicken, 188
  Sweet-and-Sour Pork
    Kabobs, 133
Barley, Curried, 341
Bean Dip, Layered, 417
Beans, Boston Baked, 64
Beef
  Barbecue Beef
    Sandwiches, 103
  Beef and Brew, 102
  Beef-Barley Soup, 108
  Beef Dijon, 91
  Beef Roulades, 95
  Beef Salad with Fresh
    Basil Dressing, 74
  Beef Stir-Fry with Orange
    Sauce, 100
  Burgers with Mustard
    Sauce, 112
  Burritos, 23
  Creamy Beef and
    Onions, 115
  Curried Beef and
    Potatoes, 101
  Curried Beef and
    Rice, 120
  Deep-Dish Beef Pie, 106
  Deviled Steak, 92

Beef *(continued)*
  Easy Green Chili, 107
  Eggplant Bake, 119
  Garlic-Wine Pot Roast, 88
  Grilled Flank Steak, 89
  Herbed Lamb Stir-
    Fry, 163
  Herbed Pot Roast, 281
  Herbed Steak and
    Onions, 97
  Individual Pineapple Meat
    Loaves, 111
  Individual Shepherd's
    Pies, 166
  Italian Beef Skillet, 96
  Italian-Style Burgers, 113
  Layered Picnic Pâté, 455
  Liver in Wine Sauce, 121
  Meatball Sandwiches, 109
  Meat Loaf with Garden
    Sauce, 286
  Mushroom-Stuffed Beef
    Roast, 87
  Mushroom-Stuffed Flank
    Steak Roll, 90
  Oriental Beef and
    Broccoli, 283
  Peanut Saté, 94
  Peppery Beef and
    Vegetables, 105
  Picadillo Rice, 137
  Pineapple Beef, 99
  Polenta with Chunky
    Meat Sauce, 284
  Saucy Spaghetti Squash
    Olé, 116
  Sherried Fillet Steaks, 93
  Spaghetti Pie, 118
  Spaghetti with Meat
    Sauce, 114
  Spicy Beef and Bean
    Burgers, 110
  Spicy Stuffed Peppers, 289
  Spinach-Stuffed Flank
    Steak, 282
  Stroganoff-Style Beef, 57
  Stuffed Cabbage
    Leaves, 117
  Sukiyaki, 98
  Sweet-and-Sour Ham
    Balls, 157

Beef *(continued)*
  Taco Salad, 75
  Tex-Mex Beef Soup, 104
  Tortilla Pie, 285
Berries
  Blueberry Gems, 380
  Calico Fruit, 408
  Fruity Yogurt Ice, 398
  Lemon Torte with
    Raspberries, 383
  Peach-Berry Punch, 433
  Peach Melba Cream Punch,
    433
  Raspberry Whip, 394
  Saucy Rhubarb and
    Strawberries, 403
  Strawberry Shortcake, 72
  Strawberry-Topped
    Cheesecake, 67
  Strawberry-Yogurt
    Pudding, 463
  Sweet-Topped
    Raspberries, 407
Beverages
  Almond Cocoa, 432
  Banana Nog, 429
  Cranberry Punch, 430
  Easy Chocolate
    Shakes, 434
  Hot Cocoa, 432
  Hot Mocha, 432
  Iced Spicy Coffee, 427
  Orange and Spice Tea, 428
  Orange-Banana Nog, 429
  Peach-Berry Punch, 433
  Peach Melba Cream
    Punch, 433
  Peppermint Cocoa, 432
  Peppy Tomato Sipper, 435
  Peppy Tomato Slush, 435
  Spicy Coffee, 427
  Tropical Banana Nog, 429
  Tropical Punch, 431
Biscotti, 388
Blueberry Gems, 380
Boston Baked Beans, 64
Boston Brown Bread, 375
Bran Muffins, 446
Bran Muffins, Berry
  Variation, 446

Bread Pudding, 387
Breads
    Apple and Oat Bran
        Muffins, 40
    Apple-Spice Loaf, 376
    Banana Bread, 377
    Blueberry Gems, 380
    Boston Brown Bread, 375
    Bran Muffins, 446
    Bran Muffins, Berry
        Variation, 446
    Bread Knots, 371
    Buttermilk Biscuits, 378
    Cheese-Topped English
        Muffin, 28
    Cinnamon Rolls with
        Orange Glaze, 71
    Corn Bread, 373
    Cornmeal and Wheat
        Germ Braids, 370
    Cornmeal Pancakes with
        Applesauce, 443
    Dill Rolls, 372
    Feathery Pancakes, 442
    Irish Soda Bread, 374
    Italian Onion
        Flatbread, 381
    No-Fry French Toast, 445
    Pancakes with Orange
        Sauce, 26
    Spicy Wheat and Oat
        Bread, 369
    Two-Bran Refrigerator
        Muffins, 379
    Whole Wheat Raisin Soda
        Bread, 374
Breakfast Blintzes, 444
Breakfast Rice Cereal, 448
Broccoli
    Baked Crab and
        Broccoli, 251
    Broccoli and Chicken
        Casserole, 204
    Broccoli Rice, 356
    Oriental Beef and
        Broccoli, 283
    Pasta with Onion
        Sauce, 338
    Pork and Broccoli
        Stir-Fry, 135
    Scallops and Broccoli with
        Pasta, 312

Broccoli *(continued)*
    Tofu and Vegetable Stir-
        Fry, 274
    Turkey Rolls Divan, 211
Broiled Chops with Italian
    Vegetables, 127
Broiled Lobster Tails, 250
Broiled Rice and Vegetable
    Patties, 266
Brownie Bites, 70
Brown Rice Pilaf, 52
Brunch Turnovers, 440
Bulgur Pilaf, 333
Bulgur-Stuffed Fish
    Rolls, 230
Burgers
    Burgers with Mustard
        Sauce, 112
    Garden Burgers, 219
    Italian-Style
        Burgers, 113
    Spicy Beef and Bean
        Burgers, 110
Burritos, 23
Burritos, Chinese, 29
Buttermilk Biscuits, 378

C-D

Cabbage
    Cabbage and Ham
        Hash, 150
    Caraway Noodles with
        Cabbage, 337
    Fruit Slaw, 33
    Hearty Italian-Style
        Soup, 461
    Roast Pork with Cabbage
        and Carrots, 125
    Saucy Caraway
        Cabbage, 363
    Steamed Sole
        in Cabbage, 306
    Stuffed Cabbage
        Leaves, 117
Caesar-Style Chicken
    Salad, 80
Cakes
    Carrot Snack Cake, 66
    Chocolate-Cinnamon
        Angel Cake, 385
    Gingerbread
        Cupcakes, 386

Calico Fruit, 408
Caraway Noodles with
    Cabbage, 337
Carrots
    Carrot and Onion
        Puff, 261
    Carrot Snack Cake, 66
    Carrots with Onions, 358
    Fluffy Dilled Carrots and
        Potatoes, 318
    Roast Pork with Cabbage
        and Carrots, 125
Cauliflower Amandine, 361
Cereal, Breakfast Rice, 448
Cheese
    Apple-Cheese Mold, 347
    Breakfast Blintzes, 444
    Cheese-and-Apple-Stuffed
        Chicken, 291
    Cheese and Vegetable
        Soup, 344
    Cheese Calzones, 272
    Cheese-Topped English
        Muffins, 28
    Cheesy Chicken Rolls, 181
    Cheesy Pepper and
        Mushroom Pizza, 270
    Cheesy Polenta
        Squares, 334
    Cheesy Scalloped
        Potatoes, 62
    Cheesy Tater Topper, 45
    Chicken Roll-Ups, 176
    Chocolate-Cheese
        Dessert, 395
    Clam and Cheese
        Chowder, 255
    Cottage Cheese and Apple
        Snacks, 420
    Eggplant Parmesan, 269
    Fruity Cottage Cheese
        Salad, 456
    Grilled Three-Cheese
        Sandwiches, 273
    Ham and Cheese
        Frittata, 151
    Ham and Cheese
        Macaroni, 152
    Mexican-Style Creamed
        Corn, 48
    Oriental Openers, 49
    Parmesan Baked Fish, 232

Cheese *(continued)*
    Rice and Beans with
        Cheese, 278
    Spaghetti with Cottage
        Cheese Pesto, 335
    Strawberry-Topped
        Cheesecake, 67
    Turkey and Cheese
        Wedges, 217
Cheesecake,
    Strawberry-Topped, 67
Chicken
    Baked Curried Chicken and
        Rice, 200
    Broccoli and Chicken
        Casserole, 204
    Brunch Turnovers, 440
    Caesar-Style Chicken
        Salad, 80
    Cheese-and-Apple-Stuffed
        Chicken, 291
    Cheesy Chicken Rolls, 181
    Chicken à la King, 297
    Chicken and Barley
        Bake, 192
    Chicken and Rice
        Salad, 458
    Chicken and Spinach
        Crepes, 202
    Chicken and Sweet Pepper
        Stir-Fry, 27
    Chicken and Zucchini in
        Mustard Sauce, 198
    Chicken Breasts with
        Curried Stuffing, 182
    Chicken Country
        Captain, 295
    Chicken Fajitas, 196
    Chicken Livers in Italian
        Tomato Sauce, 193
    Chicken Marsala, 179
    Chicken Roll-Ups, 176
    Chicken Tacos, 203
    Chicken with Grapes, 178
    Chicken with
        Mushrooms, 296
    Chicken with Mustard
        Relish, 183
    Chicken with Oriental
        Dressing, 290
    Chicken with Wine
        Sauce, 184

Chicken (continued)
  Chilled Chicken and
    Vegetable Salad, 83
  Chinese Burritos, 29
  Citrus Chicken, 292
  Curried Chicken and Rice
    Salad, 82
  Curried Chicken
    Bundles, 454
  Curried Chicken
    Casserole, 293
  Fiesta Chicken, 197
  Fried Chicken with Cream
    Gravy, 59
  Garlic-Clove Chicken, 186
  Ginger and Peach
    Chicken, 180
  Indian-Style Chicken, 187
  Lime-Sauced Chicken, 177
  Lunch Box Chicken
    Salad, 457
  Mediterranean-Style
    Chicken, 185
  Mustard and Honey
    Chicken, 174
  Nutty Chicken
    Fingers, 195
  Orange Chicken
    Tabbouleh, 81
  Oriental Chicken in
    Tortillas, 194
  Oven-Fried Chicken, 191
  Paella, 189
  Pineapple-Chicken and
    Rice Bake, 190
  Poached Chicken Breasts
    with Apples, 175
  Southwestern Chicken, 201
  Soy-Glazed Chicken, 294
  Spicy Barbecued
    Chicken, 188
  Stir-Fried Chicken
    Salad, 79
  Stroganoff-Style
    Chicken, 199
Chili, Easy Green, 107
Chilled Chicken and
  Vegetable Salad, 83
Chilled Lobster, 249
Chinese Burritos, 29
Chocolate
  Almond Cocoa, 432

Chocolate (continued)
  Chocolate-Cheese
    Dessert, 395
  Chocolate-Cinnamon
    Angel Cake, 385
  Chocolate Pears, 412
  Easy Chocolate
    Shakes, 434
  Hot Cocoa, 432
  Hot Mocha, 432
  Mint-Chocolate Chip Ice
    Milk, 396
  Mocha Soufflé, 389
  Peppermint Cocoa, 432
Cinnamon Rolls with
  Orange Glaze, 71
Citrus Chicken, 292
Citrus Dressing, Spicy, 352
Citrus Shrimp and
  Scallops, 239
Clam and Cheese
  Chowder, 255
Cocoa
  Almond Cocoa, 432
  Hot Cocoa, 432
  Hot Mocha, 432
  Peppermint Cocoa, 432
Coffee
  Coffee Ice, 399
  Iced Spicy Coffee, 427
  Spicy Coffee, 427
Cookies
  Apricot-Oatmeal Bars, 464
  Biscotti, 388
  Brownie Bites, 70
  Peanut Butter and
    Oatmeal Cookies, 426
  Pumpkin-Raisin
    Drops, 465
Coriander Turkey
  Breast, 207
Corn
  Cheesy Polenta
    Squares, 334
  Corn Bread, 373
  Corn-Bread-Coated
    Fish, 309
  Corn Chowder, 342
  Cornmeal and Wheat
    Germ Braids, 370
  Cornmeal Pancakes with
    Applesauce, 443

Corn (continued)
  Ham and Corn
    Tostadas, 149
  Mexican-Style Creamed
    Corn, 48
  Mustard-Sauced Corn, 359
  Pork Casserole with Bread
    Topping, 139
  Southwestern Chicken, 201
  Tofu and Corn
    Quiche, 265
Cornish Game Hens,
  Orange-Roasted, 205
Cottage Cheese and Apple
  Snacks, 420
Cottage Cheese-Dill
  Dip, 416
Country-Style Pork
  Stew, 132
Crab
  Baked Crab and
    Broccoli, 251
  Crab and Asparagus
    Supreme, 252
  Crab Cakes, 253
  Crab Gumbo, 254
  Creamy Crab and
    Pasta Casseroles, 315
Cranberry Punch, 430
Cranberry Sauce, Turkey
  with, 206
Cream Puffs, 69
Creamy Beef and
  Onions, 115
Creamy Crab and Pasta
  Casseroles, 315
Creamy Egg and Vegetable
  Bake, 262
Creamy Peas and
  Onions, 355
Creamy Poached Cod, 302
Creamy Potato Salad, 65
Creamy Salad Dressing, 350
Creamy Veal and
  Mushrooms, 172
Creole-Style Pork, 134
Crumb-Topped Peaches, 413
Crunchy Topped Fish with
  Potato Sticks, 227
Cucumbers, Marinated, 325
Curried Barley, 341

Curried Beef and
  Potatoes, 101
Curried Beef and Rice, 120
Curried Chicken and Rice
  Salad, 82
Curried Chicken
  Bundles, 454
Curried Chicken
  Casserole, 293
Curried Fruit Salad, 348
Curried Lamb, 162
Curried Lentils and
  Vegetables, 277
Curried Pork Chops with
  Oranges, 130
Curried Shrimp Crepes, 244
Curried Snack Mix, 425
Deep-Dish Apple Pie, 68
Deep-Dish Beef Pie, 106
Deep-Sea Kabobs, 307
Desserts
  Apple Phyllo
    Triangles, 414
  Apricot Custards, 393
  Apricot-Oatmeal Bars, 464
  Baked Apples with Cheese
    Topping, 410
  Banana Pops, 411
  Bread Pudding, 387
  Calico Fruit, 408
  Carrot Snack Cake, 66
  Chocolate-Cheese
    Dessert, 395
  Chocolate-Cinnamon
    Angel Cake, 385
  Chocolate Pears, 412
  Coffee Ice, 399
  Cream Puffs, 69
  Crepes, 202
  Crumb-Topped
    Peaches, 413
  Dried Fruit Royale, 404
  Flan, 384
  Fresh Fruit with Creamy
    Sauce, 405
  Fruit Tart, 51
  Fruity Yogurt Ice, 398
  Gingerbread
    Cupcakes, 386
  Lemon Torte with
    Raspberries, 383

Desserts *(continued)*
  Meringue Shells with
    Fresh Fruit, 391
  Mint-Chocolate Chip Ice
    Milk, 396
  Mocha Soufflé, 389
  Pavlova, 390
  Peach Daiquiri Ice, 53
  Peach Shortcake, 447
  Peach Tart, 382
  Peachy Cherry Sauce, 400
  Pineapple Flambé, 409
  Poached Pears with
    Raspberry Sauce, 37
  Pumpkin Custards, 392
  Raspberry Whip, 394
  Rum-Sauced Bananas, 401
  Saucy Rhubarb and
    Strawberries, 403
  Spicy Fruit Cup, 406
  Strawberry Shortcake, 72
  Strawberry-Topped
    Cheesecake, 67
  Strawberry-Yogurt
    Pudding, 463
  Sweet-Topped
    Raspberries, 407
  Watermelon Sherbet, 397
Deviled Steak, 92
Dill Rolls, 372
Dips
  Cottage Cheese and Apple
    Snacks, 420
  Cottage Cheese-Dill
    Dip, 416
  Fresh Fruit Dip, 418
  Garlic-Spinach Dip, 419
  Layered Bean Dip, 417
Dried Fruit Royale, 404

E-F

Easy Chocolate Shakes, 434
Easy Green Chili, 107
Eggplant Bake, 119
Eggplant Parmesan, 269
Eggs
  Asparagus Frittata, 263
  Carrot and Onion
    Puff, 261
  Creamy Egg and Vegetable
    Bake, 262
  Eggs Benedict, 61

Eggs *(continued)*
  Flan, 384
  Ham and Cheese
    Frittata, 151
  Ham and Fruit Strata, 439
  Meringue Shells with
    Fresh Fruit, 391
  Mexicali Eggs, 437
  Mexican Strata, 264
  Pavlova, 390
  Puffy Omelet Squares, 36
  Salmon-Filled Puffy
    Omelet, 438
  Tofu and Corn
    Quiche, 265
  Turkey Soufflé, 220
Feathery Pancakes, 442
Fettuccine with Creamy Ham
  Sauce, 146
Fiesta Chicken, 197
Fish and Seafood *(see also*
  Lobster *and* Shrimp)
  Antipasto Salad, 85
  Baked Crab and
    Broccoli, 251
  Bulgur-Stuffed Fish
    Rolls, 230
  Clam and Cheese
    Chowder, 255
  Corn-Bread-Coated
    Fish, 309
  Crab and Asparagus
    Supreme, 252
  Crab Cakes, 253
  Crab Gumbo, 254
  Creamy Crab and Pasta
    Casseroles, 315
  Creamy Poached Cod, 302
  Crunchy Topped Fish with
    Potato Sticks, 227
  Deep-Sea Kabobs, 307
  Fish and Peppers, 226
  Fish Soup, 235
  Fish Steaks with
    Mushroom Sauce, 303
  Fish with Cool Cucumber
    Sauce, 308
  Fish with Vegetables and
    Rice, 310
  Fried Scallops, 237
  Lime-Sauced Fish and
    Cucumbers, 234

Fish and Seafood *(continued)*
  Linguine with Clam
    Sauce, 256
  Linguine with Scallops, 50
  Orange Roughy with
    Tarragon Sauce, 228
  Oven-Fried Fish, 225
  Oyster and Spinach
    Chowder, 257
  Parmesan Baked Fish, 232
  Pasta with Seafood, 241
  Poached Fish with Orange
    Sauce, 233
  Poached Salmon with
    Caper Sauce, 229
  Salmon-Filled Puffy
    Omelet, 438
  Scallops and Broccoli
    with Pasta, 312
  Scallops Florentine, 238
  Seafood Enchiladas, 314
  Seaside Mussels, 258
  Spinach-Stuffed Sole, 305
  Steamed Sole in
    Cabbage, 306
  Stuffed Red Snapper, 224
  Stuffed Snapper, 301
  Sweet-and-Sour Fish, 304
  Swordfish with Cucumber
    Sauce, 231
  Tuna-Noodle
    Casserole, 236
  Zippy Tuna Sandwich, 452
Flan, 384
Fluffy Dilled Carrots and
  Potatoes, 318
French Toast, No-Fry, 445
Fresh Fruit Dip, 418
Fresh Fruit with Creamy
  Sauce, 405
Fried Chicken with Cream
  Gravy, 59
Fried Scallops, 237
Fruit and Pasta Salad, 349
Fruit Compote, Maple, 367
Fruit Cup, Spicy, 406
Fruit Dip, Fresh, 418
Fruit Salad, Curried, 348
Fruit Slaw, 33
Fruit Tart, 51
Fruity Cottage Cheese
  Salad, 456

Fruity Oatmeal, 450
Fruity Yogurt Ice, 398

G-H

Garbanzo Bean and
  Vegetable Salad, 459
Garden Burgers, 219
Garlic and Pepper
  Stir-Fry, 324
Garlic-Broiled Shrimp, 246
Garlic-Caraway Veal
  Roast, 167
Garlic-Clove Chicken, 186
Garlic-Spinach Dip, 419
Garlic-Wine Pot Roast, 88
Gazpacho, 462
Ginger and Peach
  Chicken, 180
Gingerbread Cupcakes, 386
Gingered Pork, 287
Glazed Ham with Sweet
  Potatoes, 145
Glazed Turkey Steaks, 210
Granola, 449
Grapes, Chicken with, 178
Greek-Style Pita
  Sandwiches, 31
Grilled Flank Steak, 89
Grilled Three-Cheese
  Sandwiches, 273
Ham
  Baked Ham and Kraut
    Rolls, 144
  Cabbage and Ham
    Hash, 150
  Fettuccine with Creamy
    Ham Sauce, 146
  Glazed Ham with Sweet
    Potatoes, 145
  Ham and Cheese
    Frittata, 151
  Ham and Cheese
    Macaroni, 152
  Ham and Corn
    Tostadas, 149
  Ham and Fruit Strata, 439
  Ham and Pasta Salad, 78
  Ham and Potato
    Skillet, 153
  Ham and Vegetable
    Soup, 34

Ham *(continued)*
  Ham and Vegetables with
    Mostaccioli, 46
  Ham Jambalaya, 154
  Ham with Honey-Mustard
    Glaze, 142
  Ham with Sweet Potatoes
    and Apples, 143
  Hot Ham and Apple
    Slaw, 77
  Oriental Ham Soup, 147
  Savory Ham and Rice, 148
  Spinach and Ham
    Lasagna, 156
  Stuffed Veal Rolls, 171
  Sweet-and-Sour Ham
    Balls, 157
  Vegetable-Bean Soup with
    Ham, 155
Hearty Italian-Style
  Soup, 461
Herbed Couscous and
  Vegetables, 332
Herbed Lamb Stir-Fry, 163
Herbed Lamb with
  Apples, 160
Herbed Pot Roast, 281
Herbed Steak and
  Onions, 97
Herbed Vegetable Toss, 25
Honey-Mustard Glaze, Ham
  with, 142
Hot Cocoa, 432
Hot Ham and Apple
  Slaw, 77
Hot Mocha, 432

I-L

Iced Spicy Coffee, 427
Indian-Style Chicken, 187
Individual Pineapple Meat
  Loaves, 111
Individual Shepherd's
  Pies, 166
Irish Soda Bread, 374
Italian Beef Skillet, 96
Italian Onion Flatbread, 381
Italian-Style Burgers, 113
Italian Tomato and Rice
  Soup, 343

Lamb
  Baked Lamb and
    Vegetables, 159
  Burgers with Mustard
    Sauce, 112
  Curried Lamb, 162
  Eggplant Bake, 119
  Greek-Style Pita
    Sandwiches, 31
  Herbed Lamb
    Stir-Fry, 163
  Herbed Lamb with
    Apples, 160
  Individual Shepherd's
    Pies, 166
  Lentil and Lamb
    Soup, 164
  Marinated Lamb
    Kabobs, 161
  Meatball Sandwiches, 109
  Oven Lamb Stew, 165
Layered Bean Dip, 417
Layered Picnic Pâté, 455
Lemon-Tarragon
  Vegetables, 357
Lemon Torte with
  Raspberries, 383
Lemony Brown Rice and
  Vegetables, 327
Lemony Herbed
  Asparagus, 32
Lemony Shrimp and
  Asparagus, 313
Lemony Turkey
  Meatballs, 300
Lentil and Lamb
  Soup, 164
Lentil Stew, 276
Lime-Sauced Chicken, 177
Lime-Sauced Fish and
  Cucumbers, 234
Linguine with Clam
  Sauce, 256
Linguine with Scallops, 50
Liver in Wine Sauce, 121
Lobster
  Broiled Lobster Tails, 250
  Chilled Lobster, 249
  Lobster Newburg, 60
Low-Calorie Shrimp
  Creole, 243

Lunch Box Chicken
  Salad, 457

M

Macaroni and Tomatoes, 336
Maple Fruit Compote, 367
Marinated Cucumbers, 325
Marinated Lamb
  Kabobs, 161
Marinated Turkey Slices, 208
Marinated Zucchini and
  Mushrooms, 421
Meatball Sandwiches, 109
Meat Loaf with Garden
  Sauce, 286
Mediterranean-Style Chicken,
  185
Meringue Shells with Fresh
  Fruit, 391
Mexicali Eggs, 437
Mexican Lentils and
  Vegetables, 365
Mexican Strata, 264
Mexican-Style Creamed
  Corn, 48
Microwave Recipes
  Almond Cocoa, 432
  Asparagus with Orange
    Mayonnaise, 362
  Baked Ham and Kraut
    Rolls, 144
  Barbecue-Sauced
    Turkey, 299
  Broccoli Rice, 356
  Cabbage and Ham
    Hash, 150
  Carrots with Onions, 358
  Cauliflower
    Amandine, 361
  Cheese-and-Apple-Stuffed
    Chicken, 291
  Chicken à la King, 297
  Chicken Country
    Captain, 295
  Chicken with
    Mushrooms, 296
  Chicken with Oriental
    Dressing, 290
  Chocolate Pears, 412
  Citrus Chicken, 292
  Corn-Bread-Coated
    Fish, 309

Microwave Recipes *(continued)*
  Creamy Crab and Pasta
    Casserole, 315
  Creamy Peas and
    Onions, 355
  Creamy Poached
    Cod , 302
  Creamy Potato Salad, 65
  Curried Chicken
    Casserole, 293
  Deep-Sea Kabobs, 307
  Fettuccine with Creamy
    Ham Sauce, 146
  Fish Steaks with
    Mushroom Sauce, 303
  Fish with Cool Cucumber
    Sauce, 308
  Fish with Vegetables and
    Rice, 310
  Fluffy Dilled Carrots and
    Potatoes, 318
  Gingered Pork, 287
  Ham and Cheese
    Macaroni, 152
  Ham and Corn
    Tostadas, 149
  Herbed Pot Roast, 281
  Hot Cocoa, 432
  Hot Mocha, 432
  Individual Shepherd's
    Pies, 166
  Lemon-Tarragon
    Vegetables, 357
  Lemony Shrimp and
    Asparagus, 313
  Lemony Turkey
    Meatballs, 300
  Maple Fruit Compote, 367
  Meat Loaf with Garden
    Sauce, 286
  Mexican Lentils and
    Vegetables, 365
  Mustard-Sauced Corn, 359
  New Potato Salad, 354
  Peppermint Cocoa, 432
  Poached Pears with
    Raspberry Sauce, 37
  Polenta with Chunky
    Meat Sauce, 284
  Salmon Cups with
    Creamed Peas, 311

Microwave Recipes *(continued)*
Saucy Caraway
Cabbage, 363
Saucy Curried Pork and
Zucchini, 288
Saucy Prunes and
Peaches, 366
Scallops and Broccoli with
Pasta, 312
Seafood Enchiladas, 314
Soy-Glazed Chicken, 294
Spaghetti Squash
Pronto, 360
Spicy Stuffed Peppers, 289
Spinach-Stuffed Flank
Steak, 282
Spinach-Stuffed Sole, 305
Spinach with Parmesan
Cheese, 364
Steamed Sole in
Cabbage, 306
Stuffed Acorn Squash, 136
Stuffed Snapper, 301
Stuffed Winter Squash, 35
Sweet-and-Sour Fish, 304
Sweet-and-Sour Ham
Balls, 157
Sweet and Spicy
Peaches, 402
Tex-Mex Turkey
Tenderloins, 298
Tortilla Pie, 285
Twice-Baked Potatoes, 317
Mint-Chocolate Chip Ice
Milk, 396
Mocha, Hot, 432
Mocha Soufflé, 389
Muffins
Apple and Oat Bran
Muffins, 40
Blueberry Gems, 380
Bran Muffins, 446
Bran Muffins, Berry
Variation, 446
Two-Bran Refrigerator
Muffins, 379
Muffulettas, 453
Mushroom and Barley
Soup, 47
Mushrooms, Stuffed, 423
Mushroom-Stuffed Beef
Roast, 87

Mushroom-Stuffed Flank
Steak Roll, 90
Mussels, Seaside, 258
Mustard and Honey
Chicken, 174
Mustard-Sauced Corn, 359

N-O
New Potato Salad, 354
No-Fry French Toast, 445
Nutty Chicken Fingers, 195
Oat Bran Muffins,
Apple and, 40
Oatmeal, Fruity, 450
Oatmeal with Fruit and
Nuts, 54
Omelet Squares, Puffy, 36
Oranges
Asparagus with Orange
Mayonnaise, 362
Beef Stir-Fry with Orange
Sauce, 100
Curried Pork Chops with
Oranges, 130
Orange and Spice Tea, 428
Orange-Banana Nog, 429
Orange Chicken
Tabbouleh, 81
Orange-Roasted Cornish
Game Hens, 205
Orange Spread, 378
Pancakes with Orange
Sauce, 26
Poached Fish with Orange
Sauce, 233
Spinach Salad, 55
Oriental Bean Salad, 340
Oriental Beef and
Broccoli, 283
Oriental Chicken in
Tortillas, 194
Oriental Ham Soup, 147
Oriental Openers, 49
Oven-Fried Chicken, 191
Oven-Fried Fish, 225
Oven-Fried Vegetables, 422
Oven Lamb Stew, 165
Oyster and Spinach
Chowder, 257

P-R
Paella, 189
Pancakes
Cornmeal Pancakes with
Applesauce, 443
Feathery Pancakes, 442
Pancakes with Orange
Sauce, 26
Parmesan Baked Fish, 232
Pasta
Broccoli and Chicken
Casserole, 204
Caraway Noodles with
Cabbage, 337
Creamy Crab and Pasta
Casseroles, 315
Fettuccine with Creamy
Ham Sauce, 146
Fruit and Pasta Salad, 349
Ham and Cheese
Macaroni, 152
Ham and Pasta Salad, 78
Ham and Vegetables with
Mostaccioli, 46
Herbed Couscous and
Vegetables, 332
Linguine with Clam
Sauce, 256
Linguine with Scallops, 50
Macaroni and
Tomatoes, 336
Mediterranean-Style
Chicken, 185
Pasta Primavera, 268
Pasta with Onion
Sauce, 338
Pasta with Seafood, 241
Pork Lo Mein, 138
Salmon-and-Pasta-Stuffed
Tomatoes, 22
Saucy Shrimp and
Pasta, 245
Scallops and Broccoli with
Pasta, 312
Spaghetti Pie, 118
Spaghetti with Cottage
Cheese Pesto, 335
Spaghetti with Meat
Sauce, 114
Spicy Pasta Pie, 215
Spinach and Ham
Lasagna, 156

Pasta *(continued)*
Spinach Lasagna
Rolls, 267
Stroganoff-Style
Chicken, 199
Tofu Manicotti, 275
Tortellini Soup, 345
Tuna-Noodle
Casserole, 236
Vegetable and Pasta
Toss, 319
Vegetarian Lasagna, 271
Wilted Greens with
Pasta, 326
Pavlova, 390
Peaches
Crumb-Topped
Peaches, 413
Ginger and Peach
Chicken, 180
Peach-Berry Punch, 433
Peach Daiquiri Ice, 53
Peach Melba Cream
Punch, 433
Peach Shortcake, 447
Peach Tart, 382
Peachy Cherry Sauce, 400
Saucy Prunes and
Peaches, 366
Sweet and Spicy
Peaches, 402
Peanut Butter and Oatmeal
Cookies, 426
Peanut Saté, 94
Pears, Chocolate, 412
Pears with Raspberry
Sauce, Poached, 37
Peas, Salmon Cups with
Creamed, 311
Peas and Onions,
Creamy, 355
Peppermint Cocoa, 432
Pepper-Rice Timbales, 331
Peppery Beef and
Vegetables, 105
Peppy Tomato Sipper, 435
Peppy Tomato Slush, 435
Picadillo Rice, 137
Pie, Deep-Dish Apple, 68
Pineapple Beef, 99
Pineapple-Chicken and
Rice Bake, 190

Pineapple Flambé, 409
Poached Chicken Breasts
  with Apples, 175
Poached Fish with Orange
  Sauce, 233
Poached Pears with
  Raspberry Sauce, 37
Poached Salmon with Caper
  Sauce, 229
Polenta with Chunky Meat
  Sauce, 284
Popcorn, Sweet and
  Spicy, 424
Pork (*see also* Ham)
  Apple-Stuffed Pork
    Roast, 124
  Barbecued Pork, 141
  Broiled Chops with Italian
    Vegetables, 127
  Country-Style Pork
    Stew, 132
  Creole-Style Pork, 134
  Curried Pork Chops with
    Oranges, 130
  Gingered Pork, 287
  Picadillo Rice, 137
  Pork and Broccoli Stir-
    Fry, 135
  Pork and Noodle Salad, 76
  Pork and Pineapple Stir-
    Fry, 131
  Pork Casserole with Bread
    Topping, 139
  Pork Chops Dijon, 128
  Pork Chops with Barbecue
    Sauce, 58
  Pork Jambalaya, 140
  Pork Lo Mein, 138
  Pork Medaillons with
    Vegetables, 126
  Pork Roast with Pineapple
    Chutney, 123
  Pork-Sauerkraut
    Supper, 129
  Roast Pork with Cabbage
    and Carrots, 125
  Saucy Curried Pork and
    Zucchini, 288
  Spicy Stuffed Peppers, 289
  Sweet-and-Sour Pork
    Kabobs, 133

Potatoes
  Cabbage and Ham
    Hash, 150
  Cheesy Scalloped
    Potatoes, 62
  Cheesy Tater Topper, 45
  Creamy Potato Salad, 65
  Crunchy Topped Fish with
    Potato Sticks, 227
  Curried Beef and
    Potatoes, 101
  Fluffy Dilled Carrots and
    Potatoes, 318
  Ham and Potato
    Skillet, 153
  New Potato Salad, 354
  Salade Niçoise, 84
  Shrimp with Tarragon
    Sauce, 240
  Twice-Baked Potatoes, 317
  Veal and Potatoes
    Vinaigrette, 170
Pudding, Bread, 387
Pudding, Strawberry-
  Yogurt, 463
Puffy Omelet Squares, 36
Pumpkin Custards, 392
Pumpkin-Raisin Drops, 465
Punch, Tropical, 431
Raspberry Whip, 394
Rhubarb and Strawberries,
  Saucy, 40
Rice
  Baked Curried Chicken and
    Rice, 200
  Breakfast Rice Cereal, 448
  Broccoli Rice, 356
  Broiled Rice and Vegetable
    Patties, 266
  Brown Rice Pilaf, 52
  Chicken and Rice
    Salad, 458
  Crab Gumbo, 254
  Curried Beef and
    Rice, 120
  Curried Chicken and Rice
    Salad, 82
  Curried Lamb, 162
  Fiesta Chicken, 197
  Fish with Vegetables and
    Rice, 310
  Ham Jambalaya, 154

Rice *(continued)*
  Indian-Style Chicken, 187
  Italian Tomato and Rice
    Soup, 343
  Lemony Brown Rice and
    Vegetables, 327
  Marinated Turkey
    Slices, 208
  Pepper-Rice Timbales, 331
  Picadillo Rice, 137
  Pineapple-Chicken and
    Rice Bake, 190
  Pork Jambalaya, 140
  Rice and Beans with
    Cheese, 278
  Rosy White and Wild
    Rice, 330
  Savory Ham and Rice, 148
  Savory Risotto, 329
  Spanish Rice, 328
  Stuffed Red Snapper, 224
  Turkey and Pepper Stir-
    Fry, 218
  Vegetable Rice Bake, 260
  Vegetarian Chili with
    Rice, 42
  Wild Rice and Bulgur
    Pilaf, 43
Rich Tomato Soup, 346
Roast Pork with Cabbage
  and Carrots, 125
Rosy White and Wild
  Rice, 330
Rum-Sauced Bananas, 401

S

Salad Dressing,
  Creamy, 350
Salad Dressing, Tofu, 351
Salade Niçoise, 84
Salads
  Antipasto Salad, 85
  Apple-Cheese Mold, 347
  Beef Salad with Fresh
    Basil Dressing, 74
  Caesar-Style Chicken
    Salad, 80
  Chicken and Rice
    Salad, 458
  Chilled Chicken and
    Vegetable Salad, 83
  Creamy Potato Salad, 65

Salads *(continued)*
  Curried Chicken and Rice
    Salad, 82
  Curried Fruit Salad, 348
  Fruit and Pasta Salad, 349
  Fruit Slaw, 33
  Fruity Cottage Cheese
    Salad, 456
  Garbanzo Bean and
    Vegetable Salad, 459
  Ham and Pasta Salad, 78
  Hot Ham and Apple
    Slaw, 77
  Lunch Box Chicken
    Salad, 457
  Marinated
    Cucumbers, 325
  New Potato Salad, 354
  Orange Chicken
    Tabbouleh, 81
  Oriental Bean Salad, 340
  Pork and Noodle Salad, 76
  Salade Niçoise, 84
  Shrimp and Fruit
    Salad, 460
  Spinach Salad, 55
  Stir-Fried Chicken
    Salad, 79
  Taco Salad, 75
  Tomato and Zucchini
    Salad, 321
  Tossed Italian Salad, 30
  Vegetable and Pasta
    Toss, 319
  White Bean and Pepper
    Salad, 339
Salmon
  Poached Salmon with
    Caper Sauce, 229
  Salmon-and-Pasta-Stuffed
    Tomatoes, 22
  Salmon Cups with
    Creamed Peas, 311
  Salmon-Filled Puffy
    Omelet, 438
Saucy Caraway
  Cabbage, 363
Saucy Curried Pork and
  Zucchini, 288
Saucy Prunes and
  Peaches, 366

Saucy Rhubarb and
  Strawberries, 403
Saucy Spaghetti Squash
  Olé, 116
Sauerkraut Supper,
  Pork-, 129
Sausage, Turkey and Apple
  Breakfast, 441
Sausage and Lentil
  Chili, 216
Sautéed Shrimp with
  Peppers, 242
Savory Risotto, 329
Scallops and Broccoli with
  Pasta, 312
Scallops Florentine, 238
Seafood (see Fish and Seafood)
Seafood Enchiladas, 314
Seaside Mussels, 258
Sherbet, Watermelon, 397
Sherried Fillet Steaks, 93
Shrimp
  Citrus Shrimp and
    Scallops, 239
  Curried Shrimp
    Crepes, 244
  Garlic-Broiled Shrimp, 246
  Lemony Shrimp and
    Asparagus, 313
  Low-Calorie Shrimp
    Creole, 243
  Paella, 189
  Saucy Shrimp and
    Pasta, 245
  Sautéed Shrimp with
    Peppers, 242
  Shrimp and Fruit
    Salad, 460
  Shrimp Ball Soup, 248
  Shrimp with Tarragon
    Sauce, 240
  Szechwan Shrimp, 247
Skillet Sweet Potatoes, 63
Snack Mix, Curried, 425
Soups
  Beef-Barley Soup, 108
  Cheese and Vegetable
    Soup, 344
  Clam and Cheese
    Chowder, 255
  Corn Chowder, 342
  Easy Green Chili, 107

Soups (continued)
  Fish Soup, 235
  Gazpacho, 462
  Ham and Vegetable
    Soup, 34
  Hearty Italian-Style
    Soup, 461
  Italian Tomato and Rice
    Soup, 343
  Lentil and Lamb
    Soup, 164
  Mushroom and Barley
    Soup, 47
  Oriental Ham Soup, 147
  Oyster and Spinach
    Chowder, 257
  Rich Tomato Soup, 346
  Sausage and Lentil
    Chili, 216
  Shrimp Ball Soup, 248
  Tex-Mex Beef Soup, 104
  Tortellini Soup, 345
  Vegetable-Bean Soup with
    Ham, 155
  Vegetarian Chili with
    Rice, 42
Southwestern Chicken, 201
Soy-Glazed Chicken, 294
Spaghetti Pie, 118
Spaghetti Squash Olé,
  Saucy, 116
Spaghetti Squash
  Pronto, 360
Spaghetti with Cottage
  Cheese Pesto, 335
Spaghetti with Meat
  Sauce, 114
Spanish Rice, 328
Spicy Fruit Cup, 406
Spicy Pasta Pie, 215
Spinach
  Cheese Calzones, 272
  Chicken and Spinach
    Crepes, 202
  Garlic-Spinach Dip, 419
  Oyster and Spinach
    Chowder, 257
  Scallops Florentine, 238
  Spinach and Ham
    Lasagna, 156
  Spinach Lasagna
    Rolls, 267

Spinach (continued)
  Spinach Salad, 55
  Spinach-Stuffed Flank
    Steak, 282
  Spinach-Stuffed Sole, 305
  Spinach-Stuffed Turkey
    Thigh, 213
  Spinach with Parmesan
    Cheese, 364
  Stuffed Mushrooms, 423
  Tossed Italian Salad, 30
  Wilted Greens with
    Pasta, 326
Spread, Orange, 378
Squash
  Saucy Spaghetti Squash
    Olé, 116
  Spaghetti Squash
    Pronto, 360
  Stuffed Acorn Squash, 136
  Stuffed Winter Squash, 35
Steamed Sole in
  Cabbage, 306
Stews
  Country-Style Pork
    Stew, 132
  Crab Gumbo, 254
  Lentil Stew, 276
  Oven Lamb Stew, 165
Stir-Fries
  Beef Stir-Fry with Orange
    Sauce, 100
  Chicken and Sweet Pepper
    Stir-Fry, 27
  Chicken Livers in Italian
    Tomato Sauce, 193
  Creole-Style Pork, 134
  Curried Beef and
    Potatoes, 101
  Garlic and Pepper Stir-
    Fry, 324
  Herbed Lamb Stir-
    Fry, 163
  Oriental Chicken in
    Tortillas, 194
  Pineapple Beef, 99
  Pork and Broccoli Stir-
    Fry, 135
  Pork and Pineapple Stir-
    Fry, 131
  Stir-Fried Chicken
    Salad, 79

Stir-Fries (continued)
  Stir-Fried Oriental
    Vegetables, 320
  Sukiyaki, 98
  Tofu and Vegetable Stir-
    Fry, 274
  Turkey and Pepper Stir-
    Fry, 218
Strata, Mexican, 264
Strawberries, Saucy
  Rhubarb and, 403
Strawberry Shortcake, 72
Strawberry-Topped
  Cheesecake, 67
Strawberry-Yogurt
  Pudding, 463
Stroganoff-Style Beef, 57
Stroganoff-Style
  Chicken, 199
Stuffed Acorn Squash, 136
Stuffed Cabbage Leaves, 117
Stuffed Mushrooms, 423
Stuffed Red Snapper, 224
Stuffed Snapper, 301
Stuffed Tomatoes, 44
Stuffed Veal Rolls, 171
Stuffed Winter Squash, 35
Sukiyaki, 98
Sweet-and-Sour Fish, 304
Sweet-and-Sour Ham
  Balls, 157
Sweet-and-Sour Pork
  Kabobs, 133
Sweet and Spicy
  Peaches, 402
Sweet and Spicy
  Popcorn, 424
Sweet Potatoes, Skillet 63
Sweet-Topped
  Raspberries, 407
Swordfish with Cucumber
  Sauce, 231
Szechwan Shrimp, 247

T-Z

Taco Salad, 75
Tex-Mex Beans with
  Dumplings, 279
Tex-Mex Beef Soup, 104
Tex-Mex Turkey
  Tenderloins, 298
Tofu and Corn Quiche, 265

Tofu and Vegetable
 Stir-Fry, 274
Tofu Manicotti, 275
Tofu Salad Dressing, 351
Tomato and Zucchini
 Salad, 321
Tomatoes, Baked
 Stuffed, 322
Tomatoes, Stuffed, 44
Tomatoes and
 Zucchini, 323
Tomato Soup, Rich, 346
Tortellini Soup, 345
Tortilla Pie, 285
Tossed Italian Salad, 30
Tropical Banana Nog, 429
Tropical Punch, 431
Tuna-Noodle Casserole, 236
Tuna Sandwich, Zippy, 452
Turkey
 Baked Curried Chicken and
  Rice, 200
 Barbecue-Sauced
  Turkey, 299
 Brunch Turnovers, 440
 Chicken à la King, 297
 Coriander Turkey
  Breast, 207
 Garden Burgers, 219
 Glazed Turkey Steaks, 210
 Lemony Turkey
  Meatballs, 300
 Marinated Turkey
  Slices, 208
 Muffulettas, 453
 Pork and Pineapple Stir-
  Fry, 131
 Pork Casserole with Bread
  Topping, 139
 Pork Jambalaya, 140
 Spicy Pasta Pie, 215
 Spinach-Stuffed Turkey
  Thigh, 213
 Taco Salad, 75
 Tex-Mex Turkey
  Tenderloins, 298
 Turkey and Apple
  Breakfast Sausage, 441
 Turkey and Cheese
  Wedges, 217
 Turkey and Pepper Stir-
  Fry, 218

Turkey (continued)
 Turkey Enchiladas, 221
 Turkey Ham and Apple
  Bake, 214
 Turkey Meatballs in
  Wine Sauce, 222
 Turkey Paprikash, 41
 Turkey Rolls Divan, 211
 Turkey Soufflé, 220
 Turkey with Cranberry
  Sauce, 206
 Turkey with Honey-
  Mustard Sauce, 212
 Vegetable and
  Turkey Sandwiches, 24
 Vegetable-Stuffed Turkey
  Roll, 209
Turnovers, Brunch, 440
Twice-Baked Potatoes, 317
Two-Bran Refrigerator
 Muffins, 379
Veal
 Creamy Beef and
  Onions, 115
 Creamy Veal and
  Mushrooms, 172
 Garlic-Caraway Veal
  Roast, 167
 Layered Picnic Pâté, 455
 Stuffed Veal Rolls, 171
 Sweet-and-Sour Ham
  Balls, 157
 Veal and Potatoes
  Vinaigrette, 170
 Veal Chops with Vegetable
  Sauce, 168
 Veal Scaloppine, 169
Vegetables (see also Carrots,
  Potatoes, and Zucchini)
 Asparagus with Orange
  Mayonnaise, 362
 Baked Lamb and
  Vegetables, 159
 Beef and Brew, 102
 Broiled Chops with Italian
  Vegetables, 127
 Broiled Rice and Vegetable
  Patties, 266
 Cauliflower Amandine, 361

Vegetables (continued)
 Cheese and Vegetable
  Soup, 344
 Chicken and Sweet Pepper
  Stir-Fry, 27
 Chicken Livers in Italian
  Tomato Sauce, 193
 Chilled Chicken and
  Vegetable Salad, 83
 Creamy Beef and
  Onions, 115
 Creamy Egg and Vegetable
  Bake, 262
 Creamy Peas and
  Onions, 355
 Curried Lentils and
  Vegetables, 277
 Deep-Dish Beef Pie, 106
 Fish and Peppers, 226
 Fish with Vegetables and
  Rice, 310
 Garbanzo Bean and
  Vegetable Salad, 459
 Garden Burgers, 219
 Garlic and Pepper Stir-
  Fry, 324
 Ham and Vegetable
  Soup, 34
 Ham and Vegetables with
  Mostaccioli, 46
 Herbed Couscous and
  Vegetables, 332
 Herbed Steak and Onions, 97
 Herbed Vegetable Toss, 25
 Lemon-Tarragon
  Vegetables, 357
 Lemony Brown Rice and
  Vegetables, 327
 Lemony Herbed
  Asparagus, 32
 Lentil Stew, 276
 Marinated Lamb
  Kabobs, 161
 Mexican Lentils and
  Vegetables, 365
 Oven-Fried Vegetables, 422
 Pasta Primavera, 268
 Pasta with Onion Sauce, 338
 Peppery Beef and
  Vegetables, 105
 Pork Medaillons with
  Vegetables, 126

Vegetables (continued)
 Skillet Sweet Potatoes, 63
 Spanish Rice, 328
 Spicy Stuffed Peppers, 289
 Stir-Fried Oriental
  Vegetables, 320
 Stuffed Tomatoes, 44
 Tofu and Vegetable Stir-
  Fry, 274
 Turkey and Pepper
  Stir-Fry, 218
 Veal Chops with Vegetable
  Sauce, 168
 Vegetable and Pasta
  Toss, 319
 Vegetable and Turkey
  Sandwiches, 24
 Vegetable-Bean Soup with
  Ham, 155
 Vegetable Rice Bake, 260
 Vegetable-Stuffed Turkey
  Roll, 209
 Vegetarian Chili with
  Rice, 42
 Vegetarian Lasagna, 271
Watermelon Sherbet, 397
Wheat and Oat Bread,
 Spicy, 369
White Bean and Pepper
 Salad, 339
Whole Wheat Raisin Soda
 Bread, 374
Wild Rice and Bulgur
 Pilaf, 43
Wilted Greens with
 Pasta, 326
Yogurt Ice, Fruity, 398
Zippy Tuna Sandwich, 452
Zucchini
 Chicken and Zucchini in
  Mustard Sauce, 198
 Marinated Zucchini and
  Mushrooms, 421
 Saucy Curried Pork and
  Zucchini, 288
 Tomato and Zucchini
  Salad, 321
 Tomatoes and
  Zucchini, 323

METRIC CONVERSIONS

By making a few conversions, cooks in Australia, Canada, and the United Kingdom can use the recipes in the Better Homes and Gardens® *New Dieter's Cook Book* with confidence. The charts on this page provide a guide for converting measurements from the U.S. customary system, which is used throughout this book, to the imperial and metric systems. There also is a conversion table for oven temperatures to accommodate the differences in oven calibrations.

VOLUME AND WEIGHT: Americans traditionally use *cup* measures for liquid and solid ingredients. The chart at top right shows the approximate imperial and metric equivalents. If you are accustomed to weighing solid ingredients, here are some helpful approximate equivalents:

1 cup butter, caster sugar, or rice = 8 ounces
 = about 250 grams
1 cup flour = 4 ounces = about 125 grams
1 cup icing sugar = 5 ounces = about 150 grams

Spoon measures are used for smaller amounts of ingredients. Although the size of the teaspoon is the same, the size of the tablespoon varies slightly among countries. However, for practical purposes and for recipes in this book, a straight substitution is all that's necessary.

Measurements made using cups or spoons always should be *level,* unless stated otherwise.

PRODUCT DIFFERENCES: Most of the products and ingredients called for in the recipes in this book are available in English-speaking countries. However, some are known by different names. Here are some common American ingredients and their possible counterparts:

■ Sugar is granulated or caster sugar.
■ Powdered sugar is icing sugar.
■ All-purpose flour is plain household flour or white flour. When self-rising flour is used in place of all-purpose flour in a recipe that calls for leavening, omit the leavening (baking soda or baking powder) and salt.
■ Light corn syrup is golden syrup.
■ Cornstarch is cornflour.
■ Baking soda is bicarbonate of soda.
■ Vanilla is vanilla essence.

USEFUL EQUIVALENTS

⅛ teaspoon = 0.5ml
¼ teaspoon = 1ml
½ teaspoon = 2ml
1 teaspoon = 5ml
¼ cup = 2 fluid ounces = 50ml
⅓ cup = 3 fluid ounces = 75ml
½ cup = 4 fluid ounces = 125ml

¾ cup = 6 fluid ounces = 175ml
1 cup = 8 fluid ounces = 250ml
2 cups = 1 pint
2 pints = 1 litre
½ inch = 1 centimetre
1 inch = 2 centimetres

BAKING PAN SIZES

American	Metric
8x1½-inch round baking pan	20x4-centimetre sandwich or cake tin
9x1½-inch round baking pan	23x3.5-centimetre sandwich or cake tin
11x7x1½-inch baking pan	28x18x4-centimetre baking pan
13x9x2-inch baking pan	32.5x23x5-centimetre baking pan
12x7½x2-inch baking dish	30x19x5-centimetre baking pan
15x10x2-inch baking pan	38x25.5x2.5-centimetre baking pan (Swiss roll tin)
9-inch pie plate	22x4- or 23x4-centimetre pie plate
7- or 8-inch springform pan	18- or 20-centimetre springform or loose-bottom cake tin
9x5x3-inch loaf pan	23x13x6-centimetre or 2-pound narrow loaf pan
1½-quart casserole	1.5-litre casserole
2-quart casserole	2-litre casserole

OVEN TEMPERATURE EQUIVALENTS

Fahrenheit Setting	Celsius Setting*	Gas Setting
300°F	150°C	Gas Mark 2
325°F	160°C	Gas Mark 3
350°F	180°C	Gas Mark 4
375°F	190°C	Gas Mark 5
400°F	200°C	Gas Mark 6
425°F	220°C	Gas Mark 7
450°F	230°C	Gas Mark 8
Broil		Grill *(watch time and heat)*

Electric and gas ovens may be calibrated using Celsius. However, increase the Celsius setting 10 to 20 degrees when cooking above 160°C with an electric oven. For convection or forced-air ovens (gas or electric), lower the temperature setting 10°C when cooking at all heat levels.